The Living Goddesses

MARIJA GIMBUTAS

The *Living* Goddesses

EDITED AND SUPPLEMENTED BY

Miriam Robbins Dexter

UNIVERSITY OF CALIFORNIA PRESS

Berkeley | Los Angeles | London

UNIVERSITY OF CALIFORNIA PRESS
Berkeley and Los Angeles, California

UNIVERSITY OF CALIFORNIA PRESS, LTD.
London, England

First Paperback Printing 2001

Library of Congress Cataloging-in-Publication Data

Gimbutas, Marija Alseikaitė

    The living goddesses / Marija Gimbutas ; edited and supplemented
by Miriam Robbins Dexter.

      p.   cm.

    Includes bibliographical references and index.

    ISBN 0-520-22915-0 (pbk. : alk. paper)

     1. Religion, Prehistoric—Europe.   2. Goddesses—Europe.
3. Neolithic period—Europe.   4. Religion—Europe—History.
5. Folklore—Europe. 6. Europe—Antiquities. I. Dexter, Miriam
Robbins, 1943– . II. Title.

    GN803.G57   1999

    291.1′4—dc21   98-46634

                                            CIP

Printed in the United States of America

09   08   07   06   05
9 8 7 6 5 4 3 2

The paper used in this publication meets the minimum requirements of
ANSI/NISO Z39.48-1992 (R 1997) (*Permanence of Paper*). ♾

CONTENTS

ILLUSTRATIONS

FIGURES

Shortly after the death of Marija Gimbutas, her daughter Živile Gimbu-tas called and asked me to finish this book, a difficult task since I would not be able to call Dr. Gimbutas to ask her questions about content, formatting, intent. She had reworked the first chapters quite a bit more than the long and very rich final chapter, which at that time formed the whole of part II. I began with my own edit of the text and then gave a more careful look at both details and the final shape the book would take. In order to make the book as up-to-date as possible, I added comments in notes (presented as "editor's notes"). (The author's own sources are given within the text.)

Dr. Gimbutas had planned many illustrations for the second half of the book, but these were not among the illustrations she left at the time of her death. Thus part I, on the prehistoric era, is richly illustrated, while part II has been left unillustrated. Illustrations of the historic-age myths and folklore may be found in editions of *Bullfinch's Mythology* and in encyclopedias of world mythology such as that of Larousse.

Marija Gimbutas always had "one more book" in her mind. This book was her final work in a prodigious writing career. She continued to edit it until she was hospitalized, ten days before her death. The manuscript manifested her love, perseverance, and hope, for she continued to work and rework it in spite of great physical pain, using her strength to shape it enough so that it could be finished by an editor.

This book was first envisioned as a popularized version of her earlier work. But, in characteristic fashion, in her last year Dr. Gimbutas decided that she must disseminate new work, and therefore she filled this new academic work with her findings from 1991 to 1993. This work therefore stands as a testimony to the research of the final years, months, and weeks of her life.

ACKNOWLEDGMENTS

Completing and editing the work of another is a daunting task, particularly when the composition has been written by one as broadly knowledgeable as Marija Gimbutas. Realizing that I could not complete this work alone, I asked several women, themselves authorities in various fields, to read the manuscript after my initial work and to offer their suggestions. I am incredibly grateful for the indispensable help of the thealogian-theologian Carol P. Christ; Susan Gitlin-Emmer, teacher of women's spirituality; the Indo-European archaeologist Karlene Jones-Bley; and the lecturer-author-biographer Joan Marler, whose prior experience in editing Marija's book *The Civilization of the Goddess* was invaluable. I also thank the Indo-European linguist Martin Huld for his willingness to confer with me on etymologies. The historian of religion Kees Bolle gave invaluable advice, as did the professor of Germanic mythology and linguistics Edgar C. Polomé.

William Oldendorf worked with Professor Gimbutas on the first draft of this book; although the work has subsequently gone through many changes, he deserves great thanks for his efforts.

Debra Eve, who edited the first versions of this manuscript together with Professor Gimbutas, was exceptionally devoted to the completion of the book. She undertook the organization of the illustrations and offered invaluable suggestions with regard to the rest of the manuscript; I offer her my heartfelt appreciation.

Most of the illustrations were produced by James Bennett. It is likely that others early on produced illustrations as well; unfortunately, their names do not appear in Professor Gimbutas' records. Further, it is quite possible that the source lists left at the time of Professor Gimbutas' death do not reflect correct sources in every case. To all of the illustrators, and sources for illustrations, I therefore extend my gratitude and my apologies.

Carolyn Radlo, director of the Joseph Campbell and Marija Gimbutas Library at Pacifica University, kindly made Professor Gimbutas' archives—books and notes—available to me; she also far exceeded the bounds of duty to search through the materials in order to unearth missing illustrations. I thank also the Special Collections librarian Richard Buchen.

I must also thank Živile Gimbutas, who with kindness and friendship encouraged this completion of her mother's work, supplying her own time and energy as well. Marija's daughter Rasa Julie Thies was also very supportive.

Irene Luksis Goddard and Valentinas Varnas carefully checked citations on Lithuanian and Latvian goddesses. Paula Coe and Angelique Gulermovich-Epstein supplied suggestions and information for the Celtic chapter. Many thanks to my research assistant, Jules Hart, for bibliographic help and loving support.

I thank Susan Gray, Sandra Golvin, and Geraldine Hannon for love and inspiration; and I give special thanks to my husband, Greg Dexter, and to my son and daughter, Jacob and Leah Robbins, for their support and encouragement to complete this project.

Finally, I am very grateful to the editors of the University of California Press, Stan Holwitz, Harry Asforis, Sue Heinemann, and Bonita Hurd, who through their encouragement and expertise were most helpful in causing this work to come to fruition.

Because Marija Gimbutas did not live to write her own acknowledgments to this book, I would like to thank, in her place, several of the people who gave encouragement and strength to her in her final months. Her daughters, Danute, Živile, and Rasa, gave her wonderful physical and emotional support. Many women in the Los Angeles community regularly visited her, including Debra Eve, Camille Ameen, Starr Goode, Susan Gitlin-Emmer, Jean Freer, Martha Wolford, Noel Lightborne, Barbara Bradshaw, Gloria Orenstein, and Ruth Barrett. Joan Marler and Vicki Noble visited frequently from the San Francisco Bay Area, as did Patricia Reis and James Harrod from Maine. These people inspired Marija to "produce, produce!"—even in her last weeks—through their inspiration and their love.

This book, which occupied Marija Gimbutas for the last two years of her life, was her last work (in English) in a writing career that included approximately three hundred scholarly articles and twenty books, translated into many foreign languages. It is different from Marija Gimbutas' other works: it is exceptionally rich in folklore and myth. The focus of the book is twofold: a synthesis of her earlier work and the addition of new research. In the first several chapters, she synthesizes much of her research on Neolithic Europe, adding information that became available after her monograph, *The Civilization of the Goddess: The World of Old Europe,* was published. (Although Gimbutas uses information dating to the Upper Paleolithic, circa 30,000–10,000 B.C., and the Mesolithic, circa 10,000–7000 B.C., she focuses her own work primarily on the Neolithic, circa 7000/6000–3000 B.C., and the Bronze Age, circa 2500–1500 B.C. She also discusses the historic cultures of the Iron Age, circa 1500 B.C. through the middle of the first millennium B.C.)

Much of Marija Gimbutas' work was grounded in her findings at the archaeological sites she excavated, including Obre in Bosnia, Anza in Macedonia, Sitagroi in northwestern Greece, Achilleion in southern Thessaly (Greece), and Manfredonia in southern Italy. These excavations led directly to three edited volumes: *Neolithic Macedonia* (Gimbutas 1976), on her excavations at Anza; *Excavations at Sitagroi I* (Renfrew, Gimbutas, and Elster 1986); and *Achilleion: A Neolithic Settlement in Thessaly, Greece, 6400–6500 BC* (Gimbutas et al. 1989).

Early in her career, Marija Gimbutas identified the "Kurgan" culture. These Proto-Indo-Europeans were a patrilineal, patrilocal, pastoral, and seminomadic group of peoples who, she believed, originated in the steppes of Russia. They were militaristic, produced weapons, and rode horses. Their religion centered upon male gods. Their agriculture was rudimentary, although as they came into greater contact with Old Europeans, they domesticated more plants and developed metallurgy. The ceramic art of these peoples was poorly developed. They buried their dead in pit graves covered with a cairn (Kurgan I and II) or an earthen mound, or kurgan (Kurgan III and IV).

Gimbutas traced their migrations from an area north of the Caucasus, in the Russian steppes, to their new homelands. These new homelands encompassed the geographic areas that became Greece, Italy, Britain, Ireland, Lithuania, Latvia, Russia, Germany, Scandinavia, Anatolia, India, Iran, and Chinese Turkestan. There were three migrations: Wave 1, circa 4400–4200 B.C. (Kurgan I–II, the Khvalynsk and Srednij Stog cultures); Wave 2, circa 3400–3200 B.C. (Kurgan III, the Maikop culture); and Wave 3, circa 3000–2800 B.C. (Kurgan IV, the Yamna or Pit-grave culture) (for a thorough discussion of the Wave theory, see Gimbutas 1977, 1980, 1985; these three articles are included in Gimbutas 1997).

When the Proto-Indo-Europeans arrived at their new homelands, they met groups of indigenous peoples who were relatively peaceful, agrarian, artistically creative, probably equalitarian in social structure, and goddess worshiping. The indigenous peoples had an advanced aesthetic: they built two-story houses and beautiful temples, of which we have clay models. They produced beautiful painted ceramic ware. They were sometimes assimilated, sometimes destroyed, by the Kurgan peoples, whose domestication of the horse and military ability gave them a strong advantage. The Proto-Indo-Europeans imposed both language and religion on the indigenous peoples, although traces of both indigenous language and religion remained as a substratum in the resulting "Indo-European" language and culture. Thus, "Indo-European" is a result of the merging of Kurgan peoples with Old Europeans.

In order to trace the Indo-Europeans, Gimbutas made use of comparative linguistics and mythology, as well as archaeology. The French mythologist Georges Dumézil had found parallels between Indo-European religious pantheons and social structure, formulating a "Tripartite" theory. According to his theory, the Indo-Europeans were divided into three social groups or "functions": priests ("first function"), warriors and nobility ("second function"), and "caretakers"—farmers, laborers, and craftspeople ("third function"). Gimbutas found sharp contrasts between the hierarchical Indo-Europeans and the equalitarian Old Europeans. Although throughout much of her early career she elaborated on the Kurgan peoples, in her last twenty years she became more and more interested in the peoples whom they assimilated: the Old Europeans. The refinement of her opinions about the Old Europeans may be traced from her 1974 *Gods and Goddesses of Old Europe* (reprinted in 1982 in updated form as *The Goddesses and Gods of Old Europe*), through her 1989 *Language of the Goddess* and her 1991 *The Civilization of the Goddess: The World of Old Europe*. In this, her final book, her thoughts have come to fruition: here we may read her final thoughts about Old Europeans and Indo-Europeans.

In the first chapter of this book, Gimbutas looks at images of goddesses and gods, including images of the bird and snake goddesses and other deities in the form of animals. Here she also discusses deified images of life and death. It is believed that the Old Europeans worshiped the full circle of birth, death, and rebirth in the form of a "great"-goddess. Unlike the early historical cultures, most of which venerated the givers of life (for example, the Greek Aphrodite), while dishonoring those who brought death (for example, the Greek Gorgon, Medusa), the Old Europeans did not divide the great-goddess into fragments of "good" and "bad." The goddess was one and many, a unity and a multiplicity. The hybrid bird-and-snake goddess was the great-goddess of the life continuum, the goddess of birth, death, and rebirth; she was the creator and the destroyer, the maiden, the crone, and the goddess in the prime of life who mated with the young god in the *hieros gamos,* the "sacred marriage," and gave birth—again and again—to creation.

In chapter 2 Gimbutas discusses another subject dear to her heart, Old European sacred script. Although translatable written language did not appear until the advent of Sumerian cuneiform writing and Egyptian hiero-glyphics, both around the beginning of the third millennium B.C., signs dating to the Old European Neolithic, and even earlier to the Upper Pale-olithic, have been recovered, carved on various objects, such as figurines and bowls. Excellent examples of Old European script are to be found on figurines from the Vinča culture, in the northwest Balkans.

In chapter 3 Gimbutas discusses the concept of the life cycle in graphic form, explaining that the tomb is also the sacred place from which new life emanates. The tomb is the womb of the goddess; the two are, in Old European religion, inextricably interconnected. There are examples in iconography showing this interconnectedness. For example, a marble preg-nant figure was found in a Cycladic grave (British Museum No. GR 1932–10.181, dating to 2800–2300 B.C.). The provenance of the tomb indicates that the figure represented a death goddess, but the goddess of death was teeming with new life. Many tombs, as well as shrines cele-brating rituals of death and regeneration, have ritual shapes: in Lepenski Vir, a site on the Danube River in the Iron Gates region, Gimbutas found small triangular-shaped structures containing statues and altars, which were associated with burials; caves such as Scaloria cave in southeast Italy con-tained evidence of ritual: pottery sherds with regenerative designs, and skeletons of mostly young women and children. The rock-cut tombs of Malta are egg-shaped, while the Maltese Hypogeum, an underground tem-ple, consists of thirty-four interconnected egg-shaped chambers; approx-imately seven thousand human bones were found there, mostly in egg-shaped niches in the lower chambers. In Sardinia as well, tombs con-sisted of rock-cut egg- or kidney-shaped chambers. Megalithic monuments, which served as places of both ritual and burial, flourished throughout western Europe. Many of these monuments were anthropomorphic in shape, representing the full figure of the goddess. Many, such as New-grange and Knowth in Ireland and the Maltese Hypogeum, were deco-rated with regenerative symbols such as the spiral and the coiled snake. These tombs, shaped like the goddess of death and regeneration, were the womb of the goddess.

In her long career, Marija Gimbutas excavated many temples—gener-ally these were found within a community, an integral part of it. In these temples or "house shrines," the hearth was often central, and home-related tasks such as baking were aligned with the sacred. In chapter 4, she dis-cusses actual temples, such as the stone temples on the Mediterranean islands of Malta and neighboring Gozo, as well as clay models of temples and other ritual equipment (more than one hundred temple models have been excavated, from much of southeastern and eastern Europe, from the Balkans to Ukraine). Some of the real temples seem to be dedicated to a bird goddess, to a snake goddess, or to a pregnant goddess of vegetation. The houselike temples of southeast Europe contained altars, statues (some life-sized), figurines (many bearing markings that indicate cloth-ing, headgear, and medallions), miniature furnishings, incense burners, and human- or animal-shaped vases. They also contained the technology of everyday life: domed ovens, grinding stones, storage jars. That they con-tained looms may be inferred from ceramic loom weights and spindle whorls (the wooden looms were destroyed by time). Gimbutas believed that the Old Europeans wove cloth, baked bread, and created pottery as sacred acts: that the ancient temples were centers of a holistic spiritual life.

Not all Old European temples were built structures. Chapter 5 exam-ines roundels (round enclosures), square enclosures, and causewayed enclosures: sacred outdoor precincts built of wood and stone and often surrounded by ceremonial ditches. In Britain, roundels such as the famous Stonehenge, Woodhenge, and Avebury in County Wiltshire date from the third millennium B.C. Earlier roundels (from circa 5000–3000 B.C.), per-haps less well known, were built by the Lengyel and other cultures of cen-tral Europe. These structures served religious, not military, purposes, since the artifacts found within them, including human skeletons (buried along with ritual objects), animal bones, vases, and figurines, indicate feasting and ritual burial. The enclosures usually opened to the four cardinal direc-tions, and they probably served seasonal rituals. They reflect cooperative work, and they served the collective community.

In chapter 6 Gimbutas discusses matrilineal inheritance, stating her belief that the peoples of Old Europe handed down their goods through the female line. In matrilineal societies, women are economically viable since they are able to inherit goods. This leads to greater female autonomy and greater respect for the female. Gimbutas relates social respect for the female to religious respect for the female—the worshiping of goddesses—and states that Old European matrilineal societies therefore honored both mortal females and female deities. Consequently, in her opinion these cultures were equalitarian in social structure, honoring both women and men.

Whereas part I considers the prehistoric goddesses and gods and prehistoric religion, part II discusses the "living" goddesses, deities who were worshiped in the early historic eras, some of which have continued to be venerated through the modern era. In the chapters of this section, Gimbutas examines the myths of several cultures, both Indo-European and non-Indo-European. She begins with southern Europe, where most of her own excavations took place. She discusses pre-Indo-European Minoan religion and then Greek religion: both its Indo-European Greek and its Old European pre-Greek components. She then examines the goddesses of the Etruscans and the Basques, two cultures that, although surrounded by Indo-Europeans, retained their non-Indo-European languages and character. Finally, she discusses the religions of northern and central Europe: those of the Celts, the Germanic peoples, and the Balts. She concludes the book with a rich discourse on the gods, goddesses, fairies, witches, and sprites of Baltic religion. Particularly in this section, Marija Gimbutas drew upon her memory, with the intention of writing down the sources later. I have attempted to add source explications wherever possible.

Marija Gimbutas' work was quite controversial, for she was an original thinker and strong in asserting her hypotheses. As a result, she had both strong proponents and strong opponents. She was a voracious reader as well, and her ideas were presented with a clear knowledge of the data and of the hypotheses of others. A dynamic scholar, she never shirked from criticism or from taking a chance. She realized the importance of interpreting findings as well as presenting them, affording us hypotheses to prove or disprove, as well as foundations of facts upon which to build our own theories. She realized that the interpretation and interconnection of data are what lead to understanding and to a deep scientific contribution.

In this book, Marija Gimbutas has made yet another rich contribution to the study of folklore and mythology and to the exciting interdisciplinary field of archaeomythology. She brings much new material to the book—for example, showing us a "Medusa" head that dates to the sixth millennium B.C., thus pushing back to the early Neolithic era this "death" aspect of the Old European goddesses. Her contributions to the field of archaeomythology are great, for she has provided the mythologist with the physical data—statues, figurines, statistics of chronology, and provenance—that give us knowledge of prehistoric religion. No less significant is her own love for the figures of folklore and myth, her own passion for the subject. It is this inextricable union of passion and knowledge that is Marija Gimbutas' legacy to us.

PART I

Religion in Prepatriarchal Europe

CHAPTER ONE

Images of Goddesses and Gods

In Neolithic Europe and Asia Minor (ancient Anatolia)—in the era between 7000 B.C. and 3000 B.C.—religion focused on the wheel of life and its cyclical turning. This is the geographic sphere and the time frame I refer to as Old Europe. In Old Europe, the focus of religion encompassed birth, nurturing, growth, death, and regeneration, as well as crop cultivation and the raising of animals. The people of this era pondered untamed natural forces, as well as wild plant and animal cycles, and they worshiped goddesses, or a goddess, in many forms. The goddess manifested her countless forms during various cyclical phases to ensure that they functioned smoothly. She revealed herself in multiple ways through the myriad facets of life, and she is depicted in a very complex symbolism.

First I will explore these forms in detail, looking mainly at goddess figures, and then I will unravel their meaning. The images of the goddess can be loosely categorized under her aspects of life giving and sustaining, death, and renewal. Although male energy also motivated regeneration and life stimulation, in both the plant and animal worlds, it was the feminine force that pervaded existence.

Figurines

Small statues, excavated from Old European settlements, cemeteries, and tombs, comprise an important source for understanding Old European religion. When the Old Europeans discovered how to fire pottery in about the seventh millennium B.C., that pottery provided a new way to express religious ideals. A variety of ceramic forms—vases, figurines, and ritual implements—displayed the spiritual symbols of Old Europe. Although Old European cultures continued to create religious artifacts in other media—stone, bone, amber, and antler—it was ceramic forms that most richly manifested the symbolic world of Old Europe.

By nature, archaeological preservation favors smaller artifacts. Chances are better for a ceramic sculpture a few inches high to survive seven or more millennia under several feet of dirt than for a life-size ceramic statue. Consequently, we often unearth small images intact and larger statues in many parts. Most of these figurines can be held in one's hand. Their makers often etched them with sacred symbols in the form of facial markings, geometric designs, and signs that may have been a form of script.

Our Neolithic ancestors not only created figurines representing certain deities, priestesses, or other mythical persona; they also reenacted rituals with these figurines. Discoveries include not only female and male figurines, which may have been made to represent goddesses and gods, but also thrones, vases, offering tables, furniture, musical instruments, and even miniature temples. Such miniature temples preserve the prototypes, adding an extra dimension to the archaeological record. Although ancient peoples created religious artifacts in other media (woven cloth and wood, for instance), except in extraordinary cases these have decayed. As a result, small ceramic objects provide some of the most important evidence for deciphering Old European religion.

Almost all archaeological sites in Italy, the Balkans, and central Europe contain these objects, spanning almost every Neolithic time period. We also find them in Asia Minor (ancient Anatolia, modern Turkey), the Near East, and to a much lesser extent, in western and northern Europe. Often where sites reach several meters deep, representing centuries or even millennia of occupation, figurines occur at almost every level. In these significant sites, we can often discern an artistic evolution from the earliest levels to the latest ones, indicating the importance of these objects to generation after generation of inhabitants.

The Neolithic, or earliest agricultural era, provides a much more fertile source for deciphering figurines than the previous archaeological periods, the Mesolithic and the Upper (or later) Paleolithic. The artifacts from this earlier time period often lose their contexts, and for the entire Upper Paleolithic, we have only about three thousand figurines. For Old Europe, with its great outpouring of religious art, so many figurines have been excavated at so many sites that we cannot possibly tabulate them accurately. Total Old European figurines may number one hundred thousand or more, counting all the broken or damaged figurines deemed unimportant in earlier excavations. Fortunately, settlements, cemeteries, and tombs, which provide excellent contexts, constitute the bulk of Neolithic sites. The innumerable Neolithic figurines preserved in their original settings intimate the richness of Old European spirituality.

The human body constituted one of Old Europe's most powerful symbols. As a result of modern cultural programming, we often associate nakedness with sexual enticement. The modern analyst naturally projects these attitudes back thousands of years and assumes that ancient depictions of the body served basically the same purpose.

Our cultural programming also leads to the assumption that female representations invariably represent "earth as fertility"; therefore all naked female artifacts become "fertility figurines." The Old European cultures certainly cared about fertility. But, as we will see, the wide variety of figurines, and particularly their Neolithic archaeological contexts, suggests that the feminine force played a wider religious role.[1] The many sophisticated Neolithic art forms accentuating the female body unveil a natural and sacred sexuality neglected by modern culture.

In religious art, the human body symbolizes myriad functions beyond the sexual, especially the procreative, nurturing, and life enhancing. I believe that in earlier times, obscenity as a concept surrounding either the male or female body did not exist. Renditions of the body expressed other functions, specifically the nourishing and procreative aspects of the female body and the life-stimulating qualities of the male body. The female force, as the pregnant vegetation goddess, intimately embodied the earth's fertility. But the sophisticated, complex art surrounding the Neolithic goddess is a shifting kaleidoscope of meaning: she personified every phase of life, death, and regeneration. She was the Creator from whom all life—human, plant, and animal—arose, and to whom everything returned. Her role extended far beyond eroticism.

The fact that these female figurines do not typically resemble an actual human or animal body belies their use as mere erotic art. The body is almost always abstracted or exaggerated in some manner. These modifications are not accidental: a brief survey of Neolithic art shows that the highly skilled ceramic workers of this time could achieve whatever effect they wished. Their intentional modifications of the human body expressed various manifestations of the inmost divine force. Before discussing the types of divinities represented by the figurines, it is necessary to focus on several peculiarities of figurine art: schematization, masks, hieroglyphs, and exaggeration of certain body parts, all of which were conventions used by the Old European artist.

SCHEMATIC FORMS

In Old Europe, schematic female and male bodies, in conjunction with other symbols, often represented the sacred force. Although many figurines

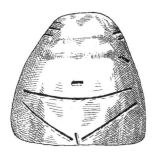  

Figure 1. Clearly the artisan had no intention of reproducing a human body on this figurine without legs, arms, or head. Attention here focuses on the large pubic triangle. One, two, or three dashes mark the figurine; a V sign and two lines are etched in back. Sesklo culture; c. 6200–6100 B.C. (Achilleion Phase III, Thessaly, northern Greece).

are ceramic masterpieces, other figurines appear strangely unfinished, sometimes resembling nothing more than a single clay cylinder with exaggerated breasts or buttocks, or a pregnant belly without arms or legs (Fig. 1). Their makers often incised them with symbols, such as two or three lines, spirals or meanders, a chevron or a lozenge. These geometric symbols may have stimulated or identified certain functions of the divinity. In fact, I believe that these schematic renderings distinctively focused attention on the symbolic message they conveyed.

Schematic figurines comprise one of the most captivating and intriguing aspects of Old European art. Although realistic, beautiful likenesses attract more attention, many more schematic figurines are excavated than lifelike ones. This should not surprise us, because prehistoric art was symbolic art. Old European artisans could create schematic figurines easily, and, like the Christian cross, in religious practice these figures communicated the same symbolic concepts as the more representational art. These simplified images do not disparage the human body, as has been commonly thought; instead, they express a sacred message.

EXAGGERATED BODY PARTS

To express different sacred functions, figurines and other ceramic art often display unusual modifications or exaggerations. Female figurines, representing the complex feminine force, particularly show such enhancements. Some figurines show exaggerated body weight, and they have been interpreted by some as obese figures or "fat ladies." Undoubtedly, this exaggerated body weight is valued, since it appears on female figurines from several different cultures. Other figurines focus on the generative organs, the breasts and vulva, as well as the buttocks. Such emphasis enhances the power of that particular part of the body. For instance, many figurines and vases prominently display breasts. The tradition of emphasizing breasts actually began much earlier, during the Upper Paleolithic, and continued much later, into the Bronze Age. Breasts symbolize the nurturing and regen-

Figure 2. Disproportionate, supernatural buttocks on this figurine reveal their symbolic importance (as a regenerative symbol related to double-egg symbolism). Her pubic triangle is marked with two lines. Starčevo culture; c. 6000–5800 B.C. (Donja Branjevina, near Osijek, Serbia).

eration of life. The depiction of breasts on ceramic vessels used in rituals clearly shows the female body, and by extension the body of the divine female, as a vessel of nourishment or renewal. Although breasts obviously embody nourishment and life sustenance, their portrayal on megalithic tomb walls also attests to the comprehensive spiritual role of the Old European goddess in death and the regeneration of life.

On many figurines, the breasts and the upper part of the body appear relatively thin and de-emphasized, while the lower parts—the buttocks, thighs, and legs—are enlarged beyond natural proportion (Fig. 2). The figurine's center of gravity, and its religious significance, rests in the lower part of the body. These figurines often display exaggerated vulvas and buttocks. Although we almost automatically think of the vulva and buttocks as sexual symbols, in Old European art they most likely signified life giving and sustenance, rather than eroticism. The symbolic value of exaggerated buttocks relates to breasts and double eggs, where the power of the life-giving symbol increases by doubling. Sometimes the artisan molded the buttocks of a figurine on egg-shaped clay cores or pebbles; thus she or he may have felt the interconnectedness of the symbols of buttocks and eggs. This symbolism was inherited from the Upper Paleolithic: on rocks dating to the Magdalenian period, in southern France (La Roche, Lalinde) and southern Germany (Gönnersdorf), artisans engraved buttocks in silhouette and marked them with one, two, or more lines. The early Neolithic figurines with egg-shaped buttocks often exhibit two lines as well, perhaps illustrating the state where one human being becomes two, in pregnancy.

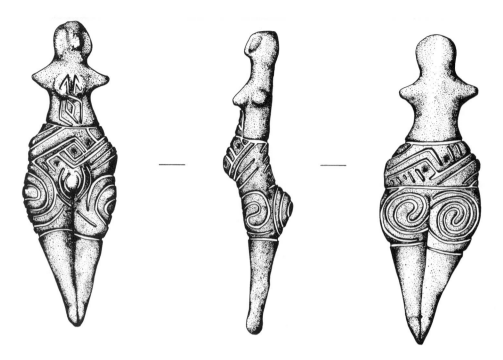

Figure 3. Interest centers on
the vulva of this terra-cotta
figurine, which is flanked by
semicircles and surrounded
by spirals and meanders. Lines
across her waist and thighs
delineate the body section that
contains these engraved symbols. The artisan carved V signs
over her breasts and a possible
script sign below them. Vinča
culture; c. 5000 B.C. (Slatino,
western Bulgaria).

In both Upper Paleolithic and Neolithic art, the vulva dominates symbolic portrayals, appearing separately or greatly enlarged on figurines and
pottery vessels. The vulva appears as a triangle, an oval, an open circle,
or even as a bud or branch—a fact that emphasizes its life-giving, rather
than erotic, role. The frequency and longevity of this symbol in the archaeological record (over thirty thousand years) speaks for its essential role
in the belief system. Three large rock-carved female figures from Angles-
sur-l'Anglin (Vienne), in southern France (dated circa 17,000–14,000 B.C.),
exhibit neither heads, breasts, arms, nor feet, but their vulvas are displayed
prominently. Giedion (1962, 178) comments on the L'Anglin frieze, saying, "Had there been a need to represent the entire body, it could easily
have been done in the space available. But apparently no such need was
felt, and so only the abdomen, the pelvic area, and the vulva have been
carved. The entire figure was not important, but only the fragment which
stood for the whole." We can easily understand why the vulva figured
so prominently among the script and symbolic messages encoded by
artisans on figurines. On one figurine dating to about 5000 B.C., semicircles enhance the oval vulva, while a meander and spirals decorate the
thighs and buttocks (Fig. 3). This symbolic combination conveys dynamism: growing, flowing, and turning. As in other symbolism, the feminine force is active and life producing. The goddess embodied the mystery
of new life.

The faces of both male and female figurines display a peculiar shape: some show severely angular jawbones, while others look perfectly oval. This feature, combined with stylized eyes and other facial features, gives these figurines an otherworldly appearance (Figs. 4 and 5; see also Figs. 13, 14, 24, 28, below). Closer scrutiny reveals that these peculiar "facial features" represent masks. For many decades, archaeologists have failed to recognize masks on figurines, even those with a distinct demarcation between the face and the edge of the mask. In fact, at the Achilleion site in northern Greece (which dates from 6400 B.C. to 5600 B.C.), we found pregnant goddess figurines with detachable masks on rod-shaped necks. In exceptional cases, figurines hold a mask instead of wearing it (Fig. 6). In contemporary cultures that still use masks in ritual, the masks serve to personify a supernatural force. The ancient Greeks employed masks in drama and in ritual for the same function: to embody the deities, as well as heroines and heroes. Masks most likely had a similar purpose during the European Neolithic. In fact, the masks of the Greeks undoubtedly descended from Neolithic times.

The Neolithic Old Europeans used actual life-sized masks in rituals and ceremonies. They probably created some masks from wood, so we have lost them to decay. But life-sized masks of ceramic and metal have been discovered from the Vinča culture and in the Varna cemetery of Bulgaria. Archaeologists have uncovered masks from Neolithic sites in the Near East, such as the Naḥal Ḥemar cave in the Judaean desert of Israel.[2] The figurines of Old Europe may represent ritual participants wearing masks, or an actual deity. Some masked figurines lack specific features, but others retain intricate details that reveal which aspect of the goddess the figurine embodies.

Figure 4. Masked figurine heads from the Sesklo culture; c. 6000–5700 B.C. (from sites near Larisa, Thessaly, northern Greece).

Figure 5. Frequently the divinity's mask is depicted in relief upon a vase neck. Starčevo culture; early sixth millennium B.C. (Gladnice near Priština, Kosovo-Metohije). Preserved H 10.4 cm.

Although Old European artists often used masks to indicate special aspects of the female divine, figurines sometimes directly assimilated animal characteristics. Figurines with animal-shaped heads occur frequently. Snake-, bird-, pig-, and bear-headed figurines have all been discovered. All of these manifestations, whether masked or not, represent the intimate relationship among humankind, nature, and the divine during the Neolithic.

By studying markings on the masks and figurines, we can discern how the divine manifested through different animals. These masks represent

Figure 6. Exceptional figurine holds a mask instead of wearing it. The figurine's left hand clasps a mask, and its right hand holds an askos (bird-shaped vase). It was unearthed in a burned aboveground building, along with four other anthropomorphic and zoomorphic figurines. Vinča culture (Phase C); c. 4700–4500 B.C. (Liubcova, Caraş-Severin, southwestern Romania). Preserved H 11.5 cm (head was inserted into a hole).

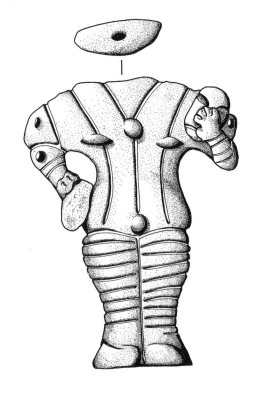

the goddess' sacred animals, and when worn by a human figure they embody a fusion of animal and human forces. Figurines take on bird beaks, snake eyes, ram horns, or bear or pig snouts. Sometimes figurines with animal bodies wear human masks (see Fig. 24, below). Deer, fish, elk, snakes, bears, frogs, rams, pigs, dogs, boars, hedgehogs, and waterbirds (to name a few) all played important parts in religious symbolism.

Life-Giving and Life-Sustaining Images

LIFE-GIVING IMAGES

The Birth-Giving Goddess

Figurines depicting birth eloquently attest to the goddess' most obvious role as life giver. Neolithic artisans rendered her seated or semireclining in the birth-giving position, with knees bent and legs raised, sometimes with a hand behind her head. Her vulva may swell in parturition, the physiologic state just before birth. The presence of masks and symbolic markings on many of these birth-giving figurines affirms their spiritual nature and the attempt of the artisan to communicate with the goddess. The birth goddess appears for more than twenty thousand years, from the Upper Paleolithic through the Neolithic. She may appear in threes, often as three Fates, in early historical religions: the Germanic Norns, the Greek Moirai, and the Roman Parcae are all threefold goddesses of fate.

Birth was sacred—in fact, it was probably one of the most sacrosanct events in Neolithic religion. In the early Neolithic, peoples constructed special rooms where birth took place. We may conceive of these rooms as birthing shrines. At Çatal Hüyük, in south central Turkey (ancient Anatolia), excavations revealed a room where inhabitants apparently performed rituals connected with birthing. They painted the room red, reminding us that red, the color of blood, was the color of life. Stylized figures on the walls illustrate women giving birth, while circular forms and wavy lines painted nearby may symbolize the cervix, umbilical cord, and amniotic fluid. A low plaster platform could have been used for actual birthing. The color and symbolism in the room suggest that people regarded birth as a religious event, and that they accompanied it with ritual. On the island of Malta in the central Mediterranean, the Tarxien and Mnajdra temple artifacts indicate similar practices; these artifacts include a model of a low couch that could have served birth giving, and a birth-giving figurine with nine lines across her back.

The connection between moisture, life, and the life-giving goddess contained deep cosmological significance. Human life began in the watery realm of a woman's womb. So, by analogy, the goddess was the source of all human, plant, and animal life. She ruled all water sources: lakes, rivers, springs, wells, and rain clouds.

The fact that the goddess birthed new life into existence explains the water symbols, such as nets, streams, and parallel lines, on many of her images. New life springs from the mysterious watery realm, analogous to the womb's amniotic fluid. Net symbolism, which continues from the Neolithic through the historic ages,[3] seems to be specifically associated with this mystical life-bringing fluid. This net symbol occurs repeatedly through time in squares, ovals, circles, lozenges, bladder forms, triangles (pubic triangles), and bands on figurines and vases, often in association with snakes, bears, frogs, fish, bulls' heads, and rams' heads.

Even in historical times, people have considered wells, springs, and ponds to be sacred places of healing inhabited by female spirits. Many early Christian pilgrims visited springs whose patron saint was female (usually the Virgin Mary or, in Ireland, Saint Brigit).[4]

The birth-giving goddess survived in classical Greek religion as Artemis Eileithyia, and in pan-European folklore as one of three goddesses or Fates. Latvians and Lithuanians celebrated birth in saunas up to the twentieth century. They propitiated Laima, the birth-giving goddess, the spinner and weaver of human life, with offerings that included a hen, or towels and other woven materials. We shall return to this amazingly tenacious goddess in the last chapter.

Mother and Child

The mother and child sculptural tradition so venerated during Christian times actually began millennia ago, and Neolithic art provides numerous examples. Just as their historical equivalents, the figurines show a mother nursing or holding her child, but the representations are distinctly Neolithic. The mother and child have human bodies, but both may assume animal masks that show communication with, or embodiment of, the divine. Some of the most touching Old European figurines show a mother tenderly embracing or nursing her child. Sometimes both mother and child wear bear masks. In addition, several bear-headed figurines display pouches on their backs, perhaps for carrying a baby.

The Bear and Deer

The bear and deer consistently appear with the birth-giving goddess. She often incarnated in these forms to assist with the birthing and nursing of the young. Ancient Greeks considered these two animals as incarnations of Artemis,[5] and other European folktales with deep prehistoric roots also connect the bear, deer, and birth-giving goddess.

The bear's history as the cosmic nurturer extends back into the Upper

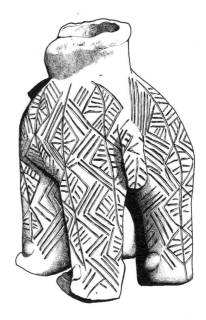

Figure 7. Bear-shaped lamp decorated with striated triangles, chevrons, and tri-lines. Danilo culture; end of sixth millennium B.C. (Smilčić near Zadar, Adriatic coast, Croatia).

Paleolithic, when people must have observed her annual pattern of hibernation and reawakening.[6] The bear was the perfect symbol of death and regeneration: when she hibernated she metaphorically entered the realm of death, and when she emerged from the cave, she was metaphorically reborn. Of course, other animals hibernate, but the bear evoked particularly powerful symbolism. She not only emerged from the cave alive, she brought forth another new life: the cub born and nursed during the winter, when it was assumed that the bear was in a deathlike sleep. Consequently, the bear, in thus representing the course of birth, death, and rebirth, would come to be connected with the goddess associated with childbirth. The numerous bear motifs used in creating exquisite lamps, vases, figurines, and offering containers reveal the ritual importance of the bear goddess. Bear-shaped lamps are characteristic of the sixth millennium B.C. (Fig. 7), and bear-legged, ring-handled vessels probably used for offerings of sacred water are also found. As already noted, the bear's likeness often adorned mother/child representations, confirming her mystical maternal role.

The deer or elk was also sacred to the birth-giving goddess. The deer's symbolic tradition equals that of the bear, extending far back into the Upper Paleolithic. (Archaeologists found deer remains dated at circa 14,000 B.C. in ritual pits at the El Juyo and Tito Bustillo cave sites in Spain.) The life-renewing aspects of the deer's antlers held great symbolic power because they appeared seasonally during spring. Archaeologists often find deer antlers, shoulder blades, and teeth in Neolithic burials. There exist exquisite vases, dating to the Neolithic, shaped like deer or with deer portrayed in relief. During the Neolithic, these vases were undoubtedly employed in rituals. Prehistoric and early historic paintings, mosaics, and tiles identified deer with wells, freshwater streams, and the water of life. Even today, northern Asiatic and European mythologies regard the pregnant doe as a mystical life-giver.

LIFE-SUSTAINING IMAGES

Birds and the Bird Goddess

Birds overshadow the numerous animals that repeatedly occur in Neolithic art. Many mythologies worldwide recount how the world originated from an egg, and certainly as a life source the bird's egg conveyed strong symbolic meaning. Bird eggs also provided extra nourishment, both during the Neolithic and earlier. The mysterious seasonal disappearance and reappearance of migrating birds and their enigmatic appearance from an egg, source of both new life and nourishment, probably contributed to their veneration.[7] Birds embodied health, fertility, and good fortune—all important to life sustenance.

Most bird goddess figurines combine the human female form with a specific species of bird: waterbirds (ducks, geese, cranes, herons); spring birds (cuckoos); or birds of prey (crows, owls, vultures). Waterbirds appear most often as figurines and vases. These birds inhabited both terrestrial rivers and lakes and the celestial environment, where rain originates. They provided a link between earthly life and beyond. Their appearance on ritual vessels connotes the life-giving power of liquids poured as libation offerings. To this day in European folklore, waterbirds such as swans and ducks bring good fortune or increase material goods.

The bird goddess often is represented as a figurine with a beaked or duck-billed mask and the body of a human female. When she lacks a mask, her face displays a beak-shaped nose. In the absence of a discernibly avian face, bird goddess figurines take on a hunched posture. Their stumpy, wing-shaped arms and exaggerated buttocks suggest the body of a bird. Small holes in the shoulders and masks of figurines may have been used to attach bird feathers, a practice recorded through modern folk custom. In Bronze Age and later representations, artisans portrayed ducks as ships or showed them pulling vehicles bearing the goddess. Whether masked or not, bird goddess figurines exhibit her symbols: chevrons, tri-lines, meanders, and streams.

Snakes and the Snake Goddess

Snakes dwell both in water and in the ground. They hibernate in the earth's body during the winter, and they return in spring. Further, their

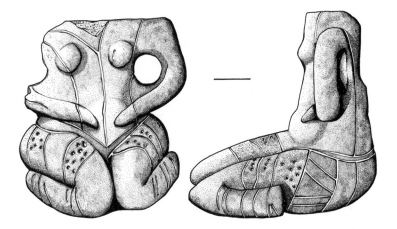

Figure 8. This squatting figurine with snake-shaped limbs has dotted bands over the hips and thighs. Vinča culture; c. 4900–4800 B.C. (Vinča near Belgrade). Preserved H 7.9 cm.

periodic molting reinforced their role as symbols of renewal. Snakes were thus thought to bring life in spring. They were also thought to embody deceased ancestors.

The classic image of the snake goddess portrays her sitting yogi-like or squatting, with snake-shaped limbs (Fig. 8). Her head appears either human, snake-like, or masked and perhaps crowned. Snake heads appear with round eyes and a long mouth on vase rims or handles. Horned snake heads were composed in relief on vases. As with the bird goddess, people associated specific symbols with the snake goddess: the snake coil, spiral, zigzag, or wavy lines, imitating the snake's movement. Other symbols resembled dotted or diamond bands, imitating the snake's skin. A snake coil often occupies the central position on painted or engraved dishes, votive tablets, or megalithic tombs. Snakes crawl or zigzag up vase sides or handles from the Neolithic, through the Bronze Age, and beyond.

Vegetation Goddesses and Gods

THE PREGNANT VEGETATION GODDESS

The annual cycle of germination, growth, and harvest held both mystery and material sustenance for early farmers. These ancient agriculturalists must have recognized the analogy between grain seeds germinating in the field and new life growing in the womb, for the representation of this analogy is found in many Old European sites. The pregnant vegetation goddess (she is popularly known as the earth goddess or Mother Earth) was one of the most-represented female figures depicted in Neolithic Old Europe. Hundreds of pregnant goddess figurines have been unearthed from Old European settlement excavations.

Many Old European cultures connected this goddess with food, especially grain and bread. Archaeologists often find pregnant goddess figurines near bread ovens. At Achilleion in southern Thessaly, Greece, my colleagues and I found altars and special stone platforms with offering pits near ovens, perhaps associated with harvest rituals. The association of this goddess with the pig also reinforces her connection with grain and the earth. The pig fattens quickly and so provides an obvious analogy to the ripening crops and fruits. Archaeologists have excavated large and small figurines and vases portraying pigs, along with exquisite human-sized ceramic pig masks. The Old Europeans may have used these masks in rituals dedicated to the pregnant vegetation goddess.

Farmers throughout prehistory and history recognized cyclical time, since they knew the annual cycle of planting, growth, and harvest. They observed festivals and rituals at appropriate times during the cycle. The pregnant vegetation goddess, who was intimately linked with this cycle, underwent her own changes as the year progressed. Figurines of this goddess, dating to the Neolithic, often show her as hugely pregnant. Later, for example in ancient Greece, this figure is represented in dual form, very likely depicting mother-daughter pairs, the spring-summer and fall-winter aspects of the goddess. The pregnant one can look young and fertile when juxtaposed next to her older, dying aspect, portrayed as a sorrowful crone.

The early Cucuteni (Tripolye) culture, which dated from circa 4800–3500 B.C., provides us with the clearest insight into Neolithic rituals honoring the pregnant vegetation goddess. At the Luka-Vrublevetskaya site on the upper Dniester River, broken pig figurines showed traces of grain, and some sixty figurines bore evidence of grain impressions on their surface (Bibikov 1953; some are illustrated in Gimbutas 1974, Fig. 165). When technicians x-rayed these very porous clay figurines, they found three grain types (wheat, barley, and millet) stuffed inside. The excavator, Bibikov, observed that the potter had tempered the clay figurines with roughly ground flour and had tossed them into the fire immediately after their manufacture, when the clay was still wet. Here we have powerful evidence for a ritual associating grain, flour, and baking with the goddess, performed in order to assure abundant bread.

Even after Old European culture disintegrated and Indo-European social and religious systems took hold, European agriculturalists tenaciously venerated this goddess. The agrarian festivals practiced in Greece and Rome continued traditions inherited from the Neolithic. Classical authors left us numerous descriptions of sowing, ripening, and harvest festivals that exude archaic ambiance. These narratives illuminate the phenomenal role of the pregnant vegetation goddess from prehistory to the present; they will be explored further in chapter 7.

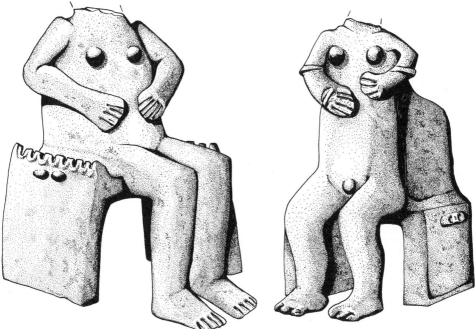

Figure 9. These enthroned male and female nudes may represent vegetation deities. The "male" god, adorned with armrings, has breasts and a penis. A rectangular vessel, perhaps for offerings, attaches to the male god's back. Although stray finds, the pair most likely came from the temple of this rich settlement; the temple yielded many enthroned female and male gods. Tisza culture; c. 4800–4700 B.C. (Szegvár-Tűzköves, southeastern Hungary).

THE VEGETATION YEAR GOD

As a divine metaphor for the cyclic growth and decay of the plant world, a male deity was worshiped as consort of the pregnant vegetation goddess. The male year god of vegetation takes on several forms that mirror the changing seasons. Thus the male force complements the female.

As a young man, the year god embodies the strength and virility needed to revive the world from winter's deep sleep. He apparently helped awaken the sleeping earth goddess. The Sesklo culture of Thessaly and the succeeding Dimini culture both made images reflecting the strong and virile aspect of the year god, portraying him nude and aroused.[8] In maturity, the year god embodied the harvest, as shown by the presence of a sickle or crook across his shoulder or attached to his belt. In wintry old age, the sorrowful year god ponders the end of his cycle. From around 6000 B.C. onward, this god appears seated on a stool or throne with his hands on his knees or supporting his chin. The Sesklo culture created many likenesses of the aging year god, dating from around 6000–5500 B.C. Just as the pregnant vegetation goddess, the year god of vegetation endured in folklore and mythology, especially in his declining and sorrowful state.

The pairing of male and female harvest deities thus goes back to the European Neolithic. The elderly female and male sculptures found in one Cernavoda grave dating from circa 4700 B.C. (representing the Hamangia culture of Romania, near the Black Sea) very likely portray such a pair. Other possible divine vegetation pairs, dating from the same period, come from the Szegvár-Tüzköves site of the Tisza culture (Fig. 9). This complementary relationship provides sharp contrast to the dominating role male deities played in later European religions.

THE SACRED MARRIAGE

Rituals uniting the sacred male and female forces may have taken place in Old European times, but we have little archaeological evidence for them. Although peculiar by modern standards, in both Europe and the Near East, ancient peoples considered this sacred male and female coupling necessary for the well-being and fertility of the land and its inhabitants. We find widespread texts describing sacred marriage rites in the earliest historical records, dating to around 3000 B.C.[9] The prevalence of the rite by that time speaks for an earlier origin, probably communal, perhaps in the Old European religious system, though little evidence exists. From Çatal Hüyük, archaeologists recovered one figurine showing a couple engaging in intercourse. Another came from the Near Eastern Natufian site, dating to about 10,000 B.C.[10] The "Gumelniţa Lovers," a statuette from the

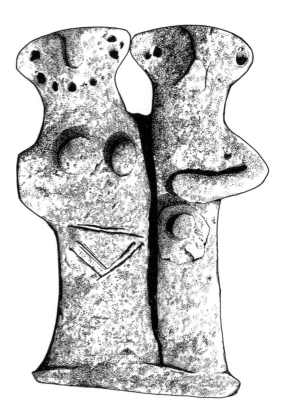

Figure 10. "The Gumelniţa Lovers," conjoined female and male terra-cotta statuette, possibly portrays a sacred marriage. East Balkan Karanovo culture; c. 5000–4750 B.C. (Gumelniţa tell, lower Danube, southern Romania). H 6.8 cm.

Gumelniţa site in southern Romania, which depicts a man and a woman tenderly embracing, might portray participants in a sacred marriage (Fig. 10).

Descriptions of sexual rituals mainly come from the earliest historical records of the Near East. These texts refer to the "sacred marriage" (in ancient Greek the *hieros gamos*), in which a couple engaged in ceremonial sexual intercourse. Ritual duties fell on only a few special individuals, priestesses (representing the goddess) and priests (representing the year god), or queens and kings, who performed the rite on behalf of their subjects.[11]

Images of Death and Regeneration

In the cycle of life, the feminine force—the goddess—not only manifested in birth, fertility, and life sustenance, she also embodied death, decay, and regeneration.[12] As death wielder, she loomed as a terrifying raptor, a poisonous snake, or the stiff white nude. For Old European cultures, however, death did not portend the ultimate end but remained part of nature's cycle. In Old European religious imagery, death was immediately coupled with regeneration. Yet regeneration continued timelessly, and special images (especially those of water creatures) specifically reminded the devotees of the goddess that she stayed with them. In this role, we see the goddess traversing both worlds—death's illusory terror and birth's sweet promise—providing a link between them.

Birds of Prey

Raptors—birds of prey—most often embody death in Old European imagery. The "Vulture Shrine" at Çatal Hüyük provides a graphic example. The walls of the shrine show painted vultures with outstretched wings swooping down on headless bodies. Several thousand miles away, in the megalithic tombs of western Europe, another bird of prey predominates. There devotees carved the likeness of the owl, specifically its eyes, into the bones and stones of the awesome monuments. This imagery also appears on the solitary standing stones known as menhirs. At both Çatal Hüyük and the megalithic monuments, additional features connect these two raptors with the goddess. Some of the vultures of Çatal Hüyük possess human feet, while the megalithic stony owl eyes stare from above a necklace and human breasts—and frequently appear with the human vulva.

The superhuman qualities and near-human appearance of the owl—its upright perch, mortal stare, fantastic vision, and nightly screams—especially evoked mystery and awe. Fascination with this bird must predate the Neolithic. The owl appears on Upper Paleolithic cave walls: three snowy owls are identified in Les Trois Frères cave, in southern France. History

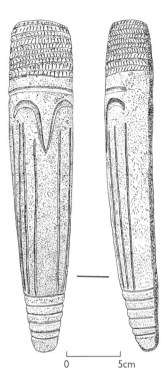

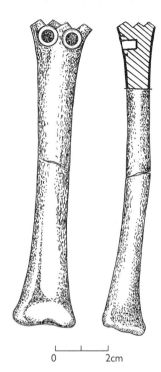

Figure 11. The death goddess' symbols of regeneration include owl eyes and beak associated with vulva and phallus. This phallic figurine with character-istic beak and eyebrow motif was engraved on a dolmen. Neolithic of Portugal; c. 3000 B.C. (Casainbos, north of Lisbon).

Figure 12. The owl goddess' role in death and regeneration speaks through these bone images that reveal the goddess' staring, round, regenerative eyes. These images were placed in graves. Here, her numinous round eyes of carefully inlaid shell gaze from the end of a cow bone. LBK culture; c. 5000 B.C. (Ensisheim, Upper Rhein).

as well as iconography connects the owl with important goddesses such as Athena, the Greek goddess of knowledge and wisdom, and Lil-Lilith, the Sumerian-Akkadian goddess whose name also appears in the Hebrew Old Testament. It has been postulated that Lilith's name may mean "screech owl." This night bird naturally rules death and the underworld.

Old European owl symbolism fuses death and life. Owl representations on tombs and statues in Brittany and Ireland have a vulva in the center. Owl-shaped urns from the north Aegean also exhibit a vulva or snake coils. Portuguese dolmens include regenerative phallic objects with the owl god-dess' features (Fig. 11). Owl and snake associations continue repeatedly throughout the Neolithic and into the Bronze Age. The owl's eyes may be considered the most impressive symbols of regeneration, especially when they are depicted on bare bones, symbols of death (Fig. 12).

An understanding of the practice of excarnation helps us to clarify the role of the bird of prey in Neolithic religion; it particularly explains its role in the death process. In this burial practice, people did not bury their dead immediately, but exposed them outdoors on platforms. There, birds of prey would strip the body of its flesh, leaving only the bones. The removal of flesh was considered necessary to complete the death process. When only the bones remained, the individual could be buried and the next segment of the cycle could begin. Two different raptors predominated in Old European mortuary symbolism, each in a different region: the vulture dwells only in the Near East and southern Europe, while the owl lives in most of Europe. Although excarnation was not universally practiced, throughout Europe and the Near East vulture and/or owl symbols represented the goddess who brought death, yet ruled life and assured birth.

The Stiff White Goddess

Goddess figurines consistently accompanied people in their graves, where the goddess lay stiff as the bare bone that symbolizes death. Her forearms are folded across her torso, assuming the same position in which corpses were often buried (Fig. 13a–f). In an obvious association with death, the figurine is bone-colored, often carved from marble, alabaster, or other white stone. Unlike other figurines, the stiff white goddess possesses small breasts, downplaying her nourishing or life-sustaining aspects. In this form, the goddess accompanies her people through their transition to her other realm. Very common depictions of the stiff white goddess are the Cycladic figurines, dating from circa 3200 to circa 2000 B.C., excavated from graves in the Cycladic Islands of the Aegean Sea. While remarkable in their geometric proportions and sometimes considered the source for later developments in classical art, the Cycladic figurines in fact have prototypes created three thousand years earlier for burials in southern and southeast Europe.

For Old European cultures, time moved in cycles, not a terminating line. This worldview applied as much to life and death as to sowing and harvest. Regeneration immediately followed death. The stiff white goddess specifically linked death with regeneration through her exaggerated pubic triangle. The proportions of the figurines draw attention to the womb, promising regeneration from the body of the goddess. So at death, when one's remains are placed in the tomb, he or she symbolically reenters the goddess' body to be reborn.

Neolithic and later sculptures of stiff figures represent the white goddess as one of her main epiphanies: the bird of prey or poisonous snake. Some sculptures feature masks with no facial attributes other than a large nose, which may symbolize a bird's beak (Fig. 13b, e, f). Some examples from western Anatolia have wings in addition to the protruding large nose.

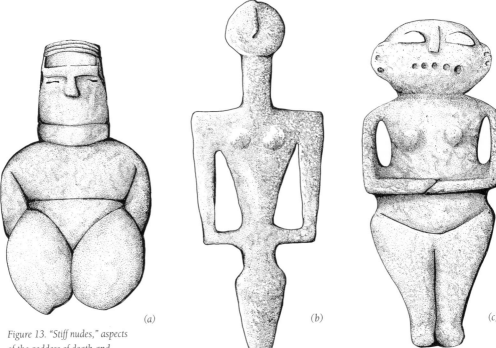

(a)   (b)   (c)

Figure 13. "Stiff nudes," aspects of the goddess of death and regeneration, belong to graves of the fifth to third millennium B.C. (a) Gray stone figurine from a rock-cut tomb. Bonu Ighinu culture; mid-fifth millennium B.C. (Cuccuru S'Arriu, Oristano, Sardinia). H 17 cm. (b) Alabaster figurine. Ozieri culture; end of fifth millennium B.C. (Porto Ferro tomb, Sardinia). H 44 cm. (c) Marble figurine. Karanovo VI culture; mid-fifth millennium B.C. (Lovets near Stara Zagora, Bulgaria). (d) One of three similar figurines found in a girl's tomb. Late Cucuteni (Tripolye) culture; c. 3500 B.C. (Vykhvatintsi cemetery, Moldova). H 18.2 cm. (e) Marble figurine. Early Cycladic culture; end of fourth millennium to early third millennium B.C. (Delos, Cyclades). H 11 cm. (f) Marble figurine. Cycladic II culture; mid-third millennium B.C. (Chalandriani, Syros Island, Cyclades).

Similar figures come from Mesopotamia and the eastern Mediterranean area. For instance, an elaborate tiara crowns the nude and winged Sumerian Lil (Hebrew Lilith), who grips her lion mount with her taloned feet (circa 2300 B.C.). Two owls flank her. Many of her eastern Mediterranean portrayals from the fourteenth to thirteenth centuries B.C. still reflected the same bearing: nude, with a large pubic triangle, an enormous owl's beak, and huge round earrings.

Other stiff white goddess masks look totally different: they lack prominent noses and instead feature teeth below a long mouth (Fig. 13c). Masks with prominent noses characterize the Mediterranean and Aegean areas, while those with emphasized mouths typify the Karanovo culture in Romania and Bulgaria. The long-mouth masks are broad and usually have pierced earlobes for attaching copper or gold earrings; they also have perforated chins for affixing copper or gold ring-shaped pendants (Fig. 14a–b). Some masks are shown with a diadem or turban (Fig. 14b). The gold ring-shaped pendants appear slightly anthropomorphized, having eyes above the central hole and a protrusion for the head. This type of mask—broad, with a long mouth and teeth—represents the face of the snake, the second main epiphany of the white goddess. Folklore provides much support for this assumption. Although in some countries (for instance, Ireland),

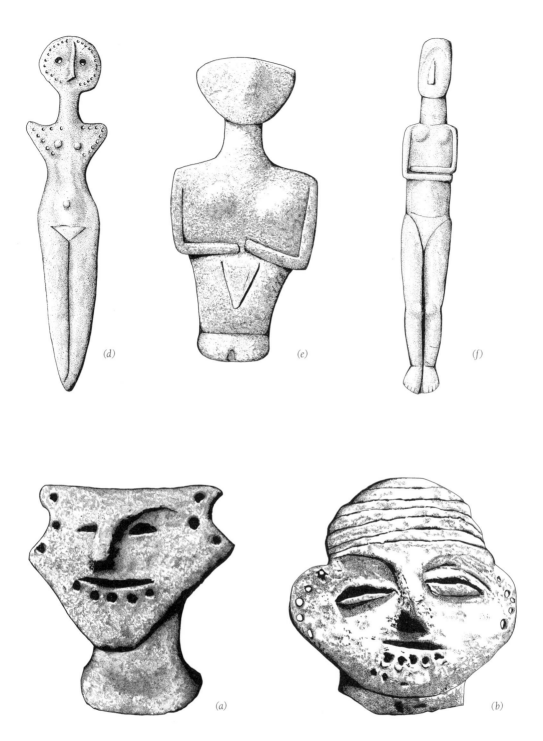

(d)

(e)

(f)

(a)

(b)

Figure 14. Figurine masks portraying the goddess of death and regeneration have long mouths above holes that could have held teeth or fangs. Both (a) and (b) relate to life-sized ceramic masks found in Varna graves. Karanovo VI culture; mid-fifth millennium B.C. (Varna Museum, Bulgaria).

the goddess of death appears as a white lady in the guise of a raptor, in other countries, particularly in eastern Europe, she appears as a poisonous snake.

The Gorgon

Some of the most remarkable masks recovered from Old European excavations very likely represent the snake goddess. Archaeologists unearthed these masks from the Varna cemetery in eastern Bulgaria on the Black Sea coast, famous for its finds of gold and jewelry dating to the mid-fifth millennium B.C. Attached to the life-sized Varna masks were gold ornaments: a diadem and ring-shaped pendants. The masks' round eyes, long mouth, and studs representing teeth were characteristic of the snake. These masks were covered with jewelry and symbolic items: rhytons; deer's teeth; ceramic dishes; triangular bone pendants; shell, stone, and gold beads; a spindle whorl; a double-egg head pin; and red ocher and a dish for crushing ocher. Despite the frightening profiles of the Varna mask, the offerings buried with them—especially deer teeth, double eggs, red ocher, triangles, and spindle whorls—symbolize regeneration and life. These symbolic grave goods suggest that worshipers conducted rituals of regeneration when they buried the goddess' mask.

The same mask type found at Varna and depicted on stiff nude figurines (Figs. 13c and 14) also appears on enthroned goddesses and anthropomorphic vases. An anthropomorphic vase from the site of Sultana (near Olteniţa in southern Romania), dating to the mid-fifth millennium B.C., furnishes further clues for deciphering this aspect of the goddess. The vase shows a goddess with a horrific face, exposed teeth, and a lolling tongue. She is the ancestress of the frightening Gorgon, familiar to us from Greek mythology. As with the Varna masks, the Sultana vase juxtaposes the image of death with symbols of regeneration: the front of the vase depicts a large vulva flanked with crescents, and the back shows spirals, bird feet, and a double egg (see Gimbutas 1989, Fig. 327). Certain Old European cul-

Figure 15. Round eyes, gaping nostrils, and a lolling tongue intensify this red-on-white-painted ceramic "Gorgon" head typical of the classic Sesklo culture; c. 6000–5800 B.C. (Thessaly, northern Greece). 1:1 scale.

Figure 16. Archaic Greek
Gorgons exhibit staring eyes,
large fangs, and extended
tongue, with vines, snakes,
and lizards emanating from
their heads. (a) Relief (Syracuse
Museum, Italy); (b) Painting
from an Attic amphora (Louvre
Museum, Paris, France).

(a)

(b)

tures, in fact, developed Gorgon imagery well before the fifth millennium
B.C. The Gorgon extends back to at least 6000 B.C., as a ceramic mask from
the Sesklo culture illustrates (Fig. 15).[13] The Gorgon is a genuinely European symbol, and she makes her presence known throughout the southeastern European Neolithic and Bronze Ages.

The Gorgon finds her most frightening realization in ancient Greek
images that date from the seventh to the fifth centuries B.C. Some of these
images, undoubtedly inherited from Neolithic times, append the grinning
mask and pendant tongue of the Gorgon Medusa to the body and wings
of a bee, an important symbol of life regeneration. Masks of her paralyz-
ing face almost always adjoin symbols of dynamic life energy: vines, snakes,
spirals, and lizards (Fig. 16a–b). The Rhodos Gorgon, dated from the late
seventh century B.C., has bee wings, yet she also clutches cranes.[14]

Greek texts record the belief that blood from Medusa's snaky locks contained magic properties that could both create and destroy. The first venomous drop from the Medusa's hair-snakes caused instant death; the second, from Medusa's veins, brought rebirth and life.[15] The death-drop of Medusa's blood may have been a transposed and distorted memory of women's powerful moon-blood, and Medusa's terrible mask could reflect menstrual fears and taboos. Even in many contemporary cultures, superstitions warn that the look of a menstruating woman can turn a man to stone, contaminate food, or endanger hunting. By the seventh century B.C., Medusa's head, chopped off by the hero Perseus, was appropriated for the aegis, or badge of divine power, intended to protect the viewer from evil. The Gorgon was frequently placed on coins, public buildings, temple pediments, individual seals, public and private roof tops, and the shields of warriors; she also adorns the breastplate of the warrior-goddess Athena.

Juxtaposition of the goddess' breasts and vulva with death symbols, particularly raptors, reflects the Neolithic belief that the goddess brought both life and death. At Çatal Hüyük, the walls of a shrine portray breasts molded in clay relief over the beaks of vultures. Until recently, researchers thought that such reliefs were confined to Anatolia, the Near East, and southeast Europe. However, recently there has been a significant find in central Europe, in an Alpine lake. Archaeologists working in Lake Constance on the Swiss-German border investigated a building of the Pfyn culture (3900–3800 B.C.), now submerged in shallow waters. Wood structures with simple clay-coated walls typify this region and time period. Unusual reliefs and paintings, however, decorated the interior of this structure, including images of breasts. The parallels between Çatal Hüyük and Lake Constance are striking. Both reveal shrines dedicated to the goddess of death and regeneration worshiped across Europe and the Near East.

SYMBOLS SPECIFIC TO REGENERATION

The spontaneous generation of nature was a major concern of Neolithic religion. This preoccupation generated the flood of Old European sacred images concerned with renewal. Most images honored various animals: fish, frogs, dogs, goats, hedgehogs, bulls' heads, all of which symbolize the uterus in some way. Some images reflected the natural world: seeds, vines, trees, phalli, plant shoots, life columns. Abstract symbols also occurred frequently: spirals, hooks, triangles, and concentric circles. We shall see how all were symbols of regeneration that embodied nascent life ready to burst forth. These symbols often fused with the ultimate symbols of regeneration: the goddess' body and procreative organs.

The Frog and Frog Goddess

The significance of the fish and frog to regenerative symbolism derives from their aquatic environment. Their habitat paralleled the uterine amniotic fluid, that watery realm where regeneration takes place. The annual spring appearance of the frog and toad and their close resemblance to the human fetus further emphasize their regenerative associations.

Neolithic art features myriad female and frog hybrids. At many Neolithic sites, artisans carved small frog-shaped goddesses from green or black stone and set them in relief on vases and temple walls (Figs. 17 and 18). The presence of the goddess' vulva accentuates the regenerative force of these images.

Neolithic pottery often stresses schematized frogs. Abbreviated into a hieroglyph, the frog or toad became an M sign. Large vases from the Vinča and Tisza cultures, dating to around 5000 B.C., bear an M sign on the neck above the goddess' human countenance. Certain peculiar handles cannot be human arms, but instead resemble frog legs (Fig. 19a–b). Frog-leg handles became a conventional feature that identified the frog goddess on anthropomorphic vases.

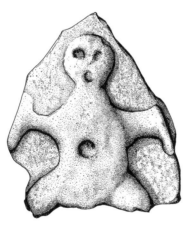

Figure 17. Reliefs of the goddess of regeneration as a frog embellish Neolithic temple walls and vases. This one is from the Cucuteni A2 (Tripolye) culture; c. 4500–4400 B.C. (Trușești, Moldova).

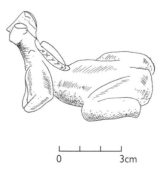

Figure 18. This terra-cotta Neolithic frog goddess figurine dates from the mid-sixth millennium B.C. (House Q.VI.5, Hacilar, western Turkey).

0   3cm

(a)

(b)

0   6cm

Figure 19. The goddess' face floats above an M sign (representing a frog or frog-leg glyph) on large vases produced by the Tisza and Vinča cultures. These glyphs signify that the water vessels were sacred to the goddess as life source and regeneratrix. Meanders and running spirals reinforce this implication. The handles of the vessels might represent the frog goddess' upraised legs (the designs have been "rolled out" on the right for easier viewing). (a) Tisza culture, end of sixth millennium B.C. (Szakálhát Komitatsrat, southeastern Hungary). (b) Tisza culture, end of sixth millennium B.C. (Jaksopart, Szentes, southeastern Hungary).

The frog and toad image, along with the frog-shaped woman displaying her vulva, appears across a wide time span, not only during the European and Anatolian Neolithic but in the Near East, China, and the Americas. Several closely related frog deity images in Egypt and the Near East help explain the function of this goddess. Egyptians revered the frog as Heket, primordial mother of all existence. In the early predynastic period (around 3100 B.C.), she was portrayed as a woman with a frog head, or as a frog or toad impersonating the goddess. "Frog" was her hieroglyphic sign. Heket controlled fecundity and regeneration after death. Heket has been connected with the Greek Baubo, probably a wet nurse, and with the Sumerian Bau, also called Baba. Bau was the Sumerian goddess of medicine and healing. A tablet from Lagash dating from circa 2500 B.C. describes a temple dedicated to her and lists seven hundred priestesses, priests, and attendants who participated in the temple's consecration.[16] Although these latter goddesses are not represented as frogs, they have connections to the fecundity of nursing and to healing.

Baubo is the goddess who displays her vulva,[17] sometimes raising her skirt in a ritual that possibly dates to the Neolithic. Skirt-raising rituals are known from Egypt; the Greek historian Herodotus describes them in his histories, recorded in 445 B.C., calling them *ana-suromai*. Diodorus, writing in 60 B.C., mentioned that he saw women enacting a skirt-raising ritual before the sacred bull, Apis, in the Serapeum temple at Memphis.

In the early twentieth century, the Egyptologist Margaret Murray hypothesized that Baubo came to Europe from Egypt via Crete and Greece. Frog-women with exposed vulvas appear in Anatolia as early as the seventh millennium, however, confirming that Baubo's origins predate the Egyptian references. Murray, of course, did not have access to Neolithic frog-woman imagery during her lifetime, so she made her connection

Figure 20. The "Sheela na gig" from medieval Ireland and England was incorporated and honored in old churches. Sheela na gig, with her round eyes and large vulva, is none other than the ancient frog or toad goddess, the birth giver and regeneratrix inherited from the Neolithic; twelfth century A.D. (St. Mary's and St. David's Church, Kilpeck, Herefordshire, England).

through myths, crafts, and other novelties imported from Egypt or the Near East. The conception of this image may even date to the Upper Paleolithic, since bone engravings of frog-women appear in Magdalenian times. Linguistic evidence also upholds Baubo's local European source. Some European languages use the root *bau* or *bo* in association with names for toads, witches, or mushrooms. In Lithuania, *baubas* and *bauba* denote a frightening witch or monster.[18] I believe these words reflect the names of the goddess of death and regeneration before she was rendered a demon. In France, the words *bo* (in the province of Haut Saone), *botet* (in Loire), and *bot* mean "toad."

The frog goddess' dynamic persistence explains a most mysterious historical image. The "impudent" Sheela na gig (Fig. 20) appears on stone

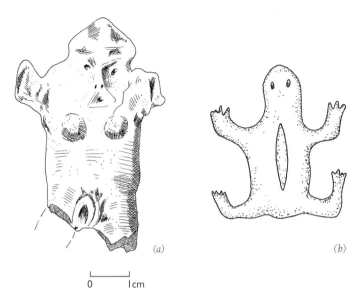

Figure 21. Portrayals of the frog or toad goddess with human face, breasts, and vulva continued through the Bronze and Iron Ages and into the twentieth century A.D. (a) Bronze Age cemetery; eleventh century B.C. (Maissau, Austria). (b) Votive painting next to Virgin Mary; dated A.D. 1811 (Bavaria).

(a)

(b)

0   1 cm

buildings in England, France, Ireland, and Wales, where she sits naked, with open, froglike legs and her hands touching her vulva. These figures were carved on castles and churches between the twelfth and the sixteenth centuries. You can usually see them above the arched entry or on church walls. The Sheela na gig's hands either point to her genitals or part her labia. Some of her sculptures have frightening heads or even skeleton-like skulls. The Sheela na gig is still highly revered but her presence, not surprisingly, is shrouded in mystery. She is none other than the descendant of the ancient frog goddess, the great regeneratrix. Many images of and beliefs about frogs and toads endured through the Bronze and Iron Ages and in European folklore and folk art (Fig. 21a–b).

Fish and the Fish Goddess

Another creature clearly homologized with the uterus and associated with aquatic symbolism is the fish. Her imagery continues through the Paleolithic and Neolithic Old Europe, the Near Eastern and Aegean Bronze Age, and the classical Greek era. In Upper Paleolithic and Neolithic engravings and paintings, fish shapes are marked with a net design, which, because it is used to capture fish in water, becomes a symbol of moisture. Engravings on bone objects dating from the Upper Paleolithic Magdalenian period frequently include fish associated with sprouts, buds, plants, snakes, does, and phalli (see Marshack 1972, 170–79, 330). These engraved objects apparently marked seasonal spring rituals of regeneration.

(a)   (b)   (c)

We can vividly see that fish represent the goddess' life-giving uterus in vase paintings portraying fish within the goddess' body. A famous vase from Boeotia, central Greece, dating from the end of the seventh century B.C., represents one such example. Here she is Artemis, the Lady of the Beasts, surrounded by lions, a bull's head, upward winding snakes, waterbirds, and swastikas, all exuding the powers of spring: the energies that reawaken life.

Fish images occur in temples and tombs: at Bugibba, a Maltese temple, archaeologists found a fish engraved on an altar stone, while in the Hypogeum, the underground tomb of Malta, a fish was portrayed in relief lying on a couch. Likewise, funerary ceramics from Minoan sarcophagi and offering vessels commonly exhibit the fish motif. The triangular temples of Lepenski Vir contained the most remarkable and unique examples of monumental fish goddess sculptures, dating from 6500–5500 B.C. (Fig. 22a–c) (see the discussion on Lepenski Vir temples, in chapter 3). The Lepenski Vir sculptures not only combine several regenerative symbols—egg and fish, or woman, fish, and water streams (Fig. 22a)—but they amalgamate a new image using the fish and goddess of death and regeneration, highlighting her breasts, her vulva, and the claws of a bird of prey (Fig. 22b).

Hedgehogs and the Hedgehog Goddess

Archaeology and folklore both connect the hedgehog with regeneration. Hedgehog-shaped ceramic objects occur throughout the Mediterranean Neolithic, Bronze, and Iron Ages. A vase lid resembling a hedgehog,

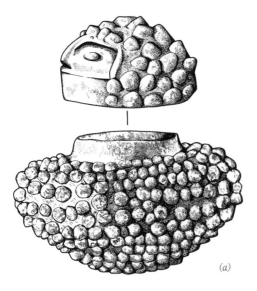

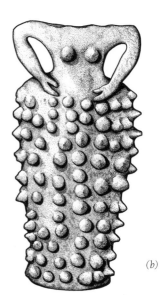

(a)

(b)

Figure 23. (a) The hedgehog goddess portrayed as a vase, her face on the lid. Karanovo-Gumelniţa culture; c. 4500–4300 B.C. (Căscioarele on lower Danube Island, southern Romania). Lid H 6.1 cm. (b) Clay figure from the pillar room of an early house. Late Minoan III culture; fourteenth century B.C. (Agia Triada, southern Crete).

depicting a face and a wart-covered body, is known from the Gumelniţa culture in Romania from around 4500–4300 B.C. (Fig. 23a); other hedgehog-shaped vases are known from related cultures. During the Aegean Bronze Age, the Minoan hedgehog goddess wore a skirt with spikes imitative of the hedgehog (Fig. 23b). The hedgehog goddess' link with regeneration is clearly shown by the early Greeks' use of hedgehog-shaped urns for infant burials. To this day in European folklore, the goddess disguised as a hedgehog appears in animal stalls. Until the start of the twentieth century, women with uterine problems carried spiked balls painted red, called "hedgehogs," to churches in Alpine villages.

The Dog, Double of the Death and Regeneration Goddess

In European mythologies, the dog accompanies or may double for the goddess of death and regeneration (Greek Hekate, Germanic Holle or Hel, Baltic Giltinė, and others). The many dog images in Neolithic sculpture and painting may evidence an analogous role in prehistory. Dog sculptures appear in clay, marble, alabaster, and rock crystal. Dog figures often decorated cult vases as protomes or handles. Vases themselves took on the dog's shape, and dog sculptures often wore human masks (Fig. 24). Many cemeteries and megalithic tombs, enclosures, and roundels (see below) have revealed dog skeletons, which attest to their profound sacrificial role. Whole dog skeletons were found within the altars of the Lepenski Vir shrines. The dog's role in regenerative symbolism can best be

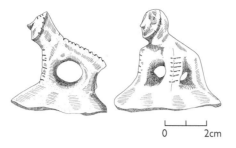

Figure 24. A dog with a human mask on a vase portrays the epiphany of the goddess as a dog. Karanovo VI culture; mid-fifth millennium B.C. (Goljamata Mogila at Gorni Pasarel, central Bulgaria).

0   2cm

Figure 25. Jumping dogs stimulate regeneration of plants, animals, and the moon in the Cucuteni (Tripolye) culture; c. 3800–3600 B.C. (Valea Lupului, northeastern Romania). H 52.8 cm.

perceived from Cucuteni vase paintings, dating from 4000–3500 B.C. Here, dogs portrayed on large pear-shaped vases jump through the air and bark at the moon. In many compositions, they flank a tree of life, a caterpillar, or a crescent and full moon—all potent symbols of regeneration (Fig. 25). The howling, barking dog apparently played a symbolic role in stimulating regeneration and succoring the growth process.

The Goat

Illustrations of goats cavorting next to sprouting plants clearly expressed the goat's prehistoric and early historic vitality. In some images, plants actually sprout from goats' bodies (Fig. 26a–c). On a Minoan seal scene, goats copulate;[19] the he-goat's sexual power represented the great stimulating force necessary to renew life, while the she-goat provides the milk used to make both cheese and yogurt.[20] In vase decorations, goats or excited men pose next to a life tree; the two exude analogous sexual power, and they play comparable roles in life stimulation. The goat's symbolic alliance with the tree of life, plants, and the moon—symbols also associated with the dog—reveals that the two played related roles in metaphors of regeneration.

Bucranium and Bull Horns

The bull epitomized regeneration during the Neolithic. In patriarchal religion, however, the bull symbolizes physical power and masculinity.

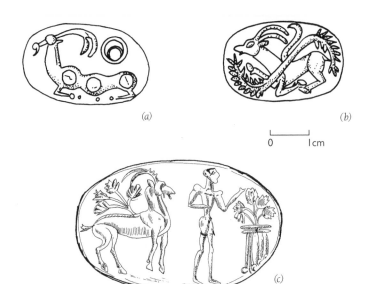

Figure 26. Minoan seals show goats associated with moons, sprouts, and burgeoning plants. (a) and (b) Minoan I-II culture; early second millennium B.C. (Phaistos, Crete). (c) Mycenaean culture; sixteenth century B.C. (Mycenae).

(a)

(b)

0   1 cm

(c)

Figure 27. Stylized female torsos revealing a bucranium in the position of the uterus and fallopian tubes; c. 6000 B.C. (Temple A.III/11, Çatal Hüyük, southern Turkey).

(a)   (b)

Figure 28. Statue-menhirs por-
tray the owl goddess wearing
a bucranium-shaped pendant;
third millennium B.C. (a) Le
Planas, Aveyron, southern
France. Upper section H 50 cm.
(b) Mas Capelier, Aveyron,
southern France. H 75 cm.

Indo-European mythologies specifically identify the bull as an animal of
the thunder god.[21] However, the key to understanding Neolithic renditions of the bull's head and horns (*bucranium* in archaeological literature)
comes through their resemblance to the female uterus and fallopian tubes.
In the temples of Çatal Hüyük, on a series of female forms there are actually depicted bucrania where the uterus and fallopian tubes should be (Fig.
27). The analogy takes on more meaning when we consider that rosettes,
often identified with bull's horns, correspond to the flowerlike ends of the
fallopian tubes. The artist Dorothy Cameron, who originally made this
observation,[22] speculates that people observed the corpse's anatomy
unfolding during excarnation, when birds of prey stripped away the flesh
and exposed the internal organs. However peculiar this symbolism may
seem, there is no denying its existence. Bucrania consistently appear associated with tombs and the goddess' womb.

   The particular sites where bucrania appear confirm their connection
to death and regeneration. We consistently find bucrania in Old European and Anatolian temples of regeneration, such as Parţa, Çatal Hüyük,
and many others. These Old European cultures also situated this image
within tombs, particularly megalithic tombs featuring the owl goddess.
This goddess stands as a statue-menhir at megalithic tomb entrances in
southern France, where she wears a bucranium-shaped pendant (Fig.
28a–b). This life-giving symbol must have strengthened the owl goddess'

Figure 29. Bucrania sculpted in relief above the entrance to a subterranean tomb. Ozieri culture; fourth millennium B.C. (Alghero, Sassari, Sardinia).

potency as goddess of regeneration. In Brittany, megaliths show rough engravings of anthropomorphic images with a protrusion for the head, probably schematic portrayals of the same tomb regeneration goddess. These outlines also appear with bucrania, horns, and hooks. The stone stela at Mane-er-H'Roeck features horns and hooks within the image's body, some placed exactly where the uterus should be. The U shapes with hooked ends and paired or single hooks encountered on interior tomb walls in Brittany and elsewhere may be streamlined bucrania or horns. Their repetition in engravings may have been necessary to evoke or ensure life powers.

Old European cultures sculpted bucrania or sacred horns above, or flanking entrances to, subterranean tombs. The Sardinian hypogea give thousands of examples (Fig. 29). The heads or horns appear in relief: some in natural form, but most in simplified geometric shapes. In Old European art, the symbolic life energy, rising from the cow's or bull's head or sacred horns, represents reborn new life or the goddess herself. She takes

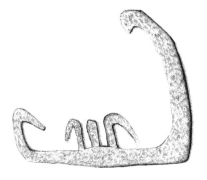

Figure 30. New life, or the goddess herself, emerges from the horns, or bucranium. Here a column of life (phallus) rises between horns on the wall of a subterranean tomb. Ozieri culture; fourth millennium B.C. (Tomb XIX, Montessu Necropolis, Villaperuccio, Sardinia).

on a great variety of shapes: a double triangle (hourglass), a human-bee combination, a butterfly with a crowned human head, or simply a plant (Fig. 30).

Phallus

In the symbolism of regeneration, the phallus represents the male force. Its energy correlates with the snake, the tree of life, the column of life, or the cave stalagmite. In depictions, the phallus emerges from the sacred horns like the tree of life. The phallus can be portrayed as a separate sculpture, or as part of a figurine or other cult object. Sometimes the phallus shows aquatic and other symbols of regeneration. In the early Neolithic (seventh and early sixth millennia B.C.), sometimes the phallus becomes the neck of a female figurine. Here it is used to enhance the goddess' regenerative powers (Fig. 31a–c). Independent phallic stands (made specially with flat bases), produced during various Neolithic phases, may have represented stimulators of life energy. They may have symbolized a phallic god similar to the later Greek Hermes. Phallic shapes frequently appear as wine-cup stems (known from the Vinča, Butmir, and Danilo cultures around 5000 B.C.). Perhaps such cups were used during the spring festivals resembling the Dionysian type known from Greek times. Festivals such as the Dionysian may have originated as early as the Neolithic.

Figure 31. Phallic energy intensifies the strength of the formidable goddess of regeneration—her upper body resembles a phallus and her lower body resembles testicles. She has red-painted locks of hair and white-encrusted chevrons incised in back; engraved on her lower front—a raptor (note the vulture's claws). Starčevo culture; c. 5600–5300 B.C. (Endrőd-Szujóskereszt, Kőrös Valley, southeastern Hungary).

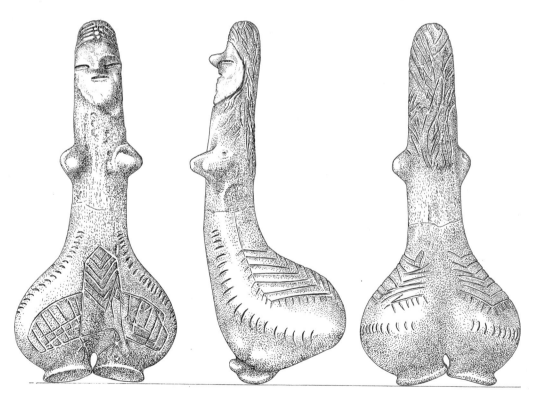

Figure 32. A triangular altar replete with meanders divides into upper and lower sections. At the bottom, the goddess' face emerges from a triangular vulva. Tri-line groups decorate the altar's sides. Tisza culture; early fifth millennium B.C. (Kökénydomb at Hódmesövá-sárhely, southeastern Hungary).

The phallus continued to be an icon of regeneration well into the historical era. In India, temples feature an upright, phallus-shaped stone, a lingam. Although these stones are obvious phallic representations, most people mistakenly regard them (and most of the goddess' images) as mere fertility or sexual symbols. In fact, these symbols—the phallus, life column, and lingam—intimately bind the male force to the goddess of regeneration.

Triangle and Double Triangle (Hourglass)

The triangle (representing the pubic triangle) has remained a central life-giving and regenerative symbol throughout prehistory and into modern times. We can see forms of this symbol from as early as the Lower Paleolithic Acheulian era (circa 300,000 B.C.) to modern triangular images of the Virgin Mary and the Christian Trinity. In Neolithic art, the triangular stone epitomizes the goddess herself. Large triangular stones stand at megalithic tomb entrances, or they stand as backstones deep within a megalith. Sometimes they display her special symbols of energy: hooks, horns, and triangular axes. In temples, large clay or stone triangles served as altarpieces. In a temple at Kökénydomb in southeast Hungary, dating from around 5000 B.C., there stood a triangular clay altar; from the smaller triangle underneath it peered the face of the goddess. Engraved meanders decorate the altar's facade, which is divided into the upper and lower "realms" by a band of larger meanders. Groups of three lines mark its sides (Fig. 32). The regenerative function of the goddess' triangular shape becomes apparent when it appears in context with other symbols of regeneration. A truly vibrant energy exudes from scenes that depict the triangular goddess on Cucuteni vases, from around 4000 B.C. (Fig. 33a–b). The illustrated example portrays a multibodied goddess with outstretched arms (which resemble bird feet) standing within a composition consisting of a turning wheel and sweeping bands of rain torrents. In this scene, she seems to command the cosmic powers themselves. This hourglass-shaped goddess frequently occurs in vase paintings from the Cucuteni (Tripolye) culture, dating from 4500 to 3000 B.C. The vases depict her as a center cartouche flanked by huge spirals, chevrons, or meanders (Fig. 34).

Such hourglass-shaped figures clearly depict either the formidable goddess of regeneration herself, or her maidens performing ring dances or regenerative rites. Certain associations and specific gestures suggest regenerative rituals, essential during the winter period. The goddess, as a bird of prey, often touches her head with one arm, while her other arm rests on her waist. Such figures have a fringed skirt; this brushlike symbol is related to the symbol of solar rays and is a powerful designation of energy (see Gimbutas 1989, 239–43). In representations painted or incised on ceramics found between Sardinia and Ukraine from the fourth millennium B.C., triangular goddess figures appear with sprouts, branches, and suns. Sometimes the round head of the goddess radiates like the sun. From the

Figure 33. Multiple triangle-bodied goddess with outstretched arms (probably bird feet) within a composition featuring a powerfully turning wheel (cross in a circle) and "rain torrent" bands. (a) Whole design on a vase. (b) Outstretched design. Cucuteni AB (Tripolye) culture; c. 4000 B.C. (Moldova). Vase H 40 cm.

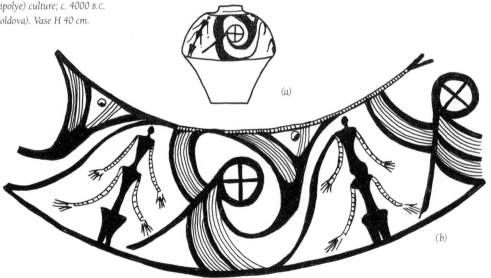

(a)

(b)

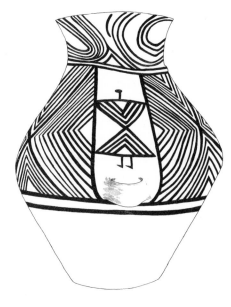

Figure 34. Two converging triangles form the goddess' image on the central panel of this vase. The balance of the vase shows large, painted chevrons and spirals at its neck. Cucuteni AB (Tripolye) culture; c. 4000 B.C. (Ghelăeşti-Nedeia, northeastern Romania).

Sardinian Ozieri culture, triangular figures have heads that seem to be radiating suns or have giant hair (perhaps a prototype of the Gorgon's snaky hair). These images also have bird feet (Fig. 35). Solar rays, brush, and hair, in combination with bird iconography, may have been interchangeable symbols; we see these symbols in combination on an early Vinča vase from about 5000 B.C.: the painted figures seem to portray a cross between the vulture goddess, with bird claws, and the sun, since rays emanate from her head.

This odd symbolic group—sprout, branch, sun, hair, spiral, raptor, hourglass, bird feet, and triangle—belongs to the same goddess,[23] who mainly functions to awaken nature's dormant life energy during the transitional period from winter to spring. When we observe the association of these symbols in context, this meaning becomes comprehensible. This association takes place repeatedly through time and space in prehistory and history, where the goddess appears in mythology and folklore identified with these symbols. For instance, the Germanic sun goddess known from runes appears with a round head and body shaped like a comb or fringed skirt representing energy.

Thus the goddess effects regeneration on the universal as well as individual plane. Just as she effects the transition of an individual from death to rebirth, so she also brings about the rebirth of all of life. This multiplicity of symbols that we have been discussing—sprout, branch, sun, hair, spiral, raptor, hourglass, bird feet, and triangle—represents the goddess

Figure 35. Vultures engraved on a dish display raptor claws, triangular bodies, and heads like suns with huge hair. Ozieri culture; fourth millennium B.C. (Grotta de Sa Ucca de Su Tintirriòlu di Maria, Sardinia).

of regeneration in her most calendric aspect, for at this time, the threshold of the new spring, she regenerates all of plant and animal life.

Conclusions

The symbolism of Old Europe was rich and varied.[24] The divine—both goddesses and gods—was represented by many images: animal, human, and abstractions.

From the time pottery was first fired in the seventh millennium B.C. in Italy, the Balkans, central Europe, Asia Minor, and the Near East, and to a lesser extent in other areas of Europe, ancient artisans began to craft figurines of humans and animals. Most of these were small enough to fit into one's hand. Many were marked with symbols that may have represented an ancient form of script.[25] Thus far, more than one hundred thousand Neolithic figurines have been found.

Symbolically, these figurines, often nude, represented much more than fertility and sexuality. They represented procreation, nurturing, death, and regeneration. The body of the figurine is usually abstracted or exaggerated in some manner. Schematic bodies often depicted the sacred force, emphasizing the divinity of the nurturing breast, the pregnant belly, or the life-giving vulva. Many of these figurines have masklike faces; the masks personify a supernatural force, many of them representing animals: snake, bird, pig, bear. Many figurines are in a birth-giving position; these figures date from the Upper Paleolithic through the Neolithic. Mother and child figurines are also numerous, often represented in connection with bear or deer.

One of the most commonly depicted animals in Neolithic art was the bird: the waterbird, the spring bird, the bird of prey. Bird figures often have large eyes, beak-shaped noses, and no mouths; many have stumpy, wing-shaped arms and exaggerated buttocks. Snake figures, too, were frequently represented in Old Europe. Because the snake sloughs its skin, it manifestly depicts renewal.

The pregnant vegetation goddess, the earth mother, was frequently unearthed near bread ovens. She personified the analogy between human and animal pregnancy and the annual cycle of plant germination, growth, and harvest. In the classical era, this figure was represented in dual form, as daughter and mother, maiden and crone, spring-summer and fall-winter. The consort of the pregnant vegetation goddess was the vegetation year god. He too went through the life cycles of young virility, the maturity that betokens harvest, and old age. The union of the goddess and god was the *hieros gamos,* the sacred marriage.

The goddess of birth and life was also a goddess of death and regeneration. She represented the full cycle of the life continuum. Representations of death goddesses imbued with the promise of new life remind us that the cycle was a totality. These are represented in both the prehistoric and the early historical eras. In the Greek Cycladic Islands were found pregnant, stiff, nude death figures (see the marble pregnant Cycladic figure, British Museum No. GR 1932–10.181; 2800–2300 B.C.), and in the Sumerian poem "Descent of Inanna," the underworld goddess, Ereshkigal, groans in childbirth as she brings forth life out of death.

In Old Europe and Old Anatolia, the goddess of death and regeneration is often depicted as a bird of prey, as a stiff, bone-colored nude, or as a poisonous snake. The bird and snake are complementary in death and regeneration as well as in life and nurturing. Many of the figures resemble the Gorgon found in later classical Greece.

Perhaps the greatest number of Old European symbols depicted regeneration: the frog and fish (historical representations of the frog goddess include the Greek Baubo or Iambe and the Irish Sheela na gig, both of whom, in frog posture, vividly display their vulvas); hedgehogs, which closely resemble the uterus; the dog (whose association with death continues into the classical era); the goat; and the bull. The phallus, too, is an important and frequently depicted regenerative symbol, as is the triangle, representing the female pubic triangle.

These symbols, taken together, represent the eternal cycle of birth, life, death, and rebirth.

CHAPTER TWO

Symbols, Signs, and Sacred Script

During the sixth millennium B.C., the Old Europeans developed a writing system; like many other Old European achievements, writing grew out of religious symbols and signs.

Paleolithic Roots

Humans have been communicating by means of symbols for a very long time. Abstract signs emerge in the Lower Paleolithic Acheulian and Mousterian periods (from circa 300,000 to 100,000 B.C.), long before the appearance of the extraordinary Upper Paleolithic art (from circa 35,000 to 10,000 B.C.). The familiar Upper Paleolithic images depict exquisite animals painted or etched on cave walls. They were also carved on bone or stone tools and made into figurines. But very few people notice the manifold abstract signs that often accompany the animals. These marks include V's, Y's, M's, P's, dots, eggs, seeds, "arrows" ($\updownarrow$ →), two, three, or more lines, branching configurations, and squares divided into four or more sections. Some of the abstract signs known from the Acheulian era, such as V, M, and parallel lines (engraved on the rib from Pech de L'Azé, France, circa 300,000 B.C.: Fig. 36), continued through the Middle Paleolithic, Upper Paleolithic, Mesolithic, and Neolithic periods.

Figure 36. Abstract signs engraved on a rib, exemplifying the deep antiquity of abstract sign use. Use of these same signs continued into the agricultural period. Acheulian; c. 300,000 B.C. (Pech de L'Azé, France).

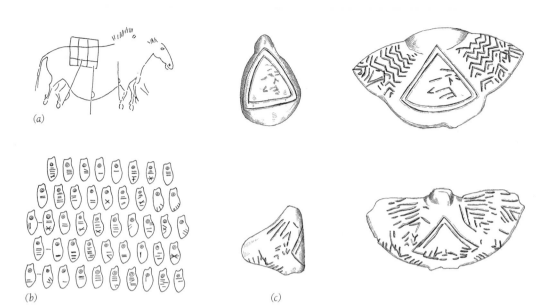

Figure 37. Signs associated with life giving. (a) A pregnant mare found painted in a passageway at Lascaux, France; c. 15,000 B.C. (b) Deer-tooth beads marked with X's and dashes from a thirty-year-old woman's grave. Out of the seventy beads found, forty-four were marked with signs. Magdalenian (Saint-Germain-la Rivière, France). (c) Outstretched design on the lower parts of two figurines with conspicuous triangular vulvas; c. 18,000–15,000 B.C. (Mezin, Ukraine, on the River Desna). Scale 3:5.

An astonishing number of symbol and sign groupings persisted for several thousand years. They must have carried various symbolic messages, and possibly the same or related meaning through time. These ancient signs still have not been systematically studied. It is thought that many symbols refer to the killing or wounding of animals. For instance, cup marks and vulvas (^) on bison are explained as "wounds" and "arrows"; another interpretation is that these signs represent the life source and life-enhancing symbols. Detailed analysis of how signs associate with one another and correspond with similar Neolithic marks will encourage more accurate interpretations. André Leroi-Gourhan's *Treasures of Prehistoric Art* (1967) made a good start along these lines by publishing "paired signs." Many sign groupings, especially if associated with vulvas, deer teeth, and pregnant mares, must be linked with life giving or life enhancement. Illustrations from the Upper Paleolithic make this apparent (Fig. 37a–c). One, found in Mezin, Ukraine, and dating to circa 18,000–15,000 B.C., represents a figurine with supernatural vulva incised with signs inside and outside; the context of the signs and their association with other pictures or symbols affirm their life-giving or life-enhancing motif.

Several thousand years before the earliest writing of the Sumerians, Old Europeans used symbolic designs and abstract signs to decorate temples, sculpture, pottery, figurines, and other ritual objects. These signs could have originally represented actual objects; for example, a triangle or "arrow" (↕) may have represented the vulva, and winding parallel lines ("macaroni") may have portrayed flowing water. During the Paleolithic, abstract signs appear beside remarkably realistic paintings of bison, wild horses,

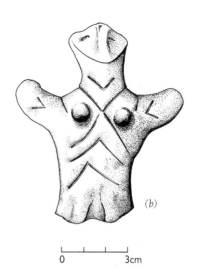

Figure 38. Special symbols— V's, X's, and chevrons (possibly an insignia or a name)—were used to decorate figurines for more than ten thousand years. These schematic bird goddess figurines date from the Upper Paleolithic and Neolithic periods. (a) Ivory figurine; c. 18,000–15,000 B.C. (Mezin, Desna Valley, Ukraine). (b) Terra-cotta figurine; c. 5200 B.C. (Turdaş, western Romania).

(a)

0   3cm

(b)

0   3cm

and other animals stampeding across cave walls. Neolithic Old Europe probably inherited these signs.

The observation that certain signs appear only on specific figurines and associated cult objects led me to decipher Old European deity types and functions. The results of this study first appeared in *The Language of the Goddess* (1989). For instance, in Old European art, bird goddess figures show X and V signs, chevrons, meanders, and parallel lines similar to those from the Upper Paleolithic (Fig. 38a–b). The longevity is amazing: the signs endure for about 15,000 years, from the Upper Paleolithic through the Neolithic. V signs and chevrons mark vases and other ritual objects through time, serving the same divinity (Fig. 39a–c).

The large animals became extinct by the Neolithic, and so their association with abstract signs also disappeared. However, we can see some

Figure 39. Chevrons and V's as a single motif appeared for thousands of years, engraved, painted, or in relief on objects used to worship the bird goddess. (a) Globular vessel from c. 6500 B.C. (Achilleion, Thessaly). (b) Globular vessel from c. 5500 B.C. (Obre I, Bosnia). (c) Vessel from c. 3000 B.C. (Troy I).

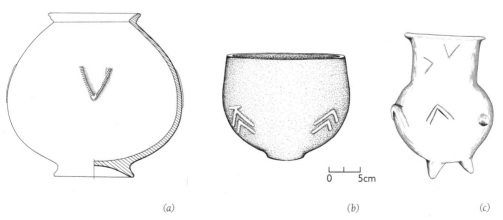

(a)   (b)   0   5cm   (c)

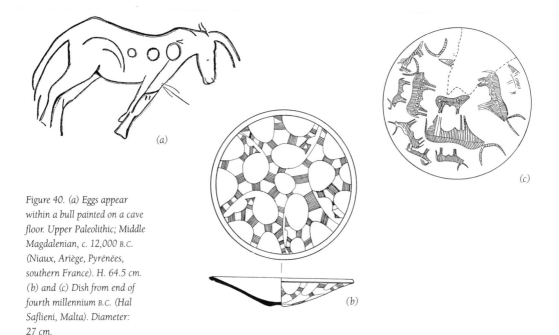

Figure 40. (a) Eggs appear
within a bull painted on a cave
floor. Upper Paleolithic; Middle
Magdalenian, c. 12,000 B.C.
(Niaux, Ariège, Pyrénées,
southern France). H. 64.5 cm.
(b) and (c) Dish from end of
fourth millennium B.C. (Hal
Saflieni, Malta). Diameter:
27 cm.

continuity: bovids with crescent horns associated with circles (that is, eggs)
continue from the Upper Paleolithic through the Neolithic and Bronze
Age (Fig. 40a–c). This grouping of symbols (cow-bull-ox, crescent, and
egg) belongs to the category of regeneration. As discussed earlier, in the
Neolithic the cow's or bull's horned head symbolizes the uterus with fallopian tubes, and it dominates temples and tombs for millennia. The
Neolithic bucrania and uteri may very well derive from the Upper Paleolithic sign, which is a U shape with turned-down ends. The M sign symbolizes the frog goddess as life regenerator. (The M sign seems to abstractly
render frog legs; it figures prominently on Neolithic pottery. See Fig. 19a–b,
above.) The very frequent M sign on Paleolithic objects may also be linked
with the frog and the human birth posture, and therefore with regeneration. A distinct group of large vases from circa 5000 B.C. bears an M sign
below the goddess' face. On this vase type, other regenerative symbols
also appear—nets, brush signs, spirals, meanders, butterflies, entrance or
gate symbols (rectangles or concentric rectangles, rhombi)—linked with
energy, the uterus-womb, and young life or transformation.

"Symbol Script" in Panels

Old European cultures produced vases with both aesthetic appeal and symbolic meaning. They expressed their symbolic designs on vases through
painting, incision, or encrustation. First, the artisan sectioned the vessel
surface into distinct areas, which would then convey specific concepts.

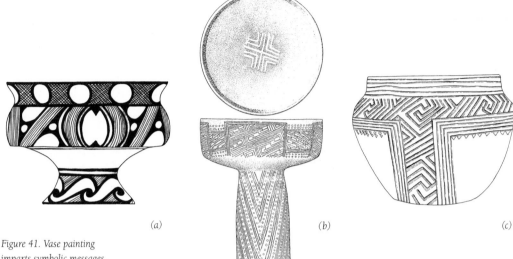

(a)   (b)   (c)

Figure 41. Vase painting imparts symbolic messages. (a) Different (though interrelated) painted symbolic designs embellish the neck, belly, and base of this vase. (Its main theme probably relates to the moon cycle.) Cucuteni B culture; c. 3900–3700 B.C. (Tîrgu Ocna-Podei, Moldavia, northeastern Romania). (b) Tisza culture; early fifth millennium B.C. (Szegvár-Tűzköves near Szentes, southeastern Hungary). (c) Rectangular panels with M and V symbols cut the "infinite" meander motif. Boian culture; early fifth millennium B.C. (Leţ, southeastern Transylvania). Scale: 1:2.

The vase's neck, foot, belly, and handles created "natural" panels for different symbolic designs (Fig. 41a). Second, the artisan repeated various-sized symbolic themes in the panels (Fig. 41b). Finally, the artisan made an "infinite design" pattern, like a textile design (Fig. 41c), as if the vase had a flat surface. Bands, panels, and metopes frame individual or multiple motifs. The border emphasizes the enclosed symbol's discreteness.

Conceptual painting and engraving effected a "symbolic script" whereby specific motifs referred to commonly understood concepts. Knobbed seals with symbols emerged in the seventh millennium, and by the sixth millennium they carry groups of signs (Fig. 42a–c). Throughout the sixth and fifth millennia B.C., single symbols (Fig. 43a) or sign groups (Fig. 43b) also appear on ceramics framed in panels.

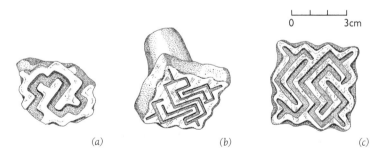

(a)   (b)   (c)

Figure 42. Labyrinth portrayed on early Neolithic handled seals. (a) Early Sesklo culture; c. 6300–6100 B.C. (Nea Nikomedeia, Macedonia). (b) and (c) Starčevo culture; c. 5500 B.C. (Tecić, former central Yugoslavia).

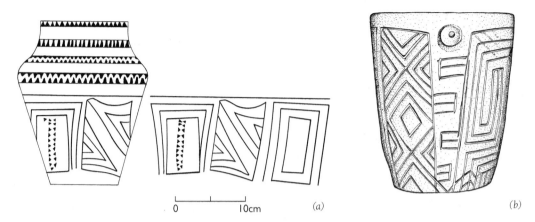

(a)

(b)

Figure 43. Old European
ceramic art typically depicted
various symbols framed within
squares or bands. (a) The
design of this vase is divided
into separate compartments,
with different symbols in each
compartment. (Outstretched
design on right.) Cucuteni
(Tripolye) culture; c. 4900–
4700 B.C. (Traian-Dealul Viei,
northeastern Romania).
(b) Different symbols mark
this spouted vase: chevrons,
tri-lines, and meanders. Bükk
culture; c. 5000 B.C. (Borsod,
northeastern Hungary).

The Emergence of the Old European Script

Around 5500–5000 B.C., intriguing combinations of signs appear in the archaeological record, contemporaneous with the conceptional symbol script discussed above. The Starčevo-Vinča culture manifested the most examples, but other Old European cultures also employed them. Some thirty abstract signs build a core set. It is important to observe that these signs indeed represent writing: instead of individual or random occurrence in pottery panels, the script signs appear in rows or clusters, with several different signs following one another (Figs. 44a–b, 45a–b, and 46).

Abstract, not pictorial, signs comprised the script. Linearity characterizes and organizes Old European writing, a trait it shares with the Minoan Linear A, Cypriot-Minoan, and Cypriot Syllabic scripts, all scripts of the pre-

(a)

Figure 44. Organized script etched on a shallow vessel
bearing inscriptions on both sides. (a) Outer side with
script signs around the figure with upraised arms made
(b) of V's and triangles. (b) Inner side with four lines of signs.
Vinča culture; early fifth millennium B.C. (Gradešnica near
Vraca, northwestern Bulgaria).

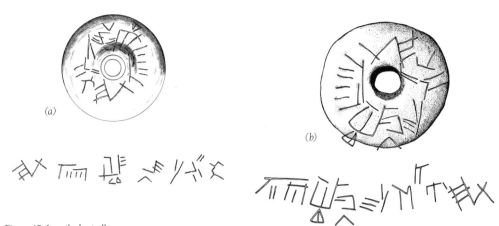

(a)

(b)

Figure 45. Inscribed spindle
whorls, with extended inscriptions shown beneath. Vinča
culture; early fifth millennium
B.C. (Fafos, Kosovska Mitrovica,
near Priština). Scale: 3:2.

classical world. All these examples use similar diacritical techniques, such
as strokes or dots to modify a basic sign. Old European script is not
"prewriting" as conceived by Shan M. M. Winn (1981). It represents a true
writing system similar to Chinese, Sumerian, Indus, and pre-Columbian
"nuclear" (logographic) writing systems.[1]

The Old European script contains more than one hundred modified
signs. The modern Latin alphabet combines a relatively small set of individual signs (or letters) into hundreds of syllables. The Latin alphabet for
English uses only twenty-six letters. But the alphabet appeared somewhat

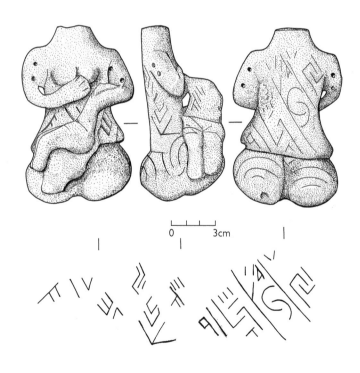

Figure 46. Mother and child
inscribed with script over front,
back, and sides. Vinča culture;
c. 5000 B.C. (Rast, western
Romania).

recently, originating around 1500 B.C. in the Near East. In ancient languages, such as Egyptian or Sumerian, one sign usually represents a syllable or whole word. When a written language represents syllables and especially words, it needs a large inventory of signs. The fact that Old European script uses more than one hundred signs suggests that these may have represented syllables and words.

Whereas commerce and trade mainly inspired the Sumerian invention of cuneiform writing, the Old European script, developed two thousand years earlier, may have developed to communicate with the divine forces. The objects that bear inscriptions include seals, vases, loom weights, figurines, spindle whorls, pendants or plaques, temple models, and miniature ex voto pots or dishes. All these objects held religious significance and occurred in religious contexts.

Although we cannot yet translate the inscriptions on these sacred objects, we can deduce their general meaning from parallels in historical times. In classical Greek and Roman cultures, and also Etruscan, Venetic, and Mycenaean cultures, worshipers dedicated objects such as loom weights, spindle whorls, figurines, and clay or lead tablets to a deity at a shrine or holy site. Termed *ex voto* or *votive*, the dedicatory offering often featured a message naming the deity and sometimes the worshiper.[2] Devotees often made dedications for improved health, greater fertility, or safe childbirth. Classical Greeks offered inscribed spindle whorls to Athena, and the Veneti, who occupied northern Italy and the northern part of the Balkan Peninsula, dedicated loom weights and lead tablets to Rehtia, their birth giver, a deity similar to the Greek Artemis. The inscriptions on the Old European artifacts, dating from five thousand years earlier, may also name deities or individuals supplicating the goddess. Classical religion inherited the tradition of dedicatory offerings, and Christianity eventually adopted the same tradition. At modern pilgrimage sites in eastern and western Europe, the faithful still leave offerings inscribed to the Virgin Mary or to saints.

DISCOVERY AND INTERPRETATION

Zsófia Torma came upon the Old European script signs, often named "Vinča script," while excavating the Turdaş (Tordos) mound near Cluj in Transylvania (northwest Romania) in 1874.[3] Miloje Vasić also unearthed numerous inscribed figurines and vessels while digging the Vinča site near Belgrade, from 1908 to 1926. In Vasić's opinion, the signs on Vinča vases, figurines, and miniature vessels resembled letters, and he saw in these inscriptions analogies to the inscriptions on Greek Archaic vases from Lesbos. Jovan Todorović excavated another Vinča site near Belgrade that revealed hundreds of inscriptions on cultic objects. He published his results in 1961. In 1963, Nicolae Vlassa wrote about several inscribed plaques discovered in an early Vinča grave at Tartaria, near Cluj. He assumed that the plaques (wrongly called "tablets") were Mesopotamian imports. In 1968, M. S. F. (Sinclair) Hood considered the Tartaria plaques "an uncomprehending imitation of more civilized people's written records." He failed to recognize, however, that Old European writing, such as that on the Vinča cultic objects, predated Mesopotamian script by several thousand years, even though several good radiocarbon chronologies existed for the Vinča culture in the late 1960s. North of Vinča, the archaeologists F. Móra, János Banner, József Csálog, and others discovered several inscribed vases and figurines at Tisza Basin sites in southeastern Hungary in the 1930s and 1940s. Further north, in Czechoslovakia, excavators unearthed inscribed vessels identified with the Linear Pottery culture, contemporary with early Vinča. In Bulgaria, during the last thirty years, many Vinča and Karanovo culture sites yielded inscribed seals, vessels, figurines, and other cultic objects (particularly at Gradešnica near Vraca in northwestern Bulgaria). Researchers now recognize inscribed and painted signs, unnoticed earlier, on Dimini, Cucuteni, Petreşti, Lengyel, Butmir, and Bükk ceramics. We can no longer point to "Vinča script" as the sole example of this phenomenon. Clearly this script characterizes the advanced and artistic civilization of Old Europe; therefore I advocate the term *Old European script.*

DIFFICULTY OF DECIPHERING

The linguistic tradition between Old Europe and the modern world has been broken, so we cannot yet translate the Old European script. Scholars have deciphered other ancient languages, such as Sumerian, Akkadian, and Babylonian, which used the cuneiform script, because of the fortuitous discovery of bilingual inscriptions. When cuneiform tablets were first discovered in the eighteenth century of this era, it was very difficult for scholars to decipher the script. Then inscriptions found in Iran at the end of the eighteenth century A.D. provided a link: these inscriptions also were written in cuneiform and in two other ancient languages, Old Persian and New Elamite: languages that had already been deciphered.[4] It took several decades, but European scholars eventually translated the ancient cuneiform script via the more familiar Old Persian language. Similarly, the hieroglyphic writing of the Egyptians remained a mystery until Napoleon's troops unearthed the famous Rosetta stone in the late eighteenth century. The stone carried the same message written in ancient Greek, Egyptian hieroglyphs, and Egyptian hieratic, a simplified cursive form of hieroglyphs. The Rosetta stone thwarted scholars' efforts for several decades in the early nineteenth century until Jean-François Champollion cracked several key hieroglyphic phrases using the Greek inscriptions. Unfortunately, we have no Old European Rosetta stone to chart the continuity between Old European script and the languages that replaced it.

The Indo-European incursions into central Europe, from the late fifth to the early third millennia B.C., caused a linguistic and cultural discontinuity. These incursions disrupted the Old European sedentary farming lifestyle that had existed for three thousand years. As the Indo-European tribes encroached on Old Europe from the east, the continent underwent upheavals. These severely affected the Balkans, where the Old European cultures abundantly employed script. The Old European way of life deteriorated rapidly, although pockets of Old European culture remained for several millennia. The new peoples spoke completely different languages belonging to the Indo-European linguistic family. The Old European language or languages, and the script used to write them, declined and eventually vanished from central Europe.[5]

Linguistic changes buried deeply in the past may make deciphering Old European script impossible. The ancient peoples on Crete and Cyprus, however, left intriguing clues hinting that Old European language and script survived the Indo-European invasions. Old European script signs also emerged on Early and Middle Helladic Greek and Aegean Island pottery during the third millennium B.C. Crete's island isolation preserved Old European culture and religion longer than did Europe's mainland. Archaeologists discovered at least three separate writing forms on Crete: Minoan hieroglyphs, Linear A, and Linear B. The earliest of these, the Minoan hieroglyphic language, dates from about 2000 B.C.[6] The latest of these languages, Linear B, dates to about 1450 B.C.; Linear B tablets were found on Crete and in Pylos, a later Mycenaean town in the southwestern Peloponnesus. All three scripts perplexed scholars for decades, until the Englishman Michael Ventris deciphered Linear B in 1952, showing that it represented a form of early Greek. In Linear B, each character represented a syllable of the Greek language. In Linear B inscriptions we find the names of Mycenaean goddesses and gods, some six hundred years before classical Greek religion. The earlier Minoan scripts—hieroglyphs and Linear A—remain a mystery.

In the eastern part of the Mediterranean Sea, on the island of Cyprus, excavators discovered several writing systems that preserve the languages used there during different eras. The earliest of these, Cypro-Minoan, dates to 1500 B.C. and resembles Minoan Linear A. Like the Minoan hieroglyphs and Linear A, Cypro-Minoan remains undeciphered. Classical Cypriot syllabic script appears later. The oldest document employing the Cypriot syllabary dates to the late second millennium B.C., but the script was not commonly used until the sixth century B.C. This fact implies that Cypriot society was bicultural and bilingual, no doubt as a result of Indo-European assimilation with or conquest of the indigenous peoples. The Cypriot syllabic script was used to write two languages: Eteocypriot, a non-Indo-European language, and a Greek dialect having close affinities to the Arcadian dialect. Researchers have translated the Greek documents written in the Cypriot syllabary, but the Eteocypriot messages remain undecoded.

These languages—Minoan hieroglyphic, Minoan Linear A, Cypro-Minoan, and classical Cypriot—contain symbols closely resembling the Old European script signs. Harold Haarmann's books, *Language in Its Cultural Embedding* (1990a) and *Early Civilization and Literacy in Europe* (1996), demonstrate similarities between Old European script signs, and Linear A and Cypro-Minoan script signs.[7] Old European elements form about half of the Linear A and Cypro-Minoan sign list. Cyprus' isolation lent itself to cultural continuity, so it retained its literacy from pre-Greek times. One can see the visual resemblance between Old European and Cypro-Minoan signs and their identical techniques in sign clusters. Parallels between Old European script and Linear A, Cypro-Minoan, and classical Cypriot scripts confirm the presence of the Old European legacy in Crete and Cyprus well into historical times.

Today, almost all of Europe and parts of Asia embrace the same family of languages, known as the Indo-European linguistic group. Indo-European horsemen, infiltrating Europe, the Near East, and south Asia between 4500 and 2000 B.C., originally spread these languages, which have branched and mutated over millennia. Early languages like Minoan and Eteocypriot (and other European languages like Scotland's Pictish and Italy's Etruscan) belong to completely unfamiliar language families, making their decipherment extremely difficult. In attempting to decipher Old European script, scholars receive little assistance from most known languages.

Older languages have left fewer records, which further hampers decipherment of pre-Indo-European languages.[8] For instance, archaeologists have unearthed about ten times more (Indo-European) Linear B inscriptions than those in (pre-Indo-European) Linear A. The study of European substrate languages constantly progresses, however, and contributes enormously to reconstructing the Old European world.

It is possible that someday, with more archaeological discoveries, Minoan Linear A and the Cypro-Minoan languages will be deciphered and that the Old European script itself might be translated. Ancient documents have already provided important clues about the goddess' role in early religion. The Linear B clay tablets, for instance, name goddesses who are probably Minoan in origin and provide some information about their rituals. Decipherment of other ancient languages and the Old European script would bequeath to us an inestimable treasure of knowledge regarding the goddess' religion.

The phenomenon of linear script among the Old Europeans confirms the very early roots of symbolic and abstract thinking. Most traditional scholars consider the classical Greeks to be the progenitors of Western logical and abstract thinking. Other researchers, however, cite the more remote Mesopotamian and Egyptian civilizations. Old European script suggests that the intellectual heritage of Western Civilization goes much farther back than we have previously acknowledged, to the ancient goddess worshipers who could think both symbolically and abstractly.

Conclusions

The prehistory of the written symbol is ancient: abstract signs date to the Lower Paleolithic, from circa 300,000 B.C. to circa 100,000 B.C. In the Upper Paleolithic, from circa 35,000 B.C. to circa 10,000 B.C., abstract signs accompany cave paintings and carvings of animals on bone and stone tools.[9] The making of these signs persists through the Neolithic.

Some animals are associated with specific signs. For example, X and V signs, chevrons, meanders, and parallel lines accompany bird figures, and the M sign is found on representations of frogs. Further, symbols and groups of signs appear on Old European pottery and figurines and may comprise an Old European script. This script is not "prewriting" but a linear script composed of more than one hundred abstract, not pictorial, signs.

Many of these symbols are found in a religious context, perhaps as inscriptions on temple models, figurines, and plaques. Thus, Old European script predated the earliest historical writings—those of Sumer and Egypt—by several thousand years. The continuity of the Old European writing was disrupted by the arrival of the Indo-Europeans; thereafter, writing disappeared along with the manufacture of finely wrought polychrome pottery and other attributes of Old European culture. Since there has not yet been a Rosetta stone discovered that can help linguists to decipher Old European script, it is as yet untranslatable. With time, we may discover a bilingual text that will enable us to translate this script and thereby reveal the intellectual heritage of the Old European peoples.

CHAPTER THREE

The Tomb and the Womb

The funerary monuments of Old Europe provide us with invaluable information on the artifacts, symbols, and contexts we need to explore the Neolithic view of death and transition. Tombs and graves exhibited a variety of forms and designs, but even in widely separated areas of Europe a remarkable underlying similarity marks the religious beliefs they express. These monuments show that the Old European view of the processes of death and transition fundamentally differed from the view of death held by many later cultures. In ancient Indo-European and Christian religions, a person's soul maintained its individual identity and traveled to the land of the afterlife. In Neolithic religion, the processes of death and transition were cyclical. As in the organic world, where new life grows from the remains of the old, birth, according to the Old Europeans, was part of a cycle that included death. Just as the goddess' womb obviously gave us birth, it also took us back in death. Symbolically, the individual returned to the goddess' womb to be reborn. Exactly what form this rebirth was imagined to take is unknown; what is clear is that Old European religion understood life and death as aspects of larger cyclic processes. Because the womb constitutes one of the most potent funerary themes during this era, we can think of the "tomb as womb." Vulva and uterus images—both natural and geometric—predominate. They can be found in the architecture of the tomb or as symbols of the tomb itself.

Throughout Old Europe one finds structures that were both tombs and shrines. These structures took the shape of the female body. In the megalithic complex at Mnajdra (circa 3000 B.C.), on the Mediterranean island of Malta, the temple complex consists of several separate structures.[1] Here, two temples manifestly took the shape of the goddess. The earlier shrines of Lepenski Vir, dating from circa 6500–5500 B.C., represented an abstraction of the goddess, a sacred triangle. Many tombs have a central passage,

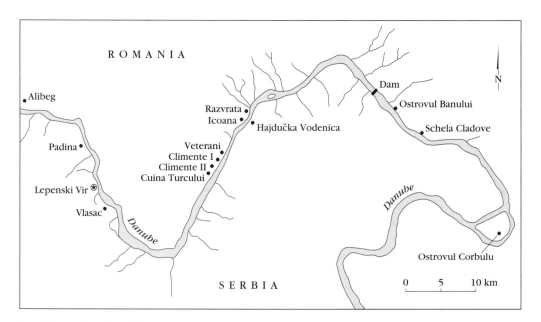

Map 1. Sites similar to Lepenski Vir found along the Danube, dating from the close of the Paleolithic to the mid-sixth millenium B.C. (Romania and Serbia).

perhaps evocative of the birth canal. In the cultures of Old Europe, the tombs are representations of the goddess of regeneration, the goddess whose womb and birth canal were the gateways to rebirth.[2]

The Triangular Shrines of Lepenski Vir

The Iron Gates region of Serbia and Romania evokes an ageless sense of awe in all who venture there. Also known as the Danube Gorge, it is where the Danube River slices through a canyon gorge in the Carpathian mountains on its tumultuous eastward run to the Black Sea. Along this stretch of river, numerous treacherous whirlpools (*virs* in Serbo-Croatian) churn the waters of the Danube. Not surprisingly, prehistoric peoples chose this enigmatic area to erect shrines dedicated to the ultimate mystery: the regeneration of life from death.

In the mid-1960s, Romania and Serbia (then Yugoslavia) entered into a joint hydroelectric development project to harness the Danube's power through the Iron Gates. The proposed dam was to flood the land to about forty-five meters above its original level, destroying any potential Danube Gorge archaeological sites. Archaeologists from both countries commenced salvage operations on fourteen sites encompassing the Upper Paleolithic, Mesolithic, and Neolithic eras (Map 1). Many of these sites distinctly differed from others excavated in the area. The first and largest site explored, Lepenski Vir, dating from 6500–5500 B.C., was located on the Serbian side and faced a tumultuous whirlpool (Srejović 1969; 1972; Srejović and Babović 1983). Padina, located north of Lepenski Vir, belongs to the same period and closely resembles Lepenski Vir (Jovanović 1971). Vlasac, three kilometers south of Lepenski Vir, was inhabited earlier (Srejović and Letica 1978). Sites on the Romanian side tended to be earlier, dating from the Upper Paleolithic and Mesolithic.

Along the riverbank of Lepenski Vir, the excavators, Dragoslav Srejović and Zagorka Letica, found the remains of more than fifty small shelters built over a thousand-year period. They dated from the mid-seventh to the mid-sixth millennia B.C. Naturally, the original wooden poles that supported the structures had long since vanished. But the floors, made of a red limestone and clay mixture, remained rock-hard and had survived millennia of Danube flooding. The shelters were quite small, about five to seven meters long, and the floor plans were neither square nor round. They looked like triangles with one corner cut off near the apex (Fig. 47). Reconstructions suggest that they were open on one end, which always faced the Danube River. The structures spread out in a long arc along the riverbank and ringed an empty space in the middle.

Skeletons found under or near many of these structures suggest that the structures had ritual purposes. Other features also indicate that they were not meant for habitation, but for rites of death and regeneration. The small size and triangular shape of the shelters would be unusual for dwellings, but not for ritual structures. The triangle symbolizes the goddess' regenerative, sacred pubic triangle, while the conspicuously red limestone floors reflect the blood of life.

These shelters seem to symbolically duplicate the female reproductive system. Each structure contained an altar built into the ground and lined

Figure 47. Excavated floor plans from triangular shrines with center stone altars at Lepenski Vir on the banks of the Danube, Iron Gates region. Shrines belong to the period c. 6500–5500 B.C.

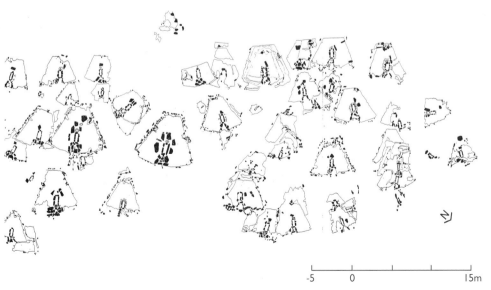

-5   0   15m

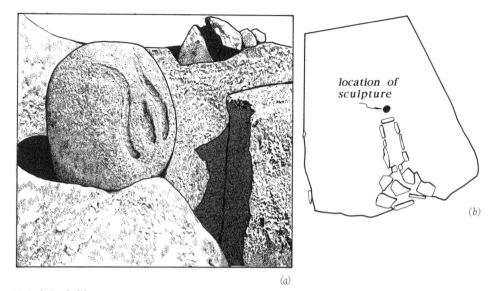

(a)

(b)

Figure 48. At the head of the altar in Lepenski Vir shrines stood one or two sculptures, usually egg- or fish-shaped. (a) An egg-shaped sculpture discloses a carved vulva. (b) The sculpture stood at the head of an altar. Lepenski Vir I; end of seventh millennium B.C. Dimensions of sculpture: 18 by 13.8 cm.

with upright stones. A trough ran down the center from the open end (facing the river) to the narrow end (facing away from the river). It probably represented the birth canal, positioned within the shelter's regenerative triangle. Many of the structures contained one or two stone sculptures, standing about fifty to sixty centimeters high, at the head of the altar. These stones exhibit important features pointing to their symbolic value in death and regeneration. First, many stones were apparently intentionally chosen for their egg- or fishlike shape. Besides the obvious implication that a bird or fish egg holds a new life source, the egg also signified the womb. Red ocher, connoting blood and the life essence, covered many of the sculptures. The triangular outline of the sanctuary representing the goddess' regenerative triangle, the altar depicting the birth canal, and the egg- (or womb-) shaped stones reflecting the uterus at the head of the birth canal together give a clear representation of the regenerative organs of the goddess.

Some of the stone sculptures were carved with labyrinthine designs or with geometric motifs suggestive of flowing water: symbols that appear elsewhere in Old European art. Some sculptures display a carved vulva (Fig. 48). But most important, many sculptures bear the combined features of woman, fish, and bird of prey. Their eyes and mouth reveal an eerie, fishlike quality. Some sculptures look like a fish-faced deity with human breasts and vulva, but with bird feet, most likely representing the talons of a bird of prey (Fig. 22, above). This combination of symbols—human female–fish–bird of prey, carved on an egg-shaped stone—uniquely

58 / *The Tomb and the Womb*

coalesces symbols of regeneration. These symbols show that the Lepenski Vir sanctuaries served the goddess in her death- and life-giving guise. Not surprisingly, given the location of these structures—overlooking the river and its treacherous whirlpools—aquatic imagery and fish play a prominent role at Lepenski Vir, and the goddess of death and regeneration takes on their shape.

But what rituals took place in these odd triangular shrines? The altars themselves harbored the remains of various animals, undoubtedly offered as sacrifices. Again, fish take an important position; most prevalent are skeletons of the larger species: carp, sturgeon, pike, and catfish. Significantly, the fish skeletons were found whole, suggesting that they were deposited intact as sacrifices, rather than cut up and eaten. Larger mammals, such as dogs and wild boar, also appear intact. Red-deer skulls and shoulder blades make up some of the sacrifices. All of these animals belong to the goddess of regeneration, and undoubtedly they were sacrificed to invoke her aid.

Beneath the red limestone floors were concealed the skeletons of newborn babies, some five or six days old. Other skeletons were buried directly outside the shrines. The skull of the deceased was set aside for special care, often protected with a box of stones. Most of the skeletons were disarticulated: the bones were not laid out in anatomical position as they would have been had the individual been buried with the flesh intact. Disarticulated skeletal bones often indicate that interment occurred subsequent to excarnation. Thus, first the body of the deceased individual would be exposed outside so that nature and birds of prey could deflesh the corpse; then the bones would be buried.[3]

Local people brought their dead to sacred sites such as Lepenski Vir and other sites along the Danube Gorge for rites of burial and regeneration. Most likely, the local inhabitants laid out their dead in front of the shrines for excarnation; bones belonging to eagles, owls, ravens, pelicans, and magpies have been found there. (This certainly occurred at the nearby site of Vlasac.) When the birds and elements had defleshed the bones, the remains were buried at the shrines.

Although the Vlasac and Lepenski Vir shrines originated with Upper Paleolithic preagriculturalists circa 11,000 B.C., several thousand years later the Neolithic agriculturalists, after occupying the sites for a few hundred years, began to use the shrines. Eventually, we find Starčevo-type pottery in the sites (from the first half of the sixth millennium B.C.), but no substantial change in the symbols of the shrines or their apparent functions. The preagricultural and agricultural peoples apparently shared the same religious beliefs and symbolic system.

Uterine and Egg-Shaped Tombs

CAVES AND ROCK-CUT TOMBS

Caves, with their hidden, cool atmosphere, stalagmites, stalactites, and underground streams, exude a mysterious quality perhaps equated to the regeneration of life itself: the enclosed spaces of caves symbolize the birth canal and womb of the goddess.

Scaloria cave, located near the town of Manfredonia in Foggia province, southeast Italy (explored by the author, Shan Winn, and Daniel Shimabuku in 1979 and 1980), provides one such example. During the sixth millennium B.C., this part of Italy supported a thriving Neolithic population with hundreds of settlements. Scaloria cave consisted of upper and lower sections. The upper cave resembled a wide hall. It contained habitation remains and several graves. The lower cave was quite long and narrow, with a number of natural features, such as stalactites and stalagmites, that would make it attractive for ritual functions. A live stream flowed near the bottom of the cave, where it widened. The narrow passage that guided visitors and ritual participants toward the sacred water may have been equated with the birth canal. Evidence collected here suggests ritual activities: excavators found potsherds that once belonged to fifteen hundred different painted vessels. The potsherd designs—eggs, snakes, plant shoots, radiating suns, and hourglass shapes or butterflies (the goddess herself)—symbolize regeneration. At the narrow entrance to the upper cave, skeletons of 137 people had been buried, but in no particular order. Most of the skeletons belonged to young women ages twenty to twenty-two years, or to children. The location of the burials, the restricted ages and gender of the skeletons, and the natural features of the cave all suggest that these burials had a distinctive ritual purpose.

Caves similar to Scaloria are known from the Adriatic Coast in Dalmatia and the Peloponnesus. Their stalagmites, like phalli, exude the feeling of mysterious life force. Some caves include rock formations reminiscent of human female figures. Many such caves contained Neolithic (sixth to fifth millennium B.C.) potsherds.

In the Maltese Islands, archaeologists consider Ghajn Abul and Mixta caves (from Gozo Island) and Ghar Dalam cave (on the main island of Malta) the earliest ritual sites. Eventually the inhabitants of Malta, and those of other Mediterranean areas such as southern Italy, Sardinia, and southern and western France, created their own underground chambers: rock-cut tombs (i.e., tombs carved from rock). The most important underground tombs date from the fifth millennium B.C. The egg or kidney shape of their chambers and the skeletons in a fetal position suggest the symbolic affinity of these tombs to the goddess' womb. As in other Neolithic tombs, the use of red, purple, and yellow ocher pigments emphasizes the womblike quality of the tombs, and the process of regeneration. The illustrated rock-cut tomb from Cuccuru S'Arriu, Oristano, Sardinia, dating from the mid-fifth millennium B.C., included a stiff nude–type stone figurine (Fig. 13a, above), and an open shell dish filled with red ocher.

The Maltese Hypogeum

Around 3600 B.C., the Maltese began building one of the most remarkable prehistoric monuments, the Hal Saflieni Hypogeum (underground tomb) located near the Tarxien temple on Malta. This remarkable monument consists of at least thirty-four interconnected chambers, carved directly out of limestone. The Hypogeum reproduces a temple underground, since its main hall looks like the facades of aboveground Maltese temples. The tomb's walls portray three upright stones holding a corbeled vault carved in relief, implying what actual Maltese temples might have looked like intact. Hal Saflieni was a dark and humid realm that would have been but dimly lit by means of burning fat or olive oil. The egg shape of the individual chambers again symbolizes the phenomenon of regeneration. Most of the egg-shaped chambers occur on the upper level, and these were probably dug first. They particularly resemble the rock-cut tombs of Malta's earlier period. Red ocher, again representing the color of life, was diluted with water and painted on many chamber walls. Red designs—spirals or vines resembling trees of life, and discs that perhaps depict pomegranates, a symbol of life—decorate the middle-level halls of the Hypogeum.

The Maltese Hypogeum illustrates the communal nature of Old European burial rites. Excavators recovered approximately seven thousand human bones, a phenomenal number considering the island's small size and its probably low population. Most bones were found in egg-shaped niches on the lower levels. The remains exhibit no evidence of a hierarchical social order. Human bones received equal treatment; the bones of different individuals were mixed together, and no one was singled out for special treatment. Grave goods do not reflect social rank but offer symbolic assistance to the process of regeneration. As at Çatal Hüyük and Lepenski Vir, the disordered state of the bones may indicate that they underwent excarnation before they were interred in the Hypogeum.[4]

Animals sacrificed in the Hypogeum—calves, kids, lambs, pigs, frogs, rabbits, and hedgehogs—symbolically facilitated the cycle of life and regeneration. One carefully sealed conical sacrificial pit in the main room contained sheep horns. Some animal remains reveal the seasonal nature of certain regenerative rites. Roe-deer skulls with mature antler racks were interred with the dead. The growth stage of the antlers demonstrates that the deer sacrifice must have taken place in the spring, the only time when deer grow antlers.[5] So at least some burial rituals took on seasonal significance.

Excavators uncovered one of Malta's most famous Neolithic sculptures, the "Sleeping Lady" of the Hypogeum, off the main hall. She reclines peacefully on her side, head in hand, in the distinctive Maltese obese-woman style.[6] This sculpture and another one shown lying on her stomach on a couch remind us of initiation and healing rites known in later classical times. During these various classical ceremonies, the initiate spent a night in the temple (or cave or other remote place). The initiate experienced a night of visions and dreams, with spiritual or physical healing taking place. We know that such rites took place at the temple of the healing god Asklepios at Epidauros, an ancient Greek city on the northeast coast of the Peloponnesus, where a healing practice consisted of preparatory washing and fasting, followed by a night in the temple. This rite probably derived from Neolithic practices that likened sleeping in a cave, temple, or underground chamber to slumbering within the goddess' uterus before spiritual reawakening. For the living, such a ritual brought physical healing and spiritual rebirth. For the dead, burial within underground chambers, shaped and colored like the uterus, represented the possibility of regeneration through the goddess' symbolic womb.

The Hal Saflieni Hypogeum shares several themes with other Old European underground tombs. First, excarnation and communal burial stressed equality, and accompanying grave goods succored life regeneration. Second, the community often aligned regenerative rites and seasonal rituals conducted at the tombs. Finally, the uterine and egg shapes of the tombs, with their symbolic embellishments and evidence of ritual, invoke the goddess' presence to speed the regeneration of life.

Sardinian Rock-Cut and Underground Tombs

As mentioned above, in the fifth millennium B.C. the Sardinian Bonu Ighinu culture carved their tombs from rock, creating egg- or kidney-shaped chambers. During the later stages of the Neolithic, identified with the Ozieri culture, Sardinia's population and trade flourished. The Ozieri people cut hundreds of tombs out of solid rock, often in dangerous vertical cliffs. They did not confine this amazing engineering feat to single chambers; in fact, cutting into the mountainside they chiseled complexes of many rooms and hallways supported by sandstone pillars. The workmanship reveals a fascinating rock rendition of wood architectural features: rafters, roof beams, pilasters, and doors with lintels.

Like many megalithic monuments in western Europe, the Sardinian hypogea were assaulted by grave robbers ages ago. Although the burial goods are long gone, the tombs themselves are well preserved and can tell us much about the Neolithic Sardinian's unique view of death. Sardinians carved one of the important Neolithic symbols of regeneration—the bovid head, or bucranium—into many hypogea walls. Bovid-head reliefs occur in the symbolically important position above the tomb's entrance, on both sides of the entrance, or elsewhere inside the tomb (Figs. 29 and 30, above). In addition to almost omnipresent bucrania and red ocher–washed walls, within the chambers and ceiling of the hypogeum several specific images emphasize the theme of regeneration: eyes, breasts, owl heads, ram horns, double spirals, and/or moon-cycle symbols.

Fortunately, a few hypogea of the Ozieri culture survived the millennia intact. At San Benedetto, Iglesias, in southwest Sardinia, archaeologists found a hypogeum that held about thirty-five skeletons. The evidence from these intact tombs shows that the Sardinian burial practices paralleled those found elsewhere in western Europe during the fourth millennium B.C. First, communal burials showed no signs of individual special treatment. Second, disarticulated and disordered bones signal exposure aboveground or previous burial before transportation to the underground tomb (that is, again, they underwent excarnation or previous burial). The famous, abstractly rendered Sardinian stiff nude or white goddess sculptures, carved in bone, marble, or alabaster, come from the Ozieri tombs.

Although Neolithic burial evidence points to excarnation in several parts of Europe, Anatolia, and the Near East, archaeologists find it difficult to pinpoint the exact locale where exposure took place. Old Europeans probably constructed wooden platforms for this purpose. These archaeologically appear only as postholes, since the wood rots. Postholes possibly indicating such platforms are known from megalithic monument sites in western Europe. In Sardinia, archaeologists have preserved a ten-meter-high platform built of earth and stones that may have been used for excarnation at Monte d'Accoddi, near Alghero. This large rectangular platform looks roughly like a pyramid with a stone foundation riveted to huge limestone blocks. A ramp leads toward the summit. Near the platform, archaeologists discovered typical Ozieri stiff nude alabaster sculptures (Fig. 13b, above), greenstone axes, loom weights, and vases richly decorated with circles, spirals, horns, zigzags, and triangles. One intriguing artifact found here—a dish depicting dancing women—tells us something about Old European rituals performed for the dead (Fig. 49). The women exhibit a form we have seen at Old European sites: an hourglass shape; their three-"toed" feet look like bird claws rather than human feet. The hourglass figures on the Monte d'Accoddi dish might portray a ritual dance once performed at the stone platform. Today we might regard joyous festivities like dancing inappropriate to the observance of death, although the

Figure 49. A ritual dance scene incised on the interior of a dish depicts five hourglass-shaped women holding hands. Ozieri culture; fourth millennium B.C. (Monte d'Accoddi sanctuary— a platform where it is assumed excarnation of the dead took place. Sassari, northern Sardinia). Scale: 1:3.

Irish wake is probably a similar ritual. But many ancient cultures, including those of the European Neolithic, may have celebrated death because it signaled the impending regeneration of life as well as reunion with the ancestors.

The Megalithic Graves of Western Europe

Megalithic ("large stone") monuments, dating from the fifth to the third millennia B.C., span Europe from Spain and Portugal in the west, through France, Ireland, and Britain, to Denmark, Holland, northern Germany, and southern Scandinavia. Unlike the cities of southeastern Europe, which lay buried for thousands of years and only came to light during the last century, the western European megaliths were observable even in Roman times, and fantastic legends regarding them have persisted through the ages. Although they may have been places of ritual, their main function was funerary; many served as ossuaries: the final resting place for bones.

Several different types of megalithic monuments exist. A common type, popularly known as a dolmen, consists of three or four large upright stones holding a horizontal stone: the cap stone. In other monuments, "passage graves," large upright stones, form a passageway leading to a round or rectangular chamber capped with other stones. The simple long rectangular tombs, or "gallery graves" (*allées couvertes* in French), are typical of Brittany. In Ireland and the Shetland Islands are found "court tombs," tombs with a semicircular courtyard in front. Examples of these types are given here (Fig. 50). Each group developed many variants during the peak era of megalithic construction, from the mid-fifth through the fourth millennia B.C. The gigantic long earthen barrows of northern Europe, built in the fourth millennium B.C. and stretching from England to Poland, usu-

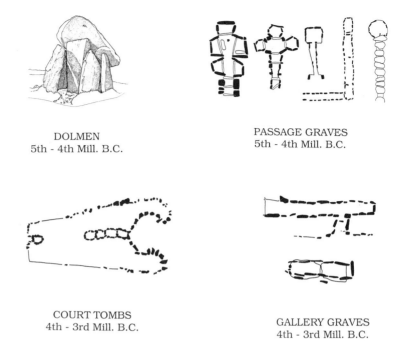

Figure 50. Main megalithic grave types found in western Europe (Brittany and Ireland).

DOLMEN
5th - 4th Mill. B.C.

PASSAGE GRAVES
5th - 4th Mill. B.C.

COURT TOMBS
4th - 3rd Mill. B.C.

GALLERY GRAVES
4th - 3rd Mill. B.C.

ally have a roughly triangular shape and cover a megalithic grave at the wide end. This grave is often anthropomorphic in outline, as in West Kennet in Wiltshire, England. The long barrows of northern Germany and western Poland have a stone or wooden chamber for burials, usually at the wider end (Fig. 51). In the Orkney Islands, north of Scotland, from the late fourth through the third millennia, inhabitants built chambered tombs in round or long mounds. The megalithic phenomenon lasted over two millennia and united most of northern and western Europe in a unique architectural representation of death and regeneration.

The megalithic tombs have intrigued people for generations, so much so that the tombs were ransacked and robbed even in antiquity. The very few monuments left intact preserve invaluable information regarding burial practices. Like the Maltese and Sardinian tombs, the western European megalithic burials make no distinctions based on class or gender. The collective burials contained no real prestige items, but instead held objects

Figure 51. A long earthen barrow supported by large stones shelters a burial chamber at its wide end. TBK culture; fourth millennium B.C. (Forst Wötz at Leetze, Salzwedel district, Magdeburg, eastern Germany).

0   3m

symbolic of the great journey after death. The megalith builders practiced both cremation and excarnation, but excarnation was most prevalent. As in other European communal burials, the inhabitants first exposed the body to birds of prey and then deposited the bones into the megalithic tomb. The disarticulated skeletons found in the megalithic tombs often lack small hand and foot bones. Often the skull received special attention.[7]

The megalithic monuments incorporated artifacts, architecture, and decoration that demonstrated their builders' preoccupation with regeneration and death. When we envision the original forms of these stone monuments, covered by large dirt or rock mounds, their symbolism becomes clearer. The passage represents a birth canal leading back into the womb, formed by the overlying mound or rock cairn. Often the passage's narrow entrance resembles a vulva. In some megaliths, the passageway remains straight throughout, but in others it opens into a round or cruciform chamber, which may have represented a uterus. The red paint found on some Portuguese megaliths seems to reinforce this metaphor. Many megaliths display the life-stimulating images noted in chapter 2: horns, hooks, spirals, and phalli. The gigantic triangular shape of the earthen long barrows seems to represent the goddess' body. Even today, legends identify the barrows with tombs of giants or giantesses. Placing a person's remains within the tomb returned him or her to the goddess' womb, from which she renewed life.

Symbols of northern European birds of prey—the owl, crow, eagle, and raven—attest to the presence of the goddess of death and regeneration in megalithic tombs. At Isbister on the island of South Ronaldsay, the southernmost of the Orkney Islands off northern Scotland, we have evidence for rituals dedicated to the goddess as a bird of prey. Here and at other sites on these isolated, windswept islands, excavators have come upon megalithic tombs still intact, containing hundreds of human bones. Skeletal analysis showed that Isbister entombed women and men in almost equal numbers. Most of their bones were disarticulated, showing that excarnation took place prior to interment or that the burials were secondary. Here, as at other megalithic tombs, a bird of prey would likely embody the goddess. At other western European megalithic shrines, we usually see the goddess as an owl, but at Isbister her presence comes through the local raptor: the sea eagle. The builders of Isbister entombed the carcasses of thirty-five sea eagles with their kinfolk. These birds had been caught or hunted and then sacrificed to the goddess of death and regeneration. Because of the sea eagle's unusual presence, the Isbister tomb has been called the "Tomb of the Eagles." Comparing the megalithic people of the Orkney Islands to modern traditional peoples, some archaeologists speculate that the eagle's significance stems from its status as a clan totem animal. Isbister's sea eagle, however, more likely paralleled the owl, vulture, and other raptors in Old Europe as a manifestation of the goddess of death and regeneration.

Other evidence from Isbister suggests that the local populace performed rites for the dead seasonally, and that they reopened the tomb during specific times of the year. Significantly, analysis showed differing degrees of weathering on the interred bones. Some displayed long exposure to the elements, while others exhibited little weathering. The individuals were probably exposed to nature when they died but interred at later seasonal ceremonies, resulting in differing periods of excarnation. Unlike the tombs of Egyptian pharaohs or Greek warriors, megalithic monuments were not hermetically sealed for eternity. Megalith builders often provided some mechanism, such as a large rock, to seal off the passageway. Reopening the megalithic tomb would still prove a difficult task, initiated only when necessary to perform new burials and seasonal rituals. Afterward, it would be resealed.

Many megalithic monuments reveal astronomical alignments that highlight the importance of the seasonal cycle to their feasts and festivals, and rituals of death and regeneration. Millions of modern television viewers have witnessed the sun's ascent on the summer solstice, the longest day of the year, at the great stone circle of Stonehenge. Many other megalithic monuments and tombs show astronomical alignments, particularly with the winter solstice, the shortest day of the year. Agricultural peoples observed nature keenly and depended closely on the seasonal cycle. So we can surmise that the summer and winter solstices, or spring and fall equinoxes (when night and day are equal), heralded significant celebrations or rituals at the tombs.

A most dramatic winter solstice alignment occurs at the magnificent passage tomb of Newgrange in the Boyne River Valley of Ireland (O'Kelly 1982). During midwinter, the days grow shorter, the weather grows colder, plants lie dormant, and animals hibernate: the world seems to die. The inhabitants of the Boyne Valley closely observed the progress of the season toward spring by monitoring the sun's position on the horizon. In the northern hemisphere, the sun rises a few degrees farther north each day as winter wears on. On the winter solstice, it reaches its northern zenith over the Tropic of Capricorn, signaling that the days will soon lengthen and grow warmer. The megalithic builders observed the exact point on the horizon where the sun rose on the winter solstice, and they constructed Newgrange so that its long passageway channeled the light onto the farthest wall of the inner chamber, for a few days surrounding the solstice.[8]

In the architectural and astronomical alignment of Newgrange, we see the connection of the seasonal cycle to rituals of regeneration. In northern countries, winter solstice marks the turning point between the death of the natural world and its return to life. When we liken the mound's passageway and chamber to the goddess' symbolic birth canal and womb, which sheltered the bones of the dead, we perceive the potency of that shaft of sunlight in the dead of winter. As it struck the chamber's inner walls, this dynamic symbol of regeneration in the goddess' womb established her as the intermediary between death and life.

The regeneration of life was a celebrated occasion, and the local populace often used megalithic tombs for feasts and offerings. Frequently there was a courtyard in front of the monument and an edifice at the entrance to the tomb. In Denmark and Sweden, completely separate structures, presumed to be mortuary houses, have been discovered. Archaeologists found food and pottery remains in front of these monuments. We can envision certain rituals transpiring upon deposition of the dead within the monument. The megalith builders also celebrated feasts or ceremonies honoring the dead at predetermined times during the year.

On the monuments, and on the artifacts found inside or nearby, are carvings that depict religious symbolism. Symbols that occur on megalithic monuments have been cataloged and studied extensively (Twohig 1981). To visitors and scholars alike, the geometric designs may seem like mere decoration, but when correlated with symbols at other Neolithic European sites they take on special significance. They graphically disclose belief in the same cycle of death and renewal evidenced in other Old European funerary monuments.

Many of the symbols engraved on tomb walls or on kerbstones (the stones that form a curb around the outer edge of an earthen mound) surrounding the large Irish mounds (particularly Knowth in the Boyne Valley: Eogan 1985) appear calendric, undoubtedly reflecting the tombs' astronomical alignments and their seasonal rituals. The crescents, circles, zigzags, and serpent forms suggest a preoccupation with time cycles: lunar months and days of the waxing moon. For instance, twenty-nine to thirty serpentine turnings suggest the number of days in a month, while thirteen to seventeen turnings may signify the days of the waxing moon. Some engravings look like modern sundials. Divisions into four, six, eight, and twelve sections occur frequently (Brennan 1983). Apart from time-reckoning compositions and such clearly recognizable symbols as suns and snakes, other more abstract engravings occur. These include cup marks, circles, wavy lines, or circles with a center dot. The action of engraving these symbols into the stone itself must have included magical intent. It was an act of communication with the divine power, essential to the monument builders.

Although some megalithic art is admittedly abstract, other symbols are clearly recognizable. For instance, there are figures that show female and

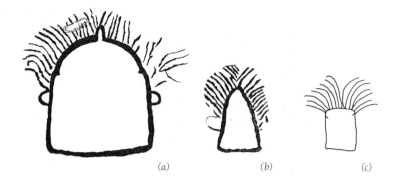

Figure 52. The rising goddess portrayed in roughly triangular, arc-shaped, or rectangular form with a protrusion (head) on top; found on passage-grave walls in Brittany. (a) and (b) Fifth millennium B.C. (Ile Longu, Larmor-Baden, Brittany). (c) Fifth millennium B.C. (Barnenez Plouézoc'h, Brittany).

(a)　　　　(b)　　　　(c)

owl features. A pair of eyes with an overarching brow gives the appearance of an owl; the figure has breasts and is adorned with a necklace. Sometimes either the breasts or the necklace appear alone. The owl goddess appears not only within the tombs but also on large individual standing stones, termed *menhirs*, near a megalithic tomb in southern France. Her round owl eyes stare from stone and bone figures deposited in megalithic tombs of Portugal (see Figs. 11 and 12 above), and on vases from passage graves in Denmark, Sweden, and elsewhere.

At Newgrange, the owl goddess' round eyes, multiple beaks, and brow ridges peer down from the ceiling. They appear in a peculiar quadrupled design and in association with snake coils, zigzags, lozenges, and winding snakes. On the entrance stone of Newgrange and kerbstone Number 52, double snake coils connected with multiple beaks replace the round eyes. Eyes and snake coils are interchangeable on many megalithic monuments. Further symbolic fusions of symbols include eyes and suns, with the sun featuring radiating rays or concentric circles with a center dot. These symbols, so elaborately engraved on stones, evoke the goddess' sacred power and energy however she was worshiped: as owl, snake, sun, or moon.[9]

The goddess also manifests through a roughly anthropomorphic shape engraved on passage-grave slabs and menhirs in Brittany. This form can look like a hill or half egg; it can be a triangular or even rectangular image, sometimes displaying a knob (a head or omphalos, a knoblike protrusion, from Greek *omphalos*, "navel") on top. Sometimes the artisan carved hair around this image, perhaps a metaphor for the goddess' power (Fig. 52a–c). The image suggests the rising goddess with her power concentrated in the omphalos. She is associated with hooks, horns, snakes, and ships, all symbols of regeneration. This same theme occurs on the masterfully decorated orthostats of the Gavrinis passage grave (on an island in the Gulf of Morbihan in Brittany). Here concentric arcs, piled on top of each other in vertical columns, constitute her image. Concentric arcs radiating from

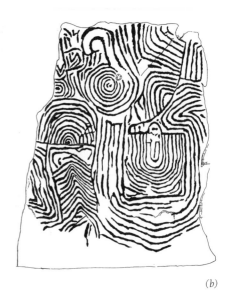

0   50cm   (a)   (b)

Figure 53. Engraved orthostats from early fourth millennium B.C. Concentric arcs radiate from a central vulvar opening. (a) Gavrinis, Brittany. (b) Larmor-Baden, Brittany.

a central vulva-shaped opening flank this rising "life column" (Fig. 53a). Another image emphasizes the goddess' rectangular shape, made up of concentric arcs and central vulva, surrounded by a flowing stream of water (Fig. 53b). This imagery exudes the goddess' inexhaustible generative force, rising from the depths of the waters.

In all of these tombs, one may feel the presence of the goddess, represented in the architecture of the monuments as well as in ritual artifacts. The goddess is present not only as she who holds the lifeless body. Within her, within her regenerative tomb-as-womb, those who were buried underwent transition to a new life.

Conclusions

The womb constitutes one of the most potent funerary themes of Old Europe.[10] In the Old European cyclical view of the life continuum, new life arose from death in the spiraling pattern of birth, life, death, and rebirth. The Old European tomb is also a womb, from which new life emanates. Often, as in the Maltese megalithic complex at Mnajdra, the tomb-shrine took the shape of the goddess. The shrines of Lepenski Vir (which date from the Upper Paleolithic through the Neolithic) were triangular, evoking the pubic triangle, an abstraction of the goddess. The floors were made of a red limestone and clay mixture, perhaps reflecting the blood of life. Many Old European tombs incorporate a long central passage that may evoke the birth canal.

Many tombs took the shape of uteri or eggs, also symbols of regeneration. Caves, such as Scaloria cave in Manfredonia and Ghar Dalam cave on the island of Malta, probably housed rituals of regeneration. Pottery left in these caves incorporates regenerative designs, such as eggs, snakes, and plant shoots. The inhabitants of Malta, Sardinia, and parts of France carved tombs with egg- or kidney-shaped chambers. In these tombs, skeletons lay in a fetal position. Stiff nude stone figurines sometimes accompanied burials, which were communal. In the Maltese Hypogeum, excavators recovered approximately seven thousand human bones, mostly found in egg-shaped niches on the lower levels. The bones of different individuals were mixed together. These tombs were not only resting places for the dead; they also housed rituals, some with seasonal significance, others perhaps for the purpose of healing and initiation. In Sardinia, the rock-cut tombs of the Ozieri people also bore clear marks of regeneration: the bucranium was carved in relief on many Sardinian hypogea walls, which were often also washed with blood-red ocher; eyes, breasts, owl heads, ram horns, and other symbols decorate the walls and ceilings of the hypogea as well. These tombs too housed communal burials and figurines of stiff nude goddesses made of alabaster.

Throughout western Europe one finds megalithic monuments: dolmens, passage graves, gallery graves, court tombs. Many of these were final resting places for bones, generally after excarnation. These burials were collective, and the grave goods were symbolic and sacred rather than prestige items. The bird of prey is often associated with the megaliths. At Isbister in the Orkney Islands, thirty-five sea eagles were entombed with human skeletons. The owl is associated with many other megalithic sites. These are manifestations of the bird goddess of death and regeneration.

Because many of the megalithic structures are oriented to the summer or winter solstice, it is likely that the megaliths were the sites of rituals honoring the cycles of the seasons. These rituals would have been closely associated with the concept of regeneration: passage tomb megaliths, used for burials, were constructed so that when the sun rose on the solstice, it shone through the long passageway and illuminated the farthest wall of the inner chamber. In nonburial monuments such as Stonehenge, the sun rises over a specific stone. At the time of the winter solstice, the longest night of the year, this shaft of light would have been a potent symbol of the renewal of light and, by extension, the renewal of life.

Again, Old European tombs reveal the holistic spirituality of the culture. The tomb was a place of healing, both of the living and of the dead; a place where the goddess not only held the lifeless body but regenerated the dead into new life.

CHAPTER FOUR

Temples

M odern archaeology has revealed that highly evolved religious beliefs and centers of worship—temples—existed in Europe and the Near East more than five thousand years before the classical eras of Greece and Rome. Religious life centered on the temple from the seventh millennium onward. During the Neolithic period, these Old European temples harbored a sophisticated spiritual system. Today, their remnants provide us with artifacts and contexts to help us unravel the Neolithic sacred system and envision the divine force in the daily lives of the people who lived in Old Europe.

Houselike Temples of Southeast Europe

For most people, the term *temple* conjures up an ornate, pillared Greek building, such as the Parthenon, set apart from the residential district. Old European temples have been neglected because the earliest temples excavated shared the same architecture as houses. Moreover, rather than being distanced from the settlement, they were integrated into it. Although these temples outwardly resembled houses, they contained features and artifacts corroborating their religious use. The Old European temple featured an altar, usually a stone or clay bench or raised platform covered with wooden boards, placed against one wall. Excavators have found assorted figurines prominently placed on these altars. The figurines can be quite large and realistically detailed, or small and schematic. Some sit on miniature thrones and chairs. The altars display ritual implements, such as portable ceramic hearths, bowls, lamps, dishes, ladles, incense burners, and human- or animal-shaped vases. Larger temples contain walls that partition the interior into four or more compartments, each containing an altar or offering place. Just as the Greeks and Romans did with their temples, some Old Europeans dedicated their sacred structures to a divinity whose statue dominated the main room; at the Parţa temple, a temple of the Vinča culture (circa 5000 B.C.), a life-sized sculpture of a double-headed goddess stood near the entrance.

DAILY ACTIVITIES INTEGRATED INTO RELIGIOUS PRACTICE

Old European temples integrated women's daily activities, particularly bread baking, cloth weaving, and pottery making, into sacred practice. Many temples contained two large artifacts used to make bread: a domed oven and a grinding stone, or quern, for making flour. Some temples emphasize the importance of this activity through the presence of large *pithoi*, storage jars, probably for grains.

Spinning and weaving constituted other activities carried on by women in temples. Although time has destroyed the wooden looms (except charred pieces remaining after fires), their presence can be inferred from ceramic loom weights. The existence of these weights implies that weavers operated vertical looms. Archaeologists also commonly find spindle whorls, used to spin thread from raw wool or other fiber, in these temples.

Old European temples have revealed many beautiful pieces of pottery, which were apparently used in temple rituals, but the connections between pottery and the temples transcend ritual use. Excavations have discovered that pottery production figured prominently in temple life. Temples might have a pottery workshop in a room adjoining the main room of the temple, or on the ground floor if the building had two levels. Two-story temples became common after 5000 B.C. They usually contained the workshops on the ground floor and a sanctuary on the upper floor. Archaeologists unearthed an important two-story temple near the town of Razgrad in northeast Bulgaria (Totju Ivanov 1978)[1] dating to the first half of the fifth millennium B.C. Time eventually buckled the second story onto the first. Second-floor artifacts included typical temple features: an altar, temple models, many figurines, and charred vertical loom parts. The ground floor of the temple had housed the ceramic workshop. One side of the workshop contained a large oven for firing pottery; the other side held a platform or work surface with instruments for decorating and polishing pottery, including flint blades and delicate deer- and bird-bone implements. In addition to the implements of the workshop, the products of the workshop were also evidenced: several high-quality unfired and finished ceramic vases. The excavation also yielded several flat stones used to crush ocher into decorative pigments.

Temple models (discussed later in this chapter) show that large ground floors with round windows (*stereobates*) were used mainly as ceramic work-

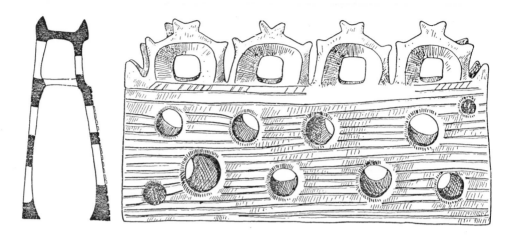

Figure 54. This clay model depicts four temples upon a huge substructure with round windows (stereobates). Horizontal lines indicate logs or planks used to construct the substructure, which must have served as temple workshops. Temples show schematically rendered gable and roof corner decorations. A walkway for worshipers surrounds the temples. This model was discovered in a burned temple. Gumelniţa (Karanovo VI) culture; mid-fifth millennium B.C. (Căscioarele, west of Olteniţa, Danube Island, southern Romania). L 51 cm; H 24.2 cm.

shops (Fig. 54). Cucuteni site excavations have revealed workshop models displaying three rooms with women making pottery, probably replicas of large temple workshops. The second floor probably held the temple proper; we have evidence of other such two-story structures.

At Herpály in eastern Hungary, archaeologists uncovered another two-story building that dates from 4800–4700 B.C.; this building preserves unusual evidence of ceramic workshops and other ritual activity. The second floor disclosed several large basins, some of which may have served as ceremonial hearths, judging from their features: neat plastering, a depth of up to one meter, and an ashlayer covering. The ground floor originally contained three rooms, one of which also held a round basin. Large ovens occupied the other two rooms. The ovens displayed a unique truncated pyramid shape. Each corner was decorated with a bucranium; bucrania also decorated the walls of the structure. Numerous exquisite biconical vases and assorted pedestaled bowls filled all of the rooms (Fig. 55).

For the twentieth-century excavator, interpreting such "houses" presents a real puzzle. Did this represent a regular dwelling filled with vases; was it a consecrated temple; or was it an odd hybrid where daily activities were considered sacred? We find such structures incomprehensible because our daily activities normally are separate from our spiritual lives. But, if we examine pottery forms and decorations, we see that they belong to a coherent symbolic system: a system that would be unnecessary if the exclusive purpose of the pottery were to look pretty. It seems more likely that Old Europeans created pottery, bread, and cloth as sacred acts, as evidenced by the proximity of the workshop to the temple itself. Our Neolithic ancestors intimately wove their secular and sacred lives together without ideological segregation. Art, craft, and religion were one.[2]

Figure 55. Two-story building with ovens, large basins, and immense amounts of ritual pottery. The three first-floor rooms contained hundreds of vases. The two rooms at right included truncated pyramid-shaped ovens, and the room at left contained a round basin. The upper floor held two large basins and vases on the right, perhaps for performing cleansing rituals. Tisza culture; c. 4800–4700 B.C. (Herpály, eastern Hungary).

FUNCTIONS OF TEMPLES AND RITUAL EQUIPMENT

Most Neolithic temples excavated so far exist in southeastern Europe. From the outset (the seventh millennium B.C.), temple symbols consistently denoted the goddess worshiped within. If she guided regeneration, then the temple walls, vases, furniture, and other cult objects displayed regenerative symbols: eggs, horns, phalli, snake coils, plant motifs, butterflies, trees of life, bucrania, triangles, double triangles, concentric circles, rising columns or snakes, and eyes: the eyes of the goddess. If she gave life and protection, symbolic decoration included V's, chevrons, spirals, trilines, meanders, snake spirals, parallel line bands, and other signs linked to the bird and snake. If she ensured fertility, the decor and equipment of the temples showed yet another set of symbols: plants, bi-lines, spirals, lozenges, and double images. Below, we shall explore several temples dedicated to these different aspects of the goddess: the regeneratrix, the bird or snake goddess, and the pregnant vegetation goddess. We shall also look at general temple functions and equipment.

Temples Dedicated to the Goddess of Regeneration

During the 1980s, while excavating a Vinča culture settlement dating to around 5000 B.C., archaeologists made a momentous discovery. At Parţa near Timişoara in southwestern Romania, they found two temples, one above the other, in the center of the settlement. The temples had survived in relatively good condition. They were rectangular, measuring 2.5 by 7 meters and 11.6 by 6 meters, respectively, and were built like the other buildings in the settlement, with timber posts and wickerwork walls daubed with clay. Both the earlier and the later temple included monumental clay sculptures, fenced offering areas, portable hearths, many tablelike altars, a multitude of vases, and bucrania attached to the timber posts at the entrance and near the statues. The rough reconstruction of the upper temple (based on a drawing by the excavator Gheorghe Lazarovici from his first report, 1989, Fig. 36) illustrates that the building was separated into eastern and western sections. These were further divided into smaller compartments that held altars, offering places, portable hearths, a loom, quern stones, and other necessary ritual objects.

In the main (eastern) hall of the upper temple near the entrance, on a podium of clay and sand more than one meter wide, towered a life-sized statue that had one torso but two heads. Unfortunately, only one head had survived. In the lower temple was another, disintegrated statue. We can reconstruct the original statue by using the abundance of Vinča double-headed goddess figurines recovered from other sites. These parallels suggest that the Parţa temple's double-headed statue portrayed a goddess with two aspects, possibly a mother-daughter or summer-winter pair. (The original excavator reconstructed the lost head as that of a bull, which is unlikely because no such parallels occur in Vinča or other Old European figurine art.) At Parţa, the archaeologist did indeed find a bucranium at the base of the double-headed statue, but this does not mean that it was part of the original statue. In other Neolithic temples, bucrania often occur near the goddess' images. For instance, in the temples at Çatal Hüyük,

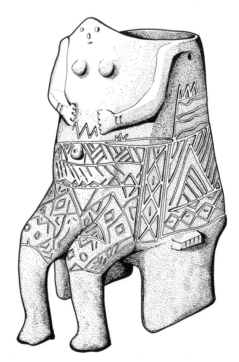

Figure 56. Vase shaped as an enthroned temple goddess, richly decorated with white incisions and encrustations—M's, X's, lozenges, triangles, and parallel lines. Grain and ash found nearby suggest that grain or bread was offered to the deity. Tisza culture; early fifth millennium B.C. (Kökénydomb, southeastern Hungary). H 23 cm.

excavators unearthed bucrania or horns below the goddess' image, and wall paintings display a bucranium in place of the goddess' uterus (see Fig. 27, above). At Parţa, other bucrania were attached to the timber uprights at the entrance. This monumental clay sculpture of a double-headed goddess, in association with bucrania (symbolizing the life-giving uterus), suggests that the temple accommodated rituals of regeneration, as did most Çatal Hüyük temples, where the double goddess usually appeared in relief or on temple walls.

In the 1960s, Vladimir Dumitrescu and other excavators exposed another temple dedicated to regeneration at Căscioarele, a Danubian island south of Bucharest. Here, the team found a two-room temple dating to the early fifth millennium B.C. Measuring ten by sixteen meters, the temple contained two clay pillars originally molded around tree trunks, and a bench along the wall. A skeleton was found between the treelike pillars. The clay surface of the pillars displayed angular spiral patterns. A painted snake coil hovered above the entrance. The temple walls were painted with regenerative symbols: red eggs, concentric circles, and snake spiral designs. The symbolic designs of the wall painting clearly disclose its purpose of encouraging regeneration.

In the fifth millennium B.C., temples in several southeast European areas exhibited large, hollow, rectangular, anthropomorphic deities. Large vases (some more than one meter tall), produced by the Tisza culture in southeastern Hungary, fit this category. The best examples come from temples of the Kökénydomb settlement, near Hódmezővásárhely, excavated by János Banner from 1928 to 1944. The goddess appears from the neck of one vase; bracelets (two parallel lines) rest on her arms, and symbols encircle the vase: triangles, lozenges, circles, extended M's, and lozenge bands with a dash in the middle (Fig. 56). Unfortunately, what the vase held remains a mystery; perhaps it held sacred water for purification. The symbolic designs link this vase with the goddess of regeneration.

Temples Dedicated to the Bird or Snake Goddess

The earliest identified bird goddess temples were excavated in Achilleion, a Sesklo settlement in northern Greece, dating from the early sixth millennium B.C., excavated by the author along with Daniel Shimabuku, Shan Winn, and others in 1973–74. We uncovered several consecutive temples, built atop one another, in the center of the settlement. These contained two rooms: a ceramic workshop and the temple proper. The altar displayed bird goddess figurines (complete or composed only of cylindrical necks with beaked heads). The temple's painted pottery was richly decorated with the bird goddess' symbols: V's, beaks,

Figure 57. Rectangular vessel-shaped deity decorated with red meanders, zigzags, chevrons, spirals, and vertical lines. Thracian Neolithic; c. 5000 B.C. (Toptepe tell, Sea of Marmara, eastern Thrace). L 35 cm; W 35 cm; H 85 cm.

chevrons, or parallel lines (illustrated in the author's books *Achilleion* [Gimbutas, Shimbuku, and Winn et al. 1989, 216] and *The Civilization of the Goddess* [Gimbutas 1991, 252]). At Porodin, a Vinča site in Macedonia dating to the sixth millennium B.C., the excavator, Miodrag Grbić, found clay temple models. Several of these models are topped with chimney-shaped hollow cylinders depicting the mask of the bird goddess; on the sides of the walls are inverted T-shaped entrances.

Archaeologists uncovered a well-preserved snake goddess temple at Sabatinivka, an early Tripolye (Cucuteni) settlement near Ulyanovsk, dating from circa 4800–4600 B.C.[3] This building measured approximately 70 square meters. An altar bore thirty-two armless ceramic female figurines with snake heads, each seated on its own miniature horned-back chair. One of them held a snake. An oven stood near the altar with a figurine placed on it, and five grinding stones sat on the floor in front of the altar, each accompanied by a figurine. The Sabatinivka temple highlighted an artifact not found at other sites: a large, ceramic horned-back chair next to the altar, facing into the room. Originally, wooden planks probably covered the chair, and we can surmise from the chair's proximity to the altar that the overseer of the temple rituals sat there. (Other temples possibly possessed similar chairs made of wood; these would have decayed.) Intriguingly, the chairs occupied by the altar figurines looked like the full-sized chair next to the altar, suggesting that miniature furniture imitated the furniture of the life-sized temples.

Another hollow anthropomorphic female figurine typical of the fifth millennium B.C. came to light at Toptepe, a tell near the Sea of Marmara in eastern Thrace, during excavations conducted in 1989 by Mehmet Özdoğan (Fig. 57).[4] The large rectangular body (85 centimeters high) combines a deity and a vessel in one. The temple, which had been consumed by flames, originally measured 7.5 by 3.1 meters. It probably contained two rooms and dated from around 5000 B.C. (based on several radiocarbon dates). The excavators found the vessel in the center of the main room near the large raised platform from which it had apparently toppled. A domed oven with an ash pit was situated west of the platform. Burnt grain and organic ash were scattered between the platform and the oven, suggesting grain or bread offerings. Upon the vessel, a goddess was painted in red with horizontal bands of zigzags, chevrons, vertical lines, meandering snakes, and spirals or snake coils. Rows of tiny triangles, perhaps imitating snake scales, girdle her upper body. Parallel lines mark her arms and zigzag bracelets adorn her wrists. This paradoxical combination of symbols points to either the bird or snake goddess.

Temples Dedicated to the Pregnant Vegetation Goddess

The pregnant goddess consecrated grain cultivation and bread baking. She was worshiped in the open and in temples. The author's excavations at Achilleion in Thessaly confirmed that at around 6000 B.C. the devotees of the goddess venerated her in an outdoor sacred space. In this fenced courtyard, we discovered a stone altar, a bread oven, a large hearth, and a clay platform with offering pits in the corners. This area also contained pregnant figurines and ritual pottery: stout vases with upraised arms. Elsewhere, pregnant goddess temple models and actual temples establish that the Hamangia culture on the Black Sea coast (from the early fifth millennium B.C.) and the Cucuteni culture in Moldavia (from circa 4000 B.C.) worshiped her.[5] The Cucuteni temple model from Ghelaeşti-Nedeia

shows the pregnant goddess seated in front of a libation pit flanked by youthful figures (possibly attendants or dancers).

General Temple Functions

A temple from Vésztö-Mágor, a Tisza site in eastern Hungary, excavated by K. Hegedüs from 1972 to 1976, provides a rare glimpse into Old European religious life (Fig. 58). The temple walls (13 meters long and 5.3 to 5.5 meters wide) revealed a framework of wooden posts interspersed with branch wattling daubed with clay, forming walls about twenty centimeters thick. Remarkably, in some places, walls up to seventy centimeters high survived. Wooden planks protected the exterior of the walls, while their inside surface was plastered and painted with red stripes. Plaster had been carefully applied to the dirt floor and had been renewed three or four times. The one-meter-wide doorway faced west. A wooden-post partition divided the temple into two rooms. The larger eastern room contained bone tools, polishing stones, loom weights, stone implements, and fired and unfired clay cones. These demonstrate that the temple served as a weaving and tool manufacturing locale. Both temple rooms contained a rimmed hearth, plastered onto the floor, perhaps used for fumigation or purification.

The finds were concentrated in several groups in the main room. The largest group includes a shattered statue that originally stood about eighty centimeters tall. (The statue may have been destroyed intentionally, since its legs, face, and an arm were found widely scattered.) Attempted reconstructions suggest either a sculpture seated on a throne or a hollow vessel related to the Toptepe containers described above, as well as statues from another Tisza site in southeastern Hungary, Kökénydomb. A large, rimmed, four-legged table about ten to twelve centimeters high stood near the statue. On top of the table, a rectangular container held a charred deer antler. A decorated jug, with a lid that looked like an open-beaked bird, stood nearby. The jug was incised with several symbols: a net, lozenge, checkerboard, and V or triangular design. Crushed white chalk filled the incisions, along with traces of red paint. Two side knobs exhibited triple protrusions. Several large vases, a rectangular three-legged offering container, and consecration horns on a flat base stood near the table. A reed mat rested on the ground near a *kernos,* a ring-shaped clay container with two small cups and two pairs of horns attached to the rim. In addition, excavators uncovered a cup, a clay disc, a flint blade, stone chisels, charred cattle bones, and a clay bird head similar to one found on the lid of the decorated jug mentioned above. Altogether, this room possessed about forty cult objects, not counting other ritual items such as charred animal bones, deer antlers, and fish scales. Although we cannot exactly reconstruct the rituals performed here, the evidence points to various ceremonial activities involving grain offerings, sacred garments, animal sacrifice, and libations, fumigations, or purifications.

Other Ritual Equipment

Various artifacts further illuminate the rich ceremonial life of Old European temples. These include lamps, ladles, kernoi, incense burners, libation vases, vase supports, three- and four-legged tables, assorted offering containers, portable clay hearths, and clay horn stands or "horns of consecration" (Figs. 59a–d, 60, and 7, above). Many small containers show possible char marks, suggesting that temple adherents burned incense and oil lamps during temple rituals.

A major artifact group specifically held liquids. Bird-shaped vases (*askoi*) with beaked spouts appear in the early Neolithic and endure until the demise of the Minoan culture. Archaeologists have unearthed several particularly fascinating seated nude female figures, each of which holds a bowl. They may portray spiritual cleansing and lustration, or the bowls may have held a liquid offering to the temple deity. The same symbols observed on sculptures of the goddess—tri-lines, chevrons, and meanders—also appear on these figurines. The great number of decorated clay ladles, possibly used in sacred food and drink offerings, corroborates the ritual use of water, milk, or other liquids. Breasts, or figurines with breasts, decorate some bowls (Fig. 61).

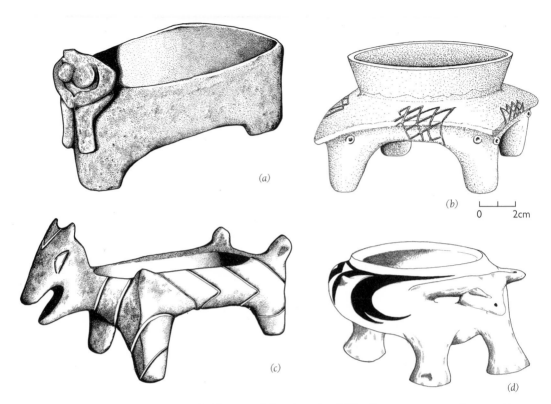

Figure 59. Offering vessels from the sixth and fifth millennia B.C. portray anthropomorphic or zoomorphic features. (a) A human female with large breasts attached to vessel front. Sesklo culture; early sixth millennium B.C. (Prodromos, Thessaly, northern Greece). H 10.5 cm. (b) Vessel with zoomorphic legs and symbolic net decoration. Starčevo culture; early sixth millennium B.C. (Donja Branjevina, near Deronj, Croatia). (c) Black-burnished, animal-shaped vessel with white-encrusted excisions; open mouth suggests a barking dog. Vinča culture; fifth millennium B.C. (Vinča, near Belgrade, Serbia). (d) Red-on-white-painted vessel with bull head attached. Gumelniţa (Karanovo VI) culture; mid-fifth millennium B.C. (Calomfireşti, lower Danube, southern Romania). L 20 cm; H 8.8 cm.

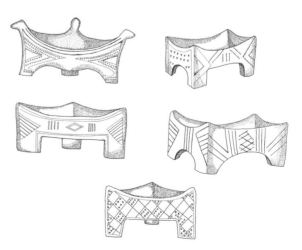

Figure 60. Elegant, symbolically decorated offering containers stand on three or four legs. Early Vinča culture; c. 5200 B.C. (Anza, central Macedonia).

Figure 61. Bowl attached to two figures with breasts, joined by a bar with large breasts on top. Cucuteni (Tripolye) culture; mid-fifth millennium B.C. (Lipkan, western Ukraine).

CLAY TEMPLE MODELS

Miniature clay temple models, unique to southeastern Europe, offer "archaeological snapshots" of ancient temple buildings and rituals. These artifacts can be small enough to hold in the palm of one's hand, but usually they range from twenty to fifty centimeters long. More than one hundred models have been uncovered from an area spanning Greece to Ukraine. These temple models not only corroborate evidence found in actual temple excavations but offer additional clues to deciphering the meaning of the temples.

Excavators have unearthed models in temples, in graves, and under house or temple foundations. Their simplest forms resemble rectangular houses, with floors, four walls, large entrances, and steeply pitched roofs. Although the models are shaped like dwellings, their symbolic decoration reveals their religious nature. Sesklo models dating from 6000 through 5800 B.C. display red-on-white painted designs with geometric motifs (checkerboards and triangles) also found on vases and figurines (Fig. 62a). Models dating to the fifth millennium B.C. exhibit sweeping painted meanders, spirals (Fig. 62b), concentric circles (Fig. 62c), and other symbolic designs. Interestingly, these cultures often painted their actual temples but not their houses.

Some models display incisions suggestive of bird plumage, as well as bird goddess symbolism. These models may not be exact temple replicas but a coalescence of structure and religious expression, perhaps manifesting the goddess in one of her forms. The shapes and decorations of the models create a clearly avian impression: the model looks like a birdhouse, an actual bird, or a combination of both.

(a)

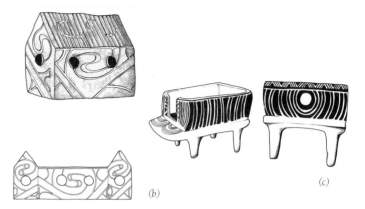

(b)

(c)

Figure 62. Clay temple models decorated with symbolic design. (a) This model displays wide apertures on four sides, and red-on-white checkerboard or triangular designs. The dedicatory deity of the model might have been placed in the roof hole. Sesklo culture; 6000–5800 B.C. (Douraki or Khaleiades, Crannon, Thessaly, northern Greece). Scale: 1:2. (b) This model features round incised windows and red-painted spirals. Karanovo culture; mid-fifth millennium B.C.(Kodžadermen near Šumen, central Bulgaria). L 34 cm. (c) Concentric circles, a symbol of regeneration, decorate this temple model painted white, red, and dark brown. Cucuteni (Tripolye) culture; c. 4200 B.C. (Vladimirivka, Southern Bug Basin, western Ukraine). Scale: 3:8.

Examples from Macedonia, on the Balkan Peninsula, strikingly illustrate the sacred nature of the temple models. As discussed above, there were several models excavated by Miodrag Grbić at Porodin, a site near Bitola, just north of the Greek border. These look like normal houses with four walls, a floor, and a pitched roof. But in the center of the roof sits a chimneylike cylinder that bears a molded mask resembling those found on bird goddess figurines; these masks have the purpose of invoking or representing the bird goddess. The chimneylike cylinder represents the goddess' neck, while the temple itself depicts her body. Moreover, the temple goddess wears a necklace: beads embossed on the roof of the model circle the deity's "neck."

A temple model dating to around 5000 B.C., from Slatino in western Bulgaria, shows a frog stretched across the roof with its head above the entrance. Frog's eggs mark the animal's body (Fig. 63). This impressive model must have exemplified a temple dedicated to the frog goddess' life-giving or regenerative aspects.

Some models lack roofs, attracting our attention inside the temple. Here we see a microcosm of temple life: the altar near its bread oven and fenced offering area. One Cucuteni open model from Popudnya in western Ukraine imparts a most remarkable picture of Old European temple ritual. Besides the small altar, oven, storage jars, and grinding stones, we see two human figurines, both female. One stands next to the bread oven and the other kneels at the grinding stone, processing flour (Fig. 64). In this model, we are shown what archaeologists rarely encounter: representations of people actually performing religious activities. This clearly demonstrates that daily life and religious life are one.

An artisan from the Dimini culture of the early fifth millennium B.C. crafted another temple model containing figurines that may suggest a hierarchical order among temple priestesses or other ritual performers.[6] The

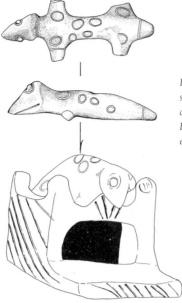

Figure 63. Clay temple model with a frog stretched across the roof. The decorative circles probably represent frog eggs. Central Balkan Neolithic; c. 5000 B.C. (Slatino, western Bulgaria).

model comes from Zarkou tell near Larisa in Thessaly (Gallis 1985). The model replicates a rectangular temple divided into two rooms. It contained a bread oven and eight figurines of various sizes (Fig. 65). The largest figurine displayed several symbols: three lines between the breasts from the neck to the abdomen, three lines across each cheek, three lines drawn ver-

Figure 64. This unroofed clay temple model includes an oven, large jars, cross-shaped platform, and sacred bread preparation scene with a figure baking bread (top right). Another figure stands at the oven (top left). The model also shows a threshold, round window, and wide entrance. Late Cucuteni (Tripolye) culture; c. 3700–3500 B.C. (Popudnya, western Ukraine). L 42.5 cm; W 36 cm.

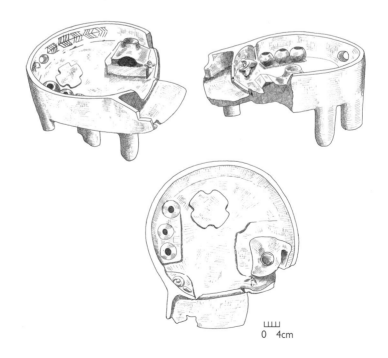

0   4cm

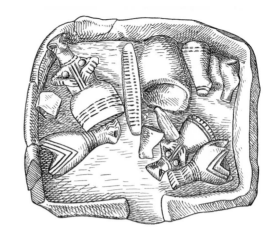

Figure 65. This model of a two-room open shrine suggests the existence of a hierarchical order of priestesses and other temple attendants. The largest figurine marked with tri-lines and chevrons (see detail) occupied the room at left together with a smaller figurine. Seven (several totally schematized) figurines were placed in the second room around a bread oven. The model probably was an offering to the bird goddess on the occasion of the foundation of the temple. Dimini culture, Tsangli phase; early fifth millennium B.C. (Zarkou at Larisa, Thessaly). H of largest figurine 8.6 cm.

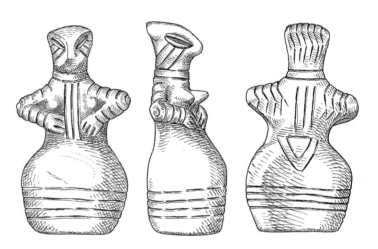

tically across the back, a large chevron on her upper buttocks, and four horizontal lines around her flounced skirt. Parallel lines decorated her arms and zigzag lines crossed over her shoulders in back. Three smaller, more schematic figurines exhibited no symbolic markings. The smallest and most abstract figurines surrounded the bread oven. The symbols of the largest figurine typify the bird goddess, known from hundreds of other Neolithic images. This ornamented figurine represents either the main priestess supervising the rituals or the bird goddess herself. The medium-sized statuettes may represent her assistants, and the smallest ones may be helpers or children, perhaps preparing sacred bread. Excavators came upon this model under the floor of a building, perhaps deposited there to honor the bird goddess upon construction of her temple. Unfortunately, archaeologists did not excavate the building itself, but only probed a small square within Zarkou tell to determine stratigraphy and habitation sequence. The purpose of this building remains a mystery.

In 1987, E. J. Peltenburg and his team brought to light a remarkable model at Kissonerga-Mosphilia, Cyprus, that reproduces temple rituals related to childbirth. This open model, found in a pit sealed by a collapsed wall, dates to the Cypriot Chalcolithic (around 3000 B.C.). The model duplicates a round building with a rectangular opening. Its red exterior and interior shows square, zigzag, and checkerboard designs. Inside, the model contained fifty objects, including pestles, pounders, pebbles, rubbing stones, a polisher, a flint blade, a conch shell, a four-legged altar, a pierced terra-cotta cone (perhaps a loom weight), and nineteen stone and clay figurines (mostly female). But the most exciting terra-cotta figurine shows a woman giving birth: from between her legs (broken off during eons under dirt) a child's painted head and arms emerge. The birth-giving figurine sits on a chair, perhaps a birth stool (unfortunately badly damaged).[7] She appears rather stiff and schematic, with arm stumps and a thick cylindrical neck topped by a round mask. The birth giver wears a red-painted neck pendant. Other schematic figurines in this tableau possess cylindrical necks and outstretched or folded arms; some stand, while others sit. They may portray various attendants in the birth-giving ritual. The tools (pestles, pounders, polisher, loom weight, etc.) indicate that temple birthing ceremonies required intricate preparations, such as preparing grain, weaving cloth, and making pottery.

This unique temple model confirms that birth took on sacred overtones associated with the temple and the goddess' life-giving functions. We know that birth rituals took place throughout the Neolithic: birthing figurines were found in the Maltese temples of Mnajdra (circa 3000 B.C.) and Tarxien (3300 to 2500 B.C.), and birthing images were painted at the Red Shrine of Çatal Hüyük, dating to circa 7000 B.C.

Temple models also tell us something about temple architecture. A particular Cucuteni model found at the Rozsokhuvatka site near Kiev, Ukraine, consists of a two-story temple (Fig. 66). As mentioned earlier, archaeologists have uncovered actual two-story temples with the sacred space on the second floor and the ceramics workshop on the first. Another model excavated on the island of Căscioarele, Romania, presents four small temples situated atop a larger substructure and suggests that some temples may have been built on a monumental scale.

We can only begin to speculate why these Old Europeans created miniature temple worlds. The actual temple locations of the models reveal their religious nature. Their exterior and interior designs further strengthen this conclusion because real temples show similar decoration. Moreover, bird plumage adornments, bird goddess symbolism, and a recurring bird-

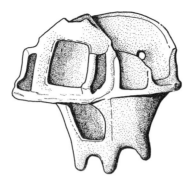

Figure 66. A two-story clay temple with one room on the ground floor and two on the second floor. Both floors display wide entrances. A platform located in front of the large portal around the second-floor temple might have allowed the worshipers to move freely. Cucuteni (Tripolye) culture; c. 4300–4200 B.C. (Rozsokhuvatka, south of Kiev, Ukraine).

houselike shape signify a strong connection between the models and the bird goddess as protectress, nourisher, and healer. Still other models exhibit regenerative symbols (suns, snakes, eggs, spirals, and concentric circles). As with genuine temples, the models must have been dedicated to a number of deities. The Old European linear script found on some of them may indicate the donor's or deity's name.

MINIATURES

Another curious group of artifacts provides additional insights into temple ritual: miniature furnishings. Old European temples undoubtedly contained full-sized ritual furniture and implements. Burial for millennia, however, destroyed most of these perishable wood and cloth objects. But the Old Europeans created miniature ceramic furnishings that have survived at some sites. At the Sabatinivka temple, mentioned above, snake goddess figurines were found seated on miniature chairs that imitated a full-sized ceramic chair in the same temple. The Ovčarovo site in Bulgaria, dating from the mid-fifth millennium B.C., revealed small drums, thrones, stools, tables, and altar screens within a temple model. Based on this and other evidence, we can assume that these clay models imitated full-sized furnishings and ritual implements. The drums, for instance, suggest that some temple rituals included music.

The miniatures may have created tableaux on the temple altar to further supplicate the deities by providing them with domestic comforts. They also may have been used to reenact rituals. In Old European temples, adherents may have effected rituals in two stages: both personal dramatization and commemoration of the rite with miniatures.

CEREMONIAL COSTUMES

Occasionally, figurines bear markings that clearly indicate clothing, bequeathing a wealth of costume detail. The Vinča culture in the Danube

River basin, from the end of the sixth through the fifth millennia B.C., left the most informative costumed figurines. These images bear deep incisions encrusted with white paste or red ocher emulating fringe, hip belts, aprons, narrow skirts, and sleeveless upper-body panels. The Vinča artisans also modeled a variety of shoes, caps, hairstyles, bracelets, necklaces, and medallions.

Figurines with clothing and ornaments appear either bare-breasted or fully clad. Several dress combinations recur persistently on bare-breasted images. Some wear only a hip belt (Fig. 67) or a hip belt supporting either an apron or an entire fringed skirt (Fig. 68a–b).[8] Others wear a tight skirt and nothing else (Fig. 69). Hip belts were made of string, textile, or leather; large buttons or discs often gird them entirely. On most clothed figurines, the incised blouse looks like several vertical panels of material sewn together. The simple V-neck in front and back results from a gap in the middle seam; the garment is sleeveless (Fig. 70). A number of figurines show black-painted panels over the shoulders and torso in front and back. The skirt, which generally begins below the waist and hugs the hips, exhibits decorative white-encrusted incisions with dots, zigzags, net patterns, or checkerboards (Fig. 71). The skirt narrows below the knee, and may have been slit in front. Some figurines wear leg wrappings. This skirt type gives the impression of constraining movement. Very likely such figurines portray priestesses in some ritual act, such as offering gifts to the goddess. Nude figurines with just hip belts or necklaces may portray participants in other types of rituals, perhaps dances.

Some figurines model hairstyles and headgear. Hairstyles received much

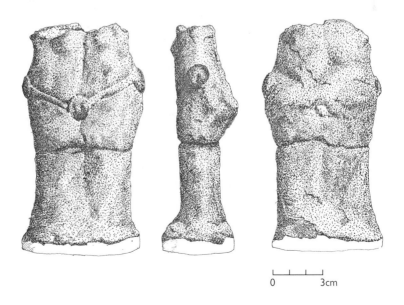

Figure 67. Nude figurine wearing a hip belt adorned with discs. Vinča culture, c. 5000 B.C.

0   3cm

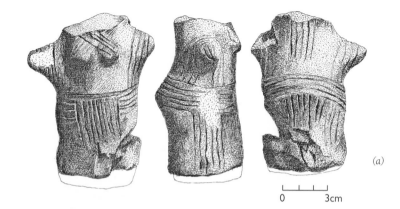

Figure 68. Nude figurines with fringed hip belts. (a) Vinča culture; early fifth millennium B.C. (b) Late Cucuteni (Tripolye) culture; early fourth millennium B.C. (Sipintsi on the upper Prut near Černovicy). Scale: 1:1. Excavated in 1893. Courtesy of Vienna Naturhistorisches Museum.

0   3cm

(a)

(b)

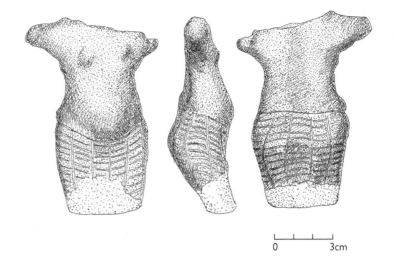

Figure 69. Nude figurine wearing a tight skirt. Early fifth millennium B.C. (Gradac, Vinča culture, central Serbia).

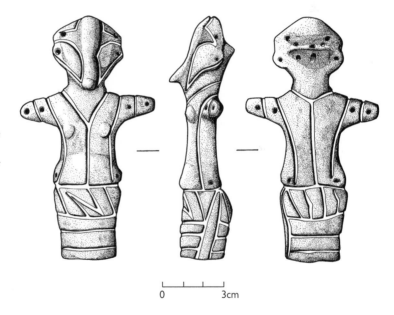

Figure 70. Several vertical fabric panels sewn together comprise the upper garment of this figurine. Both vertical and horizontal panels form the narrow skirt, which is slit on the side. Vinča culture; mid-fifth millennium B.C. (Vinča site near Belgrade, Serbia).

attention from as early as 6000 B.C. Sesklo and Starčevo figurines show hair carefully parted and pulled into a chignon. Bird goddess–type figurines frequently display the most elaborate coiffures: one or two chignons wind behind the mask. Long hair falls freely down the back or is styled into a thong or bun at the nape of the neck. There are many types of headdress, including a conical cap marked with parallel incisions, perhaps

91 / Temples

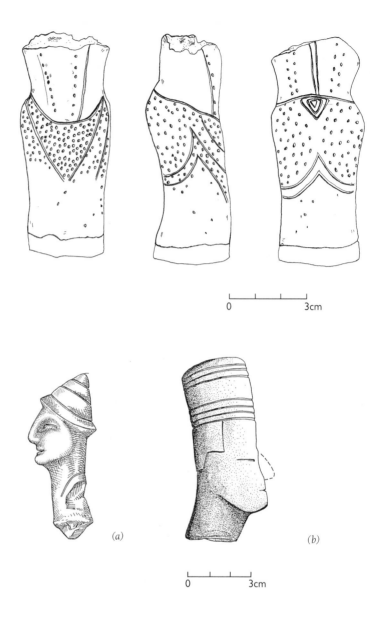

Figure 71. Figurine with a narrow skirt and apron decorated with dots. Vinča culture; c. 4500 B.C. or earlier.

0   3cm

(a)   (b)

0   3cm

Figure 72. Some fitures are depicted wearing conical or cylindrical hats. (a) Vinča culture from Vinča site near Belgrade, Serbvia; c. 5000 B.C. (b)Sesklo culture; mid-sixth millennium B.C. (Aghios Petros, Pelagos Island, northern Aegean).

representing narrow ribbonlike construction (Fig. 72a), as well as crown-shaped and tall cylindrical hats decorated with parallel lines (Fig. 72b).

Medallions have long been a favorite form of adornment; the earliest known examples of medallions come from the Sesklo culture in Greece. The author's excavation at Achilleion IV (5800–5700 B.C.) unearthed a figurine from a temple, adorned with front and back medallions. A round medallion attached to a necklace or V-shaped collar, shown on another female sculpture found in a temple, may symbolize her religious status or position. Medallions on important figurines appear throughout several millennia.

Stone Temples of Malta

The ancient cultures of the Maltese archipelago left some of the most magnificent Neolithic temples and artwork; their natural environment inspired their building traditions. The islands consist of coralline and globigerina limestone: materials easily quarried and sculpted but quite durable. Using these materials, the Neolithic Maltese expressed their religious beliefs. They created numerous megalithic temples at Ġgantija, Ħaġar Qim, Mnajdra, and Tarxien (Figs. 73 and 74). As discussed in chapter 3, they constructed the remarkable Hal Saflieni Hypogeum, with its many levels and chambers. They also sculpted statues, such as the life-sized Tarxien temple goddess (Fig. 75), which date from the fourth and early third millennium B.C.

These ancient peoples built huge temples, such as that at Ġgantija on the island of Gozo, constructed of limestone blocks weighing up to fifty

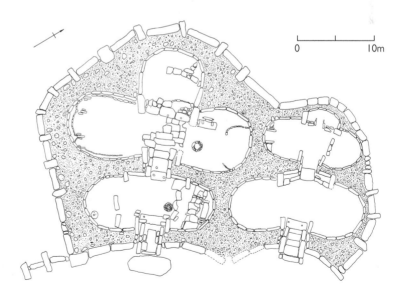

Figure 73. This double temple (one larger and one smaller) had a large area for worshipers in front. Maltese Neolithic; c. 3500–3000 B.C. (Ġgantija, Gozo, an island north of Malta).

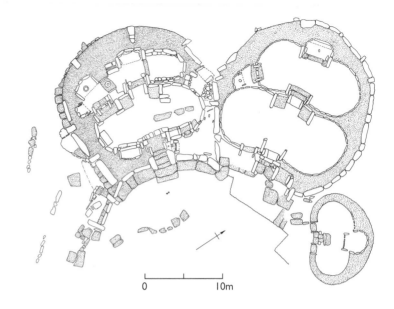

Figure 74. The double temple of Mnajdra, southern coast of Malta. End of fourth to early third millennium B.C., except the small three-apse temple to the east, which dates to the Ggantija period (Mnajdra temple, Malta).

tons. They carefully dressed the limestone into gently curving shapes that define the Maltese style of Neolithic art. Unlike the temples of southeastern Europe, which externally resembled other residences within settlements, the Maltese temples displayed a distinctive monumental architecture that only could have expressed religious purposes. A stone wall often separates these temples from their surroundings. Here the sacred stands apart.

Figure 75. The largest limestone sculpture of Malta (the height of her bottom part was 1 m; original height was probably 2.5–3 m; her upper half was quarried away). As is typical, she has egg-shaped calves. The design of the pedestal shows eggs interspersed with columns; c. 3000 B.C. (Hal Tarxien temple).

The curved lines of the temples are derived from the lobed rock-cut tombs and not from square house plans as in southeastern Europe. The earliest Maltese temples, dating from the fifth to fourth millennia B.C. (for example, Red Skorba), are three-lobed structures radiating off a central court entered through a passage.

Early Maltese temples have an egg shape evocative of the goddess' womb. Later temples, dating from the fourth to the third millennia B.C. (for example, Ġgantija, Mnajdra, and Tarxien), have four or five semicircular projections off the main room, creating an architectural design imitative of the goddess' body. Indeed, the Maltese sculptures of female figures, often called "fat ladies," mirror the temples' shape. Temple forecourts are circular or elliptical, creating a concave facade that focuses on the temple's trilithon entrance. Huge perforated stones, which have been found in the forecourts of several temples, may have been used to tether sacrificial cattle.

Like their southeast European counterparts, the Maltese temples were used for specific religious functions, particularly for rituals of death and regeneration. Maltese temples intriguingly occur in pairs, with one temple larger than the other. This can be interpreted in several ways: as representing death and regeneration, maturity and youth, or winter and spring. The temple pairs could also exemplify a mother-daughter twosome, such as that in ancient Greece exemplified by Demeter and Persephone. Figurines representing a double goddess flourish from the sixth and fifth millennia B.C. throughout Old Europe and Çatal Hüyük in Anatolia. The link between double temples and double goddesses also occurs in Malta. In 1992, at the Brochtorff Circle in Xaghra, Gozo, excavators discovered a stone statue of two goddesses joined at the hip and seated on a couch. The statue measures twenty by twenty centimeters; its weight centers in the goddesses' prominently rounded, egg-shaped hips. Like all other related figurines found in the Ħaġar Qim and Tarxien temples, the Xaghra double goddesses have no breasts.[9] One goddess' head shows neatly combed hair, but the other's head is lost. Significantly, one goddess holds a miniature figurine reflecting the same kind of double goddess, and the other grasps a cup (Fig. 76). The miniature figurine quite likely symbolizes reemerging new life.

The temple pairs may also suggest different seasonal aspects of polarity. The western temples seem larger and contain more religious artifacts and furniture. Originally, the western temples were stuccoed or painted red, the color of life and regeneration. The temples themselves were built of darker, brownish-red limestone. All this suggests that the western temples, which faced the setting sun, supported rituals of death and regeneration. The east, by contrast, represented the rising sun and new life. The

Figure 76. A stone statuette of a double goddess (two goddesses jointed at hip and shoulders) seated side by side on a couch; skirts enhance their ample hips. One holds a miniature replica of the same kind of goddess, the other, a cup. The double goddess provides a link between the paired Maltese temples and the concept of the goddesses' seasonal polarity (death/life, winter/spring). The statue was excavated from a subterranean burial complex; 3000–2500 B.C. (Brochtorff Circle, Xaghra, Gozo).

smaller eastern temples were airy and more open and constructed of paler limestone. They likely accommodated rituals of birthing and spring regeneration.

Ġgantija, on the island of Gozo, is one of the most suggestive double temples. A limestone block wall, in some places six meters high, encircles both temples. Some of Ġgantija's limestone blocks weigh fifty tons, representing an incredible engineering feat. Different rituals took place in the apses off the main rooms of the two temples; some of the stone furniture provides a glimpse of their nature. Apse 5 of the larger temple contained a large ritual basin about one meter across and a pillar carved in low relief with a snake. Apse 6 seems to have served as a triple shrine, having three altar tables and a trapezoidal slab set on edge. This shrine held several limestone blocks with several interwoven spirals engraved in low relief. Apse 2 contained a red-painted niche and also held several limestone blocks showing interlinked spirals carved in low relief. The different items of furniture, symbolic relief carvings, shape suggestive of a regenerative triangle, and red coloring of the artifacts all suggest that worshipers honored death and regeneration in the Ġgantija temple.

Mnajdra, on the southern coast of the main island of Malta, offers another glimpse into Maltese double temples. Unlike other double temples, the Mnajdra shrines almost match each other in size, although the western temple displays more elaborate architecture, with many niches and a hard torba floor. Artifacts found at this temple again suggest death, regeneration, and birthing themes. A conical stone phallus, seventy-five centimeters in height, stands near the entrance. In Apse 4, several peculiar clay objects occur, including some in a twisted shape resembling a human embryo. Figurines portrayed in the birth-giving posture again reinforce the birthing theme. It appears that at Mnajdra, rituals were for the benefit of healing and childbirth.

The Tarxien complex represents one of Malta's last great temples. The Tarxien temples preserve numerous relief carvings, ritual artifacts, and other remains that further illustrate the spiritual life of the Neolithic populace. Archaeologists have excavated many altars, as well as pottery, animal horns, and stone and clay basins. Relief carvings on altars and stone blocks display animals and plants. Among the images etched in stone, we can see a dog with thirteen pups, and a ram, pig, and four goats in procession. One wall depicts very impressive bulls with large horns. A multitude of cattle, sheep, or goat bones and horns attest to their presence as ritual sacrifices. On stone blocks are spirals and plant spirals in relief. These may symbolize the energies of plants and snakes, and the cyclical regeneration of life. The Tarxien complex also revealed ritual paraphernalia, such as stone cups, probably used in celebration or libations. A famous Maltese Neolithic statue known as "Our Lady of Tarxien," which originally stood between 2.5 and 3 meters tall, dominated one courtyard. Unfortunately, the top half of the statue was carried off long ago. The bottom half, however, portrays the plumpness characteristic of Maltese Neolithic sculptural tradition (Fig. 75, above).

Around 2500 B.C., these Neolithic Maltese architectural and sculptural traditions ceased, after enduring for nearly two thousand years. The succeeding peoples, the Tarxien Cemetery culture, cremated their dead and worshiped the goddess, but they did not build the extraordinary temples described in this section.

Conclusions

Based upon the evidence described so far, we can begin unraveling the role of the Old European temple, and we can reconstruct its rituals and activities. The Neolithic Europeans dedicated their temples to a deity and performed rituals associated with the functions of this deity. Certain themes emerge: birth, the renewal of life after death or winter, and continuing fertility for humans, animals, and the earth. The temple goddess' image appears as a wall relief, a large, hollow anthropomorphic vase, or a grand sculpture standing on a podium. The temple's interior housed one or several altars, tables, chairs, ovens, portable ceramic hearths, and fenced offering places. Offerings included food, drink, cloth, garments, incense, and temple models.

The temple epitomizes two points essential to understanding Old European religion. First, religion and daily life intimately merged. Many artifacts commonly found in temples—looms, bread ovens, and grinding stones—reflect mundane objects necessary to maintain life, but we can surmise that they manifested sacred meaning within the temple. Abstruse, arcane rituals did not take place here. The temple sanctified everyday activities. In fact, the location of the temple among dwellings further strengthens the connection between the temple and everyday life. In Old Europe, and throughout much of prehistory, people did not separate the sacred from the mundane. The sacred force imbued every activity.

Second, women's activities took on sacred meaning. In most societies, women grind grain, weave cloth, bake bread, and make pottery. This gendered labor division occurs almost universally, since these functions can be carried out while raising children. We can assume that Old Europe also adhered to a gendered labor division; it survived classical times in the Mediterranean area and remains with many agricultural societies today. Drastic cultural transformation eventually caused the devaluation of "women's work" and its removal from the spiritual sphere. In the Old European temple we see the original sacredness of women's activities. The temple evidence confirms the strong position of these groups of Neolithic women. Perhaps we can even say that the temple belonged to the realm of women, who both supervised and participated in its rituals.

In Neolithic Europe, we have no clear archaeological evidence that men took part in temple activities. But Minoan frescoes and other findings tell us that men actively participated in many rituals. Although we have not yet found direct confirmation of the presence of men in temples, no doubt they joined in ritual life, particularly in dancing. Animal-masked male figurines appear in dancing posture and as musicians. Although it appears that women played a more dynamic part in temple activities, both men and women must have shared life's everyday sacredness.

CHAPTER FIVE

Sacred Stone and Wood Ceremonial Centers

The Old Europeans invested tremendous effort in constructing huge enclosures that may have served as ritual centers for a village or clan group. These ceremonial centers—henges (roundels), square enclosures, and causewayed enclosures—were surrounded by ditches and often fences or "palisades." Several factors give evidence that these enclosures were ritual centers: the ritual nature of artifacts found in these enclosures; quantities of wild and domestic animal bones, which indicate feasting; and ritual or sacrificial burials. It would seem that the rituals contained within the enclosures honored both the dead and the goddess of death and regeneration.

There is further evidence for the fact that these enclosures served a ritual purpose. The enclosures reflect cooperation between the village and clan groups, who worked collectively. Researchers have computed impressive construction figures that support the theory that the enclosures served the collective community. For instance, the labor estimate on the Sarup enclosure in Denmark (as calculated by Andersen 1988) is as follows: ditch digging alone required 985 workdays, and the whole project took nearly 4,000 workdays. But 167 people working together could have completed the site in three months. It is possible that the people worked in concert to honor their collective ancestors, as well as the goddess.

Most activities likely flowed from an all-pervading belief in the cyclical nature of life. Certain findings in British enclosures, such as clean grain, hazelnuts, and crab apples, signify the use of the monuments in autumn or after harvest; thus seasonal rituals were most likely performed within the enclosures.

These enclosures transformed the Old European landscape. In England, circular ceremonial structures of wood or stone, surrounded by banks and ditches, were termed *henges*. Outside of England they were called *cause-*

wayed enclosures or *roundels*. Everywhere, they have inspired awe for thousands of years. In fact, one such monument, Stonehenge, in southern England, might possibly be the most famous Neolithic monument in existence. For most of the twentieth century, archaeologists operated under the assumption that henges occurred only in the British Isles. During the last two decades, new archaeological evidence has refuted this; further, evidence has shown that these enclosures were used for rituals.

These monuments first emerged around 5000 B.C. in central Europe, where the local cultures continued constructing them during the fifth and fourth millennia B.C. Only later do we find them in Britain, where most henge monuments date from the third millennium B.C. Again, as archaeological methods and theories have improved, archaeologists have come to believe that the purpose of the henges was religious and social, not military.

By historical times, legend and superstition had veiled this Old European monumental tradition. Consequently, no surviving customs or written records can elucidate the original function of the monuments. Their architecture and artifacts, however, provide us with some interpretive threads to unravel their meaning.

Roundels

The term *roundel* (from the German word *Rondel,* meaning round structure) currently is used to name large stone circular monuments of central Europe. A roundel includes a circular area surrounded by a ditch and a bank, broken at one, two, or four places by entrances. Roundels vary in size, from smaller henges measuring ten to twenty meters in diameter, to enormous monuments exceeding three hundred meters in diameter. Some roundels originally sheltered timber and stone structures within their perimeters. Although the term *roundel* is not commonly used for comparable British monuments, it is entirely appropriate to do so. About one hundred henge monuments alter Britain's countryside alone, including the famous Stonehenge, Woodhenge, and Avebury roundels, as well as the more recently excavated Marden, Mount Pleasant, and Durrington Walls (conveniently summarized by Geoffrey Wainwright in *The Henge Monuments,* 1989). Although archaeologists have discovered fewer central European roundels than British ones, many central European excavations were in process during the research and writing of this book. Though British roundels date to much later than the central European prototypes (the last British ones were built nearly two thousand years after the earliest central European ones), they nevertheless belong to the same ceremonial monument tradition.

Several central European Neolithic cultures constructed roundels. These include the Lengyel culture of the Middle Danube Basin; the Linear-bandkeramik (LBK) culture of Bohemia (also called the Linear Pottery culture), in central and southern Germany; the Michelsberg culture of the Upper and Middle Rhine Basin; and the Trichterbecherkultur (also called the Funnel-necked Beaker culture, usually abbreviated as TBK or TRB) of East Germany (the Tragtbaegerkultur in Denmark). The Lengyel culture built the first roundels in the early fifth millennium B.C., and the Michelsberg and Funnel-necked Beaker cultures continued the tradition throughout the fifth and fourth millennia B.C.

As the name *roundel* implies, Neolithic builders modeled the roundels on a near-perfect circle, carefully drawing their outline with a rope held fast at the center of the formation. A ditch, with a wooden fence or "palisade" immediately inside, surrounded the roundel. The roundel usually opened to the four cardinal directions: north, south, east, and west. Central European roundels vary in size from 40 to 240 meters across. With very few discrepancies, they are oriented along the same cardinal points (north-south, east-west); this demonstrates that the builders recognized sky and star pointers. The architects obviously wanted to correctly chart the alignments of cardinal directions, particularly with the azimuths of the solar equinox.

Some archaeologists have assumed that the ditches and fences of the roundels held back an enemy, and so they have termed them "fortified settlements." The term *fortified settlements* implies that the enclosed area contained permanent dwellings. But in reality, the central area of the roundels lacks postholes and other dwelling evidence common to settlements. Furthermore, no cemeteries have been excavated in roundels. On the basis of current evidence, the monuments are, like the henges, best interpreted as having social and religious, not military, purposes. Since the gated entrances of most roundels open to the four cardinal directions, we can envision their use in seasonal rituals; this orientation would serve no defensive function. Other evidence uncovered near or within the roundels and their ditches implies cultic activities. These finds include unusual burials; large quantities of vases, axes, flints, and figurines; and evidence for offerings, ritual burial or sacrifices, and feasting.

An excellent example of a central European roundel comes from Bučany near Trnava, southwestern Slovakia, in the Middle Danube Basin.[1] Radiocarbon analysis dated it to the second quarter of the fifth millennium B.C. Two concentric ditches encircle Bučany; the radius of the outer ditch measures 67 to 70 meters. The ditches show a V cross section where cut into the ground, and they measure up to 3 meters wide. The wooden-post palisade occupies the interior of the inner ditch. Four gates greeted the four cardinal directions. Wooden structures, perhaps towers, origi-nally occupied these openings. The northeast sector once held an unusual rectangular building measuring 15 by 7.5 meters. The building followed a north-south alignment and did not obstruct either the north-south or the east-west axes of the roundel, or its center. This attention to detail fur-ther suggests the ritual importance of the cardinal directions. Bučany's orig-inal users left several artifacts that suggest the roundel's religious nature, including anthropomorphic (human-shaped) and zoomorphic (animal-shaped) figurines deposited in pits. The anthropomorphic images are sim-ilar to early Lengyel figurines often found in settlements; they have large, egg-shaped buttocks, arm stumps, unique hairstyles, and traces of red paint.

Těšetice-Kyjovice in Moravia reveals the ritual activities of the roundels (Podborský 1985; 1988). A ditch that had four gates oriented in the car-dinal directions formed the outer boundary of the monument; the enclosed area measured 145 by 125 meters. A roundel in the center of the ditch measured about 50 meters in diameter and consisted of several palisades set inside another ditch; each palisade opened to the four directions. Exca-vators found an abundance of ritual evidence. They uncovered 314 early Lengyel-style figurines, 153 inside the central roundel and the rest either outside of it or in the outer ditch. Most important, in the central part of the roundel, excavators exposed a large ritual pit that included fragments of a Lengyel sculpture of a goddess about forty centimeters tall; ceramic vases painted in yellow, white, and red; and a human skull. Another pit also contained a human skull. Six more pits were found northwest of the inner roundel, one of which contained a young woman's skeleton buried in a contracted position. Her skull had been removed and buried under the wall of a grain pit. We do not know if this woman was buried in honor after a natural death or ritually sacrificed during harvest rites.

Additional ritual burial evidence came to light during excavations of another Lengyel roundel, built at Friebritz in eastern Austria 10.5 kilo-meters southeast of Laa an der Thaya. The two concentric ditches, 140 meters in diameter, yielded a highly unusual burial. In the very center of the roundel, where its four cardinal directions intersect, excavators found two skeletons: one of a man twenty to thirty years old and one of a woman about twenty years old. They rested stomach-down, one above the other, with the female skeleton on top. Several trapeze-shaped flint arrowheads lay at the shoulders of both skeletons (Neugebauer 1986).

The Michelsberg culture, which flourished along the Rhine River, also built roundels that contained atypical ritual burials. Archaeologists have unearthed these burials in pits outside of or at the bottom of the ditch encircling the roundel. The Bruchsal-"Aue" roundel northeast of Karlsruhe provides evidence for several ritual burials. The excavators found most individuals in a tight fetal position, with legs near the chest and hands near the forehead or shoulder. Some graves contained individual women over sixty years old. Another held a man over sixty years old. Other burials included adults and very young children (from newborn to seven years old). The children generally lay on their stomachs. Grave 5, a round pit dug at the bottom of the ditch, specifically communicates the ritual significance of these burials. Animal bones (fish, sheep, pig, cattle, and aurochs) filled its upper layers. Under the animal bones, excavators found an adult female skeleton without the skull, and below the woman, the skeletons of two children, ages five and seven. Each grave in this roundel differed from burials found in ordinary cemeteries. Thousands of potsherds and animal bones filled the ditches, indicating further ritual activities. The long bones of the animals had been split for bone marrow extraction. From this evidence, we can picture large gatherings of people feasting there at special rites, perhaps honoring death or seasonal regeneration. The presence of aurochs' horns also links these monuments with rituals of death and regeneration. (The aurochs was the wild ancestor of our domesticated cattle.) Excavators found enormous aurochs' horns near the two gates of the Bruchsal-"Aue" roundel, in the outer ditch. Originally, these horns may have been attached to wooden poles or gates. Several other horns as well were found in the ditch, near the graves (Behrends 1991).

Neolithic builders also scattered several woodhenges throughout central Europe. In plan, woodhenges resemble an enlarged roundel without the ditch and palisade structure. Instead, woodhenges have rings of wooden posts. At Schalkenburg near Quenstedt in central Germany, archaeologists detected an impressive structure with five concentric wood-post circles and gates in the four directions (Behrens 1981). The diameter of the outer ring measured about 100 meters. Excavators found nothing in the postholes. Two early Funnel-necked Beaker culture (Baalberge-type) graves, found within the inner area, may date Schalkenburg to the early fourth millennium B.C. A Funnel-necked Beaker culture (Bernburg-type) occupation dating later than the monument also helped establish its chronology.

BRITISH ROUNDELS

From 1908 to 1922 archaeologists excavated Avebury, one of the largest and best-known British roundels (located west of Marlborough in Wiltshire). A large ditch varying in depth between 7 and 10 meters encircles the village of Avebury. Outside the ditch, a bank once stood about 6.7

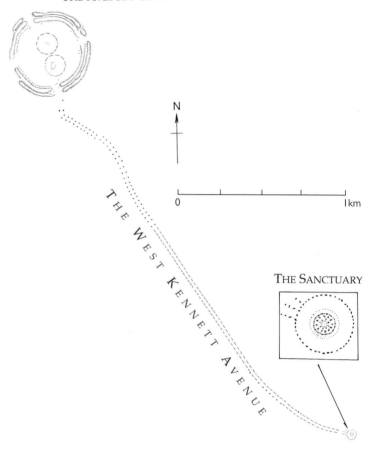

Figure 77. Avebury roundel, with West Kennet Avenue leading to the Sanctuary. Fourth to second millennia B.C. (Avebury, County Wiltshire, England).

THE WEST KENNETT AVENUE

THE SANCTUARY

N

0   1 km

meters high. Four breaks in the bank, each about 15 meters wide, open to the four cardinal directions. Avebury is huge, measuring some 347 meters in diameter, with the total ditch and bank system area covering about 11.5 hectares (28.5 acres). The ditch surrounded an impressive array of ninety-eight upright stones, some as high as 5.5 meters; two smaller stone circles stood within this array (Fig. 77).

Two serpentine stone avenues 2.4 kilometers long and about 19 meters wide travel into Avebury, joining it with other local monuments. In one approach, known as West Kennet Avenue, two hundred standing stones, in two lines, form a processional walkway connecting to a small round structure known as the "Sanctuary." The excavation of the Sanctuary (by Maud Cunnington in 1930) revealed a circular wooden building with a central post supporting the roof. Six rings of massive posts and small standing stones surrounded the structure (the shape of which resembled the South Circle of Durrington Walls). The Sanctuary had four building phases, starting around 3000 B.C. when postholes formed a circle 4.5 meters across, and ending some four hundred years later when a stone circle 40.2 meters in diameter surrounded a much larger structure. The latter joined West Kennet Avenue and eventually Avebury.

Like the continental roundels, Avebury also harbored ritual burials. Several were associated with beakers dating between 2500 B.C. and 2230 B.C.[2] Excavators came upon the crouched skeleton of a young person (probably a girl), fourteen to fifteen years old, associated with a stone-hole dating to Avebury's last phase, in the early second millennium B.C.[3]

These three interrelated monuments—the large Avebury roundel, the Avenue (formerly two avenues), and the Sanctuary—reflect very special ceremonial activities, including processions between monuments to observe specific rituals. Another monument, the West Kennet long barrow, a megalithic chambered tomb, is only one kilometer from the Avenue and only a little farther from the Sanctuary. We know that all these monuments existed contemporaneously because archaeologists found the same pottery type (Grooved ware, a grooved variety of the Rinyo-Clacton ware) at each configuration.[4]

By far the most famous English roundel must be Stonehenge, located on the Salisbury Plain. Like Avebury, it humbly began as a small ditched ceremonial site toward the end of the fourth millennium B.C.[5] Although we now see remnants of an impressive upright stone ring arranged in several concentric circles, this arrangement evolved over several generations. Archaeologists have designated Stonehenge's various phases as Stonehenge I, II, and III. Stonehenge I incorporated a small ditch outside an earthen bank broken by an entrance. A ring of fifty-six pits, Aubrey holes (after John Aubrey, the seventeenth-century antiquarian who first noticed them), ran just inside the bank. Many of the holes held human cremations. A circular building may have occupied the center of Stonehenge I. Stonehenge II marks the alteration of the monument; the construction featured an incomplete circle of eighty-two beautiful blue stones erected on an avenue to the river Avon. Stonehenge III commenced with the demolition of the blue stone circle. The final architects of Stonehenge then erected eighty sarsens (sandstone boulders) in a circle about 30 meters in diameter, joined on top by a lintel stone ring. Within this circle, they erected a U-shaped stone configuration consisting of five upright stone pairs and a lintel. Visitors today see Stonehenge III.

Like Avebury, Stonehenge has links to other local ritual monuments. Two other impressive monuments, Durrington Walls and Woodhenge, can be viewed just three kilometers northeast of Stonehenge. G. J. Wainwright and I. H. Longworth excavated Durrington Walls from 1966 to 1968, and it appears to be a ceremonial enclosure even larger than Avebury. In the interior of the enclosure, surrounded by a broad bank with two entrances, the excavators found traces of two wooden structures. In the larger building there is evidence of six concentric wooden-post circles. An avenue of wooden posts led to the smaller round structure. Woodhenge (excavated by Maud Cunnington in 1926 to 1928 and by J. Evans and G. J. Wainwright in 1970) lies just south of Durrington Walls. Woodhenge consists of a wooden structure surrounded by six concentric egg-shaped rings of postholes, all within a henge-type earthwork. At the center of the monument, the archaeologists uncovered the crouched skeleton of a three-year-old child. They also found the skeleton of a young man buried at the bottom of the ditch. One of the postholes concealed cremated human bones. Together, Stonehenge, Durrington Walls, and Woodhenge very likely formed a ritual complex similar to Avebury and its environs.

In 1969, archaeologists partially excavated another gigantic enclosure about halfway between Avebury and Durrington Walls, on the banks of the river Avon at Marden. Their survey indicated that the Marden monument, delimited by a bank with an internal ditch, enclosed some 14 hectares (35 acres). Its internal dimensions measured 530 meters from north to south and 360 meters from east to west. Originally, the earthwork contained several openings (probably four, in the cardinal directions) and a circular timber structure. Three radiocarbon determinations obtained from the bottom of the ditch date the Marden monument to the early third millennium B.C., making it contemporaneous with Durrington Walls. (Grooved ware pottery corroborated the dates of both monuments.) The archaeologists unearthed the skeleton of a young woman in the ditch.

In Dorset, England, excavations in 1970–71 uncovered yet another large monument, this one at Mount Pleasant near Dorchester. Grooved ware and radiocarbon analysis both suggest that Mount Pleasant dates to the early third millennium B.C. Within the enclosure, five concentric posthole rings suggest a large circular building. The diameter of the outer ring measured about 38 meters. Four corridors divided posthole rings into arcs. A ditch three to four meters wide and two meters deep surrounded the circular structure. After about three hundred years, a timber palisade trench with narrow entrances in the north and east enclosed Mount Pleasant's 4.5-hectare (11-acre) expanse.

To summarize the British henge monuments, each consisted of one or two circular timber structures surrounded by ditches and palisades, dating from the British Late Neolithic (the late fourth to the mid-third millennia B.C.). The earliest pottery is Grooved ware, and Beaker ware denotes the end phases of the henges. Feasting and consumption on a large scale are suggested by finds from ditches and postholes: broken pots, cups, and bowls; flint artifacts (mostly scrapers); chalk balls; antler picks; and quantities of wild and domestic animal bones, particularly those of pigs and cattle. Joints of meat, especially the hind legs of young pigs, were scattered in deposits. Archaeologists have found middens, or garbage piles, as well as extensively burned areas, on platforms outside the entrances to the sanctuaries (for instance, at Durrington Walls' South Circle sanctuary); these suggest ritual feasts and offerings. Human burials, whether by cremation (as at Stonehenge), in ditches or postholes (as at Marden and Avebury), or in the center of a sanctuary (as at Woodhenge), may have assumed dedicatory or other ritual purposes. The British roundels appear related in function to each other and to those found in central Europe, as evidenced by their similar designs, their ceremonial artifacts, and the sacrificial or ritual nature of their human remains. It is very possible that roundels were sacred places, dedicated to the goddess. Aligned with the cosmos, the territory of the roundel may have replicated a symbolic universe. Thus, a cosmic ideology may have motivated these Old European cultures to build such large-scale monuments. Through ritual in these monuments, they would have honored the Old European goddess of death and regeneration.

Causewayed Enclosures

Besides roundels, Old European cultures erected irregularly shaped ditched monuments that enclosed a specific area. Ditches and timber palisades also characterize these enclosures, but their noncircular design classifies them differently from roundels. However, like the builders of roundels, the originators of the irregularly shaped enclosures expended enormous effort to ritually transform their terrain. The fact that roundels have been found within irregularly shaped enclosures suggests that the monument types may have been related.

The shape and dimensions of the enclosure depended much on local topography. Frequently, the local Old Europeans built enclosures on promontories, on river terraces, and at the bottoms of valleys, surrounded by lakes, bogs, and streams. Sometimes they located enclosures on hills. An enclosure could be oval, subcircular, triangular, or roughly rectangular. Like other Neolithic monuments, enclosures vary enormously in dimension. The enclosed area ranged from a few hectares to sixteen hectares (a few acres to forty acres) and was surrounded by one, two, or more ditches with interruptions. Ditches could be two to eight meters wide, and one-half to three meters deep. Sometimes a palisade, made of upright posts (usually oak) interwoven with wickerwork, lined the inner side of a ditch. The builders of an enclosure felled thousands of trees for a single palisade.

As with roundels, irregularly shaped enclosures were considered a British phenomenon. In fact, the Windmill Hill enclosure gave its name to the Neolithic era in south-central England. Windmill Hill's outer ditch, interrupted by causeways, enclosed an area of about eight hectares (twenty acres). For decades, publications misleadingly called such nonsettlement sites "causewayed camps" (after Roman marching camps), which obscured their real meaning. Rather, irregularly shaped enclosures such as causewayed enclosures show evidence for ritual use comparable to that of roundels. Excavators do not find traces of settlements in irregularly shaped enclosures, and artifacts recovered from the ditches include pottery, human and animal bones, substantial food remains, white chalk balls, and flint and bone tool deposits. Hence, causewayed enclosures cannot be confused with hill forts or settlement enclosures. Causewayed enclosures uniquely characterize Old Europe, and they have no historical parallels. By now archaeologists have recorded and/or systematically researched hundreds of enclosures not only in England and Ireland, but across continental Europe. Their interpretation will reveal a great deal about the social and spiritual lives of their builders.

A detailed look at artifacts from the ditches of the irregularly shaped enclosures shows that these artifacts recur wherever enclosures are found, and that they are related to materials found in roundels. Irregularly shaped enclosures conceal votive offerings that include complete pots, and stone or bone tools, especially axes. Mysterious deposits of organic material now appear as dark humus-colored layers at the bottom of a ditch. Charcoal, cups and bowls, and masses of animal bones (cattle, pigs, and sheep) speak of large-scale feasting. Rituals might have included animal sacrifices. At the Bjerggård enclosure in Denmark, excavators unearthed four dog skulls that had been placed on a stone paving.

Several human skeletons suggest ritual burial or sacrifice. Human skulls and isolated jawbones are common (as in Sarup, Denmark: Madsen 1988; Andersen 1988). The site of Champ-Durand revealed a number of unusual burials: in addition to children's skulls, excavators came upon five complete juvenile and adult skeletons. A niche dug into the wall of the ditch harbored the remains of a young man and a young woman. Other skeletons included a thirteen- to fifteen-year-old boy, an eighteen-year-old youth, and an adult woman found in the debris of a fallen wall with a mass of pottery. The cause of death of these individuals remains a mystery, so we do not know if these were human sacrifices or ceremonial burials of honored individuals who died natural deaths.

Skulls, jaws, and skeletal parts found in enclosures may have been remnants of excarnation rites. As discussed earlier, certain Old European cultures exposed their dead to nature and scavengers before actual burial in order to remove the flesh. Enclosures may have been the places where such excarnation rites took place. After the relatives and survivors feasted

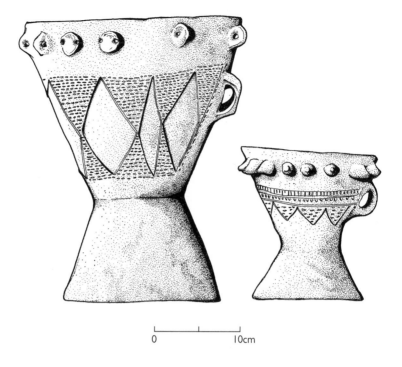

Figure 78. Clay drums decorated with hourglass figures (symbol of the goddess of regeneration) and breasts. Baalberge group; early fourth millennium B.C. (Dölauer Heide, Langer Berg, central Germany).

and performed rituals, they collected the skeletons and deposited them in the ossuaries in the megalithic tombs. Some disarticulated bones might have been left in the ditch. Some skeletons, particularly those of the young, might have been left behind for ritual purposes. If this scenario holds true, then the enclosures would be part of a complex funerary ritual. Several artifacts support linking the enclosures with death and regeneration: the pottery and its decoration, white chalk balls (probably replicas of eggs), and types of animals sacrificed. All these symbols belong to the goddess of death and regeneration. Some vases deposited in ditches or special votive pits portray symbols associated with the goddess of death and regeneration, such as round owl eyes, triangles, or hourglass shapes. The same symbols appear on funerary monuments such as the passage graves. Excavators discovered clay drums decorated with breasts and hourglass shapes (schematic contours impersonating the goddess) at the Dölauer Heide enclosure in central Germany (Fig. 78).

In Denmark, research reveals that one enclosure occupied the center of a megalithic tomb cluster dating from 3500 to 3200 B.C., which suggests the relation between enclosures and tombs. A similar situation has been reconstructed in the Orkney Islands. In Wessex, England, an enclosure and long barrow group appear related. In Neolithic society, death rituals were an enormous force that governed social interaction.

Other artifacts and skeletons recovered from the enclosures confirm their religious nature, and particularly their connection with death and regeneration. One enclosure revealed anthropomorphic figurines and clay thrones for figurines. Sacrificed dogs confirm that rituals relating to death and regeneration took place, since the dog belongs to the goddess of death and regeneration. Many funerary monuments in widely separated locations across Europe, such as Lepenski Vir (circa 6500–5500 B.C.) and the Orkney Islands (third millennium B.C.), disclosed whole skeletons of sacrificed dogs. The motif of a dog or hound accompanying the goddess echoes throughout history. The dog accompanied Hekate in Greece, and throughout Europe the hound serves the white lady—the goddess of death—still said to appear in some villages.

Square Enclosures

In addition to the roundels and irregularly shaped ditched enclosures, archaeologists have discovered square enclosures in central Europe. Like the roundels and irregularly shaped enclosures, square enclosures do not contain settlements and they lack defensive character. One example is Makotřasy in Bohemia. The principles employed in constructing square enclosures provide more distinct evidence for abstract conceptual planning. These sites, attributed to the Funnel-necked Beaker culture (Baalberge group), in existence during the first half of the fourth millennium B.C., yielded several ditch systems, including one near-perfect square measuring three hundred by three hundred meters. The geometric regularity of the square enclosures suggests an astronomical orientation parallel to the alignment of the roundels.

Towns Conceived as Replicating the Universe

The concept of a "miniature universe," first applied to ceremonial sites, seems to have been applied to some settled towns as well. In several settlements of the Karanovo people of northeastern Bulgaria, for example Poljanica and Ovčarovo, town plans reflected squares with strict geometric regularity and gates in the four cardinal directions. Several palisade rows, like those found in roundels, surrounded Karanovo towns. Like the entrances to the roundels, the main streets aligned north-south and east-west, with houses grouped in four quadrangles. Such towns are, of course, labeled "fortified settlements." It seems that here, however, as in roundels, the palisades served a symbolic purpose rather than a defensive one.

Conclusions

The roundels and enclosures discussed here were strictly nonsettlement sites, void of habitation debris. They were therefore ceremonial in nature. Aligned to the cardinal directions, these structures may have represented the cosmos. This concept was first applied to sacred ceremonial places. Subsequently, the concept was transferred to towns, such as the Karanovo settlements described above.

Much of the architecture of Old Europe was religious. The motivation behind these amazing structures appears to be the satisfaction of an obligation to the ancestors, alignment with the cosmos, and honoring of the goddess of birth, death, and regeneration. Rather than being defensive, these structures were monuments reflecting the spiritual life of Old Europe.

CHAPTER SIX

Matrilineal Social Structure
as Mirrored in Religion and Myth

The Parthenogenetic Goddess-Creatress

During the Paleolithic and Neolithic eras of prehistory, the worship of a female deity as the creatress of life mirrors the matrilineal, or mother-kinship, system that most likely existed in these times. The religious symbolism is permeated by symbols based on the life-creating female body. The mother and the mother-daughter images are present throughout Old Europe, while the father image, so prevalent in later times, is missing. The goddess is nature and earth itself, pulsating with the seasons, bringing life in spring and death in winter. She also represents continuity of life as a perpetual regenerator, protectress, and nourisher.

The role of the father in prehistoric antiquity was either not fully understood or not as highly valued as that of the mother. The female body gives evidence of maternity, while the male body does not give evidence of paternity. Further, in many societies females did not mate for life with their male sexual partners. This would lead to an inability to establish paternity, the identity of the exact biological father of a woman's child. Establishing paternity is one of the cornerstones of later patriarchal cultures, which insisted on controlling women's reproductive behavior. This inability to establish paternity has an effect on social structure because, when the biological father cannot be determined, the mother and her kin automatically are the focus of the family, and the family structure is matrilineal.

The woman's body was regarded as parthenogenetic, that is, creating life out of itself. This ability was celebrated in religion. In Neolithic times and earlier in the Upper Paleolithic, religion centered on the feminine power, as shown by the abundance of female symbolism. Just as the female body was regarded as the goddess creatress, so too the world was regarded as the body of the goddess, constantly creating new life from itself. The

112

imagery of Neolithic art is overwhelmingly feminine: the female body, and particularly its generative parts—vulva and uterus or womb—are predominant. These symbols appear not only on figurines or larger sculptures of goddesses, but also on vases, cult equipment, and in tomb and temple architecture.

Mother as Progenitor of the Family and Woman's Role in Religion

Given Neolithic religious symbolism, it is extremely difficult to imagine that Old European society would not be matrilineal, with the mother or grandmother venerated as progenitor of the family. In fact, the spiritual and social worlds were intimately intertwined: part of Old European religion was ancestor worship, in which the oldest women in the family, progenitors of a particular branch of the family, were venerated. This is shown strikingly by the burials of older women beneath houses and temples and under long barrows, by the spatial arrangements of graves in some cemeteries, and by the particularly rich symbolic artifacts buried with women.

Obviously, the burial underneath the house had a specific purpose. Archaeologists consider these types of burials to be a form of ancestor worship, in which the presence of an especially revered ancestor beneath the dwelling ensures the blessing of that ancestor or the continued presence of the spirit. In this way, the continuity of the family and its dwelling was ensured.

An analysis of the skeletons found underneath Old European houses or near them reveals two important facts essential to understanding Old European social structure and religion: first, these burials were almost always women, and second, the women were usually of an older age. This is the type of evidence we would expect to find in a matrilineal culture in which the women were heads of families and extended clans. An older woman was the ancestor whose blessing was sought to ensure continuity of the family she had started, and who was honored by burial beneath one of her houses or temples. At Çatal Hüyük, in south-central Turkey, the skeleton of an older woman was found beneath the floor of one of the largest shrine rooms, under the wall with a painting measuring eighteen meters across depicting Çatal Hüyük itself. She had been buried with a great deal of care, covered in jewelry. This particular burial was undoubtedly a revered ancestor. After 5000 B.C., the tradition of burying important individuals underneath or near houses continued, but in addition the Old Europeans began to dispose of their dead extramurally, or outside of their settlements, in cemeteries. At first, groups of five to ten people were buried near each other. Unlike the intramural burial, or burial *within* a settlement, where a single important individual was buried for religious reasons, the extramural cemeteries contain more of a cross section of Neolithic society. Perhaps the most notable feature of Old European graves and cemeteries is a lack of emphasis on material goods. In the Linearbandkeramik (LBK) cemeteries of central and eastern Europe, for instance, only 20 to 30 percent of graves possess grave goods: tools, pottery, jewelry, and other symbolic items. The relative poverty of the cemeteries contrasts sharply with the richness in art and wealth of Old European settlements, and suggests again that in the treatment of the dead, the concern was with spiritual functions rather than display of individual wealth.

While characteristics suggesting hierarchical class structure are absent, this does not mean that some sort of division of labor between the sexes did not occur, or that some individuals were not distinguished for reasons other than wealth. The 20 to 30 percent of graves that do contain artifacts tell us some important facts about the trades and activities, and something of the place and role of men and women in the social structure as well. In the LBK culture, for instance, males were buried with stone celts (a woodworking tool), jewelry made from imported spondylus shells, and flint scrapers and arrowheads. These items seem to reflect the participation of these men in trades: they were woodworkers and house builders, hunters, and craftsmen fashioning jewelry from spondylus seashells. In inland areas, seashells were obviously an item that had to be traded over long distances, and the presence of seashells in graves suggests that trading, too, was the province of men. In the Lengyel culture, men were buried with tools and other artifacts suggesting trades and mining: stone axes and hammer-axes made from antler and with nodules of flint and obsidian. The latter were mined in the nearby Carpathian Mountains. Artifacts found with women also show particular occupations. Some women's graves contained quern stones, suggesting grinding grain and baking. Tool kits for decorating pottery were found in several graves. But the types of artifacts found in male graves versus female graves are not subject to a strict division of labor. In some cemeteries, the same types of artifacts—quern stones, axes, chisels, or copper and shell jewelry—appear in both male and female graves.

Significantly, women's graves demonstrate the important role of women in religion. After 5000 B.C., when cemeteries appeared, older women in cemeteries continued to be accorded high status. Their connection to home and temple life is attested by the high concentration of symbolic items in their graves. Among cemeteries of the LBK group, women's graves often contained decorated pottery, ocher, and palettes, all notably religious artifacts. Particularly rich grave goods were found in women's and young girl's graves in the late LBK (Stroked Pottery phase) and Lengyel culture. In this area, several graves of women were distinguished from those of men by the presence of many vases and, especially, jewelry: copper, shell, and bone beads, and beautiful geometrically decorated bone bracelets. Two graves from Krusza Zamkowa, western Poland, belong to an older and a younger woman. The exceptional richness of these two graves suggests the important position of the women in the society; perhaps they were a revered spiritual leader and her daughter. One remarkable grave showing the importance of females in Old European religion and society was excavated in the cemetery at Aszód, north of Budapest, Hungary. Here, a teenage girl was buried with a large clay temple model (N. Kalicz 1985; illustrated also in Gimbutas 1991, Fig. 3-39). The temple model shows that this teenage girl was closely connected with the temple and its family group and was an important member of the lineage of women within the family.

Kinship Evidence from Cemeteries and Settlements

In the early cemeteries, dating to the millennium between 5000 and 4000 B.C., graves were grouped together in clusters. In the earliest cemeteries, graves were clustered together in groups of five to ten, a pattern that suggests a family unit. At the Aszód cemetery, graves were clustered together in three groups of about thirty each, which may reflect kin-related groups. Studies of megalithic tombs in northern Europe also reveal groupings of twenty to thirty individuals. The study of skeletal material has shown that individuals of each group were interrelated genetically (according to the study of bones from megalithic tombs of the Walternienburg group in central Germany, conducted by H. Ullrich). Megalithic tombs of northwestern Europe often include two or three chambers instead of one. These may represent subgroups within a larger kin-group. Keith Branigan studied Cretan circular tombs, *tholoi,* which dated to the third millennium B.C.; he found that they are burial places of extended families with a living membership of about twenty persons. At many sites, two or three tombs are built alongside one another at about the same time. One tomb of the group is architecturally superior to the others, which suggests that one family claimed primacy or preeminence and that communities already knew a degree of social ranking. Groupings in twos and threes with a noticeable preeminence of one house are also recognizable in settlements, where often two houses (one larger and one smaller) or groups of three houses (one larger and two smaller) stand together.

Research in Denmark, Wessex, and the Orkney Islands has shown that a single ditched enclosure appears in relation to a cluster of tombs within a particular area. Such territorial groupings, consisting of a large, ditched enclosure and some ten to twenty megalithic tombs, were mapped in central Jutland, Denmark.[1] If we assume that one tomb belonged to a village, then a group of villages (up to twenty) very likely were responsible for building the enclosure, which served as a communal and religious center.

In the Orkney Islands north of Scotland, the remains of large and small monuments offer insight into the relationship of villages to monuments. Here, a number of large chambered cairns still stand, as well as smaller cairns (see Fraser 1983; Biaggi 1994, 59 ff). The spatial distribution tells us something about who used the monuments: no two of the large monuments are found near each other.[2] Rather, each of the large cairns seems to be part of a topographic unit and probably served the villages in this area. The more numerous smaller cairns were located near individual villages, and it seems that each village had a cairn. The larger cairns more likely served as meeting and ritual sites on important occasions throughout the year, and were constructed and maintained by people from several villages.

In studies of spatial distributions of settlements and monuments in the Orkneys, Denmark, Wessex, and elsewhere, there is no evidence of a patriarchal chiefdom society at work. In the past, it has been assumed that the labor to construct these monuments must have been directed by a ruling class, and that the monuments themselves served some secular purpose: as royal courts or tombs. But as we saw with ditched ceremonial centers, in chapter 5, these monuments are religious in nature and were built by collective effort. No individual monument stands out as the seat of a chieftain.

The study of spatial distribution of graves in Old European cemeteries and tombs suggests the existence of family lineages. The same is provided by the study of blood groups. Remarkably, it is possible to determine blood type from the bones of people dead for thousands of years. Certain cemeteries of the Lengyel culture in Hungary have been studied by István Zălai-Gaál and Imre Lengyel, who analyzed the blood types of the skeletons—men, women, and children. The adult females and children were found to have been related by blood group, but the adult males in the same cemetery were found to be unrelated. This is the type of pattern we would expect in a matrilineal society, with the mothers and daughters maintaining residence and ownership of property, the young men leaving to enter another family, and males from another kingroup marrying into the matrilineal family.

Another type of spatial distribution that distinguishes Old European society from later patriarchal cultures is found in Old European settlements. In excavations of Neolithic sites, houses are sometimes found that are larger and better built (with many floor renovations) than the rest. Often, a large house is in the center of a cluster of smaller buildings. Naturally, archaeologists have often interpreted these to be a sort of "big man's" house, and the small houses as being the quarters for vassals and servants. This view is clearly inaccurate: evidence for a hierarchical type of patriarchal society is totally lacking in settlement evidence just as in cemetery evidence or in any other facet of Old European life. A large house was the central house of a "core family" of a lineage.

At a number of Old European sites, temples are found within a cluster of several buildings. At the early Neolithic site of Nea Nikomedeia in northern Greece, the largest building, distinguished not only by its size but by the number of ritual objects found within it, was surrounded by six smaller houses. In the Tisza and Vinča cultures, similar arrangements of houses and temples are found. Most likely, the houses held members of a kin-related group descended from one female ancestor. The shrine would be kept by the female members of the families living in the surrounding houses. The temple was in essence a family shrine maintained by members of the extended family. The tradition of several related families tending a common shrine is still found among the Christian Orthodox on islands of the Aegean. Significantly, this activity is carried out by the women of the families.

We see from the above discussions that the obvious signs of patriarchal societies were absent from the Old European cemeteries and settlements. Nowhere do we find the evidence we would expect to find in patriarchal societies: individual burials of male nobility buried in a manner that would reflect their worldly status.[3]

The Male Role in Symbolism and Myth

The male element in symbolism was significant but far from being prominent. In the Old European symbolic system, male animals and humans stimulate and enhance life, particularly plant growth. They are an important part in the process of becoming but do not actually create life. The phallus (not the semen) is an important symbol. The phallus as a spontaneous life energy is depicted alone or is shown to spring out of the female uterus or from between horns (a metaphor for the uterus). In Maltese temples, double or triple phalli appear in niche-shaped altars. In the sculptural representations of the early Neolithic, the phallus as divine energy is often shown fused with the life-creating female body: for example, the goddess sometimes has a phallic neck. Clearly, in this religious system the two sexes complement each other and thus invigorate the powers of life.

In Neolithic art and in myth, the male deities appear as partners of the goddesses. Alongside the mistress of animals is the master of animals, who may be descended from the Upper Paleolithic image of the half-human/half-animal found in caves and associated with animals. In Çatal Hüyük wall paintings of the seventh millennium B.C., a male figure holds a bird in each hand: an image parallel to that of the mistress of animals known from the Neolithic and later times, who was portrayed grasping geese, cranes, or other birds in each hand. In both the Neolithic and the historical era, the earth fertility goddess sometimes was portrayed with a male partner. The female and male deities discovered in a grave of the Hamangia culture from the early fifth millennium B.C., on the coast of the Black Sea, very likely represent a sister and brother pair rather than a married couple, since in European mythologies the female and male deities are known to be sister and brother pairs (for example, the Lithuanian earth mother, Žemyna, has a brother, Žemininkas, and the Scandinavian great-goddess, Freyja, has a brother, Freyr).

Another important, but different, role for the male god is that of consort of the great-goddess; he appears in festive rites of sacred marriage, the *hieros gamos*. This ritual mating ensured the smooth process of the vegetation cycle and secured fertility and happiness for the land. This rite is well known from historical times, but although images of copulation date back to the Neolithic, such images are rare (see chapter 1, on the *hieros gamos*). In the early historical era, the *hieros gamos* was celebrated in erotic hymns in Sumer and other Near Eastern cultures and in India. In myth and ritual it persisted throughout history and into the twentieth century. In myth, especially in the Irish Celtic tradition, the kingdom was conceived anthropomorphically as a female figure who symbolized not only the fertility or prosperity of the land but also the spiritual and legal dominion.[4] Irish legends from the Ulster cycle preserve strong vestiges of a prehistoric ritual in which the goddess conferred prosperity on a people by choosing one of its male members as her mate.

The iconography of the sacred marriage is recognized in frescoes, gems, and ivory reliefs found in Indo-European Mycenaean and later Greek art. The repeated theme is that of the bridegroom who comes in his ship from overseas to fulfill the sacred wedding in the sanctuary of the goddess. The gold ring from the Mycenaean citadel of Tiryns depicts the arrival of the bridegroom in a ship with a cabin and the encounter of the divine couple at the entrance of the bride's sanctuary. The famous Ship Fresco of the West House of Akrotiri, Thera, according to Gösta Säflund (1981), may represent the arrival of the bridegroom elected for the sacred wedding festival to be celebrated in the sanctuary.[5] The Building Complex B, in which the Ship Fresco was found, is considered to be a sanctuary since it displays loggias with large windows (as in Minoan clay models of temples), verandas, and balconies, one of which is crowned by horns of consecration. The priestess-goddess who plays the part of the divine bride appears on this balcony. She has her right arm raised: she seems to welcome the arriving fleet and ship carrying the bridegroom. The main priestess, as well as other women standing on the balconies and on the roof (very likely attendants of the sanctuary), is portrayed on a larger scale than are the men. Below the building, a procession of young men carries animals for sacrifice. The bridegroom is identified by Säflund as a male figure in the ship seated in an elaborate cabin, decorated with symbols of the goddess: pendants of stylized crocus blooms, butterflies, and sunflowers; lions and dolphins are depicted on the side of the ship. Important here is the fact that in this fresco, as well as in other portrayals of the same and later periods, the bridegroom comes to the bride's quarters. There is no sign of the bride leaving her home: the divine wedding of the goddess with a foreigner (who comes from over the sea) takes place in her own temple. This matrilocal tradition is also preserved in ancient Greece in the *hieros gamos* rite of Hera performed in the sanctuary of the goddess at the Argive Heraion and at Samos. An ivory relief from the sanctuary of Orthia, dating to the sixth century B.C., also depicts the bridegroom arriving in his ship and being tenderly received by the goddess.[6]

Priestesses and Women's Collective Power

From the early phases of the Neolithic onward, the goddess whose part is played by the priestess is portrayed crowned or enthroned. In early historical records and in folklore she is called queen, mistress, matron, or lady. The priestess-goddess is assisted by other priestesses and helpers, numbering from two, three, four, or nine, to a whole college. The attendants performed a variety of duties in rituals and temple maintenance. Priestesses and temple attendants are shown in a variety of sizes and are marked with different symbolic designs. Next to the goddess were the priestesses who may have formed a council important for decision-making. Councils of nine women are mentioned in early historic records and exist in European mythologies. The Scandinavian magician-priestess known as the Vølva had a council of nine wise women. Assemblies of nine priestesses or muses are well known in ancient Greece. A splendid example of a group of temple attendants is the model of an open temple from Zarkou in Thessaly dating from the early fifth millennium B.C. (see Fig. 65, above). It includes nine figurines of various sizes and workmanship. One priestess (or the goddess) is shown much larger than her attendants, and she is richly decorated with her special symbols: chevrons and tri-lines.

Another cache of twenty-one figurines was recovered from an early Cucuteni shrine dating to the early fifth millennium B.C.; it is particularly interesting because the figurines may represent a grouping in a temple ritual. (Excavated at Poduri-Dealul Ghindaru, Moldavia, in northeastern Romania, these figurines are illustrated in Gimbutas 1989, Plate 9.) Most probably used for the reenactment of earth fertility rites, the figurines measure from six to twelve centimeters in height. In addition to the figurines themselves, excavators found fifteen miniature chairs or thrones on which the larger figurines could be seated. The three largest ones are painted ocher-red, with opposing snake coils on the abdomen and lozenges on the back, dotted triangles and lozenges over the ample thighs and legs, and cartouches with chevrons over the buttocks. The medium-sized figurines have a striated band across the abdomen and stripes over the thighs and legs. The small figurines were rather carelessly produced and are not painted with symbols. Only one figurine out of the whole assembly has human arms; her left hand touches her face, while her right hand clasps her left arm at the elbow. The other figurines have schematized, stumpy arms. The differences in size and quality among the figurines may reflect differences in cult roles, ranging from goddess or priestess to various levels of assistants and attendants.

Communities of priestesses and women's councils, which must have existed for millennia in Old Europe and in Crete, persisted into the patriarchal era, but only in religious rituals. In the earth fertility ritual of the Thesmophoria (the festival of Demeter) in ancient Greece, women did choose a presiding person and form a council in which decisions were voted by majority rule. Men were not allowed to participate.

Communities of priestesses having great collective power are well known in early history as sisterhoods of enchantresses (known from Gaulish inscriptions), and as colleges of priestesses living on islands to which men are not admitted (mentioned by Strabo and Pomponius Mela in the first century A.D.). Priestesses as oracles, prophetesses, and magicians are known up to modern times in folklore and in myth. Groups of fairies who dance in circles and in meadows or around stone rings, creating enormous energy, appear in folklore from Scotland to Bulgaria even in the twentieth century. The magician-goddess, who was originally the goddess of death and regeneration but who was later considered a magician or a witch, survives up to the present as Basque Mari, Irish Macha or Medb, Baltic Ragana, Scandinavian Freyja, and German Holla. These goddesses appear alone or with large groups of assistants, and they exercise supernatural power in control of nature: the moon, the sun, eclipses, storms, hail. They destroy or create fertility of fields and control male sexuality. They themselves are endowed with an inexhaustible sexual energy. Irish Macha can run faster than the swiftest horses, while the sight of Queen Medb is sufficient to deprive men of two-thirds of their strength. Those who served the Inquisition in fifteenth-century Spain destroyed huge numbers of "witches": those who practiced the rites of the goddess and who had knowledge of medicinal herbs and other healing arts. Among many complaints about the powers of witches given by a soldier to the Inquisitor there is this notable sentence: "They have such power by reason of their arts that they have only to command and men must obey or lose their lives" (cited by Baroja 1975, 149). Myths and beliefs describe the female as the stronger gender, one endowed with magical powers.

Remnants of Matrilineal Social Structure in Minoan Crete, the Northern Aegean, Etruria, and Iberia

After reaching a flowering of culture in the fifth millennium B.C., the Old European way of life became submerged. Elements of the Indo-European culture—its religion, economy, and social structure—came to dominate life in Europe. The French mythologist Georges Dumézil (1939, 1958) made the fundamental observation that deities of Indo-European religion can generally be categorized into three classes: sovereign, warrior, and laboring (this class also included artisans and general "fertility" figures). Indo-Europeanized Europe fostered hierarchical societies, which were divided into these three classes. Patriarchy, class society, and warfare became the norm. But the Old European culture was not entirely eliminated everywhere. One way in which the Old European influence was felt was in the status of women in certain European societies in the early historical era. The survival of Old European customs is recorded in historical accounts that not only provide a confirmation of the matrifocal nature of Old European society suggested by archaeological research but also provide details of matrifocal customs which archaeology cannot preserve.

One of the regions that preserved elements of Old European culture the longest was the Aegean, where records were found that capture descriptions of matrilineal customs. The Minoan culture of Crete, as a result of its geographical location, preserved matrilineal customs much later than its counterparts on the mainland. A vast amount of religious art, architecture, and sepulchral evidence of Minoan culture attests to the importance of the female and the matrilineal inheritance patterns of the culture. Even after the arrival of the Indo-European Mycenaeans, the matrilineal traditions remained strong. In the first century B.C., the Greek historian and geographer Strabo describes matrilocal marriage in Crete, and the existence of this custom is confirmed by evidence from the marriage laws preserved in the Law Code of Gortyna (fifth century B.C.). The laws state that the woman retained control of her property even after marriage, and that she could choose to divorce at her will. Another aspect of the Old European matrilineal system, the avunculate—the important role carried out by the woman's brother—is described in the same inscriptions. Among other responsibilities, the brother was responsible for the upbringing of his sister's children.[7]

Another area that preserved elements of the matrifocal system is Sparta. Although Sparta embodied many elements of Indo-European social structure, such as an emphasis on war, the isolated location of the city-state in the center of the Peloponnese Peninsula of Greece helped it to preserve Old European elements.[8]

The Etruscans of central Italy also preserved matrifocal customs; this culture flourished from the eighth century B.C. onward, but it fell into decline after the fifth century B.C., when it began a gradual assimilation into the Roman Empire. The Greek historian Theopompus, who wrote during the fourth century B.C., was shocked by the freedom and power of Etruscan women. Theopompus recorded that Etruscan women would often exercise unabashedly in the nude with men and with other women. They liked to drink, and they dressed in a manner similar to that of men. They even wore symbols of citizenship and rank: mantles and high shoes. The names of Etruscan women reflected their legal and social status, in sharp contrast to Roman customs, where a woman had no name of her own. In fact, before a Roman woman was married, she was known as her father's daughter, and after marriage she was known as her husband's wife. In contrast to Roman women, Etruscan women played important roles as priestesses and seers, and they were a force in politics.

Many other aspects of Etruscan society reflect matrilineal succession and a matrifocal household. Theopompus recorded that Etruscan women raised their own children, whether they knew the father or not. This matri-focality was probably related to the woman's right to own property and to matrilineal succession. Matrilineal succession was reflected in the naming of individuals: in Etruscan inscriptions, individuals are referred to by the mother's name only. (For more on the role of Etruscan women, see chapter 9.)

The survival of matrilineal practices is not simply a peculiarity of the ancient Greek, Aegean, and Mediterranean worlds but is also found in the peripheral areas of northern and western Europe, where the influence of the infiltrating Indo-European tribes was weaker. Among the ancient and modern cultures that preserve this aspect of Old European heritage are the Basque culture of Spain and France, the Iberians, and the Picts of Scotland. Other cultures that were predominantly Indo-European, but which also preserved matrilineal traits, were the Celts, the Teutons, and the Balts. One of the most remarkable cultures that preserves Old European roots is the Basque, which survives to the present day in northern Spain and southeastern France. The Basques have a completely non-Indo-European culture, with its own non-Indo-European language, folklore, legal code, and matrilineal customs descended from Old European times. Basque law codes give the woman high status as inheritor, arbitrator, and judge, in both ancient and modern times. The laws governing succession in the French Basque region treat men and women entirely equally. Another Old European culture on the Iberian Peninsula was the Iberian, whose matrifocal practices were discussed by the Greek historian and geographer Strabo in the first century B.C.: "Among the Iberians, the men bring dowries to the women. With them the daughters alone inherit property. Brothers are given away in marriage by their sisters. In all their usages, their social condition is one of gynaecocracy."[9]

Farther north in Europe, ancient written records preserve memories of Old European cultures in the British Isles. The area of present-day Scotland was inhabited by a tribe known as the Picts, who spoke a non-Indo-European language and who escaped Indo-Europeanization until quite late because the Roman Empire never extended farther north than Hadrian's Wall. The Picts also preserved matrilineal laws and the goddess religion and its symbols. In this culture, transmission of property was matrilineal. Another Pictish custom, one still practiced in parts of the Scottish Highlands into the early twentieth century, was that of the woman remaining in her parents' house, even after marriage.

Much of Britain and Ireland was occupied in pre-Roman times by Celtic tribes who, although speaking Indo-European languages, still retained many Old European customs, such as goddess worship and matrilineal succession. Traditional Irish narratives describe marriage as being essentially matrilocal. Early Irish and Welsh literature preserves legends of Celtic heroes who, like the Greek heroes, leave home to seek an heiress to marry and thus share rule over her lands. The laws of ancient Ireland and Wales reflect an important role for the maternal brother, who represented the maternal kin, as well as an important role for the sister's son, who inherited the estate. Most probably, matrilineal succession was the rule in ancient Celtic society.[10]

Generally speaking, ancient records and archaeology both reveal the important social role of Celtic women, who had personal prestige and could possess property, even though the Celtic legal system was founded in patriarchal Indo-European custom. The region of Gaul (modern-day France) was inhabited in Roman times by Celtic tribes. In the first century B.C., the Greek author Diodorus Siculus describes Gaulish women as being "not only equal to their husbands in stature, but they rival them in strength as well."[11] One of the best-known Celtic historical figures was Boudicca, a Celtic queen who lived on the island of Britain. She was actually the widow of a Celtic king, and she instigated a rebellion against the Romans in order to reclaim her inheritance. The Roman Dio Cassius describes her in awe: "She was huge of frame, terrifying of aspect. . . . A great mass of bright red hair fell to her knees: she wore a great twisted golden torc [around her neck], and a tunic of many colors, over which was a thick mantle, fastened by a brooch."[12] Archaeological excavations in eastern France and the Rhineland have revealed remarkably rich graves of Iron Age Celtic women, dating from the seventh to the fourth centuries B.C.; these women belonged to the Celtic Hallstatt and La Tène cultures.

In ancient times, matrifocal traits also persisted in the Scandinavian and the Germanic areas, where the maternal relationship was considered more important than the paternal. Among the Thuringians, a man's property passed to his sister or mother if he died without children. In Burgundy, the estates and titles of royal houses passed through the women. Among the Saxons, a claim to the throne was not considered complete until the aspirant had married the queen.[13] In various Germanic tribes, matrilineal succession was the norm, and the kingdom was inherited through marriage with the queen or princess. As late as the eighth century A.D. in Scandinavia, a kingdom passed to the daughters and their husbands. The earliest historical documents of the Nordic and Germanic tribes tell that men were often named according to their mother's name, rather than their father's: the same practice we saw among non-Indo-European cultures of the Aegean area.

In the ancient cultures of the early historical period, many elements of Old European culture remained. One of the most visible is matriliny and the inheritance of property through the female line of the family; the succession to the throne or position of power also passed through the female line, from mother to daughter. We see the importance of the female lineage in the naming of individuals, who are named after the mother rather than the father. Of particular importance was the sister-brother relationship; even marriages between brother and sister are known, for example in ancient Egypt. The sister had a greater loyalty to her brother than to her husband. The brother was directly involved in the rearing and education of the children. In many places, marriage was endogamous: that is, people married within their culture groups.

In the Indo-European cultures we are most familiar with, the patriarchal society, with its emphasis on warfare and the value of weapons, is mirrored in religion by warrior-deities and in religious symbolism by the emphasis on weaponry. The hierarchical stratification of Indo-European societies is reflected in the hierarchy of Indo-European deities. In Old Europe, the social structure of society was different. This is one of the primary reasons that Old European religion had a nature fundamentally different from the more familiar Indo-European religions.

Conclusions

The reconstruction of the pre-Indo-European social structure of Old Europe is possible if various sources from different disciplines are used: linguistic, historical, mythological, religious, archaeological (especially the evidence from cemeteries and settlements). Evidence from these disciplines shows that the Old European social structure was matrilineal, with the succession to the throne and inheritance passing through the female line. The society was organized around a theacratic, democratic temple community guided by a highly respected priestess and her brother (or uncle); a council of women served as a governing body. In all of Old Europe, there is no evidence for the Indo-European type of patriarchal chieftainate.

The Living Goddesses

Old European Religious Continuity through the Bronze Age,
Early Historical Period, and into Modern Times

The contact between Old European and Indo-European cultures, quite opposed in social structure and ideology, resulted in the European cultures that we recognize from historical times through today. Indo-European language, beliefs, and social structure predominated, but they did not eradicate indigenous Old European religion and customs everywhere. The contact between the two cultures resulted in their amalgamation. Old European religion and customs remained a strong undercurrent that influenced the development of Western civilization. In some areas, like Minoan Crete and the Aegean Islands, a completely theacentric, gynocentric[1] civilization and religion endured through the first half of the second millennium B.C. Elsewhere, cultures still worshiped Old European divinities, although they adopted a hierarchical social structure. The Mycenaeans of Greece, Etruscans of central Italy, and Celts of central Europe, Britain, and Ireland exemplify this case, as do the Baltic, Slavic, and Germanic cultures to a certain degree.

Old European religion and customs survived because the Old Europeans themselves endured. In geographical areas where the Indo-Europeans assimilated with the Old Europeans, the pastoral Indo-Europeans became the ruling warrior caste; the Old Europeans remained agriculturalists and craftspeople, retaining their beliefs and customs. In time the two groups adopted each other's deities and practices, fusing the characteristics of deities from separate cultures into one.

Powerful goddesses inherited from the Neolithic occur throughout Europe, but their preservation differs from region to region. Most tenacious are the birth and life bringer and the goddess of death and regeneration. The continuity of her major prehistoric characteristics demonstrates their universality. Historical records, literary works, and survivals in folklore flesh out the archaeological evidence, allowing a more complete reconstruction of these prehistoric images. Hence the heirs of Old European goddesses and gods, assimilated into the early historical patriarchal cultures, help us to understand the Old European deities and their eventual destinies.

I will not describe here every deity of Old European descent from the Bronze Age to modern times. A selection from various regions and periods will suffice. For our purposes I have chosen the following cultures to discuss:

FROM SOUTHERN EUROPE:

The Minoan on Crete, to illustrate the undisturbed continuity throughout the Bronze Age

The Greek (beginning with the Mycenaean Bronze Age), to show the persistence of Old European religious structure under Indo-European rule, as well as the hybridization or change of certain deities

The Etruscan in Italy, which demonstrates the continuity of indigenous elements merged with the Indo-European influence via contact with the Greeks[2]

The Basque in northern Spain and southern France, which exemplifies the persistence of the indigenous religion of western Europe

FROM CENTRAL AND NORTHERN EUROPE:

The Celtic of central Europe, Britain, and Ireland: a culture with very strong Old European undercurrents

The Germanic, mainly Scandinavian, Christianized after A.D. 1000, where sagas describe two categories of deities: the Vanir (indigenous goddesses and gods) and the Aesir (Indo-European deities), their wars, and reconciliation

The Baltic, pagan almost to the sixteenth century A.D., which preserves Neolithic mythical figures up to modern times despite the presence of an Indo-European superstratum

CHAPTER SEVEN

The Minoan Religion in Crete

The upheavals that followed the Indo-European infiltrations into Europe from 4300 to 2900 B.C. transformed different regions at different times and to differing degrees; a few areas were left relatively unaffected. One such region is the Aegean area to the south and east of mainland Greece. The Aegean civilization consisted of many small islands in the Aegean Sea, including the Cycladic archipelago and the small island of Thera. It also included the large island of Crete south of the Aegean in the Mediterranean Sea. Here Old European and Anatolian[1] religion and social structure remained strong, as evidenced in art, pottery, architecture, and burial customs.

In the Old European Neolithic, the mainland and island peoples spoke a common language or several closely related languages that were non-Indo-European. Linguists recognize at least six thousand ancient European words that can be identified as non-Indo-European. Geographical place-names are found in non-Indo-European words such as "Zakynthos," the ancient name of Zante, an island in the Ionian Sea to the west of Greece; and "Hyakinthos," a pre-Greek god; or names with "ss," as in "Knossos," one of the most important ancient cities of Crete.[2]

Crete and the other Aegean Islands were among the areas that remained unaffected by the infiltrations of Indo-European-speaking tribes during the third millennium; these islands may owe their cultural survival to the fact that Indo-European peoples depended heavily on the horse and were, at least in their early stages, not well acquainted with navigation. The distance to Crete and the Aegean Islands, combined with the difficulty of transporting horses and soldiers by sea, contributed to the continuity and preservation of indigenous culture on Crete and the other Aegean islands. While Old European cultural development on the mainland was diverted by Indo-European influences, the Aegean Islands, particularly Crete, encapsulated the evolution toward Old European high civilization. It is important to remember that the Minoans flourished for some two thousand years after most Old European cultures in east-central Europe had disintegrated through contact with Indo-European cultures.

Cretan civilization remains the best-known Aegean culture. It was excavated fairly early in the history of archaeology, along with the famous Egyptian and Mesopotamian excavations. Sir Arthur Evans implemented the first excavations of Crete in 1900, and over the next twenty-five years he uncovered the large site of Knossos, on the north shore of the island near the modern city of Herakleion. He named the advanced Cretan culture "Minoan," after the legendary King Minos of Knossos, known from later Greek mythology.

Since it first came to light, Minoan culture has fascinated twentieth-century poets, writers, and historians, who saw its art as spontaneous, sensuous, and life affirming, in contrast to the structured forms of classical Greece and Rome. Although scholars of the early and middle twentieth centuries explained the origin of Minoan culture and religion by diffusion from the Near East (which occurred to a certain extent), its life-affirming, goddess-inspired art and religion stem from its Old European–Anatolian heritage. Because the Minoans lived some two millennia after the height of Old European civilization, they possessed more advanced artistic and architectural technologies than the Neolithic east-central Europeans. Therefore, their civilization and religious expression appear more distinct.

The same peoples inhabited Crete from the early Neolithic through the Bronze Age; Crete possessed small agricultural communities as early as the seventh millennium B.C. Between 6000 and 3000 B.C., these communities produced pottery and figurines similar to those found on mainland sites. Traditionally, Minoan culture is considered a "civilization" only since around 2000 B.C., when it satisfied two of the criteria traditionally required for such status: the building of true cities or religious centers (at Knossos, Mallia, Phaistos, and later at Zakros) and the construction of monumental structures. Early in this century, when excavators such as Sir Arthur Evans first exposed Minoan sites, at each site they found notable central buildings with large central courts. Drawing on knowledge of Near Eastern cities and sites on mainland Greece, where large central buildings usually housed royalty or warrior chiefs, the excavators termed the large Minoan buildings *palaces,* even though large portions of these structures clearly accommodated religious rituals. Evans even remarked that the buildings seemed to resemble temples more than palaces. Unfortunately, the term *palace,* with its connotation of a hierarchical society, has stuck. The evolutionary phases of Minoan culture are still classified with reference to the "palaces." After the "early palatial" period (1900–1700 B.C.), Minoan culture progressed in architecture and arts, reaching its apogee in the "late palatial" phase (1700–1450 B.C.). At this time, the Minoans expanded and adorned their "palaces" with beautiful frescoes, paved their streets with cobblestones, and built towns with two-story villas and plumbing.

At their height in the sixteenth century B.C., the Minoans were one of the most important trading powers in the eastern Mediterranean, forming a network with Greece, Egypt, Asia Minor, the Levantine Coast, and other Aegean Islands. Although Minoan culture centered on Crete, the largest island in the Aegean cultural group, the same culture extended across the Aegean. The island of Thera lies just 112 kilometers north; its remarkable city, Akrotiri, also contained two-story buildings and temples with beautiful frescoes.

The Minoans used two writing systems, which came into use by at least 1700 B.C. The first included a series of pictorial symbols, termed *Minoan hieroglyphs*. The second involved a set of signs written in straight lines across clay tablets, termed *Linear A*. Unfortunately, as mentioned in the earlier chapter on writing, neither the Minoan hieroglyphs nor Linear A have been deciphered (that is, none of the efforts to date have been well accepted), because these signs represent a non-Indo-European language, and there are no fully deciphered languages to which we may compare Linear A or the hieroglyphs. A third Minoan script, Linear B, came into use about 1450 B.C., at a time when Crete had succumbed to or assimilated with the mainland powers. For decades a mystery, the secret of Linear B was finally revealed in 1952 when Michael Ventris, in collaboration with John Chadwick, advanced a strong case that Linear B was an early form of Greek. By 1400 B.C., Crete had lost its sovereignty to mainland powers who brought with them the Greek language. Although the Linear B tablets are decipherable, they give us less information about Minoan culture than we would like. Similar to the earliest written records of Mesopotamia, Linear B tablets consist of short lists and inventories, not extensive myths and legends. However, they provide valuable information regarding the names of deities worshiped in Minoan times, many of whom were venerated into the classical era, both on Crete and on the Greek mainland.

The Minoan civilization differed strikingly from Near Eastern civilizations. Its advanced technical achievements in arts, crafts, and architecture rivaled and, in many ways, exceeded, those of contemporaneous Egyptian and Mesopotamian cultures. The inhabitants of Minoan city-states lived with one another in apparent peace: no Minoan city possessed extensive defensive walls. Further, Minoan culture differed in its religious expression. The Minoans' competence in arts and architecture expressed a world-view entirely different from that evident in the ancient Near East: the world-view of Crete reflected its Old European–Anatolian roots.

Temple Complexes

Since 1900, when excavation of Minoan cities began, researchers have focused much attention on the large central buildings found in most Minoan cities. These central buildings were certainly marvels of engineering: the first and largest structure, excavated at Knossos, covered about two hectares (five acres), stood two or three stories high, and included expansive skylights. As mentioned previously, excavators labeled these buildings "palaces," by analogy to the large "megarons" of the Greek mainland and the royal palaces of Near Eastern cultures. But as already noted, the concept of a "palace," "megaron," or "big man's house" set aside for the warrior nobility did not exist in Old Europe. However, since excavators on Crete have found no separate administrative centers, it appears that religious and administrative functions were consolidated. These structures were in fact religious-administrative-economic complexes, not palaces. Even the earliest excavators, while calling the buildings "palaces," noted that large sections of the structures encompassed ritual use. With all of the connotations in mind, we can use the terms *temple complexes* or *temple-palaces* to designate complexes that, in addition to myriad ritual spaces, also contained administrative buildings. Into this category fall the "palaces" of Knossos, Phaistos, Mallia, and Zakros; these, in fact, are conglomerates, or labyrinths, of many temple complexes.

Rodney Castleden used the term *temple-palace* in *The Knossos Labyrinth* (1990) (see also Nanno Marinatos 1993). He claims that Knossos may have functioned very much like a medieval monastery, acquiring great wealth, supporting a large hierarchy, and acting as a redistribution center. He suggests that priestesses may have presided over the complex, with any king acting only in subordination to them.

The spectacular temple complexes, with hundreds of "horns of consecration" (models of bulls' horns) lining their roofs and terraces, unequivocally attest to the active ritual life of the larger Cretan towns. However, archaeological evidence also reveals that shrines and temples distinguished smaller Cretan towns and even the countryside. The Minoans venerated the same deities everywhere and performed related rituals. Further, the spiritual and secular ways of life were closely intertwined.

Nearly a century after the discovery of Knossos, scholars have finally agreed that the term *palace* merely connotes a convention. It does not define the functions and meanings of these magnificent complexes, which were embellished with ubiquitous scenes of goddess worship and which embraced an entirely female-oriented symbolic system. Along with the realization that the term *palace* did not really apply, it has also become obvious that no king or priest-king dominated Knossos. In fact, the very name *Minoan* is a misnomer. Sir Arthur Evans originally envisioned the legendary King Minos sitting on his throne at Knossos, long before we ascertained the true nature of Minoan and Old European culture. The early correlation of kingship with the Knossos temple complex created a major stumbling block to our perception of Minoan culture.

The "dethronement" of King Minos revolutionized our views on this most female-oriented culture. As Dorothy Cameron says in her forthcoming book, *The Lady and the Bull: An Interpretation of Minoan Art,*

The evidence of feminine influence and sensibility in Minoan art and religion—in architecture and artifact, in the wall paintings which depict ceremonies connected with the worship of a feminine deity, in the priestesses who surround her represented in figurines and paintings and in the thousands of sealstones depicting ritualistic scenes in her honor—is too strong to be dismissed. The male presence shown on sealstones and in wall paintings during this peak period was as "adorant," the description used by Evans throughout his early volumes. The adorant was shown most frequently worshipping the female deity at shrines in the sealstones. In the wall paintings, a procession of males carrying ritual objects usually follows behind two female figures. It was not until the slow absorption of Mycenaean influences that this characteristic rendition of the male changed into what Evans described as a more formal "militaristic" presence. Shields began to replace ritual objects and less attention was given in religious aspects, an influence which began after the peak of Minoan artistic culture had been reached.

Cameron has interpreted the architectural structure of the Knossos temple complex, particularly the disparity between the west and east blocks, as reflecting the different spiritual functions I explored in our earlier examination of Neolithic religion. The west block of the temple complex reflects regeneration (from death or winter), while the east portion embodies birth and life giving. These themes also have parallels on Malta, where twin temples differed from each other in function. Evans (1921–36, Vol. 1) has himself observed that the west wing of the "palace" was little more than a conglomeration of small shrines of pillared crypts designed for ritual use. In chapter 3 of this book I mentioned the prehistoric European belief in the sacred, womblike, regenerative qualities of caves, and the Old European efforts to build temples of regeneration that imitated caves. The dark, pillared crypts of the Knossos temple complex, like the cave (and womb), embodied regenerative qualities. These crypts preserved repositories of precious cult objects and traces of offerings of grain and animals. The main symbol was the double ax, consisting symbolically of two triangles joined at the tips. Archaeologists unearthed bases for holding the huge ceremonial double axes and found ax images engraved on three or four sides of pillars. The term *crypt* in Christian times denoted a room underneath a church that also sheltered tombs. The Knossos crypts did not safeguard human remains, but their womblike character is reminiscent of actual Minoan tombs containing the same symbols of regeneration: double axes and horns or bucrania. The pillars found in crypt shrines are also important symbols of regeneration. They are symbolically related to the stalagmites that occur naturally in caves: both symbolize rising earth energy. Elsewhere in Minoan art, pillars and columns alternate with the tree of life or with the goddess herself. As we know from the Neolithic, the triangle and double axes were prime symbols of the goddess of death and regeneration: both were symbols of becoming. In Old European times, ax images adorned megalithic tomb walls and western European menhirs. In the west temple of Knossos, we find other symbols of regeneration: the cores of roe-deer horns (one of the animals of the goddess in her life- and birth-giving functions), and ivory and bone inlays fashioned into a pomegranate motif. These further confirm the symbolism of rebirth. Some of the most beautiful examples of Minoan art are the exquisite faience snake goddess or snake priestess figurines. Of two figurines crowned by tiaras and attired in ritual costume, their breasts exposed, one figurine lets snakes wind around her arms, while the other holds snakes in her hands. Found in a floor cyst repository, a storage area for sacred objects, these figurines further stress regeneration and the chthonic aspect.

Symbolism in Minoan crypts suggests seasonal rites of renewal. Additionally, personal rites of passage, a ceremony in which the initiate was "reborn" or healed, cannot be excluded. I believe that rituals that occurred in the dark crypts of the Knossos temple complex relate, on the one hand, to those performed one or two thousand years earlier in the large tomb shrines of Old Europe: Newgrange and Knowth in Ireland, and the Hal Saflieni Hypogeum in Malta. On the other hand, they mirrored those enacted in classical times, such as the Mysteries of Eleusis in Greece. The ceremonies of initiation at Eleusis, accompanied by music and dance, symbolically imitated death and resurrection.

While the crypt-shrines of the west wing of the Knossos temple complex possessed a dark, womblike atmosphere appropriate to regenerative rites, the east quarter projected an entirely different ambiance. This wing held no basements and no darkness; instead, it reflected light and gaiety and extravagant color. It contained halls, "reception rooms," open light areas, and the so-called Queen's Megaron, with murals and painted reliefs. Breasts decorated cult vessels; spirals and breasts adorned ceilings; dolphins, spirals, and rosettes enhanced walls. This wing celebrated birth and life. A giant wooden statue of the goddess measuring about three meters tall and adorned with bronze locks of hair stood in the great East Hall. It parallels the immense statue of the goddess in the Tarxien temple of Malta (Fig. 75, above). The presence of the large statue of the goddess in the East Hall confirms that the east quarter was dedicated to the goddess; the vivid breasts, dolphins, rosettes, and spirals evidence that the goddess was worshiped in her life-giving aspect.

A significant feature of the west wing of the Knossos temple complex is the "throne room," which contains an elevated seat obviously intended for some important ceremonial function. In the decades since Arthur Evans uncovered Knossos, the throne was considered the seat of honor for a king (such as the mythical Minos), which gave Minoan culture an undeservedly militaristic and patriarchal quality. But a number of researchers, including Helga Reusch, Sinclair Hood, Emmett L. Bennett, Henri Van Effenterre, W. D. Niemeier, and Nanno Marinatos, have challenged the plausibility of assuming a Minoan culture based upon male royalty, whose ceremonial power would have focused on the "throne room."

In fact, the symbolism of the frescoes surrounding the throne does not represent a king at all: it is the symbolism associated with the goddess known from many other representations of her. The throne and the door leading to a preparation room are flanked by palms and griffins (mythical beings with the head of a bird and the body of a lioness). In the frescoes, the griffins have crests of plume, curled as spirals; a rosette on the body; necklaces; and groups of three lily stems over their bodies. The heraldic scene of the goddess between the animals (dogs, griffins, lions) is repeated many times on Minoan seals. The seat back of the throne has curving sides decorated with semicircles and a protrusion on top (it is actually roughly anthropomorphic). As Castleden has suggested, the throne mirrors the shape of a mountain summit, as portrayed on a rhyton from Zakros where it is flanked by he-goats. It is quite possible that the mountain summit symbolized the goddess herself. In fact, a hill with a protrusion or an omphalos is a well-known symbol of the goddess in megalithic western Europe (Fig. 52a, above), in ancient Greece, and in later cultural areas as well. The seat face displays an omphalos with the full moon: symbols of concentrated life force. Moon, triads, spirals, lilies, omphalos: all familiar symbols of the goddess inherited from earlier times.

The "throne room" obviously served ceremonial, not secular, purposes. We can easily envision the rituals that took place here. In the adjoining preparation room, the priestess was dressed in festive, symbolic attire. She appeared at the door, flanked with sphinxes, and then advanced to the throne, where she received offerings brought through the same door from the service section (a suite of rooms that included tables, benches, and low stone seats next to the preparation room). The priestess became the earthly representation of the goddess.

A lustral basin stood across the room and down several steps. Its presence reveals a ritual that may have included descending to be cleansed with water and fragrant oils, and ascending again, renewed. Many lustral basins occur in Knossos and other Minoan temples. They convey that the worship of the goddess involved a ritual of cleansing and renewal, and that it was continually practiced. Lustral basins have predecessors in Malta, Newgrange, and Knowth, in the fourth millennium B.C. This type of ritual was another aspect of Minoan religion inherited from Old Europe.

The functions served by temples in Crete during the early and mid-second millennium B.C. have deep roots in Old Europe and Old Anatolia. The large edifices at Knossos, Phaistos, Mallia, and Zakros seem to have functioned mainly as "temples of regeneration" that concerned the passage from death to life. They joyously celebrated birth and the flowering of life. The presence of the goddess radiated from the west and east quarters through her thrones, sculptures, and, especially, her symbolism. Minoan temple complexes grew to gigantic architectural proportions and great ceremonial complexity, but at their core they closely resembled the temples of regeneration in Europe and Anatolia dating some three to four thousand years earlier.

Cave Sanctuaries

Worshipers used caves as sanctuaries from the Upper Paleolithic through the Neolithic. These caves are an important part of the Minoan archaeological repertoire.[3] Not every cave was sacred. The Minoans regarded only those caves with special properties important: specifically, those that contained chambers, passages, stalagmites, wells of pure water. Their particular shape, darkness, and damp walls symbolically connected the cave to the tomb and the womb. The pillared crypts in Minoan temples resembled human-created caves. But caves themselves made more dramatic and powerful religious sanctuaries than crypts, with their often remote settings, fantastically shaped stalagmites and stalactites, and shadowy interiors illumined only by torches or lamps. Some giant temples maintained their own cave sanctuaries. Phaistos used the Kamares cave, located at an altitude of 1,524 meters and only accessible during certain seasons. Knossos was served by the huge Skoteinó cave and the smaller Eileithyia, both of which were special regional cult locales. The larger religious centers appear to have organized pilgrimages to these sacred places.

Exploration of the cave sanctuaries has brought to light several religious artifacts, such as altars, vessels, offering tables, and symbolic objects that reflect the same regenerative themes as tombs and crypts. Pottery from the Middle and Late Minoan periods constituted the most ubiquitous find, including Kamares "eggshell" cups and magnificent vases produced in the Phaistos temple complex. Other artifacts recovered from cave sanctuaries include the familiar manifestations of the goddess of death and regeneration, including sacred horns, double axes (of gold, silver, and bronze), and seals and plaques engraved with a tree of life growing from the center of the sacred horns. Some finds suggest the presence of pilgrims and priestesses in caves. Archaeologists have uncovered votive offerings, some with inscriptions, and a considerable number of figures of male votaries saluting with their right arm. A seal from the Idean cave shows a priestess holding a triton shell standing in front of an altar bearing a pair of horns, with a tree of life in the middle and individual trees flanking the horns on either side.

Several Cretan caves are clearly associated with birth giving: the Eileithyia cave at Amnissos (the harbor town mentioned by Homer in *The Odyssey*) and the Dikte cave in the Lasithi Plain. To this day, these caves carry their ancient names. The goddess Eileithyia (which is not a confirmed Indo-European name), to whom offerings of honey were made, is mentioned as early as the Linear B tablets from Knossos (around 1400 B.C.). In classical Greek myth and ritual she is known as Artemis Eileithyia, the Artemis who presides over birth. Rites of renewal and celebrations of the birth of the divine child were most likely performed in caves.

Peak Sanctuaries

Like caves, mountain peaks evoked a sense of power and sacredness. Many legendary deities lived on mountaintops, and even recently Greek peasants believed that a tall goddess dwelled there. In Minoan Crete, peak temples appeared around 2000 B.C. and continued throughout the second millennium, in some cases into Greek and Roman times. Archaeologists have discovered several impressive temples on Cretan mountain peaks, such as those at Juktas (located near Arkhanes, not far from Knossos), Petsofas (near Palaikastro in eastern Crete), and Traostalos (north of Zakros). These temples contained three or more rooms and were decorated with horns.

We can deduce what peak sanctuaries symbolized from their portrayals on stone rhytons found in Zakros and Gypsades (near Knossos). Each of the buildings depicted has a tripartite facade and walls topped with horns. The anthropomorphic hill or mountain embodying the goddess herself, flanked by pairs of mountain goats, decorates the central niche as depicted on the Zakros rhyton. Birds top the smaller side niches. The rhyton further illustrates several kinds of altars below the shrines on stairs or rocks, suggesting that votaries left offerings. The Gypsades' portrayal of a peak sanctuary even includes a worshiper or pilgrim depositing offerings in a basket placed on a rock. At peak sanctuaries, archaeologists have found accumulations of offerings not only on altars but also, in the case of Juktas, in crevices and deep chasms. Ash layers attest to great bonfires that were lit on special occasions.

Symbols unearthed in peak sanctuaries correlate with those found in caves and crypts: horns, double axes, bulls, birds, beetles, and anthropomorphic figurines. These again indicate the presence of regenerative rites. Some female figurines exhibit snakes in their crown or headdress; many other figurines simply seem to depict worshipers (votaries) with crossed arms on the chest. Certain artifacts suggest additional functions of the peak sanctuaries. In the temple of Juktas, excavators found small models of birthing women, a female with a swollen leg, and women with deformed bodies. Other figurines portrayed sheep and cattle. (For illustrations of ex votos, see Rutkowski 1986.) These shrines apparently offered healing and help in delivery, in addition to serving as sites of the main rituals of life renewal. The goddess portrayed on seals as standing on a mountain peak holding a power symbol is obviously the same regenerator and healer found in crypts, caves, and temples.

A widely reproduced *National Geographic* article (see Sakellarakis and Sakellarakis 1981) portrays peak sanctuaries as places of blood sacrifice that was performed before an impending natural catastrophe to propitiate the goddess. The excavations of Yannis and Efi Sakellarakis (1981) promoted this scenario. They unearthed the small triple temple of Anemospilia on the northern slope of Mount Juktas, dating from about 1700 B.C. In the central shrine, a life-sized wooden statue stood on an altar; the northern shrine held an altar-shaped sacrificial table. On this table rested the remains of a seventeen-year-old youth tightly folded up, feet to buttocks. His throat, the excavators presumed, was slit with the bronze dagger engraved with a boar's head that sat beside the boy. A robust, thirty-year-old man lay on the floor beside the body. The excavators imagined that the man may have killed the boy minutes before the building collapsed. They also exhumed a woman's body nearby. Outside the doorway to the central shrine, where the statue stood, the archaeologists found yet another male or female skeleton. All of them were entombed in situ during the earthquake that coincided with the ritual. Is this a clear case of a human sacrifice? According to Nanno Marinatos, the evidence for human sacrifice is far from conclusive.[4] We certainly need much more evidence to conclude that this civilization practiced human sacrifice.

Cult Equipment

The ritual artifacts found in Minoan caves, temples, and mountain peak sanctuaries continued the rich Neolithic religious tradition, reflecting beliefs and ways of worship that the Minoans inherited from Old Europe. Both the Minoan and the Old European–Anatolian cultures shared several categories of ritual objects: tripods, rhytons, and movable altars; special tables with depressions for offerings; benchlike altars along the wall which held vases, figurines, and symbolic items; *kernoi* uniting several (as many as nine) cups to a common base (for offering different kinds of grain, legumes, oil, honey, milk, wool, etc.); ornithomorphic (bird-shaped), zoomorphic, and anthropomorphic vases for libations or other purposes. This continuity in ritual objects evidences a long-lasting tradition in ritual functions. Much of the Minoan cult equipment (rhytons, for example) exhibits superb beauty and workmanship that surpasses Neolithic equipment. Some Old European artifacts, however, such as their ornithomorphic, zoomorphic, and anthropomorphic vases, equal those of the Minoans.

Bull-Leaping

Preoccupation with bulls characterizes Minoan religion, as attested by the famous bull-leaping frescoes and depictions on sealstones dating from the fifteenth century B.C. Other bull-related artifacts, particularly the "horns of consecration," occur in religious contexts at many sites on Crete. The bullfighting tradition of modern Spain, Portugal, Turkey, and elsewhere very likely derives from Minoan bull games. The modern bullfighting "sport," however, is cruel. Minoan portrayals do not show infuriating injuries inflicted on the bulls; they depict only an elegant sport. The Bull Leaper fresco from the Knossos labyrinth shows three acrobats performing: a youth (shown in black), who leaps from the direction of the bull's horns over its back with hands pressing down on the bull's spine and body arched over the bull's tail; and two girls (shown in white): one holds the bull's horns, while the other waits with outstretched arms behind the bull to catch the youth.[5] Another exquisite representation shows the bull with its forelegs resting on a large rectangular block and a youth vaulting through the horns. Having the bull's forelegs on a block certainly would have made it easier for the acrobat to make his or her jump through the horns. A large stone block was found in the central Phaistos court. J. W. Graham (1987) assumes that the acrobats used it in the beginning of a bull game, and that bull games may have taken place in the central courts of temple complexes.

The Minoan preoccupation with the bull and its horns reflects an Old European tradition. In Old Europe, the bull was sacred to the goddess of death and regeneration; the bucrania and bull's horns were symbols of her regenerative powers, present in tombs and temples of regeneration. In Minoan Crete, the presence of the bull and its horns in so many aspects of Minoan life—frescoes, sealstones, and architecture—simply expresses their belief in regeneration.

Goddesses and Gods

Because Minoan religious continuity with Old Europe survived unbroken, Minoan religion embraced many deities descended from Old European goddesses and gods. The best-known Minoan goddess, portrayed in seals, rings, frescoes, and sculptures, is the young goddess whom we identify with the Neolithic goddess of regeneration. Depictions show her surrounded by animals and plants. Minoan art abundantly reflects regenerative symbols: double axes, butterflies, bucrania, and trees (or columns) of life. An exceptional portrayal of this goddess comes from the Xeste 3 temple on the island of Thera. Here, the Fresco of Crocus Gatherers pictures this goddess seated high on a throne on a tripartite platform, flanked by a griffin and a monkey. Young girls bring her flowers in baskets. She is exquisitely dressed in a crocus costume and adorned with necklaces of ducks and dragonflies. Large golden hoops hang from her ears. Her dress harmonizes with the marshy landscape; she is mistress of nature. Nanno Marinatos (1984) more specifically describes her as the spring renewal of the mistress of nature. Ritual vases from the same Theran temple depict flying swallows, lilies, and crocuses. Scenes of nature depicted in frescoes and painted on vases at Knossos and Thera allude to the concept of spring fecundity and abundance.

The young, strong, bare-breasted goddess is also portrayed on sealstones flanked by griffins or lionesses. The sealstone from Knossos shows her standing on a mountain peak holding a scepter; a worshiper salutes her and a columnar temple with sacred horns, perhaps Knossos, appears behind her. Another seal from Knossos depicts her seated on a tripartite platform with lions flanking her. A seal from the cave of Dikte displays the tall, strong goddess holding triple horns above her head. Several seals depict her holding waterbirds.

On other seals and rings, the goddess receives gifts while seated. On the seal from Knossos, a woman, probably a priestess, brings her a large vase with two circular handles. In this scene, the goddess sits under a lush tree and holds her bare breasts with her left hand. A large double ax appears between her and the priestess, and a crescent moon and sun (or full moon) float in the sky above her.

A common Minoan religious symbol related to the goddess of regeneration is the *labrys,* or double ax. It frequently appears in crypts, tombs, and temples, often depicted emerging from between the sacred horns. It is the main symbol of this goddess in her regenerative aspect. Often the ax is portrayed in an anthropomorphic form with a human head; at other times the ax stem is shown as a tree. This goddess embodied by the double ax was the major deity worshiped at the Knossos temple complex. One of the Linear B (Mycenaean Greek) tablets recovered from the Knossos archive refers to a honey offering dedicated to "da-pu-ri-to-jo po-ti-ni-ja." Linguistically, Mycenaean Greek *da-pu-ri-to-jo* is related to the classical Greek word *laburinthos* (labyrinth), a name attributed to the Knossos temple complex. *Po-ti-ni-ja* (potnia) means "lady" or "queen." The offering of honey was bestowed upon "Our Lady (or Queen) of the Labyrinth" (i.e., the Knossos temple complex).

This goddess figures most prominently in the art of Middle Minoan Crete. Arthur Evans called her the "Great Minoan Goddess." She survived into the subsequent Achaean and classical Greek periods, and writings left by Greek and Latin authors have preserved her names. In classical antiquity, different names and epithets identified the same deity in different localities, and the Minoan goddess of regeneration too has many names. One of her names was Britomartis, "Sweet Virgin" (or "Sweet Maid"), which stresses her youthfulness and beauty. On the island of Aegina, she was worshiped as Aphaia. Another of her names was Diktynna, which some scholars link to *diktyon,* "net." Legends recount that this goddess was saved by fishermen after she had thrown herself into the sea to escape pursuit by Minos; but this may be a false etymology. In fact, the connection of the goddess with the net possibly began much earlier than this Greek legend. The net symbol, which begins in the Paleolithic and continues throughout the Neolithic and Minoan eras, correlates with birth giving, life-giving water, and amniotic fluid. The names of the Cretan cave Dikte and the mountain Dikte very likely derive from the worship of this goddess in caves and on mountain peaks.

The connection with life-giving fluid leads to her aspect as the goddess of childbirth, Eileithyia. This name is connected with the cave at Amnissos. She is described by Homer as *mogostokos,* or "goddess of the pains of birth." Another of her epithets, Phytia, means "she who stimulates growth." On Roman coins from imperial times, Diktynna is shown holding a youth: Zeus (the Cretan Zeus was a divine child; the Greek Zeus was a latecomer who replaced the pre-Indo-European divine child).

Artemis, worshiped in both classical and Hellenistic Greece, is the same goddess and is associated with the cave on Akrotiri in western Crete. This cave is called Arkoudia, "Cave of the She Bear," in our times still sacred to the Virgin, who has a local name, Panagia Arkoudiotissa, "Our Lady, the (Sweet) Bear." Even in the classical era, Artemis is linked with the bear, as we shall discuss later. Thus we can see a link between Artemis and the bear mother, well evidenced in Neolithic sculptural art. The names used for this goddess through various places and periods shed light on her many aspects: she is young and beautiful, she is goddess of childbirth, she has the power to stimulate growth, and she is the bear mother nursing the divine child.

In the earlier chapters on Old European religion, I recounted the close connection between life and death: the goddess was life giver as well as death wielder. With symbols of regeneration figuring so prominently in Minoan art, we would expect the death aspect of the goddess to be manifest in the dark cave sanctuaries and crypts of Crete. But this is not the case. Life, rather than death, primarily characterized Minoan culture. Nevertheless, the image of the vulture goddess presented one aspect of the goddess of death to the Minoans. On seals and rings she exhibits a vulture or raptor head with large wings, but she also may have large bare breasts: a sign that she is the goddess not only of death, but of regeneration. Clearly, she derives from the Neolithic bird goddess and gives rise to the Greek Athena. Athena's name, which is not Indo-European, appears in the texts of Mycenaean Crete. One Knossos tablet (V, 52) contains a dedication to *a-ta-na po-ti-ni-ja,* "Lady (Mistress) Atana."[6] The stiff nude of marble or alabaster, the tomb goddess inherited from the Neolithic, represents the same goddess. She wears a mask with a large nose[7] and has a large life-regenerative pubic triangle (Fig. 13, above), so again, the emphasis is on life and regeneration.

The Minoan snake goddess possesses snake limbs or snakes writhing in her crown, as in the Neolithic. The famous faience sculptures from the Knossos temple repositories appear beautifully attired, with bare breasts, and snakes crawling up their arms, entwined around their waist, or held in their hands. These sculptures may represent the snake goddess or priestesses performing snake dances or other rituals connected with life's regeneration after the winter season. Figurines holding birds or portrayed with a dove on the head and with upraised arms, as found in the Tomb of the Double Axes (this is both a tomb and a shrine) at Knossos, also harmonize with the theme of spring regeneration.

The pregnant vegetation goddess, whose figurines inundate European Neolithic sites, is absent in Cretan archaeological remains. But her memory is preserved in legends and written sources, which record two Cretan goddesses of vegetation: Ariadne and Demeter. According to the Homeric Hymn to Demeter, this goddess came to Greece from Crete. Each married a god: Ariadne was wed to Dionysus,[8] and Demeter married Iasion.[9] At Naxos, Ariadne had two festivals, one of them celebrating her marriage, the other mourning her death. This goddess died annually, as did her consort, the god of vegetation, in order to bring new fertility in the spring. The classical myth depicting the death of both female and male vegetation deities very likely derives from Neolithic Europe, as shown by burial of the pensive female and male figures (perhaps representing deities) in a Cernavoda grave of the Hamangia culture in Romania, dating from the early fifth millennium B.C. The death of the female vegetation goddess is a local tradition, and it is unlikely that the Old Europeans imported it from the Near East. Mourning and lamentations of female deities do not occur in Eastern cults, in whose myths only the male god dies. In Greek myths of Demeter the mother and Persephone the maid, Persephone, the spirit of the grain, dies and is born again. Seeds from harvest time were kept in underground pits so that they could be fertilized by contact with the dead. Persephone symbolized dying vegetation, as her mother, Demeter, represented revived and growing vegetation.

Another Minoan deity whose primary evidence comes from legends and written records, but whom archaeology also supports, is a young dying god who is born in a cave, the cave of Dikte, and nursed by the goddess Dikte. Minoan seals depict the young god. One seal from Kydonia shows the god rising from horns like a tree of life and flanked by mythical animals: a winged goat and a "daemon" with an animal head who holds a pitcher. Other seals or sealings depict him as a "master of animals" holding animals or birds, a parallel image to the goddess as "mistress of animals." Another male deity well known in Neolithic imagery, the sorrowful dying god, does not occur in Minoan portrayals. But like the young god born in the cave, the sorrowful god inhabits legends that recount the death of Dionysus, Linos, Cretan Zeus, Velchanos, and Hyakinthos. Minoan Velchanos endured into the classical period as one of the titles attributed to Zeus on Crete: "Zeus Velchanos." Here he was a *kouros*, a "young man."[10]

Poseidon, the principal Mycenaean god, ruled not only the sea and the earth but also horses and earthquakes. Originally, he may have been a Minoan god, a counterpart of the earth mother. In Homeric Greek his name was Poseidaon; the earlier form was Poteidaon. This name allegedly etymologizes as "lord of the Earth" from Indo-European *potis*, "lord," and *da,* "earth" (cf. Demeter from *da mater*).[11] This etymology and his association with horses suggests an Indo-European influence for Poseidon's origin, but the association with the sea and earth suggests earlier (i.e., pre-Indo-European) roots. Analogous pre-Indo-European deities occur in other European regions: for instance, Germanic Njǫrðr, god of the sea and earth, a male counterpart of Nerthus, the earth mother. Linear B tablets found at Pylos recount Poseidon receiving sacrificial offerings, in several cases alongside a female deity, *po-si-da-e-ja* (dative case: Posidaeiai). Together they receive an offering of a cow, ewe, boar, and sow: typical offerings to the earth mother known from later Roman rituals.

In Castleden's estimation (1990), a clay sealing known as the "Master's Impression" from Khania, dating to 1500–1450 B.C., depicts the Minoan Poseidon as commander of the sea. In this scene, Poseidon stands on top of a coastal temple. The god is young and strong; one arm is outstretched and his hand holds a long staff. He has long flowing hair, and he wears a necklace and bracelet. A gold ring from Knossos portrays the same type of god, longhaired and holding a staff. He is shown hovering next to a pillar and tree shrine. Clearly, this god inspired Minoan iconographers, but we need more evidence to identify him with Poseidon. Generally, in Minoan art, male deities appear as vegetation gods and are associated with animals. In these aspects, they are counterparts of the female deities. Even the strong god holding a staff has an iconographic parallel in the goddess standing on a mountain peak holding a staff, her symbol of power.

Burial Rites

As in Old Europe, the archaeological evidence of Cretan funeral rites imparts many details about the social structure and religious beliefs of Crete. During the Neolithic era on Crete, the usual burial rite involved rock-cut tombs or caves, as in Malta or Sardinia, or circular-chamber *tholos* tombs. *Tholos* tombs occur mostly in the Mesara Plain of southern Crete. These tombs hold hundreds of burials, which date to the Early Bronze Age (the third millennium B.C.). It seems that clans used the tombs, and often two tombs stand together. They house collective burials, with individual remains treated in the same way.[12] The custom of collective burial in Crete relates to the collective burials in western European megalithic graves during the fourth and third millennia B.C. As in the western European case, the Cretan burials reflect a society based on clans. Some of the collective tombs had pillared chambers reminiscent of cave stalagmites and pillared crypts. Offerings left outside the tomb indicate funereal feasts or memorials celebrated on specific days after the deposition of the bones. Typically, finds include stone *kernoi* and libation cups. Excavators also found clay models of shrines with pillars, such as that at Kamilari, near Phaistos. Here, an open model of a rectangular building with two pillars framing the facade contained four human figures seated on stools in front of offering tables, while votaries entered the shrine carrying cups. Another model of a round building, possibly a copy of a *tholos* tomb, included two people sitting on either side of a low table. The models seem to replicate funereal meals. Such feasts did not honor individuals but communally celebrated the return of the dead to their ancestors and the ancestral home. In some southern Cretan areas the custom of collective burial lasted until the end of the fifteenth century B.C. We have discovered no royal tomb from the period before about 1450 B.C.; small tombs and single burials appear in Crete only after this time. The change from collective tribal burial to individual interment coincides with the appearance of Mycenaean influences from mainland Greece.

However, there were some exceptionally rich burials among the Minoans, in which individuals were buried in sarcophagi,[13] on which the symbolism of regeneration appears. As in crypts, horns of consecration with a double ax (or butterfly) rising from the center dominate the iconography. Next to the double axes, surrounded by plant, fish, and marine motifs, and by wavy lines, are vertical columns of spirals, arcs, semicircles, or snakes. Some sarcophagi portray winged griffins, and octopuses with human faces or even with breasts. Several sarcophagi from Rethymnon, now in the Khania museum, feature painted bulls on birds of prey: a remarkable combination of a bull with the vulture goddess.

The most celebrated sarcophagus, dating from the Mycenaean occupation of Crete (circa 1400 B.C.), from Hagia Triada, southern Crete, has been reproduced many times by various authors. The painted scenes on all four panels constitute a treasure trove for interpreting burial rituals. One of the long sides portrays several women, probably singing, preceded by a male flute player. The center bears an ornate sacrificial scene: a bull is tied to a table and his blood pours into a vessel; below the table two goats wait to be sacrificed; to the right, in front of an altar, a priestess places a vessel with offerings; a libation jug and a fruit basket with fruit appear above the altar, behind which stands an obelisk crowned by a double ax on which perches a bird; in the background appears a structure topped by horns enclosing a tree of life. One of the narrow sides shows the arrival of two goddesses at the shrine, in a chariot drawn by winged griffins. A large bird perches on the wings of one griffin. The other long side pictures an armless dead man behind a stepped altar in front of his tomb (or shrine). Three men carry offerings to him: a boat and two calves. To the left, several people appear in a procession, including a male lyre player, a woman carrying pails, and a priestess pouring liquid into a vessel between two poles, which have double axes on top. The second narrow panel includes again two females in a chariot drawn by wild goats. The two are very likely the same goddesses linked with death and regeneration, perhaps a mother-daughter pair.[14]

Over the years, researchers have offered two interpretations of the scenes on the Hagia Triada sarcophagus. They may portray the burial of the armless man. Alternatively, the scenes could depict the resurrection of the vegetation god (Veiovis, according to Gjerstad 1973) in the spring. Which is right? The participation of the goddess (or goddesses), bull sacrifice, libations, double axes on columns, and trees of life seem to belong to regenerative rites. The boat offered to the man very likely supported his journey across the water to the other world. Funerary rites also entail processions with music. So we have more justification for burial rites than for the rebirth of a young god.[15]

Fall of Minoan Culture

Minoan civilization reached its height during the two and a half centuries between about 1700 B.C. and 1450 B.C., in spite of natural and human-made disasters that afflicted the island of Crete. One of the most calamitous natural disasters recorded in historical times played a part in Crete's downfall. One hundred and twelve kilometers north of Crete is the island of Thera, which was either a Minoan outpost or an independent people possessing a closely related culture. But the island itself was actually the tip of a long-dormant volcano. Probably in 1628 or 1627 B.C., the volcano erupted with a force comparable to the 1883 explosion of Krakatoa Island in Indonesia.[16] Krakatoa's explosion created giant waves that devastated large portions of the South Pacific Islands. The volcanic eruption on Thera decimated much of that island, leaving a water-filled volcanic crater some 12.8 kilometers across and nearly 400 meters deep. On the remaining portion of the island, two-story buildings in the community of Akrotiri survived under tons of volcanic ash. We are reminded of the Italic cities of Pompeii and Herculaneum, which met the same fate over a millennium later. Like Pompei and Herculaneum, Akrotiri would also remain buried intact under volcanic debris for millennia until excavations in this century.

The explosion of the volcano at Thera produced a giant tidal wave that swept the coasts of mainland Greece and the north shore of Crete. Devastation occurred along much of the north shore of Crete, which held many large Minoan cities. Both the existence of the volcano at Thera, and the fact of its eruption in prehistory, were only recently discovered, in the 1960s, by Spiridon Marinatos, the excavator of Thera. At first some scholars speculated that this eruption may have completely explained the fall of Minoan culture, which occurred shortly thereafter. But closer analysis shows that the eruption did not totally annihilate Minoan culture. Settlements inland and on the south shore of the island remained unaffected.

On the ravaged northern shore, excavations confirm new layers of construction over the devastation. For at least fifty years after the explosion, then, the Minoans continued to rebuild their culture.

Although Minoan culture may have been weakened by Thera's catastrophic explosion, its ultimate collapse came through human, not natural, intervention. For many centuries, Crete had escaped the fate of mainland Greece, which had been engulfed by Indo-European tribes. But around 1450 B.C., chaos assaulted Crete, not only along the coast but across the entire island. All communities show signs of burning and destruction, as if ransacked by invaders. Many locales repeat the pattern of earlier Old European sites: the Old European layers end abruptly with a destroyed stratum, buried beneath a new occupation that possessed different artifacts, architecture, and artistic styles. During this phase, known archaeologically as the "late palatial," the resulting Cretan culture was an amalgam of Old European and Indo-European elements.

Conclusions

The Minoan culture flowered for several hundred years. The period of Minoan "civilization," which meets the criteria of advanced artistic and architectural technologies, dates from circa 2000 B.C. Minoan culture had deep roots in Old Europe and Old Anatolia, evidenced by its artistic creativity, its theacentric social structure, and its symbolism of griffins, spirals, palms, lilies, moons, snakes, birds, and the *labrys,* the double ax. Minoan art celebrated life and nature; we have evidence of the goddess of birth and life: standing on a mountain peak; on a tripartite platform flanked by lions; holding waterbirds. Thus the Minoan goddess or goddesses continued Old European traditions. Although female figures greatly outnumber male figures in excavated Minoan artifacts, the Minoans also depicted, in their iconography, the young year god.

The peoples of Crete also invented two writing systems, a hieroglyphic script and a linear script, Linear A; upon the latter, the Mycenaeans built their own script, Linear B. Many of the deities whom we know from archaic and classical Greece—Hera, Artemis, Athena, Poseidon, and others—are listed in the Linear B inscriptions, giving evidence of their long continuity.

The centers of Minoan culture were originally thought to have been palaces, with the hierarchical and patriarchal connotations implied by that term. Now we know that those "palaces" were in reality temple complexes, and that the culture was goddess-centered. Whereas the temple complexes were administrative as well as religious centers, cave sanctuaries and mountain-peak sanctuaries probably focused upon ritual. In these sanctuaries were found sacred horns, double axes, and seals engraved with a tree of life: all themes of regeneration. The Minoans celebrated the passage from death to rebirth.

Thus, the Minoans continued the Neolithic artistic and goddess-centered cultures. Further evidence of this continuation is to be found in the Minoan tradition of collective burials, distinct from the single burials of the Indo-European cultures.[17]

With the fall of the Minoan culture, the last of the Old European—Anatolian civilizations disappeared. But the Minoans and other Old European cultures would strongly influence the ancient world: an influence that has lingered through the modern era.

CHAPTER EIGHT

The Greek Religion

The classical era of Greece flourished almost a millennium after the first Greek culture developed in Greece. The first Greek culture, known as the Mycenaean, flourished about 1300 B.C.; its writing system, Linear B, was derived from the yet-undeciphered Linear A of the Minoans, and its art is quite similar to that of the Minoans as well. This chapter discusses the two forms of Greek culture.[1]

The Mycenaean Period

Most scholars agree that the Mycenaeans, whose culture formed in Greece in the wake of earlier Indo-European incursions, conquered the Minoan cities. The Mycenaeans came to prominence in the Peloponnese around 1600 B.C., and their centers consisted of heavily fortified cities on the Peloponnese Peninsula. The most notable is Mycenae, whose massive fortified walls still stand. Prior to the mid-nineteenth century, scholars assumed that the Mycenaeans only existed in Homer's *Iliad* and *Odyssey*. Heinrich Schliemann first uncovered the existence of the Mycenaeans as an actual people. He started excavating the ruins of Mycenae in 1876, after completing his excavations of Troy in Asia Minor. From the beginning, Schliemann sought to prove the historical reality of the Homeric poems.

The Mycenaeans adopted many elements from Minoan culture. Clay tablets written in Mycenaean Linear B occur both on Crete and in Mycenaean cities on the mainland. The tablets mostly preserve short lists and inventories, but importantly, they include names of deities worshiped in later classical Greece, such as Zeus, Hera, Athena, Artemis Eileithyia, Poseidon, Dionysus, Ares, and possibly (under a different name) Apollo. Unfortunately, the tablets only give us the names of goddesses and gods. They reveal little about their mythologies or the characteristics the Mycenaeans attributed to these deities; in fact, the Greeks did not transcribe their myths and legends until the eighth century B.C.

The Minoans also endowed the Mycenaeans with a style of arts and crafts. The highly skilled Cretan artists apparently moved to the mainland where, under their Mycenaean masters, they produced pottery and frescoes in the Minoan style. Many of the same symbols appear on the mainland as on Crete, and, in fact, the art of this time in the Aegean and on the mainland is often referred to as Mycenaean-Minoan art.

The art, architecture, and written records of the Mycenaeans reveal a fascinating mixture of Old European and Indo-European elements. There is no doubt about the Indo-European ancestry of the Mycenaeans. They glorified war, and male warriors held prominence in society. Carrying on the Kurgan burial tradition, Mycenaean graves feature a prominent male warrior buried with his weapons, the dagger and sword, as well as with remarkable gold artifacts.[2] Their pantheon featured male warrior deities. At the same time, the archaeological evidence shows that the Mycenaeans retained strong Old European–Minoan beliefs. Much of the artwork—frescoes, signet rings and seals, pottery, and figurines—is quite similar to the Minoan. The same goddesses and symbols—the mistress of animals and mountains, the snake and bird goddesses, the horns of consecration, and the double ax—all occur in mainland Mycenaean art. We find both male and female deities in sanctuaries, with the female deities outnumbering the male. The Mycenaeans produced thousands of goddess figurines, which descend directly from Old European motifs. Full-sized ceramic models of snakes, recovered from shrine storerooms, number among the most remarkable Mycenaean artifacts. They clearly indicate the importance of the snake cult at this time.

The Mycenaean civilization demonstrates that significant worship of the goddess persisted in Bronze Age Europe, even within heavily Indo-Europeanized cultures. The Mycenaeans represent an important transitional phase between Old European gynocentric culture and the classical Greek culture, where the male element came to dominate almost completely.

The Mycenaeans, who were themselves descended from earlier Indo-Europeanized tribes from the north (central Europe), eventually succumbed to more militarized Indo-Europeans. Around 1200 B.C., a new wave of peoples from central Europe swept through Greece and the Aegean Islands. Subsequently, the Greek and Aegean Islands fell into a Dark Age, from which, centuries later, the civilization of classical Greece would rise.

Classical Greece

During the centuries-long Dark Age that followed upon the Mycenaean civilization, the art of writing in Linear B script disappeared, the beautiful Minoan-Mycenaean artistry vanished, and the great Mycenaean hill forts, devastated by the invasions, fell into ruin. The post-Mycenaean Greeks lived in small, scattered settlements. In spite of the cultural decay, however, the Mycenaean elements shifted to later Greek culture in several ways. The Mycenaeans spoke an archaic form of the Greek language, as demonstrated by the Linear B tablets. We can assume that Greek in some form was spoken in this area during the centuries of the Dark Age. Religious activity also endured, since many of the same Greek gods and goddesses known from classical times occur several centuries earlier in Mycenaean written records. Also, many Mycenaean cult sites, such as the sanctuaries of Delphi and Eleusis, continued in use through the Dark Age, flourishing during the classical era. Even the epic poems of Homer, the *Iliad* and the *Odyssey*, though written down in the seventh or eighth centuries B.C., are set in earlier Mycenaean times.

The Greek culture that arose after the Dark Age differed significantly from the Mycenaean. We can only speculate as to the reasons for this contrast, but one major influence came from the peoples who overran the Mycenaeans, whom Greek tradition calls the Dorian tribes. The second influence emerged from Anatolia and the Near East, during the so-called Orientalizing period.[3]

The diminished role of women in society constituted the most radical change. In the earlier Mycenaean and Minoan civilizations, the feminine played a central role, and (at least in Minoan Crete) women held significant positions in society. But this had changed dramatically by the classical Greek era. Classical Athenian society excluded women from public life. Women participated in almost no significant social, political, or intellectual activities. Classical Greek religion also narrowed the scope of the feminine. Greek goddesses, while fulfilling roles similar to earlier Minoan-Mycenaean ones, now served male deities. Rather than a central feminine force guiding the world, male powers dominated it. The hierarchical Greek pantheon reflected Greek society. Zeus, the chief male deity, was descended from the typical Indo-European warrior-god. Yet the Greek pantheon also uneasily synthesized Old European goddesses and gods with deities created by the pastoral Indo-Europeans.

Although Greek society and religion relegated the feminine to inferior roles, study of Greek religion assists our understanding of Old European spirituality and its fusion with the Indo-European religion. The Greeks left detailed written records of their religion and customs. Two of the earliest bodies of literary works date from about the eighth and seventh centuries B.C.: the Homeric epics, the *Iliad* and the *Odyssey;* and the *Theogony* of Hesiod. The Homeric epic poems actually are set several centuries earlier in the Mycenaean era and recall the adventures of the heroes of the Mycenaean city-states, their legendary ventures against Troy, and their journeys home. Because the epics are set in Mycenaean times, it is tempting to use the Homeric poems as sources for Mycenaean religion. But we should remember that the Homeric poems recount the mythology of eighth-century Greeks, which Homer then projected onto the earlier Mycenaeans. Although a warrior society themselves, archaeological evidence shows that the Mycenaeans still retained strong beliefs in the goddess, beliefs closely related to those of Minoan Crete. Catastrophic changes befell the mainland during the four to five centuries between the fall of Mycenaean civilization and the rise of Archaic Greece, and the feminine role eroded to yield the familiar religion presented by Homer, where goddesses were subordinate to gods.

A second important literary work is the *Theogony* of Hesiod. Whereas Homer wove the intervention of Olympian deities into entertaining stories, the *Theogony* was a strictly theological work. Hesiod wrote it to explain the origins of the world and the deities, and the relationships of the Greek goddesses and gods.

These works, as well as later written sources, give detailed accounts of Greek religion, including the familiar pantheon of goddesses and gods and how they interacted with each other and the human world. The polytheistic Greeks worshiped many deities, whose home had been removed from the earth and transferred to lofty Mount Olympus. Male deities of the Greek pantheon dominated both Mount Olympus and the human world. Their primary ruler was Zeus, a form of the Indo-European sky and thunder god. The formerly independent goddesses, while still fulfilling important roles, become wives and daughters to the gods. Legends narrate the rape of the goddesses by Zeus and other gods, which can be interpreted as an allegory for the subjugation of the local goddess religion by the invaders' patriarchal pantheon. In fact, the Greek pantheon, with its many Indo-European gods, had now become decidedly belligerent; some of the goddesses inherited from Old Europe were militarized.

By examining the written texts depicting Greek goddesses, we can gain valuable insight into the Old European forebears, since archaeology alone does not preserve details comparable to the comments of ancient writers. Some of the deities were clearly continuous with Neolithic and Minoan times. We should remember that the amalgamation of Indo-European and Old European culture, which took place over several millennia, engendered the goddesses and gods of classical Greek religion. During this time, the life-affirming goddesses of Old Europe progressively mutated, taking on Indo-European traits. This becomes obvious in the centuries before the rise of classical Greece, during the periods known as the Archaic, Geometric, and Protogeometric. The classical period in Greece began around 500 B.C.; it was preceded by the Archaic period, dating from the seventh to the sixth centuries B.C., and by the Protogeometric and Geometric periods, which date from the tenth to the eighth centuries B.C. Although the goddess lost her primal place in the religious worldview of these times, strong goddesses were worshiped in classical Greece.

Goddesses, Gods, and Supernatural Creatures

Hekate

Hekate in her multiple forms was descended from the Old European goddess of life, death, and regeneration. Through Mycenaean and Greek times she remained powerful and was worshiped with ecstatic dances. From written sources and from what manifested in vase painting and sculptures, she represented many phases of life: the birth giver and motherly protectress, the youthful and strong virgin, as well as the fearsome and dangerous crone.[4] These aspects are analogous to the moon's phases—crescent, waxing, and full—and to the cycle of life, death, and regeneration. The writer Porphyry, in the third century A.D., tells us that the ancients called her the "moon."[5]

Hekate mostly, however, personified death. She is a remorseless killer who travels above graveyards collecting poison. Her animal, the dog, sometimes appears with her: she is portrayed holding a torch, and she sweeps through the night followed by her dogs. Sometimes the goddess herself is a howling hound. In Caria, western Turkey, supplicants sacrificed dogs to her and performed orgiastic dances in her honor. Greek writers describe her as the mistress of night roads or crossroads who leads travelers astray. She sometimes wears a nest of writhing snakes in her hair. Hekate's statues had enormous magic power, according to Pausanias (III: 16.7). The resplendence of her statue in the temple of Ephesus forced those who looked at it to cover their eyes (Ginzburg 1991, 131). Her favorite herbs were poppy, mandragora, smilax, and aconite.

Artemis

The young and strong Artemis was goddess of spring, giving life to all nature. As in Crete, she was revered as mistress of mountains, forest, stones, animals, springs, and healing waters. She was especially worshiped in Arcadia (an region where Indo-European influence was less pronounced than in other areas of Greece), where she was known as *kallisto,* "the most beautiful," or *agrotera,* "the wild one." From Pausanias, in the second century A.D., we hear that her statue in the Arcadian temple of the Despoina was clothed with a deer pelt.[6] She lived in the wild, untouched forests, surrounded by stags and hounds: the lady of free, virgin, untamed nature. As a maiden, she raced across the mountains with her nymphs, dancing and showering her arrows, exulting in the chase. Her nymphs dwelled in brooks, streams, and flowers. She was Potnia Theron, "lady of wild animals," and the "stag huntress" in *Homeric Hymns.*[7] Her portrayals on vases, ivory plaques, and elsewhere show her winged, holding cranes or geese with her hands, flanked by stag and dog or lion. In the historical era, Artemis, the mistress of wild things, received sacrifices of all kinds of wild animals; in the second century A.D. Pausanias mentions deer, fawns, boars, birds, wolf cubs, and bear cubs.[8] Mycenaean Linear B tablets from Pylos record the name Artemis as A-ti-mi-te, A-ti-mi-to.

As in Crete, Artemis remained birth giver, appearing at the birth of a child or animal. The medicinal herb artemisia (mugwort) encouraged delivery. Diana, the Roman equivalent of Artemis, was "the opener of the womb." In Thessaly, pregnant women sacrificed to her as Enodia,[9] to ensure her blessings at birth. Offerings to her included loom weights, spindle whorls, and figurines seated in the birthing posture. As birth giver, Artemis was a Fate who spins and weaves human life. The association of the birth-giving Artemis with the bear constitutes another link with earlier religion. Classical sources convey that Kallisto was turned into a bear, later becoming Ursa Major, and that Athenian girls danced as bears to honor Artemis of Brauronia, a town in Attica. The motherly qualities of the bear, who is a fierce defender and careful nurse of her young, made this animal, from at least the Neolithic, the double of the birth-giving and protecting goddess.

Artemis also represents regeneration. As in the Neolithic, her epiphanies are the bee and butterfly, or those animals associated with the vulva, fetus, and uterus: frog or toad, hedgehog, fish, and hare. As was mentioned earlier, the goddess was worshiped as a toad in Egypt, Italy, and Lithuania. The toad has powerful qualities similar to those of the goddess: she can release a virulent poison that can kill people, but at the same time she can heal.

One of the richest regenerative scenes involving Artemis-Hekate comes from an egg-shaped amphora found in a Boeotian tomb, dating from 700 to 675 B.C. Here the goddess is surrounded by birds, swastikas, a bull's head, a bladder-shaped object, howling lions (or ferocious hounds), and upward-winding snakes in separate columns. The fish holds the central symbolic position in this scene. It floats within the body of the goddess, equated with the womb. The goddess manifests some characteristics of an insect, perhaps a bee: serrated lines around the lower part of her body, and zigzagging lines on each side of her head, resemble insect antennae more than human hair. Her outstretched arms without hands suggest insect legs. The panel on the other side of the amphora includes a large bird, clearly mythical: it has the body of a net-patterned fish. (See Gimbutas 1989, Fig. 405.) A hare and net-patterned triangles appear below the bird. Snakes, spirals, swastikas, and more birds add energy to the dynamism of this regenerative scene. The two panels on the Boeotian vase, dating from just before the dawn of classical Greece, offer almost a full catalog of regenerative symbols familiar to us from the Neolithic era.

In a fragment of a Greek tragedy by Aeschylus, the priestesses of Artemis appear as bees (in Greek, *melissai*); the bee is another important regenerative symbol inherited from Neolithic and then Minoan times. In the third century A.D., Porphyry relates that souls are bees,[10] and that Melissa draws down souls to be born. He also equates the moon with the bull (another symbol of regeneration) and makes the fascinating assertion that cows beget bees.[11] The goddess as a bee appears in Greek jewelry of the seventh to fifth centuries B.C. from the islands of Rhodes and Thera. Gold plaques portray her with human head and arms, but she has wings and the body of a bee, as well as a ridged abdomen. At Ephesus, Artemis was associated with the bee as her cult animal, and the organization of the sanctuary in classical times may have rested on the symbolic analogy of a beehive, with swarms of bee-priestesses, *melissai,* and *essenes,* "drones," who were eunuch priests.[12] The bee, much as the Egyptian beetle or scarab, symbolizes eternal renewal.

Artemis had many insect epiphanies: the bee, the moth, the butterfly. Her butterfly epiphany is an image descended from the Neolithic era and then the Minoan period in Crete. It is very similar to the image of the Cretan *labrys,* the double ax. When anthropomorphic features are added to the double ax—a circular or crowned head on a stick, a plant or a human body in the middle, and triangles as wings—then the image is transformed into the goddess in the aspect of a butterfly or moth. In Mycenaean times this image was still popular, although in a more rigid form than in Minoan art. In the Protogeometric, Geometric, and Archaic periods of Greece, the motif became progressively more abstracted. It was integrated into ornamental design as rows of double axes (two triangles joined at their tips) or as X's separated by a group of vertical lines.

Athena

Athena represents another deity descended from Old European and Minoan prototypes. She was a popular Greek goddess venerated in many places besides Athens, especially in the Peloponnese (Argos and Sparta) and western Turkey (Troy and Smyrna). Athena was descended from the Old European bird and snake goddess; she was also the community protectress and life sustainer, and she was associated with Greek cities. By the fifth century B.C., she had become firmly established as Athens' official municipal goddess. She acquired military characteristics during the Bronze Age, and she became the victim of a rather preposterous Olympian myth, in which she is described as a daughter of Zeus, having sprung fully armed from his head. The image of Greek Athena merges features acquired from the Old European vulture goddess with several Indo-European martial attributes, such as a shield, crested helmet, and long spear. On Greek vases and in statues she appears with birds (doves, ducks, gulls, swallows, and sea eagles, but mostly owls and vultures). Homer, in the *Odyssey,* tells us that Athena can change into a vulture.[13] This goddess intervened as an owl in the battle against the Persians and helped, it was believed, to conquer them. In vase paintings, we can see her as an owl armed with helmet and spear. Sometimes both are shown: Athena as an anthropomorphic goddess and behind her the owl. Homer called her "owl-faced."[14]

One of Athena's important personas is that of giver of crafts, which she seems to have inherited from Neolithic times. This association (explored by the author in *Language of the Goddess*) can be traced in Old Europe through signs and inscriptions incised on artifacts such as spindle whorls, loom weights, crucibles, and musical instruments. According to Greek myth, Athena invented the flute, trumpet, pottery, metallurgy, spinning and weaving, and many other aspects of civilization. A series of Greek terra-cotta plaques shows an owl with human arms spinning wool. Spinning, weaving, twisting, and sewing were as commonly associated with Athena and her Roman counterpart, Minerva, as with the Old European goddess. Priestesses in Athena's temple wove the peplos (a type of robe or shawl) for the goddess. Athena is also associated with metal workshops. In one house inside the Citadel of Mycenae, in a room adjoining a metal workshop, excavators discovered a fresco of a goddess, most likely Athena. Minoan culture also linked the goddess with metallurgy. The cave of Arkalokhori, south of Knossos, served as both a sanctuary and a workshop for bronze smiths.[15] As an inventor of crafts and protectress of cities, Athena personified the mother of civilized life.

Sirens and Harpies

Two supernatural creatures of Greek mythology that also manifested the traits of birds were the Sirens and Harpies.[16] These creatures, with their antecedents in the Neolithic bird goddess, incorporate a human head, bird's body, and vulture's feet. In Homer's *Odyssey,* the Siren possesses the sinister ability to lure humans to their death with her song. The Sirens are associated with music in Plato's *Republic*. His tale of Er narrates the role of music in the physical universe: the heavenly bodies dangle in transparent, concentric spheres that turn around a spindle, like a vast spindle whorl. Each sphere possesses a Siren who sings its particular note, creating the mystical Music of the Spheres.[17]

Hera

Hera (Roman Juno), a tall, majestic, and beautiful goddess, ruled pastureland and seafaring. The most important temples of Hera are known from Argos, Perakhóra in Corinth, the islands of Samos and Lesbos, and Sybaris and Foce del Sele in Italy. Artists often portrayed her as a powerful queen positioned between two lions, comparable to the Minoan goddess standing on the mountain. A Cycladic clay relief *pithos* from around 680 to 670 B.C. depicts her with a crown, from which grow sinewy branches heavy with grapes; howling lions flank her powerful figure, and her arms are uplifted. Two priestesses attend her sacred net-patterned robe. One of the most ancient Greek religious festivals, one in which only women were permitted to participate, was held in honor of Hera; it took place at Olympia every fourth year. For this occasion, sixteen chosen women wove a resplendent robe for the goddess. The main event was a famous foot race featuring virgins who ran in order of age: the youngest first, and the eldest last. The winning virgin received an olive branch crown with an olive wreath, and a share of a horned cow that had been especially sacrificed to Hera.

In art and legend, Hera often consorts with cows and snakes. The latter association suggests a link with the prehistoric snake goddess, the protectress of family life and particularly of cows. Hera roamed the fertile plains with cattle herds, and she accepted oxen sacrifices at her temples. Homer called her "cow-eyed."[18] Calves, horned animals, anthropomorphic figurines with large eyes, and figurines of snakes number among the votive offerings to her. Portrayals reveal her hair curling like snakes and her eyebrows in the shape of horns. Spirals, circles, and zigzags decorated her dress. A northern European sister of Hera is Mārša or Māŗa, preserved in Latvian mythological songs, called the "Mother of Cows," "Mother of Milk," or "Fate of Cows." I will discuss her further in the last chapter, on Baltic religion.

In the Olympian pantheon, Hera was both elder sister and wife of Zeus. Some time in the later Bronze Age, they were married, but many pictorial representations continued to show Hera occupying the throne while Zeus stood at her side. She can also be seen standing over him with her arm raised like a great-goddess, while he sits in the suppliant son-lover pose. The *Iliad* called her "Hera of the Golden Throne." After centuries of unsuccessfully pursuing Hera, Zeus won her hand through deception. According to one myth, he disguised himself as a little cuckoo to be warmed against Hera's breast.[19] Having gained access to Hera's body, Zeus immediately revealed himself and threatened to rape her unless she married him. Thereafter Hera personified the archetypal nagging and jealous wife; however, she never entirely lost her powers.

Classical Greece continued the mystery ritual known as *hieros gamos,* or "sacred marriage," between Hera, or the great-goddess, and Zeus. This reunion of goddess and god caused the earth to revive and blossom. The *Iliad* contains a beautiful passage about the influence of the marriage of Zeus and Hera: "There underneath them the divine earth broke into young, fresh grass, and into dewy clover, crocus, and hyacinth so thick and soft it held hard ground away from them."[20]

Demeter and Persephone

Different aspects of the Neolithic pregnant vegetation goddess can be recognized in Demeter, the queen of grain, as well as in her daughter Persephone, who is both grain maiden and queen of the dead. Persephone is also known as *Kore,* "maiden." *Kore* is the feminine form of *koros,* which means "sprout" as well as "young boy." Demeter's sacred animal, the sow, also came from Neolithic symbolism.

Demeter is the goddess of the earth's fruits; she was called "the green one," "the bringer of fruit," "the one who fills the barn," and "she who brings the seasons." In the *Homeric Hymn* to Demeter, when the goddess comes to Eleusis disguised as an old woman, she tells people that she came across the sea from Crete. Hence, it seems that both the Minoan and the Greek Demeter were the same goddess. However, in the later Olympian myth, Demeter became incorporated into the Olympian pantheon; she became sister to Zeus, Poseidon, and Hades. Zeus agreed to hand his daughter Persephone over to Hades, and in some versions Poseidon raped Demeter Erinyes (the "angry Demeter") during her search for her daughter Persephone. Despite the Indo-European addition of the rape, Demeter continued to be revered as "mother of the grain," and "mother of the dead," since seeds must fall beneath the earth to grow again. Plutarch, in the first century A.D., called the dead "Demeter's people," Demetrioi.[21] Such a belief must have been in sharp contrast to the Indo-European view of the underworld as a gloomy and shadowy realm where bloodless souls reside.[22] Homer speaks of "dread Persephone" as "Queen of the Dead," married to Hades. Yet, in visual art of the fifth and later centuries, Persephone sits enthroned, holding a dove, a pomegranate, a torch, and/or ears of corn. Her torch light quickens the grain: the seed does not die, but continues to live in the underworld. This image epitomizes the essential difference between Old European and Indo-European ideologies. In Old European belief, life continues in a hibernating state (being in nonbeing), while in Indo-European belief, life is diminished or extinguished. The Eleusinian Mysteries prominently reflect Old European beliefs: the *zōé*, the "life force," suffers no interruption and permeates all things.

Demeter and Persephone are sometimes called Demetres, a name that stresses the oneness of their divinity. In vase paintings and sculpture, it is sometimes difficult to distinguish who is mother and who is daughter, so similar do they appear, and so close is the bond between them. In fact, the two images represent one goddess in two guises, her older and younger aspects. In spring, the two are joyously reunited. Persephone returns to the world of light with the child Brimos-Dionysus. The divine child is birthed from the confrontation between darkness and light, and life continues.

The story of Demeter and Persephone recalls much earlier Neolithic depictions of the two goddesses, or the goddess portrayed as Siamese twins. Sources as seemingly disparate as figurines dating from the seventh through the fourth millennia B.C., and Maltese temple layouts, preserve both versions. In both double figurines (Fig. 76, above) and the Maltese temples (Ġgantija and Mnajdra, Figs. 73 and 74, above), the two elements that comprise the image or structure are not equal: one is slightly larger than the other. It is likely that the double images and temples symbolize spring-summer and fall-winter seasons in a cycle of constant renewal.

Linos

Chapter 1, the discussion of the pregnant vegetation goddess and the year god, investigated the importance of both male and female deities to the perpetuation of the agricultural cycle. Not only did the Greeks adopt the Old European vegetation goddess, they adopted the male rising and dying vegetation deities as well. One such deity is Linos, the flax god, who is born from the earth, grows, blossoms, and later is tortured and dies. Annual ceremonies lamented Linos' "premature" death, described by several writers. Homer's *Iliad* mentions the "Linos dirge" or "Linodia."[23] Hesiod, in the middle of the seventh century B.C., tells us that all singers and lyre players recite the Linos song at banquets and dances.[24] Other classical authors repeatedly allude to the "Linos dirge" or "doom Linos."

Dionysus

Another year god is the bull-born or water-born horned Dionysus. He appeared in spring brimming with virility and was most favored by women. He thrives, marries the queen (the goddess), and finally dies. Many temples and sculptures evidence his cult. Festivals, such as the Anthesteria, the Lenaia, and the Greater Dionysia, reenact an orgiastic scenario with phalli, phallus-shaped cups, ladles, and cult dishes, and the bull-man Dionysus marrying the queen. The Lenaia festival, held in January, woke the slumbering vegetation. The City Dionysia festival in March acted to ensure fertility, indicated by the presence of a phallus: one of the Greek cities sent a phallus-shaped object as a tribute to this festival.[25] The Anthesteria was a festival of flowers, which included drinking and rejoicing.[26] It concluded with celebration of Dionysus' marriage in an ox stall, attended by women. Ritual artifacts similar to those from classical Greece—phalli, cups with phallic handles, and bull-man sculptures—also surface in southeastern Europe, dating from the sixth and fifth millennia B.C. They suggest that Dionysian-like festivals existed five thousand years before classical Greek civilization, and that they endured for a very long time. Other evidence for the longevity of the Dionysian cult comes from the island of Keos, excavated by M. E. Caskey, who discovered a sanctuary of Dionysus dating back to the fifteenth century B.C. This sanctuary had been used for more than one thousand years. The Keos finds included terracotta figurines portraying women in a dancing posture, dressed in festive attire, with exposed breasts, snake collars, and belts. They may represent maenads, the devotees and ecstatic dancers in the Dionysian festivals.

According to Orphic religion, the god Dionysus was killed and dismembered. He, like Persephone, receded into the dark depths of the earth and remained there as a seed. Women saved the seed or phallus, laid it in a winnowing fan, and performed the reawakening ritual of the god.[27] In the myth, Zeus entrusted the limbs of Dionysus to Apollo, who set them beside his own tripod (the symbol recalling the feminine trinity) at Delphi.[28] The omphalos marked this holy place, the center of the Greek universe. Apollo, the healer and bringer of light, eventually revitalizes the dismembered, suffering, temporarily mad Dionysus. Each god needed the other, for they represented the complementary aspects of darkness and light. This reunification brought bliss to the earth.

Hermes

The pre-Olympian god Hermes, also associated with the phallus and the snake, stimulated plant growth and animal fecundity. He was a likely descendant of Old European phallic nude figures. A youthful god who brought luck, he was particularly worshiped in Arcadia. His cult monument is known as the phallus-herm, a square pillar crowned with a human head and decorated with a phallus. A Greek traveler would commonly see herms by the roadside. As an anthropomorphic deity, Hermes carried a staff, the *kerykeion,* a magical wand with snakes twisted about it. He also ruled the underworld; with his *kerykeion* he summoned the souls from the grave. Homer relates that he put men to sleep and also awakened them. He was a psychopomp, and thus a regenerative god. The phallus and the snake, his main symbols, are quite appropriate.

Asklepios

Another male deity associated with snakes is Greek Asklepios, the savior-healer. A snake coils around his magic staff, as around Hermes' *kerykeion;* in some representations he stands next to a snake, or a snake crawls over his body. The function of Asklepios' snake is healing, while that of Hermes' snakes is hibernating and awakening.

Zeus Ktesios

Snakes also guard the household and multiply wealth. The male household snake in Greek mythology is Zeus Ktesios. Even here Zeus has penetrated! As guardians of *penus* (food and provision) in Roman mythology, these male snakes, *penates,* are known from countless wall paintings.

Kronos

The pre-Hellenic god Kronos, often shown as an old man seated on a chair holding a curved object, possibly a sickle, also guides the vegetation cycle. His festival, Kronia, was a harvest celebration. Old European sculptures and figurines of seated men holding a curved object likely depict predecessors of Kronos. These images may originate in the pre-Greek Sesklo (early sixth millennium B.C.) culture of Thessaly and the Tisza culture (early fifth millennium B.C.), which flourished in the regions that became eastern Hungary and Croatia.

Pan

The Greek god Pan clearly has pre-Hellenic roots. He was god of the forest, who existed outside the pantheon of great gods and goddesses. He was a shepherd, and he protected wild animals, hunters, and beekeepers. His attributes included a syrinx (Pan's pipes), a shepherd's crook, and a pine tree twig. More than one hundred recorded cult places identify with Pan's name, which demonstrates his popularity. His association with wild nature suggests his deep roots in prehistory, perhaps even before the invention of agriculture.

Conclusions

The above survey of Old European deities that influenced classical Greek mythology illustrates that even after twenty-five hundred years of Indo-

European domination (from the early third millennium B.C.), Old European religious concepts remained vital. The most important Old European goddesses—who became Artemis, Hera, Athena, and Demeter—found their way into the Olympic male pantheon. The Greeks built magnificent temples for these goddesses, as they did for the Indo-European gods. However, the independent, parthenogenetic (creating life without male participation) goddesses gradually became the brides, wives, and daughters of the Indo-European gods, albeit not always successfully or consensually. In Greek mythology, Zeus rapes hundreds of goddesses and nymphs, Poseidon rapes Demeter, and Hades rapes Persephone. These rapes in the divine sphere may have reflected the brutal treatment of Old European mortal women during the transition from prepatriarchy to patriarchy.

Earlier, during Neolithic millennia, goddesses controlled birth giving, life sustenance, death bringing, and regeneration. The Old European goddesses carried out these functions powerfully, as reflected by their physically strong portrayals in figurine and sculptural art. By classical times, the Old European goddesses were eroticized, militarized to various degrees (especially Athena), and made subservient to the gods. Aphrodite (Roman Venus) loses all functions but love and sexuality.[29] This new feminine image diminished the physical power present in Old European goddesses, replacing it with frail beauty and physical weakness. This notion of female deficiency, present in both religion and society, would be inherited by modern western cultures. It continues to plague secular and religious art up to our times.

Some fusions of old and new male deities took place: Zeus and the divine child, or Zeus and the snake (Zeus Ktesios). These fusions are strange since Zeus represents a powerful, autonomous Indo-European thunder god (or thunder god fused with the god of the shining sky). His entry into the mythological realm of the divine child (born in a cave and cared for by the goddess) and the chthonic household divinity (the snake) is quite incredible. Other Old European male deities—the fertility and vegetation spirits, as well as the protectors of wild animals and forests—persisted into Greek times almost unaltered.

CHAPTER NINE

The Etruscan Religion

Another ancient culture that retained Old European–Anatolian traditions is the Etruscan. The Etruscans inhabited a region of Italy north of Rome in an area roughly corresponding to modern-day Tuscany, known in Roman times as Etruria. The Etruscans possessed the earliest civilization on the Italian peninsula, predating the Romans and contemporary to the Greeks. During the height of their power in the eighth through the sixth centuries B.C., the Etruscans ruled Rome, traded widely in the western Mediterranean, and established colonies in southern Italy.

The origin of the Etruscans is somewhat enigmatic. During the past century, scholarly debate has focused on whether the Etruscans originated in Italy or emigrated from Asia Minor. Herodotus states that the Etruscans emigrated from Lydia in Asia Minor in the thirteenth century B.C. One artifact from the island of Lemnos in the northern Aegean Sea, a stela engraved in a dialect related to the Etruscan language, lends weight to this argument. However, the Etruscans could have evolved from the local Iron Age culture known as the Villanovan.

Etruscan Language and Culture

The Etruscans spoke a non-Indo-European language, even though Indo-European speakers surrounded them on the Italian peninsula. Their Indo-European neighbors included the Latins (later Romans) and the Umbrians. When the Greeks began to colonize portions of the western Mediterranean,[1] their trade extended into the Tyrrhenian Sea west of central Italy and brought them into contact with the Etruscans; Greek pottery is found in Etruscan excavations of this time. The Etruscans adopted a number of Greek innovations, including the Greek alphabet, which the Etruscans modified slightly to write their own language.

Some thirteen thousand Etruscan inscriptions have been recorded, and because we know the phonetic sounds of the Greek alphabet we can reconstruct roughly what the Etruscan language sounded like. The Etruscan language has been deciphered, but most Etruscan texts remain obscure. This is partly because Etruscan bears little relation to other known languages and partly because most of the many inscriptions are short dedications on tombs, mirrors, or pottery.[2] Extensive texts are rare. The longest inscription is a liturgical calendar of sacrifices and prayers from a sacred book written on linen, parts of which were preserved because they were recycled as wrappings for Egyptian mummies. A Croatian traveler in the last century bought the linen, and it now resides in the Zagreb National Museum. It contains some twelve hundred readable words. Ancient languages are often bilingual: they are translated through inscriptions that contain the same message in two languages: one of them already deciphered, the other unknown. But only one bilingual (more exactly, close to bilingual) inscription is known, written in Etruscan and Phoenician. This inscription is written on three gold tablets found at Pyrgi in 1964, at the Greek harbor of Caere, dating from about 500 B.C. The tablets, which will be detailed later, include only an inscription to the goddess Uni, not enough to solve the enigma of the Etruscan language.

The Etruscans differed socially from surrounding Indo-European cultures. Both Greeks and Romans noted the elevated position of women in Etruscan society. Women drank, danced, attended the theater, and participated in public life. Etruscan women were literate. One of the better-known Etruscan women was Tanaquil, wife of Tarquinius Priscus, the first Etruscan king of Rome. The Roman writer Livy recorded that she was learned and well versed in the practices of divination.[3] The Etruscans constructed some of their most elaborate tombs for rich noblewomen or priestesses. One example is the Regolini-Galassi tomb at Caere, which dates from the seventh century B.C., richly equipped with gold jewelry, ivory pyxis, silver table service, and dice. Artifacts from this tomb can now be found in the Vatican's Museo Gregoriano.

While the existing Greek and Roman literary evidence gives us some idea of Etruscan social life, we know little of Etruscan religion, for several reasons. First, a distinct Etruscan society had died out by the time Rome reached its glory, so later cultures did not preserve its traditions. Second, no extensive Etruscan written religious records have survived. Consequently, we have no literary evidence for Etruscan mythology comparable to that of the Greeks and Romans. We do know that, in addition to their own pantheon of deities, the Etruscans adopted Greek goddesses, gods, and myths. Inscriptions mention a number of Etruscan deities, some of which carry Etruscan names; others come from Greek or Latin. Much of our knowledge comes from secondhand accounts by the Greeks and Romans, and from archaeological evidence of the later Etruscan period (the fifth to the second centuries B.C.). Despite these obstacles, something can be learned about Etruscan religion and its Old European inheritance.

Temples

The existence of altars, sculptures, temples, temple models, and hundreds of votive offerings speaks clearly of continuity with the Old European–Anatolian tradition. This continuity especially occurs in the Etruscan sacred architecture. Etruscan temples typically accommodate a triple-cella (triple alcove) reminiscent of Maltese temple triple-cellas (as in Ġgantija) and Minoan triple-cella mountain peak sanctuaries. Moreover, the Etruscans, not the Indo-Europeans, originated the cult image in Italy. In fact, prior to Etruscan influence, the Romans did not make images of their deities. The earliest wood and terra-cotta sculptures have succumbed to time, but smaller votive figures—reduced copies of cult statues—survive in considerable numbers. The Etruscans formed divine triads, an inheritance from the Old European triple goddesses and the general sacredness of the number three. Outside Veii stood a Portonaccio temple dedicated to three goddesses: Minerva, Aritimi, and Turan.[4] The Etruscan Tarquin kings built and dedicated the Capitoline temple in Rome to the triad formed by Tinia, Uni, and Menerva (Jupiter, Juno, and Minerva). Later, after the Etruscans had been driven from Rome, the Capitoline temple became the religious center of the whole Roman world. According to tradition, every Etruscan city must include a tripartite temple. A new Etruscan city could not be established without three sanctuaries and three gates.

Goddesses, Gods, and Spirits

The Etruscan pantheon of deities is related to that of the Greeks in that both comprise Old European and Indo-European gods and goddesses. The way in which the two pantheons were formed is, however, different. Earlier in this chapter, I examined how classical Greek culture and religion emerged from the forcible conquest of Greece and the Aegean Islands by Indo-Europeanized tribes. By contrast, the Indo-European deities present in the Etruscan pantheon evolved through peaceful influences, as a result of trading contacts with the Greeks.

Inscriptions on various artifacts, as well as historical sources, provide the names and some information about Etruscan deities.[5] References by Roman historians dating from the fifth and fourth centuries B.C. indicate some of the major goddesses of a number of Etruscan cities. For instance,

Juno Regina was the great-goddess of Veii, while Juno Curitis was the chief deity of the Etruscan Falerii.[6] Greek authors mention that the Etruscans worshiped the goddess in the great sanctuary at Pyrgi, on the coast near Cerveteri (Caere); they gave her the Greek names Eileithyia, a childbirth goddess, and Leucothea, a sea goddess.[7] We know from bilingual inscriptions that Juno is the Latin name for the Etruscan goddess Uni. (In Greece she is known as Hera.) Eileithyia and Leucothea perhaps became aspects of the life-giving functions of the goddess Uni. Bilingual gold tablets from Pyrgi, dating from circa 500 B.C. and inscribed in Etruscan and Phoenician, record a text of gratitude from the ruler of Cisra (Caere) to the goddess Uni, identified as Semitic Ashtarte (Štrt) in Phoenician. Although inscriptions say nothing about her functions, the various sources seem to agree that Uni was the most revered goddess, like the great-goddess of the Minoans. Depictions of this goddess in Thera and Crete frequently show her flanked by dogs, lions, or griffins. Early Etruscan art, from the period around 700 B.C., echoes the Minoan portrayal, picturing Uni between two winged sphinxes (as on, for instance, the ivory pyxis from Cerveteri, now in the Walters Art Gallery, Baltimore).

Significant religious artifacts include Etruscan mirrors, produced from 530 through 200 B.C. and inscribed with names of deities and Greek mythological figures.[8] One favored divinity on these mirrors is Menerva or Menrva (Roman Minerva), adopted from the Greek Athena along with her militarized features. Portrayals of Menerva from the fifth century B.C. show her winged, with the head of a Medusa, in the company of Hercle (Herakles), Turms (Hermes), or Pherse (Perseus). On mirrors dating to around 300 B.C., she appears engraved in full regalia: crested, flowing-maned helmet, with Gorgon-headed aegis and spear. Other goddesses identified on mirrors include Aritimi or Artumes (Artemis) and Turan, goddess of love, known in Latin as Venus and in Greek as Aphrodite. Etruscan mirror inscriptions also mention male deities; among them are Fufluns, who correlated with Greek Dionysus and Roman Bacchus. A bronze mirror from Chiusi, dating to the late fourth century B.C., reveals a young Fufluns with his partner, Areatha (Ariadne), flanked by Fufluns' mother, Semla (Semele), and a satyr named Sime, "snub-nosed."

A bronze model of a sheep's liver may constitute the most unusual artifact inscribed with names of divinities. The model dates from approximately 150 B.C. and came to light near Piacenza in the Po Valley in 1877. This rare find provides evidence for Etruscan divination, a practice that made the Etruscans famous in the ancient world, and that, after the Romans conquered them, they were still called upon to perform. One of the practices of divination was *haruspicy* (or *hepatoscopy*), in which an animal (usually a sheep) was sacrificed and its internal organs, particularly the liver, were examined. The Etruscans must have viewed the liver as a microcosm of the universe. On the bronze model from the Po Valley, the outer margin contains sixteen regions, corresponding to sections of the sky, and the interior is divided into twenty-four regions. The deity names inscribed on the liver, known mostly from earlier sources, are Uni, Tin (Tinia), Fufluns, Hercle, Selvan (Silvanus), Cel (a mother goddess), Celsclan (son of Cel), Catha (a sun god), Usil (the sun), and Tivr (the moon).

From the inscriptions and portrayals of goddesses and gods, it appears that an overwhelming number of Etruscan divinities stem from Old European deities. Notwithstanding their Indo-Europeanization via Greek and local Italic influences, they retained an almost complete Old European tradition. Among the female deities are Uni, most likely the life giver and regenerator; Aritimi (Artemis), the nature goddess, who may have been the same as Uni; Menerva (Roman Minerva; Greek Athena), a militarized Old European bird goddess; Turan (Roman Venus; Greek Aphrodite),[9] goddess of love; Semla (Greek Semele), earth goddess;[10] Cel, the mother goddess (who could have been a mother aspect of Uni or related to Semla). Among the males were Fufluns (Dionysus); Turms (Hermes); Selvan (Silvanus), protector of forests; and the divine child. Regarding the latter, it seems that Etruria developed the divine child image along the lines of the Cretan Zeus. On an Archaic scarab from Etruria, a winged goddess carries a young male figure; the inscription identifies them as Turan and Tinia (Tinia was the equivalent of Zeus). Here, as in Crete, the major Indo-European god was converted into a child.

The magnificent Etruscan tombs also preserve the Old European concepts of life, death, and regeneration, especially during their earlier period.[11] Death goddess images that have Old European roots continue throughout the whole of Etruscan history. Etruscan statues of nude goddesses, standing erect with feet together (such as that found at Orvieto, dating from the sixth century B.C.), may derive from the Neolithic stiff nudes. As late as the fourth century B.C., a vulture deity—who may be related to the Neolithic vulture goddess, albeit in male form—appeared as a death demon in Etruscan tomb paintings. In the tomb of Orcus at Tarquinia, a painted scene illustrates a fearsome winged monster with a vulture's beak, an ass' ears, and snake-infested hair, hovering above a seated Theseus. Written beside the monster is his name: Tuchulcha. Another winged demon portrayed with the hooked nose of a vulture and snake hair and armed with a hammer is Charun. He is related to the Greek Charon, the ferryman of the dead. Winged Vanths—young, fair women wearing short skirts, crossed baldrics, and hunter's boots—assist Charun in his shepherding of the dead. Like the Germanic Valkyries, the Vanths linger at battles and accompany the dead to the underworld. Some mingling with Indo-European elements occurs on Etruscan tombs later, in the fourth and third centuries B.C., when Rome ruled the Etruscan cities. But early tumuli clearly reflect Old European concepts.

Although the frightening demon is present in the Etruscan tombs, there is nothing mournful or sinister in tomb paintings. Most Etruscan death shrines celebrate life and regeneration, depicting joyful scenes of nature, featuring ducks, playful dolphins, trees of life, bulls, erotic scenes, and banquets with drinking, music, and dancing. Consider one painting from the Tomb of the Lionesses: the side walls illustrate a banquet. Above, on a frieze, flying ducks and dolphins plunge into a ruffled sea; young men lie stretched out, their long hair wreathed with green leaves. One man holds an egg in his right hand, obviously a symbol of regeneration. The end wall of the tomb shows a gigantic crater wreathed with vine leaves. On either side stand the musicians: a piper and a citharist. To the left, a woman dances, her red-lined blue cloak swinging with her movement. To the right, a boy and girl dance opposite each other; the girl makes the gesture of the horns with her left arm while the boy swings a jug. Other tombs show funereal games with wrestlers, boxers, gladiatorial combat, and horse and chariot races. Feasts with music and dancing, and presumably with games and races, very likely originate in the funereal rites of Neolithic Europe. Remnants of feasts, drums, and dancing scenes on vases imply a joyful celebration of the deceased's reunion with the ancestors. Etruscan tombs preserved the final chapter in the Old European philosophy of life and death, in which they viewed death as a joyful transition necessary for the renewal of life.

Decline of the Etruscans

Toward the end of the sixth century B.C., the fortunes of the Etruscans declined. First, in 509 B.C. the Romans expelled the Etruscan Tarquin kings from Rome. Several decades later, in 474 B.C., a fleet from the Greek city of Syracuse in Sicily decisively defeated the Etruscan fleet off Cumae in southern Italy. Subsequently, the colonies in southern Italy slipped from Etruscan control. Shortly thereafter, the Romans began their expansion northward, and the closest Etruscan city to Rome—Veii—fell in 396 B.C. In the first few decades of the fourth century, disaster also visited the Etruscans from another direction: Celtic tribes from the Alpine region infiltrated the northern Italic peninsula and reduced the once-powerful Etruscan city-states. Over the next century and a half, the Romans conquered all Etruscan cities, and Etruria remained within the Roman sphere for the duration of the Roman Empire.

The Roman conquerors adopted several significant features from the

Etruscans, such as the Greek alphabet, which they used for writing Latin. The Romans also inherited a number of architectural innovations: the basic temple plan, the Etruscan-style Doric column, and the practice of designing towns along a north-south grid. Etruscans even influenced Roman dress: the famous Roman toga was borrowed from the Etruscans. In religion, the Etruscans inspired the Roman art of divination.[12] The Etruscan language, though not in daily use after the beginning of the Christian era, may have survived in certain Roman rituals until the end of the fourth century A.D.[13]

Conclusions

The Etruscans were an ancient Italic people who were surrounded by Indo-European speakers and yet spoke a non-Indo-European language and preserved a non-Indo-European culture.[14] Etruscan women, unlike most classical Greek and Roman women, participated in public life, were literate, and were often buried in elaborate tombs, which may reflect high status.

Etruscan deities were an amalgam of Indo-European and non-Indo-European; many deities, such as Uni (Roman Juno), Menerva (Roman Minerva), Tinia (Roman Jupiter), and Aritimi (Greek Artemis; Roman Diana) have much in common with their classical counterparts. But the continuity with Old European–Anatolian culture is evidenced by Etruscan altars, sculptures, and temples built with triple alcoves similar to those in temples in Malta and Crete.

Etruscan tombs seem to reflect the Old European concept of regeneration, depicting joyful scenes taken from nature; scenes of music, dancing, and lovemaking; and trees of life. The Etruscans produced art evocative of Old Europe. Menerva was portrayed with wings, while Uni was flanked by winged sphinxes: both continued the iconography of the Neolithic bird goddess. Thus, the Etruscans preserved an island of Old Europe within an Indo-European sphere.

CHAPTER TEN

The Basque Religion

In western Europe, several cultural islands continued Old European traditions throughout the millennia: the Basques in the western Pyrenees (now northern Spain and southwestern France), the Iberians of eastern and southeastern Spain, and the Picts in the Scottish Highlands. This chapter will focus on the Basques, whose non-Indo-European language, social structure, and, to some extent, ancient religion have been preserved to this day.

Basque Language and Culture

The Basque language is a pre-Indo-European relic of the ancient western European languages. It is the only indigenous language to survive the Indo-European invasions and cultural influences of the last three thousand years. The Basque people themselves have retained a remarkable ability to integrate new influences without losing their cultural identity. Indeed, they remain the great exception to all the laws of European political and cultural history. There is no doubt that the Basques are living Old Europeans whose traditions descend directly from Neolithic times. Many aspects of Old European culture—goddess religion, the lunar calendar, matrilineal inheritance laws, and agricultural work performed by women—continued in Basque country until the early twentieth century. For more than a century, scholars have widely discussed the high status of Basque women in law codes, as well as their positions as judges, inheritors, and arbitrators through pre-Roman, medieval, and modern times.[1] The system of laws governing succession in the French Basque region reflected total equality between the sexes. Up until the eve of the French Revolution, the Basque woman was truly "the mistress of the house," hereditary guardian, and head of the lineage.

The Basque Goddess and Her Offspring

Christianity arrived late to Basque country. The populace was only superficially Christian in remote rural areas during the fifteenth and sixteenth centuries. Even in the twentieth century, some mountainous regions escaped Christianity. There, belief in the goddess remains a living reality.

ANDRE MARI

The primary Basque goddess worshiped today is known as Mari, often combined with Andre, "Lady." She also preserves local names derived from places where she appears, usually at caves: Lady of Anboto; Andre Mari Munoko, "Lady Mari of Muno"; Txindokiko Mari, "the Mari of Chindoqui"; and others. Her image and functions are known from living beliefs. They are richly documented in collections of folklore (primarily the twenty volumes by José Miguel de Barandiarán).

Andre Mari continues many characteristic features of the prehistoric magician goddess of death and regeneration. She is the vulture goddess, tomb goddess, and regenerator who appears in a multitude of zoomorphic shapes, similar to those she manifested during the Neolithic. Basque folklore recalls that she was also a prophetess who ruled over natural phenomena and guarded moral conduct. Although the Inquisition ruthlessly persecuted devotees of the goddess as "witches," the goddess somehow escaped destruction here, as well as in northern Europe, where the Basque Mari closely parallels the Germanic Holla and Baltic Ragana.

Basque mythology recognized the underworld as the realm of the goddess. Rivers of milk and honey flow in this delightful region, where everything is abundant. The underworld communicates with the upper world by means of apertures: wells, caves, and abysses. Souls of the dead emerge occasionally through winding cave galleries and abysses. Devotees also leave offerings to the dead and to the goddess at caves. Mari generally takes on bird form in her subterranean abodes: she flies out of caves as a crow or a vulture. In the great cave of Supelegor in the mountain of Itziñe (Orozco), she appears as a vulture with her companions.

Legends revere Mari as a prophetess and oracle. Devotees sought her advice at cave entrances, where she would appear if called three times. Her caves shelter a fire and bread oven, since she bakes bread on Friday. She appears at the entrance to the cave spinning thread with a bobbin of gold, or combing her hair with a golden comb. In her cave at Anboto, she makes skeins of golden thread using the horns of a ram as bobbins, and elsewhere she combs her hair while mounted on a ram. Mari's habitations are richly adorned with gold and precious stones, but when robbers take this wealth outside, it turns to coal or rotten wood. These legends bequeath the goddess with the power to control human greediness and to magically transform substances, a power also possessed by the goblins, her avatars, who can increase or decrease wealth.

Mari also upholds law codes. She is herself the lawgiver, ruling over communal life and watching jealously to see that her commandments are kept. She condemns lying, robbery, pride and bragging, the breaking of a promise, and lack of respect for people, houses, and property. In this capacity, she ensures a high standard of moral conduct.

Mari rules natural phenomena: hail, winds, drought, lightning, and rainstorms. She creates storms or droughts to chastise disobedient or evil people. She appears crossing the sky with a cart, as a woman who emits flames, or as a woman enveloped in fire. She sometimes even drags a broom or rides mounted on a ram. As an incarnation of lightning, she is frequently seen as a sphere (or bundle) of fire, or as a sickle or stick of fire. Folklore recounts that she throws storms down from the caves. Conjurations and offerings can placate the goddess, and the Basques have even celebrated Catholic masses and performed exorcisms near the mouths of certain caves. If pleased, she protects her flock by keeping winds and storms locked up in the underworld.

Mari is associated with the moon. To this day, people of Azcoitia province view her as a great woman whose head is encircled by the full moon. This belief provides a link between Mari and the Greek Artemis-Hekate, who is also an incarnation of the moon. Basque folklore that elucidates Mari's power over celestial phenomena gives us information regarding this important Old European goddess that archaeological sources could not provide.

MARI'S OFFSPRING

Basque mythology has preserved mythological figures that have names related to Mari and are associated with stones, tombs, and ancestors. These are Mairi, Maide, and Maindi. The Mairi are builders of the dolmens, megalithic structures that consist of two upright stones and a capstone. The male Maide are mountain spirits and builders of the cromlechs, the ancient structures consisting of single stones encircling a mound. The Maindi are souls of ancestors who visit their old hearths at night.

Still other relatives include the Lamiñak, which appear in human form but with chicken, duck, goose, or goat feet (just as the goddess herself appears with bird or goat legs). The elflike Lamiñak correlate with the Baltic Laumas; both are extensions of the powers of the goddess. Lamiñak are female counterparts of the cromlech-building Maide. They increase and decrease wealth, assist industrious women, and control moral behavior and male sexuality. Their tomb-building activities in the area more than anything else speak for deep antiquity and link these creatures with the West European Neolithic.

Conclusions

Like the Etruscans, the Basques were surrounded by Indo-European speakers, but they too retained their non-Indo-European language, culture, and religion.[2] Remarkably, the Basques have maintained their uniqueness into the modern era.

Similarly to the Etruscans, the Basque women held important positions in society, inheriting equally with Basque males. The major Basque deity was Mari, a goddess who appeared in the form of a vulture or crow: a goddess of death and regeneration, a prophetess, a lawgiver, and mistress of natural phenomena. Her realm was the underworld, a region of abundance rather than terror. Mari liked to spin and bake. She thus incorporated many of the attributes of the Old European goddess. Her offspring, the builders of megaliths and cromlechs, also connect her to Old Europe.

CHAPTER ELEVEN

The Celtic Religion

Religious Continuity in Central and Northern Europe

From about 3000 B.C. until the end of the first millennium B.C., much of central Europe was a hybrid of Indo-European and Old European culture. The Indo-European influence can be seen in the importance placed on combat and the production of weapons. In many regions, burial rites carried on the Indo-European tradition, which featured a single male warrior interred with his weapons. The horse played an important role in society, being a sign of wealth and mobility. Indo-Europeanized society was stratified, with the king and warrior-nobility at the top and farmers and other nurturers forming the lowest stratum. The Indo-Europeans depended heavily on metals for trade and for their own weapons and tools. Throughout their history, the smiths were renowned for their metallurgy, and the craft of shaping metal would take on mystical proportions. Yet the art of later Bronze Age cultures and the early Iron Age Hallstatt culture in central Europe (sixth century B.C.) revealed an imagery that could only have been inherited from Old Europe. The degree of Indo-Europeanization varied markedly in different geographical regions.

Although the Kurgan element is widespread in central Europe, the Old Europeans also left their mark on the central European funerary monuments. Figurines incised with symbols of regeneration appear in graves down to the middle of the second millennium B.C. Urns and accompanying vases are also richly decorated with Old European symbols. There is a strong presence of owl and duck imagery. Bird-shaped vases and bird figurines continued to be produced with exceptional skill. Images with other divine animals, especially pigs, boars, deer, and snakes, comprise the rest of the funerary repertoire.

There still existed a farming culture along the Danube Valley west and east of present-day Belgrade throughout the first half of the second millennium B.C., an "island" of Old European culture almost devoid of Indo-European elements. This remarkable repository of Old European traditions extended from the Tisza and Mureş (Maros) basin in the west, along the Danubian valley, and across the provinces of Banat and Oltenia. (The names of the culture groups used in archaeological literature are Periam, Pecica, Verbicioara, Vattina/Gîrla-Mare, Cîrna.) Their permanent agricultural settlements formed tells as in the Neolithic, and there are no Kurgan (round barrow) graves in this area. The burial cemeteries of the early second millennium B.C. and cremation cemeteries of the mid-second millennium B.C. yielded elegant and delicate vases, thin-walled, well-baked and burnished, incised and white-encrusted with Old European symbols: snake coils, spirals, hooks, horns, V's, M's, X's, zigzags, bi-lines, tri-lines, snake spirals, combs, and others. In about thirty cemeteries that harbored cremation urns, excavators found terra-cotta statuettes placed inside the urn or on its shoulder. The figurines continue the Old European tradition, representing the goddess of death and regeneration. They have small abstracted heads, but some are clearly bird-beaked and have round owl eyes. The statuettes are portrayed in a standing position with arms folded above the waistline. The upper body is flat, and the lower part is bell-shaped, suggesting a flounced skirt. Incised designs suggest diadems and strings of necklaces, many with attached semicircular pendants (replicas of gold pendants were widespread during the mid-second millennium B.C. in east-central Europe).

Other symbols dominant on grave goods include concentric circles, alternating spirals, and snake coils, as well as double and triple snake coils, rows of hatched triangles or triple triangles, vertically flowing zigzag bands, and combs. Some of these symbols recall those from western European funerary monuments such as Newgrange (particularly the triple-snake-coil motif). They also are similar to symbols incised on schist figurines from Portuguese megalithic passage graves, which included rows of hatched triangles. Snake coils forming the limbs of the goddess frequently decorate sarcophagi of postpalatial Crete.

From Dupljaja, northeast of Belgrade, which belongs to and dates from the same culture that created the cremation urn cemeteries, come terra-cotta wheeled carts drawn by ducks, with a goddess standing on the platform. She has a beaked head, a flounced skirt (as on other figurines), and double-spiral ornaments. Concentric circles and rows of hatched triangles decorate her skirt. Another cart holds a standing deity with incised circles and concentric circles flanked with swastikas. The cart carrying the deity, drawn by waterbirds, reflects a belief in a goddess who accompanied the dead to the afterworld beyond the waters. Many graves contained duck-shaped vases standing near the urns, together with the figurines. In a Korbovo cremation cemetery (comprising the eastern group of this culture), one grave held five vessels filled with bones of a fowl. The important role of the waterbird and the regenerating functions of the deity cannot be doubted. Model carts carrying female deities brought their significance into the succeeding centuries of the central European Hallstatt. That the Dupljaja deity represents the sun god Apollo, as Belgrade archaeologists assume, is doubtful.

An outstanding four-wheeled bronze funerary cart, thirty-five centimeters long, was discovered in 1851 at Strettweg in eastern Austria, in a Hallstatt mound cremation grave with stone construction. It dates from the seventh century B.C. This impressive bronze work portrays the goddess standing in the center, twice the size of the other figures around her. She holds a gigantic dish in her upraised arms, perhaps a container of regenerating life-water, or water in which the goddess herself was cleansed in order to be reborn. Stags with huge antlers stand at the front and back of the cart, surrounded by naked men and women. There are two pairs of shielded horsemen and an ithyphallic man holding an upraised ax. The front and rear of the wagon platform displayed pairs of horse heads. The Strettweg cart reflects a spring regenerative ritual akin to that of the Germanic goddess Nerthus, described by Tacitus, in which the goddess was carried in a cart through her land.[1]

These few examples show that the goddess, in the aspects of death and regeneration, continued to be worshiped throughout the two millennia before the Christian era. Her owl, duck, and snake guises were popular. The cart-riding motif is an innovation, but the association of the goddess with basins, cleansing, and renewal originated with the life-bringing Neolithic goddess. Another aspect of the goddess, extremely popular in early Iron Age iconography, and descended from the Neolithic, is the "mistress of animals": the winged queen holding rabbits or geese, flanked by lions, and associated with snakes and birds of prey. Around 600 B.C., this image was widespread throughout the Mediterranean regions of Greece, Etruria, France, and even north of the Alps.

The Celts

The Celts constitute one of the interesting Indo-European-speaking cultures that formed from the meeting of Indo-European and Old European cultures during the Bronze Age. According to archaeological evidence, the Celtic tribes migrated south and west from their central European homeland in the eleventh to tenth centuries B.C., settling across modern-day France and the Iberian Peninsula. In the ninth and eighth centuries, they moved throughout Europe, mostly westward. They came to prominence during the eighth and seventh centuries B.C., and by the fourth to third centuries B.C., the Celts had covered much of Europe. Consequently, they significantly influenced the development of subsequent European culture, contributing an advanced knowledge of metalworking and a significant body of ancient oral literature.

Records of Celtic presence in the British islands and in Ireland date from the sixth to fifth centuries B.C. Ample archaeological evidence in burials and metalwork confirms that by the fourth to third centuries B.C., the Celtic confederation had extended from the British Isles to the Alps. In the early fourth century B.C., several Celtic tribes from central Europe overran the Italic peninsula, contributing to the weakening of the Etruscan city-states. A Celtic group sacked Rome in 387 B.C. By 225 B.C., the Roman military machine had finally defeated the Celts and had driven them out of the Italic peninsula. The Celts also expanded into southern Europe, impinging on the Greeks and pillaging the holy Greek sanctuary of Delphi in 279 B.C. Several tribes migrated into the Balkan Peninsula, eventually crossing to Asia Minor, where they settled and became known to later history as the Galatians. During the first century B.C., the fortune of the Celts changed. Julius Caesar conquered the Celtic tribes in Gaul (modern-day France), and Germanic tribes invaded much of the remaining Celtic territory in central and eastern Europe.

In the early stages of Celtic culture formation, Old European influence can be seen in the relatively high status of Celtic women.[2] Rich burials of women mark the Hallstatt period, particularly the burial of a Celtic woman near Vix in east-central France, dated to around 525 B.C. Like Celtic noblemen, the woman—perhaps a princess—was buried with a funerary wagon, surrounded by jewelry, Greek and Etruscan pottery, silver bowls, and bronze basins. One of the most spectacular items found in a Hallstatt grave was a giant krater, or mixing bowl, used for funereal feasting. The huge vessel is more than 1.5 meters high and almost 4 meters in circumference, with a capacity of about 1,250 liters.

Later, in the historical era, Irish women upheld their prominent positions. When an Irish woman married, she retained ownership of her own property, which she took with her if the bond dissolved. Ancient writers noted the willingness and zeal with which Celtic women fought alone or alongside their husbands in battle.

OLD EUROPEAN DEITIES DURING THE PERIOD OF CELTIC
DOMINANCE IN CENTRAL EUROPE AND ROMAN TIMES

Some remarkable pieces of art, undoubtedly related to Celtic religion, date from when the Celts pressed into eastern Europe. One celebrated find is the silver Gundestrup cauldron, dated to somewhat before 100 B.C. Accidentally discovered in 1891 in a peat bog near Gundestrup, northern Jutland (Denmark), it encompasses motifs influenced by art from many different regions: Celtic, Thracian, and Hellenistic. Consequently, it was probably produced in an area central to all these regions, most probably northwestern Bulgaria and adjoining southern Romania, the homeland of the Thracian tribe, the Triballoi. This tribe was influenced by the Celtic Scordisci tribe, which settled along the banks of the Danube. In this region, a mixed Celtic-Thracian society thrived. The Gundestrup cauldron reflects both Celtic and Thracian artistic styles and mythological figures. Art historians have documented the technique and the material—fine hammered silver work with human and animal figures beaten into high repoussé— from the Thracian and Dacian area, but not from Celtic western Europe. Even the details of dress on the Gundestrup cauldron have exact parallels on an important silver artifact from southeast Europe: a gilded *phalera* (a metal disk worn as a sign of military rank), found in a grave at Stara Zagora in central Bulgaria, also dating from the first century B.C. On this *phalera*, the costume of Hercules corresponds exactly with that of a male figure, claimed to be Cernunnos, on the cauldron: tight-fitting trousers, linearly striped, which stop just above the knee. (To learn more about the origin and interpretation of mythological elements, see Kaul et al. 1991.) Several other stylistic features of the Gundestrup cauldron confirm its place of origin on the border between the Celtic Scordisci and the Thracian Triballians. The Germanic Cimbri raided this territory in 118 B.C. and sent the cauldron to Denmark, probably as war booty, and then their counterparts set it into a peat bog, possibly as a religious offering. Iron Age tribes commonly offered valuable weapons and art works to deities by throwing them into rivers or placing them in peat bogs.[3]

Several plates, ornamented in relief, comprise the cauldron itself. Each of the seven outer plates portrays an anthropomorphic figure in half-length portrait, without doubt representing a deity. Four depict bearded men who have upraised arms and clenched fists. Three illustrate women. One outer plate is missing, and it too probably depicted a woman. The female figures have long hair, which falls down against the shoulders to both sides. Two of the female figures hold their hands on their chests, below their breasts; the third raises her right arm, upon which sits a small bird. Two servants or priestesses, depicted in a smaller size, attend this latter figure: one sits on her right shoulder, while the other arranges her hair. Eagles (or other birds of prey) fly near each side of her head. A pair of anthropomorphic male figures flanks one of the females. All of the females and two of the males wear torques (neck rings), a typical Celtic ornament regarded by the Celts as having magical properties in warding off evil. Two of the five inner plates portray similar males and females surrounded by wild beasts. The female is flanked by jumping griffins, rosette-shaped wheels, and elephants (Indian elephants were used in the armies of the Hellenistic rulers). The third inner plate portrays the stag god Cernunnos with large antlers. He sits on the ground, legs drawn up, clothed in a tight-fitting pant costume, wearing a torque around his neck, holding a torque in his right hand and a large ram-headed snake in his left. A stag stands to his left and a wolf to his right. The fourth inner plate depicts three bulls, each with a man in front holding a sword (the three bulls are to be sacrificed). The fifth inner plate, the richest in figures, shows a troop of horsemen and a row of marching warriors holding a long tree with the tips of their swords, and a scene of human sacrifice.[4] The base plate from the interior of the cauldron discloses a large prostrate bull and a jumping priestess with spurs on her feet above it, about to plunge a slashing sword (*machaira*) into the neck of the beast; this scene thus depicts a bull sacrifice.

The portrayals of female and male figures—again, perhaps deities—on this cauldron reveal a syncretistic religion with elements inherited from both Old European and Indo-European religions. Except for the stag god Cernunnos (portrayed on the inner plate and also in one of the portraits holding stags aloft), the male deities are Indo-European, probably Celtic Taranis (or Thracian Perkunas), the thunder god; and Ares or Esus, god of war and fertility. The female portraits are in no way Indo-European. They represent the familiar Old European goddess in several of her aspects. On one panel, she is the life bringer in spring, surrounded by wild beasts; on another, she is the goddess of death and regeneration, associated with birds of prey.

Nanny de Vries (in Kaul et al. 1991) identifies one Gundestrup goddess with the Phrygian goddess Kybele, who was also very popular in Thrace. There Kybele fused with the local goddess Rhea-Bendis. In Greek literary sources, Kybele is referred to as "great-goddess," "mother of the gods," "mountain mother," and "queen of the wild beasts." The *taurobolium*, or bull sacrifice, represents the most important ritual honoring this goddess. The day of the sacrifice was considered to be the day of rebirth. The bull's male organs were offered as a dedication to her. In Thracian art from the fourth to the first centuries B.C., Kybele appears as a winged figure holding lions or riding a lion. On a silver jug from the treasure of Rogozen, Bulgaria, she sits enthroned, flanked by two lions or centaurs. On the Rogozen jug, she is "queen of the wild beasts," holding dogs (like the Greek Artemis); on the Gundestrup cauldron, she is surrounded by a number of wild animals and flanked by elephants. Both portrayals are associated with the bull sacrifice.

The antlered god Cernunnos also embodies regenerative symbolism.

The figure sitting on the ground in cross-legged position with closed eyes and open mouth appears to be singing. The antlers and serpent he holds in one hand symbolize rebirth. The torque around his neck characterizes him as divine. This iconography is Celtic, but the tale itself, as Best argues (Kaul et al. 1991), may be that of the divine Thracian singer Orpheus, whose voice enchants animals of prey as well as other beings animate and inanimate.

The stag god depicts the Thracian version of the Old European master of animals or "lord of wild things." He is also carved in rock at Val Camonica, in the Alps of northern Italy. Scholars have dated the engraving to the fourth century B.C., the era when the Celts occupied this area. A number of stelae reliefs of the horned god associated with a stag and bull or with a ram-headed serpent are known from Roman Gaul. The name "Cernunnos" appears in a relief carving from Paris, above a representation of an antlered god (although the god could have had other names elsewhere). Some of the Gaulish portrayals associate the horned god with material prosperity. A stela relief found at Reims portrays the god seated Buddha-like near a stag and a bull. He holds a sack from which cascades a stream of coins. The Celts in Britain and Ireland preserved this god as keeper of the forest and the animals. The medieval Welsh "Four Branches" (Tales) of the *Mabinogi* contains the tale of Owain, which includes a vignette of a huge dark man sitting on a mound; as keeper of the forest, he can summon all animals through the bellowing of a stag. The tale narrates that they do obeisance to him "as humble subjects would do to their lord."

After the Romans conquered Gaul, they wrote descriptions of the Celts and their religion. These Roman writers (including Caesar himself), however, describe them from a Roman perspective using Roman appellations. In *Gallic Wars,* Caesar lists the principal deities of the Gauls.[5] Mercury, who possesses the most images, invented all the arts, guided travelers, and encouraged commerce. After Mercury, Caesar continues, the Celts honored Apollo, Mars, Jupiter, and Minerva. Apollo drives away diseases, Mars controls the issues of war, and Jupiter rules the heavens. Mars and Jupiter are Indo-European gods, but Apollo may have been fused with a local youthful healing god. In Caesar's description, Minerva teaches the first principles of the arts and crafts; dedications to Minerva are found in Gaul and in Britain.

The Romans mention many sanctuaries at the sources of Gallic rivers: for instance, a sanctuary dedicated to Dea Sequana at the Seine's source, and a sanctuary honoring Matrona near the source of the Marne. At the source of the Seine were found many ex votos, including 190 wooden objects. Some represent complete human figures while others represent diseased parts of the body, reflecting the worshipers' great expectations that the goddess would heal them. The goddess herself was portrayed in bronze standing on a duck-shaped boat. She wears a loose, folded garment and a crown, her hands stretched before her in blessing. (The statue is 61.5 centimeters high and is housed in the Musée Archéologique de Dijon, Cote-d'Or, France.)

The Celts called the great-goddess Matrona. Some inscriptions bear the name *matronae,* "the mothers," and they frequently portray the goddess as a triad, a group of three. They carry baskets of fruit, cornucopias, and babies. On a recently discovered Gaulish inscription the goddess is called Rigantona, "the great queen"; this name appears in the Welsh *Mabinogi* as Rhiannon. In the *Mabinogi* there is the character *Mabon ap Modron:* that is, Maponos son of Matrona. Maponos, "the youthful one" or "divine youth," is a Gaulish and British god. That he derives his name from his mother emphasizes the importance of the female line.

Related to Matrona and the Greek Artemis was the bear goddess Artio ("the bear" in Gaulish was probably *artos,* in Irish, *art*).[6] In the second or third century A.D., a woman named Licinia Sabinilla dedicated a bronze sculpture group to the goddess Artio (it was rediscovered in fragments at Muri near Berne, Switzerland, in 1832). In its present form at the Historical Museum in Berne it shows a seated female divinity with her lap full of fruit, holding a bowl in her right hand; a female bear (measuring 12 centimeters high), its back to a tree, faces her. The pedestal bears the inscription DEAE ARTIONI LICINIA SABINILLA, "For the goddess Artio, Licinia Sabinilla [dedicates this offering]." A more thorough examination of the sculpture reveals that instead of a group, originally there was only the bear, Artio, crouched in front of the tree. Epigraphs dedicated to the goddess Artio have also been found in the Rhinish Palatinate (near Bitburg), in northern Germany (Stockstadt, Heddernheim), and in Spain (Sigüenza or Huerta).

Another form of the Gaulish-Celtic goddess who gained great popularity in the Romano-Celtic world was Epona, protectress of horses. She was most often represented riding sidesaddle on a horse, sometimes accompanied by a dog, a bird, or a foal. She is an Indo-European creation, since the Indo-Europeans considered the horse to be sacred. One of her Gaulish centers of worship was Alesia in Burgundy, east-central France. Epona was imported into Britain and Ireland during the period of Roman dominance. Here, her equivalents are the British Rhiannon and Irish Macha, both of whom show marked equine associations. For instance, an Irish Macha, the wife of the peasant Crunnchu, races against the fastest horses in the land—and wins—while on the verge of giving birth to twins.

With the decline of the Celts on the European mainland, the British Isles became the last stronghold of Celtic culture. Much of our evidence for Celtic art, religion, and social structure comes from these islands. Britain and Ireland lend us particularly significant information because, as islands, they remained insular and less influenced by changes on the continent. Although the Romans conquered Britain as far as southern Scotland, disrupting those Celtic cultures in the defeated areas, the Romans left Ireland untouched. Here, the Celtic heritage and oral tradition continued uninterrupted.

The Irish oral tradition became a written one because Ireland and Britain converted to Christianity in the fifth century A.D. With the building of the monasteries, Ireland became a center of European learning, and the Christian monks introduced writing to the Celtic peoples. Although mainly concerned with copying Christian beliefs, the scribes, many of whom were Irish, also wrote down pre-Christian pagan legends in the scriptoria of the monasteries. The transcription of Irish oral tradition had begun by the end of the sixth century A.D., but only a few manuscript fragments survive from before A.D. 1100. Like Ireland, the Celtic country of Wales maintained great manuscript compilations, the earliest from around the end of the twelfth century A.D. The Welsh compilation, the *Mabinogi,* constitutes one of the most important sources for British mythology.

It is remarkable that, in spite of both Indo-European and Christian influence, the Irish and Welsh oral tradition and historic records preserved the primary Old European goddesses—especially the life giver and death wielder—with little change since Neolithic times. Some of their ancient features survived up to the eighteenth century. Some are remembered to this day in folk beliefs and rites. These goddesses, whose attributes sometimes overlap, are known as Brigid, Ana (or Anu or Danu), the Morrígan, Macha, and Badb.

In folk beliefs, Brigid (Brighid; Scottish, Bride) still walks and visits houses in Irish villages. Her presence is felt in sacred wells, streams, trees, and stones. Brigid is an Old European goddess consigned to the guise of a Christian saint. Remove the guise and you will see the mistress of nature, an incarnation of cosmic life-giving energy, the owner of life water in wells and springs, the bestower of human, animal, and plant life. Her myths reveal that she assists at birth, as does the Cretan Eileithyia. She spins and weaves human life. Today people still leave woven offerings to her, such as rags, towels, and ribbons, on trees, or on bushes at her wells or streams. Her wells are sacred, and they contain the great miraculous healing power of the goddess. Ring dances around wells and menhirs are performed to evoke her powers. Her very ancient features are especially visible when nature awakens, around February first. Then she, the queen, appears as a snake from the mound ("This is the day of Bride, the Queen will come from the mound" are words that come from a song still heard around 1900). Her feast on February first, Imbolc, celebrated the first signs of spring and the lactation of the ewes, symbolizing new life. It was the day of purification and homage to the goddess. People poured milk on the ground as an offering and baked special cakes. Girls carried dolls in her image in procession through the town, and each house welcomed the goddess. These celebrations endured well through the Christian era, when Imbolc became St. Bridget's Day.

The death goddess, the Neolithic vulture goddess and tomb goddess, became known in Old Irish tradition as Ana (or Anna, Anu, or Danu). She gave her name to the legendary Túatha Dé Danann (or Anann) tribe, the "People of the goddess Danu (or Anu)" (genitive case: Anann).[7] As Anu, she was "mother of gods." This ancient name for the goddess is well attested in the Mediterranean and Near Eastern world as meaning "mother" or "foster mother." Ana and Annia appear as names for caves and tombs. She was the mother of the dead and the regenerator of nature as well. Her life-giving, nourishing breasts are identified with a pair of hills in County Kerry, "Dā Chích Anann," the Paps of Ana.[8] This appellation recalls the megalithic tomb era five thousand or more years earlier, when people sculptured breasts on tomb walls and menhirs.

The legend of the Caillech Bherri, "The Old Woman of Berre," documented Ana in a character well known in modern Irish folklore. Her name connects her with a peninsula in southwestern Ireland, but her folkloric presence is much deeper, extending throughout Ireland and Gaelic Scotland. Legends tell that she created cairns in County Meath by dropping stones from her apron, that she moved islands in west Kerry, and that she carried rocks in her creel to build mountains in Scotland. Additionally, she was "queen of Limerick fairies." She is closely connected with the great megalithic monuments of Knowth in County Meath.

In other traditions, Caillech Bherri becomes a divine ancestress with numerous offspring, an embodiment of longevity who repeatedly experienced the cycle of youth and old age. This goddess was not only intimately related to the land and its prosperity; she also symbolized spiritual and legal dominion over the land and the king. She was the goddess of sovereignty, known in myth as Flaith and in saga as Queen Medb, "the intoxicating one."[9] This goddess symbolized the land to whom the king is wedded. As Medb of Leinster, she cohabited with nine kings of Ireland, and of her it was written: "Great indeed was the power and influence of

Medb over the men of Ireland, for she it was who would not permit a king in Tara unless he had her for his wife" (*Book of Leinster,* 380a).

The same goddess appears in tales as the Morrígan or Macha or Badb, a crow goddess, a death messenger perched on pillars or trees. She can be one or three, either all named Macha or each with a separate name: Neman, Macha, and the Morrígan. The Morrígan possesses many faces. At one time she is a most beautiful queen; at another time, she is a beaked, gray *badb,* a "crow." As a shape changer, she can become a greyhound, an eel, a red hornless heifer, a red-haired woman driving a cow, and an old woman milking a three-teated cow. Like the Greek Athena, the Morrígan was militarized: in Gaul she already appeared as a war goddess, and the process of her militarization could have begun earlier, perhaps as early as the Bronze Age. Literary records describe the Morrígan or the triple goddess (Macha, Neman, and the Morrígan) as terrible Furies, able to confound whole armies. In battle, they appear as crows, shrieking and fluttering furiously over the heads of warriors.

During the battle of Magh Tuiredh (described in the *Book of Leinster,* 93: 2), Badb, Macha, and the Morrígan manifested fog-sustaining shower-clouds and poured down enormous masses of fire and streams of red blood from the air. Described at the battle of Almu near Kildare,[10] they appeared as red-mouthed, sharp-beaked, croaking *badbs* over the warriors' heads, creating panic and lunacy.

In Irish folk tradition of the last centuries, the death messenger appears as a little woman dressed in white, or sometimes as a tall, slim, and ugly woman. She is heard as a bird's cry, lonesome and mournful, frequently repeated three times. As a harbinger of death she takes the shape of a bird that sits on the windowsill where an ill person sleeps. As a death messenger she also manifests as a washerwoman, and in the eighteenth century, she merged with the image of a banshee,[11] an anthropomorphic fairy.

Conclusions

Both Old European and Indo-European deities comprise the Celtic pantheon.[12] The Gundestrup cauldron portrays female figures associated with birds, and male and female figures surrounded by animals. The former represent the Old European goddess of death and regeneration, and the latter represent the Old European mistress and master of animals.

After the Romans conquered Gaul, they wrote descriptions of the Celtic pantheon, using Roman names to describe Celtic deities: Mercury, Apollo, Mars, Jupiter, and Minerva. Statues inscribed to Matrona or the triple matronae, the Celtic "mothers," have also been discovered. Matrona was most likely the great-goddess in both her singular and multiple forms. The

Celts also worshiped Dea Artio, "bear goddess," a descendant of Old Europe, and the horse goddess Epona, probably an Indo-European creation.

Historic deities among the Irish Celts include descendants of the Old European bird goddess: the Morrígan, Macha, and Badb. The multifunctional goddess Brigid was descended from the Old European great-goddess and assimilated into Irish Christianity as Saint Brigid.

Other Celtic forms of the Old European great-goddess of birth, death, and rebirth include Queen Medb, an epicized goddess who represented the sovereignty of the land, and the triple Macha. The goddess of death survived into later Irish folklore, where she was known as the Caillech Bherri, the "Old Woman of Berre," and the *banshee,* the woman of the fairy mound.

CHAPTER TWELVE

The Germanic Religion

The origin of the Germanic-speaking peoples of Europe and the formation of their culture have much in common with the cultures of the Celtic, Baltic, Slavic, and Italic peoples. Linguists have discovered that their languages shared several terms that did not appear in other sister-languages: Indo-Iranian, Greek, and Armenian. This supports the hypothesis that a northwestern Indo-European linguistic community once existed that shared inherited terms from the same cultural substrate. Archaeological evidence shows very much the same phenomenon. All of these Indo-European branches, which formed in northern and central Europe after 3000 B.C., are derived from an earlier culture: the Globular Amphora culture of the second half of the fourth millennium B.C., which occupied the area north of the Carpathian Mountains, between Denmark and western Ukraine. This culture formed after the Kurgan peoples infiltrated the area from the region north of the Black Sea, a result of the Kurgan superimposition and gradual amalgamation with the Old European substratum (the Cucuteni and the Funnel-necked Beaker cultures). Radiocarbon dates confirm that the Globular Amphora culture coexisted with the Funnel-necked Beaker culture in Germany and Poland for nearly one thousand years. Such a long coexistence must have greatly influenced the formation of linguistic families. The next wave of Kurgan infiltration (Kurgan Wave 3) into east-central Europe, in the early third millennium B.C., forced the Globular Amphora people to shift northwestward into southern Scandinavia, and northeastward into southern Finland and central Russia.[1] Archaeologically, the spread of the Corded ware (subsequent to Globular Amphora) cultural artifacts traces this movement, marking the beginning of the Indo-European presence in northern Europe. The new population expanded from central Europe to the north and initially constituted a mere superstratum to a long-established group of peoples. A long coexistence was followed by gradual intermingling and intermarriage of the local population with the newcomers. This amalgamation gave rise to the nuclei of two northern European Indo-European language families: the Germanic in the northwest and the Baltic in the northeast.

In the Bronze Age, northwestern Europe—Denmark, southern Scandinavia, and northwestern Germany—comprised a Proto-Germanic cultural area from which many tribal groups branched off.[2] This cultural area differed distinctly from its central European and eastern Baltic neighbors in tools, weapons, ceramics, burial rites, ornamentation of bronze artifacts, and many other phenomena. Throughout the whole second millennium B.C., the northwestern European culture developed gradually and apparently peacefully, with no major migrations. Such migrations, beginning in the early Iron Age, would change the course of European history.

By the time of Julius Caesar in the first century B.C., the Germanic peoples had established themselves west of the Rhine and had invaded southern Gaul and northern Italy. After their initial defeat by the Romans, some Germanic tribes were incorporated into the Roman Empire. But in A.D. 9, the Germanic peoples, led by Arminius (Hermann), revolted against Rome. The victorious Germanic peoples destroyed the army of Publius Quinctilius Varus in the Teutoburg Forest (identified by excavation north of Osnabrück). This constituted the first major disaster for the Romans at the hands of the Germanic peoples.

In the closing centuries B.C., the Vandals, Gepidae, and Goths descended from southern Sweden to the southern Baltic coast, and from there expanded farther west and south, at the expense of the Celtic peoples. The Goths migrated southeastward to Ukraine and Romania in the second century A.D.

The southern Germanic tribes were converted to Christianity much earlier than those in the north. The Goths already had a bishop by A.D 325. The Germanic peoples who moved into the Roman provinces before the fall of the western Roman Empire were Christianized during the fifth century A.D.: the Vandals in Spain (409–429), the Burgundians in eastern Gaul (412–436), the Ostrogoths in Pannonia (456–472), the Rugii north of the Danube in Austria (before 482). Farther north, conversion came later. England became a Christian country in the seventh century, and the Old Saxons on the continent converted to Christianity during the second half of the eighth century. Missionaries succeeded in converting the Scandinavians during the course of the tenth and eleventh centuries. Iceland was officially Christianized in A.D. 1000 but remained faithful to the ancestral religion until the thirteenth century. This enabled thirteenth-century Christian humanists to record ancient beliefs and preserve them for posterity. Sweden was the last Germanic stronghold of both Old European and Indo-European paganism.

These conversions were far from smooth. The brutality of forced conversion reached its climax in the year A.D. 772, when the Frankish emperor Charlemagne massacred thirty thousand Saxons who refused to accept Christianity. In addition, the Irminsul, the sacred ash tree that symbolized the mythic world-tree, Yggdrasil—the holy axis—was cut down. (Such a desecration could be comparable to the destruction of St. Peter's for Catholic Christians.) We shall now turn to these northern regions, where the populace still upheld pagan customs and beliefs in the thirteenth century, when monks finally transcribed the sagas.

The main sources for Viking Age mythology are the poetic *Edda,* a collection of poems and other fragments compiled in Iceland during the thirteenth century, and the prose *Edda,* a handbook for poets written by the thirteenth-century humanist Snorri Sturluson (this is the best introduction to Norse mythology); Saxo Grammaticus' *History of Denmark,* completed around 1215, in which the author describes the Scandinavian mythological tradition and gives somewhat different versions of myths depicted in the prose *Edda;* Adam of Bremen, who chronicled Swedish pagan festivals in his *History of the Bishops of Hamburg* (1074–83); reports of other Christian authors; and the skaldic poetry and sagas. Some information also comes from the Old English epic poem *Beowulf,* dating from around 1000 B.C., which tells of the exploits of a Scandinavian hero.

Very few sources exist before the Viking Age, except for the runes; their magical and religious messages are particularly interesting.[3] I believe that they continue, at least to some degree, the tradition of Old European sacred script, and that their importance lies in the fact that they stem from prehistory. The oldest form of runic writing, the Elder Futhark, was practiced as late as the early Christian era. (The oldest object with runic writing is the Meldorf brooch, dating to around 50 A.D., found on the west coast of Jutland.) The twenty-four-sign alphabet appears on a standing stone in Kylver, Sweden, dated to about the fifth century A.D. Runic writing lasted until around A.D. 1000. There are several important efforts to incorporate runes as a viable source for Old Norse mythology (cf. Gitlin-Emmer 1993).

The following text focuses on gods and goddesses of Old European descent who survived until the thirteenth and later centuries, despite the strong presence of Indo-European male warrior deities and the introduction of Christianity.

Germanic Deities: The Vanir and Aesir

The world of religious myth reflects social reality. Earlier chapters discussed how Indo-European religion, with its emphasis on male warrior deities and the sky, reflected the mobile, patriarchal culture of the steppes, as well as how Greek mythology mirrored the violent takeover of Old European cultures by Indo-European tribes on the Greek peninsula.

In Germanic religion, the coexistence of two religions, the Old European and the Indo-European, is clearly distinguished by two separate families of deities: the Vanir and the Aesir. The Vanir represent the indigenous, Old European deities, fertile and life giving. In contrast, the Aesir embody the Indo-European warrior deities of a patriarchal people. The principal Vanir deities were Nerthus, the earth mother, who does not appear in Scandinavian myth but is described by the Roman historian Tacitus in his *Germania* during the first century A.D.; the sea god, Njǫrðr; Freyja, the life giver and protectress of young life, and the magician goddess of death and regeneration; and her twin brother, Freyr, the god of peace, abundance, and fertility. The principal Aesir deities, those of Indo-European descent, were Tyr, Thor, and Oðin (Wotan). Tyr was a god of war and justice similar to the Roman Mars; Thor (or Donar) was a strong, brave thunder god who fought against monsters; and Oðin was not only god of death and the underworld, but also the god of poets, prophetic seers, and warriors. Oðin's name is derived from the Old Norse word *óðr,* "possessed," and thus connected to inspiration, trance, ecstasy, intoxication, and rage.[4] Myths refer to Oðin-Wotan as "All-Father"; he helped to create the world. Throughout Germanic mythology, as told in the *Eddas,* the Vanir and the Aesir met in continuous rivalry and occasionally combat, but, quite surprisingly, the conflict is resolved: a ritual reconciliation takes place and "ambassadors" are exchanged. The peacemaking between the two sets of deities may reflect the gradual reconciliation over centuries between the local Old European population and the Indo-European invaders. Interestingly, the Aesir male warrior deities did not rape Vanir goddesses (as Zeus raped Greek goddesses and heroines), but they did intermarry. We can particularly discern the Vanir influence on Aesir deities in the realm of magic and prophecy (for example, Freyja taught *seiðr,* "witchcraft," to Oðin; see below) and in belief in the underworld.

THE VANIR DEITIES

The Vanir deities, who were descended from Old European goddesses and gods, lived in Vanaheim, west of the central plain of the world-tree, in the land of fruitful fields, abundant fresh waters, and luxuriant green plant growth, a land of peaceful pleasure, of magic and creative play. The Roman historian Tacitus, in the first century A.D., left us valuable information about a vegetation festival held by the seven tribes of the lower Elbe River. He says,

The tribes revere in common Nerthus, the earth mother (*Nerthum, id est Terram Matrem*), and they believe that she intervenes in human affairs and that she rides among their peoples. In an island of the ocean stands a sacred grove and in the grove stands a cart draped with a cloth which none but the priest may touch. The priest can feel the presence of the goddess in the holy of holies, and attends her, in deepest reverence, as her cart is drawn by cows. Then follow days of rejoicing and merry-making in every place that she honors with her advent and stay. No one goes to war; no one takes up arms; every object of iron is locked away; then, and then only, are peace and quiet known and prized, until the goddess is again restored to her temple by the priest, when she has had her fill of the society of men. After that, the cart, and, believe if you will, the goddess herself, are washed clean in a secluded lake. This service is performed by slaves who are immediately afterwards drowned in the lake.[5]

Tacitus does not tell us what kind of image the tribes carried on the cart. Most likely it held a wooden statue of the goddess. He also does not mention when this event took place, but it resembles a spring celebration of an agricultural goddess, perhaps similar to the Greco-Roman festival, Sementiva, dedicated to the pregnant grain goddess. The procession of the goddess' statue would have served to protect the sown fields and secure vegetal prosperity. The goddess was apparently ritually bathed once each year. (Kybele, a Magna Mater of Asia Minor introduced into Rome in 204 B.C., was also celebrated in an early spring procession and bathed in a stream. Cleansing the goddess symbolized purification and renewal of the goddess' powers.)[6]

The Norns

The three Norns, the old, wise Germanic fates, harken from deep antiquity. Sometimes they mysteriously appear as three mighty women. They emerge from the spring beneath the world-tree, Yggdrasil. The *Vøluspá*, the "Prophecy of the Seeress," says, "From there came three women, great knowledge they had . . . [T]hey carve the stones, they determine the fates of human children, the length of their lives."[7] Even the Aesir deities feared this Germanic triple goddess, inherited from Old Europe. According to the *Vøluspá*, the Aesir deities were sitting around happily playing board games, with not a care in the world, when three powerful females came along and spoiled the game. The women's power overrode the decisions of the Aesir deities! These were the three Norns, later named Urð, Verðandi, and Skuld. *Urð* means "fate" or "destiny"; *Verðandi* indicates to "turn," to "become"; and *Skuld* means "shall," "must," "a debt," in the sense of fate, law, and duty. In Snorri Sturluson's time, during the thirteenth century A.D., and in subsequent centuries, the populace strongly believed that these three goddesses represented the three basic determining forces of human lives. In folk beliefs up to the twentieth century, it was said that their mysterious powers exerted influence on every human being.

Vǫluspá verse 21 speaks of the "origin of war," when the Aesir attacked the Vanir sorceress Gullveig. The Aesir speared and burned her, again and again and again, in the war-father Oðin's hall.[8]

Freyja

The most renowned Vanir goddess was Freyja, who clearly preserved several features of the Old European great-goddess: life giver, life taker, and regeneratrix. In Germanic areas, she retained several names. In Denmark she is Gefion; her name is related to Old Norse *gefa*, "to give." Hence, she is a giver, most likely in the sense of "giver of all" or "giver of new life in the spring." The cuckoo, the messenger of spring, is sacred to Freyja. Bulls, which are animals replete with life energy, were sacrificed to her. She oversees the birth of children; women in labor invoke her. This attribute clarifies her relationship to the Greek Artemis-Eileithyia, giver of life, and the protectress of young life. She is one and she is three, inseparable from the Norns, the supernatural women, spinners of fate, the "three maidens sitting on three chairs," who determine the destiny of the newborn child.

According to Snorri Sturluson, Freyja married an absentee husband, Oðr, for whom she weeps and searches worldwide. This behavior may be interpreted as mourning for the dead lover with whom she mated in a sacred marriage, but who consequently died (or was killed) as a dying vegetation spirit. Besides her life-giving and womb-opening capacities, Freyja safeguards the sexuality of youth and protects marriageable girls.

Not less importantly, Freyja's powers extended into the world of death and magic. On the battlefield, half of the dead belong to her, the other half to Oðin. She appears as a falcon or a she-goat, traveling in a carriage drawn by cats or riding on the back of a boar, the animal associated with death. The boar or sow is her special animal. Her legend recounts that she was the first to teach witchcraft, *seiðr,* to the Aesir; in fact, Oðin's shamanism very likely is derived from Freyja's.

Freyja was clearly one goddess of the entire life cycle. Her counterparts in other parts of Indo-European Europe usually comprise two goddesses, or one such goddess having two names, such as the Greek Artemis-Hekate or Baltic Laima-Ragana. She manifests herself as life and birth giver. Being full of life powers, she is also goddess of love.[9] However, her powers encompass death and magic, though she is not a frightening destroyer like Hekate, Ragana, or the Russian Baba Yaga. With such a wide range of functions and manifestations, it is obvious why Freyja remained the most important Nordic deity.

The Vølva

Sturluson and other sources disclose that Freyja closely identified with the chief practitioner of *seiðr,* the Vølva: a wise woman, seeress, and authority in rites of divination who was surrounded by nine female sages. The Vølva is described as wearing a costume of animal skins, including boots of calfskin and gloves of catskin, perhaps in the likeness of Freyja's costume. The goddess seems to have been a formidable shaman and the divine predecessor of both later wise women and demonized witches.

Frigg

Another Germanic goddess is the Swedish Frigg. She was wife of Oðin (German Frija—a name distinct from Freyja—wife of Wotan/Wodan), whose special day was Friday, "Frigg's day." Marrying an important Indo-European god placed this goddess within the patriarchal pantheon, but otherwise she retained features similar to Freyja's. Frigg is referred to as "the mother of all the gods," a title associated with the great-goddess in several mythologies. Her handmaiden, Fulla ("abundance"), who has long golden hair, distributes gifts from Frigg's coffer: a metaphor for the womb of the goddess, similar to Pandora's box in Greek mythology.[10]

Valkyrie

The death goddess appears in other European regions as a battlefield raptor, such as the Irish Morrígan or Badb (crow), or the Greek Athena (owl). But in Norse mythology, she becomes the battle maiden, Valkyrie, who echoes the Old European vulture goddess. Her name, *val-kyrja,* means "corpse-choosing." As a destroyer, she brings hail that damages or kills crops and livestock. On the other hand, she is linked with renewal and regeneration. In myths, multiple Valkyries appear as swan maidens who sometimes throw off their swan guises and become human maidens who bathe in secluded streams. These waterbirds, returning to the north from their southern migrations, symbolize seasonal renewal.

Skaði

Still another death-winter goddess, Skaði, inhabits Old Norse mythology. Her name may be identified with the Old Norse noun *skaði,* "harm, death." Her sacred animal is the wolf, who eats the bodies of the dead. She travels on snowshoes and loves the lands of ice and snow.

Hel/Holla

The oral tradition of Germany preserves the ancient goddess of death and regeneration in many forms: in the figure of Hel/Holle, Holla (best known as Frau Holla from Grimms' fairy tales) and as Holda, Berchta, and Perchta. Myths portray her as nightmarish and fearsome, like the Greek Hekate. She appears with her wolf-dogs, who rip the flesh from the corpse. As mother of the dead, she escorts the dead to the otherworld in the inner depths of mountains and caves. Holler, Holder, Hollunder is the name for the elder tree, sacred to Holla, under which the dead reside. Although an ugly old hag with long, powerful hair, Holla is also a regeneratrix. She brings out the sun, and as a frog, she retrieves the red apple, symbol of life, from the well into which it falls at harvest. When ice melts in the spring, Holla sometimes appears as a beautiful nude woman bathing in a stream or lake. Then she personifies the returning powers of life after winter, as the dangerous death hag turns into a young spring maiden.

The images of Freyja, Valkyrie, and Holla witness the continuity of the Old European goddess as life giver, death wielder, and regeneratrix. She can be young, beautiful, and strong, or old, ugly, and powerful, representing a full cycle from birth to death to rebirth. As the most influential magician goddess, she rules over both the living and the dead.

Freyja and Freyr

Snorri Sturluson recounts that Freyja and Freyr were chief deities of the Vanir and calls Freyr "god of the world," much loved by the Swedes. They invoked Freyr to bring good crops and maintain peace. He journeys through the land during autumn to bless the season. In accordance with Freyr's peacekeeping role, he banned weapons from his temples. Bloodshed on his sacred land angers him. Strongly at odds with the Indo-European male warrior deities, Freyr, like his sister, Freyja, is connected with childbirth and marriage. According to Adam of Bremen, who lived in the eleventh century A.D., Freyr's image in the temple of Uppsala was a phallic one. This phallic portrayal recalls Hermes, the Greek god who led souls to the afterworld; he was god of commerce, communication, and luck, bringer of wealth and joy, whose cult monument was simply the phallus. Just as Hermes was a god of the underworld and regeneration, Freyr too has links with death and regeneration. Typically, his totem is the boar, an animal incarnation of the death goddess or god. Another of his symbols is the ship *Skiðblaðnir*, a vessel large enough to hold all the gods and capable of being folded up when not in use. His ship could have been used in processions for ceremonies of blessing the land and also for regenerative rituals in funerals. Like Freyja, Freyr also possesses oracular powers and foretells the future.

In Uppsala, as Adam of Bremen reports, Freyr erected the great temple that became Sweden's religious center. There, he was honored every nine years by nine-day-long sacrificial rites.

The brother and sister pair, Freyr and Freyja, as the major Vanir deities, clearly stem from the Neolithic or even earlier. Their rare preservation up to medieval times documents a balanced pair of male and female deities that had long since disappeared in other parts of Europe. Their equal importance sheds light on the balance in Old European society before the advent of the Indo-Europeans.

Conclusions

Historic records preserve no other deities of the pre-Indo-European Vanir with any clarity, except for memories of the divine child, and the vegetation god, who is born, matures, dies, and is lamented for his premature death. For instance, in the opening section of the Old English poem *Beowulf*, the royal ancestor of the Danes, Scyld, came across the sea to Denmark as a child, became a king, and then departed again over the sea. Another version of the story relates that the child came over the sea with a sheaf of corn. Baldr, one of the most beloved of those in Ásgard, is said to be the son of Oðin. But an impressive description by Snorri Sturluson of his death, and the grief and lamentation it caused, discloses that Baldr may have been a god of vegetation in the Vanir family. Like the Greek Linos and Adonis, the Egyptian Osiris, and the Mesopotamian Dumuzi and Tammuz, the goddess destined him to die to renew the land.

When scholars have applied Georges Dumézil's tripartite division[11] to Norse gods, the Vanir deities have traditionally belonged to the third category of "fertility" gods. This classification is rather misleading. The Vanir do not represent a third and lesser class of Indo-European deities; they exemplify Old European deities whom the Indo-Europeans elaborately assimilated into the Germanic pantheon.

CHAPTER THIRTEEN

The Baltic Religion

The Baltic region, comprising Lithuania, Latvia, Finland, and Estonia, perhaps represents the greatest repository of Old European beliefs and traditions. Here, pagan religion persisted not through millennium-old historic sagas but via oral traditions and customs that endured to the twentieth century. The Balts were the last pagans of Europe. Christianity came to Lithuania, not in the fifth century, as in Ireland, but at the end of the fourteenth century. In fact, it reached farming people some two to three hundred years later. As a result, the Christian layer of beliefs among the Balts is very thin.

The Baltic speakers originated (as a distinct linguistic family of the Indo-European "family tree") much like the Germanic speakers did. Both formed in northern Europe from the gradual amalgam of immigrants from central Europe—the Corded ware people—with the local inhabitants. From about 2900 to 2500 B.C., the northeastern branch of the Corded ware culture spread as far north as southern Finland and as far east as central Russia, even beyond the modern city of Moscow. A Proto-Baltic culture formed during the course of the late third and early second millennia B.C. out of the East Baltic Corded ware culture and the Fat'yanovo and Middle Dnieper cultures in central Russia. This new fusion gave rise to a number of regional groups that continued throughout the Bronze and early Iron Ages. Thousands of river names of Baltic origin evidence the presence of Baltic speakers over a large area between Pomerania in modern Poland and central Russia. The maritime Balts formed from the substratum of the Neolithic Narva culture. In this large area of northeastern Europe, no territorial changes took place until the migrations of the Germanic Goth in the second century A.D. and the Slavic movements northward into the Dnieper Basin during the sixth to seventh centuries A.D. During the eighth to twelfth centuries A.D., Slavic language and culture came to dominate about half of the eastern Baltic lands. The Baltic western coastal territories (the lands of the Prussians, Curonians, Lithuanians, and Letts) remained the most prosperous throughout prehistory. The Romans in particular prized Baltic amber and traded extensively with central Europe.

The situation changed drastically in the early thirteenth century when Teutonic knights set out to convert "the last pagans" (at sword point, of course). The Prussians and Lithuanians refused to accept Christianity, since the war not only included conversion to a new creed; it was also an aggression, a Drang nach Osten,[1] and a cruel ethnic extermination. During the thirteenth century, the knights finally conquered the Prussians, leaving few survivors. (The Prussian language, a western Baltic language, could be heard on the Samland peninsula until about 1700.)[2] The knights moved on to Lithuania, on the river Nemunas, where the invasion continued intermittently throughout the fourteenth and early fifteenth centuries. The Germanic aggression was stopped, except for the colonization of the northern Baltic territories via the Baltic Sea. In 1201 a bishopric was founded in Riga, which remained a German stronghold for centuries to come.

The Endurance of Old European Beliefs

Lithuania officially became a Christian country in 1387, when the Lithuanian grand duke Jogaillo married Jadwiga, a Hungarian princess who had become queen of Poland two years earlier. The duke's baptism, however, was not copied by the peasants. Christian missionaries remained foreigners with no understanding of the local language, so they found it difficult to communicate with and convert the peasants. Pagan beliefs continued unhindered for centuries. A letter by Bishop Merkelis Giedraitis to the Jesuit General, dated 1587, vividly illustrated the strength of the ancient religion at the end of the sixteenth century: "You would not find a single man [sic] in the greater part of our bishopry who would go to confession and take communion, know prayers (Pater Noster) or how to cross; you would not find a man who has any understanding of the secrets of our [Christian] creed. They make sacrifices to Perkunas [a thunder god], they worship serpents, and hold oak-trees sacred. They offer food to the dead and many other strange things more from ignorance than ill will . . ." (Ivinskis 1986). Many other authors from the sixteenth to the twentieth centuries described pagan rituals, especially concerning harvest customs and the worship of Žemyna, the earth mother, and Laima, or fate, who governs human life, controlling birth and death.

The study of Baltic mythology and religion draws upon historical, archaeological, ethnographic, and folkloric sources. References to pre-Christian Baltic religion begin with the Roman historian Tacitus in the first century A.D. and continue from medieval times through the seventeenth century. Many of the historical records concerning the ancient religion have been published (most important is W. Mannhardt's *Letto-Preussische Götterlehre,* 1936), but they remain insufficient for the reconstruction of a more complete picture of this religion. The wealth of folkloric-mythological songs (richly preserved in Latvia), tales, riddles, charms, and rituals that continued into the twentieth century hold the key to understanding these ancient beliefs.[3]

Lithuanian and Latvian written and oral sources did not separate pre-Christian deities into two groups like the Vanir and Aesir in Scandinavia. Rather, the Old European matristic and the Indo-European patristic deities existed side by side for millennia with little intermingling. The Baltic Dievas, the Indo-European god of the shining sky; Perkunas, the thunder god; and Vėlinas or Vels, god of death and the underworld, could not transform the Old European goddesses into lovers, wives, and daughters. Laima, the life giver and fate, appears not as a wife but as an equal partner with Dievas, both blessing the fields at summer solstice. Mother Earth Žemyna was a powerful goddess of plant and human fertility; after assimilation with the Indo-Europeans, folkloric beliefs attributed her insemination to the thunder god, Perkunas, via the first lightning of early spring. This was clearly a patriarchal addition to Žemyna's mythology. Ragana, now a witch, was originally a goddess of death and regeneration. Her magic, shamanism, and omniscience influenced the Indo-European Vėlinas, as Scandinavian Oðin was influenced by Freyja.

The following sections focus on the goddesses and gods of Old European origin and disregard Indo-European deities associated with the sky, horses, cattle, weapons, and physical power. The goddesses take their creative energy from water, the earth, the moon, stones, and plants. They gather in clans headed by a queen. Some goddesses have male counterparts, usually brothers, typical of a matrilineal social structure. They maintain their dual and triple natures, as in the Neolithic. The same goddess may appear as young and old, as a mother and daughter, or as two sisters. She can be a life giver and a death wielder. The triple goddess appears as three Fates or three white ladies.

Baltic Goddesses and Gods

LAIMA

Known in Latvian as Laima and in Lithuanian as Laimė, the most powerful Baltic goddess controls the cosmic life energy, as well as the powers of creation. Laima is Fate. The length of a life, happiness and unhappiness, wealth and poverty, all depended on her pronouncement. Laima, whether known singularly or as a triple goddess, remains one and the same deity. If the first two Laimas decree ambiguously, the third Laima's pronouncement is final.

Lithuanian and Latvian dictionaries of the seventeenth and eighteenth centuries witness her existence as both "goddess of Fate" and "goddess of birth." Her solid presence in folk beliefs and customs concerning birth endured as late as the early twentieth century. People believed that at the birth of a child, Laima, or three Laimas, as Fate or the three Fates, appeared beneath the window to forecast the child's fate.

Birth rituals at the end of the nineteenth century and the beginning of the twentieth century included offerings to Laima. In Latvia, the birth ritual, in which only women participated, was called *pirtižas,* from *pirtis,* meaning "sauna," since it took place in the sauna. The grandmother presided over the ritual, which included bathing before the birth and a feast immediately after the birth. The ritual included the sacrifice of a hen or a sheep and the presentation of towels, belts, or other woven materials to Laima. Records from the end of the seventeenth century indicate that the hen was killed with a wooden ladle. This certainly must be a very ancient custom. It evokes the beautifully decorated Neolithic wooden ladles carved in the shape of water fowl, usually a duck or goose, often found in peat-bog sites.

Baltic beliefs recall the ancient relationship of Laima with the bear. As late as the mid-twentieth century, a pregnant woman or mother recently confined was called the "Bear." The women congregated in the sauna pronounced the formula, "The Bear is coming," upon seeing the young mother soon after the birth giving. In the Baltic area, the birth-giving goddess may have been imagined as a bear, just as she was in Old Europe.

Laima is identified with several sacred trees. In the following Latvian mythological song, she is identified with the linden tree:

> A branchy linden tree grew
> In my cow stall.
> This was not a linden tree,
> This was Laima of my cows.   (Biezais 1955, 256, no. 29172)

This tree was considered sacred in earlier days and was surrounded by a ditch. From other songs we learn that sheep and goats can be born directly from Laima's trees, as the following song testifies.

> All roadsides were covered with Laima's trees:
> From a birch a ewe was born,
> From an aspen-tree, a little goat.   (Biezais 1955, 192, no. 28963)

It is indeed fascinating to see how life is born from any living creature—bug, snake, hen, or tree—and that there are no boundaries between them. The same unifying creative power is in all of creation.

In addition to taking human form, Laima can be a bear, a tree, a hen, a menhir, or a waterfowl. She has one more important incarnation: the cuckoo, associated with the spring aspect of this goddess.[4] The cuckoo forecasts a person's life span, happiness, and marriage. The cuckoo gladdens people's hearts in the spring. Peasants rise eagerly on the days of the first cuckoo's call, for luck follows the person who hears that cuckoo. A superstition still prevails that a person will live for as many years as the cuckoo repeats its call. Just as Laima spins and weaves human life, so too the cuckoo spins, weaves, or sews with golden or silken threads while perched on a golden throne:

> Sing, O cuckoo,
> Tell me, cuckoo,
> Perching on a green spruce,
> Sitting on a golden throne,
> Herding the horses of the brothers,
> Weaving a silken scarf,
> Sewing with golden threads,
> Counting my years,
> How long shall I live?   (Lithuanian Folklore Archive, V, 917: 9417)

Another folk belief relates that the tree on which the cuckoo sits becomes sacred and imbued with the powers of the goddess. If a person peels a piece of bark or breaks a branch of this tree, he or she will know the cuckoo's prophecies. Since the cuckoo is an oracle of the spring, it represents the end of winter's dominion. After the spring, the cuckoo vanishes and then returns as a hawk. The belief in the cuckoo's transformation into a hawk is widespread.

Laima-Dalia

Laima also apportions material goods: she gives a person his or her share. Lithuanian folklore recognizes this attribute by her double name Laima-Dalia, for *dalis,* "share." In this aspect, she manifests as a swan or a ram. Tales abound of swans who turn into beautiful maidens. If a poor man marries a swan-maiden, she will make him rich and happy. Or one may, by chance, obtain one of Laima's enchanted rams and magically become rich. If Laima does not allot a share, it cannot be obtained by other means. Even a stone can represent Laima's share. If an unlucky man gets a stone, assuming that it might be his "share," the stone will shrink little by little each day.

Cow Laima

The "Cow Laima" evokes a sense of deep antiquity. She is preserved in Latvian mythological songs as Māṛa, Mārša, or Māršaviṇa (also written Mārṣaviṇa). Her titles include "Cow Laima" or "Cow Mother" (in Latvian, Govu Laima or Māte), or "Mother of Milk," or "Shepherdess of Cows." She owns the spring of life, which is the source of milk in cows. Māṛa primarily gives birth to calves. She presides in animal stalls during delivery, not as an anthropomorphic deity, but as a black serpent, a black hen, or even a black bug. The color black here accentuates fertility, birth, and multiplication. A number of mythological songs identify the black snake, hen, or bug in the cow stall as Cow Laima or Cow Māršaviṇa, as in these examples:

> A black snake crawled into the stall of my cows.
> She was not a black snake:
> She was the Cow Mārṣaviṇa.[5]

> A black (or white) hen crawled into
> the stall of my cows.
> She was not a black hen,
> She was my Cow Mārṣaviṇa.[6]

The hen (that is, the goddess) magically shakes herself and a stall full of calves appears:

> The black hen shook herself
>
> In my cow garden [stall];
> For herself—a full nest [of eggs?]
> For me—a full stall of calves.[7]

Peasants offered Māṛa-Mārša black hens until the eighteenth century. Lithuanian farmers, upon building a new house, would allow a healthy egg-producing black hen and a black rooster into the dwelling to ensure the fertility and happiness of the people and cows. The pair was privileged, untouched, well-fed, and never killed. Snakes, too, were honored: if a snake came to a stall, it was allowed to stay as a good omen, even if it milked the cows.

Māṛa can produce gigantic, magic cows, as in this song:

> Mārīṇa (dim. of Māṛa) gave me a cow
> Big, big, wide, wide.
> Her horns were too large for my stall
> And there was no place in the garden.[8]

Other songs mention supernatural cows: they swim in the sea, and they display four large horns. They give

> So much milk as there is water in the sea,
> So much butter as there is sand in the sea.
>
> (Biezais 1955, 248, unnumbered)

Māṛa-Mārša is clearly a protectress and bestower of cow fertility and abundance of milk. It is obvious that she and Laima (Fate) are one and the same goddess of birth and mistress of life-giving fluids. The name Māṛa (in the diminutive, Māriṇa) or Mārša (in the diminutive, Māršaviṇa/Mārṣaviṇa) is of Old European origin, related to the series of names of goddesses with the root Mar- (Mara, Mari, Mora, Morė, and others); it does not derive from Christian Maria, although in several songs she appears as Māṛa Magdalena: clearly a result of assimilation with the name Mary Magdalene.

Gabija

Gabija, the hearth-fire deity, may represent another aspect of Laima. She resembles the prehistoric bird goddess. It was believed that she protected the house and family, brought fertility and happiness, and stimulated cattle and crops. The Lithuanians called this goddess Gabija, from the verb *gaubti*, "to cover" or "to protect." Latvians have *uguns māte*, "mother of the fire."

The Balts imagined the hearth-fire deity as an anthropomorphic goddess but also as a stork or a cock. The stork protected the house from fire and thunderstorms and safeguarded the hearth, family, and village community. The stork was the metonymy and epiphany of the goddess. Each day the hearth-fire deity was fed. When food was prepared, some of it was thrown on the hearth. A common offering to the fire was bread and salt. As late as the first decades of the twentieth century in Lithuania, the mother of the family, while baking bread, first prepared a little loaf for Gabija, marking it with a fingerprint. The anthropomorphic Gabija was treated as a human being. "To make a bed for Gabija" meant to cover the charcoal with ashes in the evening. When the family moved into a new home, they first carried the ancestral hearth fire from the old house to the new.

SNAKES AND THE SNAKE GODDESS

Up to the mid-twentieth century, harmless green snakes often shared the house with people. They occupied the place of honor, the sacred corner of the house, and were fed milk in addition to their regular diet. The snake protected the family, or more exactly, symbolized its life force. Cows also had their own snakes, symbolizing the life energy and fertility of the cow. Since the snake embodied life energy, it could not be killed. It was believed that whoever killed the snake would destroy the happiness of the whole family and would be paralyzed for the rest of his or her life. If the house snake lived in the children's area, it was especially important that the snake not be harmed or killed. If it were, the child would die. The serpent's vital influence extended not only to fertility and increase but to the regeneration of dying life-energy. Combined with magic plants, the snake possessed potent powers in healing and creating life. Snakes hibernate from the fall until the end of January or early February. In Lithuania, up to this century peasants celebrated a sacred day of snakes (*kirmių diena*) around January 25, when snakes symbolically awakened and abandoned the forests for the houses. This special day marked the beginning of everything, the awakening of nature. On this day farmers shook the apple trees so that they would bear fruit, and knocked at beehives to awaken the bees.

During the Neolithic, portrayals of the snake goddess consistently featured a crownlike headpiece. This feature lives on in Baltic and other European folklore in the belief that some snakes will appear crowned; these crowns are the symbol of wisdom and wealth. Folktales narrate that a person who struggles with a huge white snake will acquire a crown. The crown enables one to know all, to see hidden treasures, and to understand the language of animals. The crowned snake is the queen; fairy tales recorded three hundred years ago recount the meetings of hundreds of snakes ruled by a crowned snake. Clearly, these dim memories of the sacredness of snakes harken back to the Neolithic snake goddess.

AUSTĖJA

Austėja, the bee goddess, mentioned in the sixteenth century, is both woman and bee; she promotes fertility in humans and bees. Her name is connected with the verb *austi,* "to weave,"[9] and also "to dart," "to fly." Offerings were made to her by jumping while tossing the oblation upward to the ceiling or into the air.

Austėja appears as the idealized bee mother, a responsible homemaker figure. She ensures that the families (as every beehive community is commonly called) under her guardianship multiply and increase. Apiculture can be understood in these beliefs as a metaphor for the human family where the mother-housekeeper has the most prominent role.

GODDESSES OF DEATH AND REGENERATION

Giltinė

Giltinė is death, sister of Laima. Her name relates to a whole group of well-known words: *gelti* (the verb "to sting"), *gylys* (the noun meaning "sting"), *galas* ("the end"), *geltonas* ("yellow"), and *geltligė* (yellow jaundice, a dread disease). A century ago, she was described as follows: "This is Death in human form, a woman with a long nose and long tongue, filled with deadly venom. Draped in a white sheet, by day she roams the cemeteries seeking coffins of the dead, licking corpses with her tongue to extract the poison which she uses to destroy the living."[10] She bites human beings; she strangles, suffocates, or kills them in other ways. Giltinė can be one or three, and sometimes she appears as a group of white maidens. Giltinė knows no obstacles: she can penetrate anywhere. Fences mean nothing to her; doors open by themselves. She wanders around like a shadow, appears on a bridge, in the field, or comes out from behind the barn. At times she cannot be seen, but she can be heard in the sound of a whip whistling three times in the air. Or you will hear a strange clattering noise; dishes may rattle, doors mysteriously open and close. If a shiver goes through your body, it may be that Giltinė has looked you in the face (or teeth, in the Lithuanian expression). You can deceive Giltinė for some time. For instance, you can catch her in a box or a nutshell when she takes a diminutive shape. In fairy tales about Giltinė and a doctor, the doctor tries to turn the bed so that Giltinė stays at the feet and not at the head of the dying man, which means that the man will not die for a while. However, all these measures are temporary: Giltinė will come out of the nutshell one way or another. She is Fate and you cannot escape her.

Ragana

Ragana, a goddess of death and regeneration, can be felt especially at night and at the dark moon. Although degraded to a witch and pushed deep into the forest during the Christian era, she maintains characteristics of a very powerful deity. The name Ragana derives from the verb *regėti*, meaning "to see," "to perceive," "to divine," or "to foresee." The Lithuanian word *ragas*, "horn," as in *ragas mėnulio*, "moon's horn," "crescent moon," suggests Ragana's relationship with the moon, regeneration, and transformation. She can become a crow, a magpie, a swallow, or a quail, but she can change her shape into any animate or inanimate form. Ragana also carried the energy of a snake: if a Ragana died, you might see her hair curl, like a Gorgon's, into snakes, and little snakes crawl out of her mouth.

Multiple Raganas

Ragana appears as one goddess, but very often legends mention a whole crowd of raganas, who can take the shape of crows, usually at meetings on a mountaintop. However, one of the raganas is addressed as "Lady," the leader of the group. All others are her assistants in their nightly actions. They wait for instructions from the "Lady." After smearing ointment on themselves, they fly to the mountains or fields, following the directions of their leader.

As a dangerous hag, Ragana continuously inflicts damage: she ties rye ears into knots at harvest time, shears too much wool from sheep, stops milk in cows, places rocks on wells. At weddings she can "spoil the bride"—make her sterile—or turn the bridegroom into a wolf or dog. On a cosmic scale, she can cut the full moon in half or even cause an eclipse of the sun. Ragana oversees the cyclicity of nature: she balances the life-energy. She stops blossoming and growing lest plants and the moon grow forever. Ragana also controls male sexuality. She dominates men, often utterly exhausting them after a night's orgy. She kills the life power in order to secure the cyclical renewal of life energy. She knows the magic of herbs: with them she heals the sick, regenerates life, restores life to the dead.

The main epiphany of Ragana in the function of death and regeneration is the toad (see below), but she often takes the shape of a fish, snake, hedgehog, sow, mare, dog, magpie, swallow, quail, moth, or butterfly. Early in the spring, Ragana appears in brooks or lakes as a beautiful nude woman, combing her golden hair.

Žverūna

Thirteenth-century records describe the goddess Žverūna (from *žvėris,* "wild animal").[11] She is said to be a dog. Žverūna seems to parallel the Greek Hekate, who also has a dog epiphany. Both must have been related to the ancient image of the "lady of the beasts," who holds geese or is flanked by wild animals. Later sources confirm that Žverūna is the same as Ragana, because the names *Ragana* or *Ragaina* are often substituted for Žverūna.

Baba Yaga

A similar goddess is Baba Yaga, known in Russian folklore as a witch and an ogress. But she is the ancient Slavic goddess of death and regeneration. In Slavic folktales (mainly Russian), Baba Yaga lives in nocturnal darkness, deep in the woods, far from the world of men. Folktales inconsistently depict her as an evil old hag who eats humans, especially children, and as a wise, prophetic old woman. She is tall, bony-legged, and pestle-headed in appearance, with a long nose and disheveled hair. The bird is her primary animal image, but she can turn instantly into a frog, toad, turtle, mouse, crab, vixen, bee, mare, goat, or inanimate object. Baba Yaga never talks; she either flies in a fiery mortar or lies in her hut: on top of the oven, on a bench, on the floor, or stretched from one end of the hut to the other. The hut, supported on bird legs and able to turn on its axis like a spindle, is, in fact, Baba Yaga herself.

Linguistic analysis of Baba Yaga's compound name reveals prehistoric characteristics. *Yaga,* from Proto-Slavic **(y)ęga,* means "disease," "fright," and "wrath," in Old Russian, Serbo-Croatian, and Slovene, respectively.[12]

It correlates with the Lithuanian verb *engti* ("strangle, press, torture"). The early form may be borrowed from Proto-Samoyed **nga,* meaning "god," or "god or goddess of death." The Slavic etymon *baba* means "grandmother," "woman," "cloud woman" (a mythic being who produces rain), and "pelican." The last points to Baba Yaga's avian nature, comparable to that of the archetypal vulture and owl goddess of European prehistory, who personifies death and regeneration. In Russian tales, Baba Yaga eats humans by pecking like a bird (Shapiro 1983). In East Slavic areas, Baba Yaga has a male counterpart, Koshchei Bessmertnyi, "Koshchei the Immortal." His name, from *kost'* ("bone"), evokes the notion of a dying and rising god: that is, a deity who cyclically dies and is reborn. In tales where Koshchei appears, Baba Yaga is either his mother or his aunt.

Rupūžė, the Toad

To this century, the toad (*rupūžė* in Lithuanian) is as prominent as Ragana in beliefs concerning death, healing, and regeneration. Her name is often used as a swearword. As omen of death, the toad recalls the white lady (Giltinė) and the birds of prey. If a toad (or frog) croaks in a farmer's house, someone will die. If, in the spring, a toad jumps in front of you on the road, then you will die. (See also Gimbutas 1989, 256.) However, the toad can be a healer. If one finds a toad, dead or alive, and places it on a sore, it may help heal it. The drink made of toad and vodka, *rupūžinė,* is a panacea, and it is widely used in Lithuania today.[13] Sometimes, a live toad was attached to the neck of a cancer patient and carried, dead or alive, until the cancer disappeared.

Lauma

Latvian Lauma (Lithuanian Laumė), a fairy, is Ragana's earthly extension. She rises from expanses of water at night, singly, in threes, or in a large group. She is a sexually attractive woman with superhuman characteristics. Often she is a bird; she looks like a woman with long hair and pendulous breasts but has bird feet or even a hen's body. Lauma may also change into a goat or a mare. At night, Lauma may work all sorts of mischief: she shears too much wool from sheep, milks cows dry, rides horses and wears them out. However, she is not entirely evil: she sometimes does good work. But her goodness is conditional and may immediately turn into a threat of destruction and death. Multiple Laumas come in groups in the evenings, bringing their spinning wheels, particularly on Thursday nights. They spin very rapidly and are likely to spin everything in sight, once they have finished with flax, tow, and wool. They may seize the moss and fiber used to stuff chinks in the walls, the hair of women, and even human intestines or veins.

About a quarter of all stories dealing with Laumas describe their relations with men. Like Raganas, they dominate men sexually. They can exhaust men until the men drop dead, or they can tickle men to death. If a man should accost a Lauma, annoy her, or make fun of her, she pursues him to his detriment. Lauma's physical appearance vividly reflects her Paleolithic origins. She has bird feet and a bird body combined with a woman's breasts. Her sexual superiority and manifestations in threes and in groups clearly stem from the pre-Indo-European social order. Analogous beings found in other European cultures include south Slavic Vilas (Vily), Russian Rusalki, Polish Boginki, Basque Lamiñak, and Greek Lamias.[14]

EARTH POWER

The second group of Baltic goddesses and gods of Old European origin manifests both wild and cultivated nature, and the fertility of crops, animals, and humans. The main divinity is Lithuanian Žemyna (Latvian Zemes Māte). Her name comes from *žeme, zeme,* "earth." She personifies Mother Earth: moist, fertile, black (the color of the fertile earth), and strong. This goddess has close parallels with the Greek Gaia-Demeter, Thracian Semele, Roman Ops Consiva, Slavic Mat' Syra Zemlya, "Mother Moist Earth." Her counterparts include incarnations and guardians of wild nature (male and female), dying and resurrecting male deities, and the subterranean manikins: the Kaukai. These amazingly archaic creatures are the manifestations of earth life itself, located between death and birth. They have their patron god Puškaitis, god of the elder bushes, who breathes and exhales earth life force in the form of foul smells.

Žemyna

The functions of the goddess Žemyna concern fertility and multiplication. She creates life out of herself, performing the miracle of renewal. This act accords with the Old European belief that seasonal awakening, growing, fattening, and dying were interdependent among humans, animals, and plants. As indicated by ritual practices, her veneration continued to this century. From late-seventeenth-century sources (as described by Praetorius in Lithuania Minor in 1690), we hear that a black suckling pig was offered to Žemyna (as it was to Demeter in Greece) during the harvest feast presided over by a priestess. Offerings to her are of the utmost importance: grave consequences are expected if offerings—bread, ale, and black animals or birds—are not made at regular intervals. In such a case, as recorded in 1582 in eastern Lithuania, a family member or an animal of the household may be paralyzed, or a huge snake will obstruct the entrance to the house. Offerings of bread to Žemyna continued through the early twentieth century. A loaf or piece of bread was left in a rye, wheat, or barley field at the first spring plowing to ensure a fertile year, or at harvest's end to secure abundance for the next year. At the end of harvest, the mowers had to find the bread and circle it three times. Then they ate a piece and buried the rest in the ground.

The earth mother was worshiped on mountain summits crowned with large stones. The summit stone represents the omphalos, a concentrated power center of the earth.[15] The earth mother was similarly worshiped in many ancient cultures throughout Europe. In Brittany, she became a hill topped with an omphalos, illustrated by passage graves in Brittany (see Fig. 52a–c, above). In Crete, the British Isles, and the eastern Baltic area she was also the sacred mountain.[16] A large stone crowns the sacred hill of Rambynas on the bank of the Nemunas River in western Lithuania. It has been considered sacred at least since the fourteenth century. A sixteenth-century source conveys that women coming to Rambynas seeking fertility should be very clean. Even in the nineteenth century, newly-wed couples seeking fertility at home and good crops in the field made offerings there. Those stones of the earth mother are not upright pillars, but large and flat. In Germany and the Scandinavian countries, flat stones with polished surfaces are widely known as *Brautsteine*, or bridestones. Young brides visited these stones to sit on them or crawl over them, seeking fertility. In Rome, large stones with flat surfaces dedicated to Ops Consiva, the Roman goddess of earth fertility, were kept in holes in the ground (*sub terra*) and covered with straw. They were uncovered only once a year during the harvest feast. About fifteen hundred years later, Jesuit annals recorded the same tradition in Lithuania. In A.D. 1600, they described large stones with flat surfaces dug into the earth and covered with straw: they were called *deivės*, "goddesses." Thus, we learn that the stone is the goddess herself.

Earth is justice, the social conscience, as represented by the Greek Themis, Russian Mat' Syra Zemlya, and Lithuanian Žemyna. The wide distribution of this concept reveals its prehistoric roots. The earth mother listens to appeals, settles problems, punishes all who deceive or disrespect her. She does not tolerate thieves, liars, or vain or proud people. In legends and tales, sinners are devoured by the earth, along with their houses or castles; the earth closes over them, and a lake or mountain appears on the site. For centuries peasants settled legal disputes relating to landed property by calling on the earth as witness. If someone swore an oath after placing a clod of earth on his head or swallowing it, that oath was considered binding and incontestable.

Medeina: Goddess of the Forests

Although few records described Medeina (Lithuanian Medeinė), they recognized that she was related to the Greek Artemis and Roman Diana. Actually, fifteenth-century records call her Diana, guardian of forests. She first appeared in the Russian chronicles of Hypatius, in the thirteenth century A.D. Her name derives from *medis,* "tree," and *medė,* "forest." In early historical times, as well as in prehistory, she was a prominent goddess of forests, perhaps an incarnation of the powers or fecundity of wild nature. Her sacred animal was a hare, an animal also special to Artemis and Diana. Folk beliefs relate that this alert, quick little animal helped the goddess to protect her forests, especially by leading hunters astray. The sight of a hare in Medeina's forests created fear. Even the Lithuanian king Mindaugas (who lived in the thirteenth century A.D.) would not hunt in the forest if he saw Medeina's hare. Clearly, the animal was sacred, a double of the goddess.

One nineteenth-century folktale from northern Lithuania speaks of "the lady of the forests" dressed in silk, living in a huge mansion and assisted by strong young priestesses.[17] At their mansion, they kept a bull whom each of the young girls struck with a rod upon entering the house. When the last and the most beautiful of the priestesses arrived, she hit the bull with such force that the animal died. The peculiar ritual of killing the bull may represent a memory of bull sacrifice, the *taurobolium.* The bull was the primary animal sacrificed to Artemis and Kybele, in order to ensure the rebirth of nature.

Vaižgantas: Dying and Resurrecting Flax God

The god Vaižgantas appears in the form of flax from the earth. He is tortured, dies, stays in the earth as seed, and is reborn. The sixteenth-century text of Lasicius records the following prayer to him: "Vaižgantas, . . . don't let us go naked." Lasicius also speaks of certain rituals to Vaižgantas performed during the feast of the dead, Ilgės: a girl climbs on a chair with an apron full of cakes, which she holds in her left hand. In her right hand is the bark of a linden tree. Standing on one foot, she invokes the god, asking him to make the flax grow as tall as she is now and so plentiful that she could totally cover herself with flax (Mannhardt 1936, 532). Thus, Vaižgantas is not only the god of flax in the narrow sense, but also the one who "clothes naked people." Vaižgantas also symbolizes the general renewal of vegetation, specifically related to flax. In sources dating to the sixteenth and seventeenth centuries, Vaižgantas is mentioned as "god of women and libertines," comparable to the Greek Dionysus, who was known as the "god of women." The Greek flax god, Linos, closely parallels Vaižgantas, which suggests a common origin for both the southern and northern European flax gods in an early agricultural period. Linos is the dying god, similar to the Mesopotamian Dumuzi-Tammuz, described in greater detail in chapter 8.

The name Vaižgantas is a compound, the first part of which, *vaisà*, is "fruitfulness," or "reproduction." In Praetorius' description of Lithuanian paganism in Prussia at the end of the seventeenth century, Vaižgantas is called "god of fertility," to whom a lamb and a rooster are sacrificed (ibid.). Although the sources are scanty for a full reconstruction of Vaižgantas' image, we can sense this god's rich dimensions: he was not only a sorrowful god destined to die; he was also a blossoming young god who influenced plant growth and the marriage of girls.

Kaukai: Manifestations of Earth Power in the Cycle of Death and Life

In Lithuanian children's books, Kaukai appear as bearded gnomes. But they are far more than gnomes: they are little creatures the size of a human head who look more like tadpoles than humans. Sixteenth- and seventeenth-century records described them as "little men who eat vegetarian food." To this day they are believed to help people by increasing grain and hay.

Lexical evidence substantiates the chthonian origin of *kaūkas* (sg.) (Greimas 1979, 36 ff.; 1992 in English translation). Numerous words stem from the root *kauk-: kāukolas, kāukolis,* and *kaukuolys,* which denote a dry or frozen clod or lump of earth. Through analogy, we can see this imagery in representations of *kaūkas:* for example, "a *kaūkas* is as big as two fists, round like a ball."[18]

Additional words make direct reference to *Kaukas. Kaūkas, kaukelis,* or *kaukoras* is a name for a certain type of aromatic root, *Mandragora officinarum.* "Kaukas' comb" is a name for a plant shaped like a hand. This plant possesses magical powers and has connections with the underworld: "Comb your hair with it, and make sure that not a single piece breaks off—you will then have knowledge of all that is hidden in the earth."[19]

Kaukai make their abode underground. Housewives often make a loose garment from a single thread and bury it in a corner of their house in order to entice a Kaukas to dwell there. Since the Kaukai are earth-born, they live in basements or dark storehouses.

Before humans and Kaukai made an agreement, Kaukai lived in the forest. Lexical evidence sheds some light on this arrangement. For example, many words that have the root *kauk-* relate to mushrooms: *kaukagrybis* (*grybas* = mushroom) refers to a whole group of mushrooms, *Phallus impudicus; kaukatiltis* (*tiltas* = bridge) represents a place where many mushrooms can be found; *kaukoratis* (*ratas* = circle or wheel) is a cluster of mushrooms. There is a saying: "Don't light any fires on *kaukoratis,* because *Kaukeliai* (diminutive of *Kaūkas*) might come there at night."

Kaukai accept only vegetarian food, and they give only earth's products. They increase wheat and rye (this is connected with their bread eating) and hay (this is connected with their milk drinking). The Kaukai never bring money.

If a Kaukas leaves you a single straw of hay on a few kernels of grain, never-ending fortune will be yours. A Kaukas does not bring material fortune, but symbolic increase (Lithuanian *skalsa*), which imbues objects with a mythical abundance so that they seem inexhaustible. Kaukai are believed to increase property. The expression "*Kaukas yra skalsas*" ("*Kaukas* is increase") implies that the Kaukas himself embodies the idea of infinite material supply.

Various written sources mention *bezdukai,* or *barstukai,* another name for Kaukai. Their patron divinity is the god Puškaitis, who lives under the elder bush. Praetorius explains that this tree or bush was also called *bezdas.* These facts help explain why *bezdukas* describes the forest-dwelling Kaūkas. He lives in or near an elder bush and smells characteristically foul. A certain rank root plant also called *kaukas* provides further evidence regarding the Kaūkas olfactory association. As Greimas has shown, the root for the god Puškaitis is *pušk-,* and it may belong to the same word group that includes the verb *pūškuoti,* "to exhale, to breathe heavily." This kind of etymology discloses that the god Puškaitis embodies the earth and, by alternately breathing deeply and spreading odors with the help of *bezdai* (elder trees), gives birth to chthonic beings: *bezdukai* and *Kaukai.*

The name *Kaūkas* relates not only to roots, mushrooms, and dirt clods but also to "glands" (*kaukos*) and a "boil" (*kaukas*). The boil is round, soft, and damp, which connects it to the spheroid form of the Kaūkas (Greimas 1979, 51). A further explanation of the origin of the name allies it with the boar, an animal that the Old Europeans associated with death. Kaukai can be hatched from a boar's testicles. One must slaughter a seven-year-old boar, cut off his testicles, and hatch them, keeping them in either a warm place or a hole in the wooden post of the porch doorway. The newborn Kaukas announces his hatching by rapping and tapping. The wooden porch doors represent the passage from the "natural" exterior to the "cultural" interior, from forest to house. "Boar" in Lithuanian is *kuilys,* derived from *kuila,* a rupture or hernia.

Kaukas has further linguistic associations with "skull" (*kaukolė*), and "head, mask" (*kaukė*). The name for skull (*kaukolė*), in addition to the Kaukas' head- or skull-sized dimensions and his embryonic, glandular form, place the Kaukai in the time between death and birth. They temporarily rise to the surface and affect human life, then return to their pre-birth state underground, where they belong. Jan Lasicius, in the late sixteenth century, described *Kaukai* as "souls of the dead" (*"kaukie sunt lemures"* [Lasicius 1969, 44]).

A common belief, originally Old European, maintains that the skull contains the life principle; therefore, people often cared for and buried the skull separately. The association of Kaukai with the skull and the head as the soul's abode, their association with roots and mushrooms, and their glandular, embryonic appearance leave little doubt about the essence of these chthonic beings. The Kaukas is a creature about to be born, yet unborn, belonging to an intermediary realm between death and birth. This sacred time of the earth's pregnancy is imbued with mysterious energies that may manifest themselves aboveground as Kaukai, bringing ever-increasing material goods. Kaukai, with their patron god, Puškaitis, reveal the earth's constant cyclical energy as the forest's "breathing power."

Conclusions

We can see that the Baltic pantheon remarkably preserves an almost complete Old European family of goddesses and gods. Neither the presence of the Indo-Europeans nor the five centuries of intensive war between paganism and Christianity exterminated the oldest layer of Baltic beliefs. Best preserved are the goddesses, who were life and birth givers, healers, protectresses of households and communities, bringers of earth fertility, death messengers, and life regenerators. Until recently, people kissed Mother Earth as if she were a human mother, in the morning and in the evening, before Christian prayers were said. You could kiss Mother Earth; you could see Laima in an anthropomorphic form or in any animal manifestation; you could touch the goddess as a stone, or hear her as a cuckoo. You could sense the death goddess Giltinė's approach as a sliding snake or see her in human shape standing at the head of a sick person. Until very recently, the goddess was a living entity. She diminished only in the mid-twentieth century, with the infiltration of technology and political upheavals. Sadly, many residues of past ages were wiped out rather suddenly. Virgin Mary partially replaced Laima and Žemyna and continued to be passionately worshiped as a savior of fallen humanity. In May, she is still showered with flowers. In August, she is expected to bless the harvest. Ragana still exists as a witch; her name is a curse word, as is the name for her main incarnation, *Rupūžė*, "the toad." The snake, the symbol of life energy for millennia, has finally vanished from homes and house foundations. The Lithuanian sorrowful god—the old vegetation god—still sits calmly supporting his chin with his hand at farmsteads, in forests, along roads, or in chapels, wondering if regeneration is still possible.

Marija Gimbutas concluded this, her final book, with the goddesses, gods, and spirits of the Balts. It is perhaps fitting that she ended this book with a long section on Lithuanian folklore, since it was the Baltic goddesses, particularly the Latvian and the Lithuanian, with whom she had felt a kinship since her childhood. Throughout her life, her native country, its folklore, language, and customs, remained foremost in her heart.

When she was a child, she learned of the Lithuanian goddesses, gods, and spirits honored even in the early part of the twentieth century. These deities peopled the landscape of her spirit, enriching her love for the land, waters, flowers, trees. Marija Gimbutas was an ecologist decades before the word became popularized, and her home in the hills of Topanga, California, reflected her love of nature. This love became a foundation stone in her own philosophy of life and her personal spirituality.

In her last decade of life, Marija Gimbutas' own ecological and spiritual beliefs found resonance in the growing spiritual and ecological movements in the United States and abroad. Her books, as well as her presence, became a strong focus in ecological movements—so much so that many people, perhaps without intending to, learned quite a bit of archaeology. Marija Gimbutas' philosophies—describing a world where men and women might live in harmony with one another and with their environment—found a home in the hearts of thousands of people, helping to shape the ideas of a new generation of ecologists. Women and men in the fields of ecological science, anthropology, folklore, and mythology, as well as archaeology, have been touched and transformed by the works of Marija Gimbutas.

Chapter One   /   Images of Goddesses and Gods

1. This is a common theme in Marija Gimbutas' work, misunderstood by many, who assert that she advocated a single unidimensional deity for both the European Upper Paleolithic and the Neolithic, a "fertility" or "mother" goddess. For an excellent explication of the various functions and manifestations of ancient female figures, see Rice (1981); Rice contends that what are called Upper Paleolithic Venus figures are really figures of women of all ages, from young women to pregnant women to old women.

2. Artifacts found in this cave date to the seventh millennium B.C. See Bar-Yosef (1985, 15). According to the author, the cave must have been used as a store for cult objects in a Neolithic ritual.

3. See Barber (1994, Figs. 2.1, 2.5, 2.8).

4. In Ireland, holy wells are still visited and honored. See Brenneman and Brenneman (1995).

5. In the festival of Brauronian Artemis, a female celebrant, wearing a yellow robe, would portray Artemis as a bear. See Dexter (1980, 26).

6. This is not true hibernation: although in winter the bear lives off of the fat that it stored in summer and autumn, its body temperature remains high and it leaves its den and walks on mild days.

7. Further, birds were able to fly freely through the air, between earth and heaven; since they could thus communicate with the heavens, they were perhaps therefore identified with those deities who inhabited the heavens.

8. The Sesklo culture flourished c. 6500–5500 B.C. in Thessaly and southern Macedonia. The Dimini culture flourished c. 5500–4000 B.C. in Thessaly.

9. These are Sumerian texts.

10. This site was located on the eastern Mediterranean coast.

11. See Leick (1994, 150–51) for another viewpoint.

12. According to Mircea Eliade (1954; 1991, 52), among all cultures there is the concept of the periodic regeneration of life, at least on the cosmological level, presupposing a repetition of the cosmogonic act. Life, and time itself, are cyclically regenerated.

13. Although this figure does not exhibit all of the features that one recognizes in more classical Gorgons, its wide mouth and lolling tongue are hallmarks of the "death goddess" that later became the Gorgon.

14. In other representations Medusa is winged. She is both bird and snake, and she thus represents both death and the promise of regeneration. See Dexter in Dexter and Polomé, eds. (1997, 124–54).

15. See Apollodorus, *Bibliotheca,* III.x:3.

16. Bau/Baba was the city goddess of Lagash. She bore septuplet daughters, the clouds, to her husband Ningirsu. Lubell (1994) discusses Baubo and similar goddesses. Marija Gimbutas wrote the foreword to this book.

17. For iconography of Baubo and Isis-Baubo displaying her vulva, see Lubell (1994): Figs. 1.4 (from Alexandria, Egypt), 8.2–3 (from Priene, Asia Minor), 9.2–3 (from Alexandria, Egypt), and 9.4 (from southern Italy).

18. These could be related to Lithuanian *boba,* an old woman or wife, and *bobausis,* an edible fungus.

19. See Reynold Higgins, *Minoan and Mycenaean Art* (London: Thames and Hudson, 1967), 52, Fig. 50. The scene takes place on a gold signet ring made between 1700 and 1550 B.C. According to the author, the hoop is too small for the ring to have been worn on the finger. Thus, one would presume religious or ritual significance.

20. See Walberg (1986, 104), Figs. 122 and 123, where she-goats nurse their young.

21. The warrior god was represented by a bull in other ancient patriarchal religions as well; for example, the Semitic Ugaritic peoples of northern Syria called one of their gods "bull El": *tr il* (cf. Cyrus Gordon, *Ugaritic Manual,* "Hymn to Anat" Pl. X.v.22 et passim). We should be aware, however, that the cow, the she-goat, and the sheep are powerful epiphanies of the female deity. Thus both Hathor and Hera are given cow imagery and epithets, while sheep are regularly associated with the great-goddess: for example, the Iranian Anahita. Thus we must not too readily assign male gender to horned bovines. Carol P. Christ (personal communication) believes that the connection between cows' horns and the uterus is more likely than a connection between bulls' horns and the uterus.

22. See Cameron (1981).

23. This goddess may be associated with the winter sun. See Monaghan (1994, 232–44) on the Gorgon Medusa and the sun.

24. This concluding section has been written by the editor in order to maintain consistency, since Marija Gimbutas had written conclusions only to some of the chapters by the time of her death. Since her conclusions frequently take the form of summaries, this section is a summary as well.

25. This script is well evidenced on the Vinča and other Balkan figurines (described in this chapter and more thoroughly in chapter 2). It is also evidenced, and has been the subject of some controversy, at the French site of Glozel. See Biaggi et al. (1994).

Chapter Two / Symbols, Signs, and Sacred Script

1. This system may have been similar to Sumerian. In Sumerian, the earliest form of writing, sentences are not always syntactically complete; some sentences seem to follow a set of rules; others, missing various elements, seem to be a sort of shorthand. But we have no way of knowing if Old European writing too may have represented sentences, complete or otherwise. The Old European writing system may have been ideographic: its symbols may have indicated whole words or even concepts.

2. The term *ex voto* is Latin, meaning "from a vow," an object given in fulfillment of a pledge to a deity.

3. See Roska (1941) for the text used by Marija Gimbutas. Also see Zsófia Torma (1894).

4. Old Persian was an ancient Indo-European language, similar in many ways to the ancient Indic language Sanskrit; Akkadian and Babylonian were

Semitic languages; and both Sumerian and Elamite have no known linguistic affiliations.

5. However, the Old European languages remained as "substrates" of the new Indo-European languages, affecting the new languages in many ways, including the phonology, or individual sounds, of the language and the vocabulary as well. See Huld (1990, 389–423), who gives evidence for an Old European *Sprachbund,* a collection of languages that share similar phonological and other patterns, particularly an initial *b,* open syllables, and gemination of stops. See also Polomé (1990, 331–38) on prehistoric northern European substrate words for plants, animals, and activities characteristic of Neolithic cultures.

6. For a discussion of the different Minoan scripts, see Packard (1974).

7. Marija Gimbutas read the unpublished form of the latter of Haarmann's books in manuscript.

8. In archaeological terminology, "pre-Indo-European" refers to indigenous peoples occupying areas to which the Indo-Europeans migrated. Thus, they were peoples who lived in areas *before the advent of the Indo-Europeans.* However, in linguistic terminology, the term "pre-Indo- European" or "Pre-Indo-European" refers to the form of the Indo-European language preceding the Proto-phase: thus, it means *a very early phase of Indo-European.* Marija Gimbutas uses the term in its archaeological sense.

9. This concluding section was added by the editor.

Chapter Three / The Tomb and the Womb

1. For a discussion of the Mnajdra megaliths, see chapter 4.

2. We may think of the Sumerian goddess Ereshkigal, queen of the underworld and the dead, who in the "Descent of Inanna" is in the process of giving birth.

3. Carol P. Christ (personal communication) reminds us that, alternatively, there may have been a second burial some years after the first, as in contemporary Greece.

4. Again, an alternative notion is that they may have undergone a previous burial.

5. An alternative theory is that the antlers were retrieved without sacrificing the deer.

6. Most of the female figurines and statues found in Malta are large-bodied, with distinctively heavy arms and legs.

7. Skulls were often buried separately from the other bones of the skeleton. They have been found stacked along the walls of a tomb; sometimes the skull, hands, or feet are missing from a burial. At other times, skulls have been found in a special area of the cemetery, separated from the other skeletal bones and buried along with the skulls and jaws of animals: deer, ox, goat, and pig. See Gimbutas 1991, 283.

8. It is a tribute to the engineering abilities of these people that "the sun has shone [into] the chamber ever since the date of its construction and will probably continue to do so for ever [sic], regardless of secular changes in the obliquity of the ecliptic." See Jon Patrick in O' Kelly (1982, 124). Thus the phenomenon has endured for more than five thousand years.

9. There is no general agreement on the interpretation of Megalithic art. Numerous alternate interpretations have been advanced. See O'Sullivan (1986) for a brief survey and bibliography of the various approaches, including his own.

10. This concluding section was added by the editor.

Chapter Four / Temples

1. I have been unable to find this article.

2. According to Carol P. Christ (personal communication), "The creation of pottery from clay and fire, bread from wheat, water and fire, and cloth from flax or wool were no doubt viewed as transformative mysteries, analogous to and governed by the goddess' transformative power."

3. This town, on the west side of the Urals, is on the Volga River.

4. Mehmet Özdoğan pointed out to Joan Marler, the editor of Marija Gimbutas' *Civilization of the Goddess,* that the anthropomorphic vessel was actually a grain storage container (Marler, personal communication).

5. Moldavia is the Soviet name; the post-Soviet name is Moldova.

6. However, there are scholars who believe that there was no hierarchy in Old Europe. See Christ (1997, 59).

7. The chair has great significance in ancient iconography. It represents the goddess herself (for example, the Egyptian Isis was the throne, as her hieroglyph demonstrates). By sitting in the chair, a mortal was invested with the power of the goddess, thereby receiving the right to rule. The birthing stool, by playing an important role in childbirth, would have participated in the sacrality both of the throne and of birth and regeneration.

8. Barber (1994) discusses string skirts evidenced from Upper Paleolithic artifacts through contemporary folk costumes; she believes that these skirts were associated with—and therefore an icon of—childbearing.

9. Although these figures are without breasts, they are identified as female by many archaeologists because they are steatopygous: that is, they have characteristic accumulations of fat on the buttocks. See Gimbutas (1989, 163) on steatopygous Upper Paleolithic female figurines. She believed that the steatopygia was a "metaphor for the double egg or pregnant belly: intensified fertility." Also see Malone et al. (1993, 81), who state that the figures found in the Maltese site of Tarxien, dating to c. 2800 B.C., were "almost certainly female because of the distinctive accumulation of fat on the buttocks." The authors believe that the female figures have an underworld, rather than a fertility, aspect; see also Trump (1972, 25).

Chapter Five / Sacred Stone and Wood Ceremonial Centers

1. Although the earlier stages of the roundels, such as that represented at Bučany, did not contain settlements, there is evidence that in the Lengyel II culture of Slovakia (c. 4400–4200 B.C., calibrated dates), at the Žlkovce site, there was indeed a settlement associated with a palisade fortification. Perhaps because of climatic changes, there are no known fortifications dating from the Lengyel III or IV stages. See Pavúk (1991).

2. See Burl (1979, 190). Further, a dwarflike woman, her head aligned to the south, was buried in the middle of a group of small sarsens in the southern part of Avebury henge, and very large sarsen slabs were placed over her. See Burl (1979, 66).

3. See Burl (1979, 197–98).

4. The Avebury complex has not been fully excavated, although there are plans to continue excavation in the near future. Many of the megalithic stones of Avebury were discovered buried within the henge, and it is assumed that the new excavations will unearth many more megalithic stones.

5. Stonehenge I dates from c. 3100 to c. 2300 B.C.; Stonehenge II lasted from c. 2150 to c. 2000 B.C.; Stonehenge III, in several phases, dates from c. 2100 to c. 1100 B.C.; and Stonehenge IV dates to 1100 B.C. See Chippindale (1983, 267–71).

Chapter Six / Matrilineal Social Structure

1. See Madsen (1988, 301–36). According to Madsen, the period in which the causewayed enclosures were built coincides with the period of concentrated tomb building: both date from c. 2700–2450 B.C. (these are uncalibrated dates). Following calibrated dating of Andersen (1988, 337, 354) and Gimbutas (1991, 138), we may postulate calibrated dates of c. 3400–3200 B.C.

2. On environmental factors in the spatial distributions of cairns, see Davidson in C. Renfrew (1979, 16–20); on "sacred space" in the disposition of Orcadian cairns, see C. Renfrew (1979, 215 ff.).

3. On burial practices of the patriarchal Indo-Europeans, see Jones-Bley (1997, 194–221). Jones-Bley analyzes the eight elements that, according to Marija Gimbutas (1974a, 293–94), identify an Indo-European burial.

4. To the Irish Celtic tradition of the sovereignty goddess Flaith, and the epic heroine Queen Medb, we may compare the Indic goddess Śri Lakshmi in her particular role as *rāja-lakshmī*, "kingly fortune"; without her the king cannot remain sovereign.

5. Another opinion is offered by Morris (1989, 511–35), who interprets the frescoes as a pictorial narrative "transforming history into art," including generic landscapes and motifs that complement the literary epics of Homer as well as earlier epic poetry that she believes was in existence in the early Mycenaean period, c. 1500 B.C. Thus the frescoes would tell of scenes of battle, council, and arrival and departure by sea, juxtaposed to scenes of everyday, peaceful life among peoples about to be besieged.

6. Thus, although we cannot be certain of an Old European *hieros gamos,* there is great evidence for the myth of the *hieros gamos* in most early historical (and early patriarchal) European and Near Eastern cultures.

7. The custom of the avunculate was preserved in both matrilineal and patrilineal societies.

8. The fact that the Spartan men were often away from home, at war, must have contributed to the autonomy of the Spartan women, who of necessity occupied a very public role in society—unlike their Athenian sisters.

9. Strabo, *Geography* 3.4.18. The Greek word used actually is *gynacocracy:* γυναικοκρατίαν. The people referred to in the passage are the Cantabrians, an Iberian subgroup.

10. Another possibility is that succession among the ancient Celts was matri-patrilineal. See Dexter 1997a.

11. Diodorus Siculus, *Bibliothecae,* V:32.2 ff.

12. Dio Cassius, *Roman History,* Epitome of Book, LXII2:3–4. Marija Gimbutas takes the translation from James E. Doan, *Women and Goddesses in Early Celtic History, Myth, and Legend,* 20. In Indo-European tripartite symbolism, red is the color of the warrior class.

13. For example, Procopius, in the *History of the Wars* (VIII:20.20), tells us of Hermigisil, king of the Saxon Varini, who, on his deathbed, ordered his son Radigis to marry his stepmother, the queen: "Let my son Radigis be married to his step-

mother henceforth, just as the law of our forefathers decrees." Similarly, Canute the Dane overthrew Ethelred and then married his queen.

Part II / The Living Goddesses

1. Marija Gimbutas had recently begun using the term *gynocentric,* "woman-centered." This is not a universally accepted term, but one she used to attempt to convey an idea still in flux.

2. Marija Gimbutas did not include a section on Roman religion, preferring that her attention to Italy be focused on the Etruscans and their religion.

Chapter Seven / The Minoan Religion in Crete

1. Marija Gimbutas refers here to prehistoric cultures such as that of Çatal Hüyük, which she discusses in the early chapters.

2. On pre-Indo-European place-names, see Haley (1928, 141–45), with map; and Blegen (1928, 145–54); both include a review of the literature. The authors cite names ending in *nthos* and *assos* as part of an Aegean-Anatolian substratum borrowed by Greek. Haley identifies a movement from Asia Minor to Greece, and Blegen, citing archaeological evidence, hypothesizes that these pre-Greek place-names are to be associated with the early Bronze Age. See Gimbutas (1991, 388) for dates: c. 2900–2250 B.C.

3. On Cretan cave sanctuaries, see Christ (1995).

4. Marinatos (1993, 114) believes that the ritual implements may have belonged to a temple official, who could have been the owner of the house; thus the implements need not point to a sacrifice committed within the building. Consequently, all four people may have died when the earthquake caused the building to collapse.

5. There has been some disagreement whether the white color is an adequate indicator of gender in Minoan Crete; Nannó Marinatos argues that both the red-brown-colored (sometimes termed "black") and the white-colored bull leapers are male, citing both their anatomy and their ritual dress, which includes a codpiece with phallus sheath (1993, 218–20).

6. The Linear B syllabary did not indicate aspirated consonants such as *th,* so *a-ta-na* can indicate Athana, classical Greek Athena.

7. This large, beaky nose is a characteristic of the Neolithic bird goddess.

8. Hesiod, *Theogony* 947–48; Apollodorus, *Epitome* I.8.

9. Homer, *Odyssey* V:125–26; Hesiod, *Theogony* 969–71.

10. On fourth-century coins of the Cretan city, Phaistos, Zeus Velchanos (Ϝελχανός) is depicted sitting on a stump holding a rooster; his form is very youthful, similar to that of the classical Dionysus. See Farnell (1896–1909, I:109).

11. Although this etymology seems rational, there is one difficulty: the uncompounded word *dā, dē,* "earth" has not been securely attested. See Chantraine (1966–70, II:272–73).

12. At Mesara, Mochlos, Archanes, and other places, graves were periodically cleansed and fumigated; then parts of the skeleton were reburied. This is known as secondary burial. In the case of secondary burial, only certain bones, such as the skulls and femurs, were kept; others were discarded. Secondary burial is still practiced in Greece. See Marinatos (1993, 22–23, 26–27).

13. Such secondary burials in sarcophagi, or *larnakes,* were found in the cemetery of Phourni at Archanes in central Crete. See Marinatos (1993, 22).

14. In Egypt, this pair of goddesses is represented by the sisters Isis and Nephthys, who both protect the dead and nurse the living.

15. We should keep in mind that this sarcophagus dates to the Mycenaean era. Thus, it may not depict Minoan rites at all.

16. The dating of the Theran eruption is very recent; see Sinclair Hood (1996); archaeologists arrived at the date through radiocarbon dating calibrated with tree-ring analysis. Hood, in his earlier work (1971, 147) gives c. 1500 B.C.; Marinatos (1993, 4) also dates the eruption at 1500 B.C. For another opinion see Renfrew (1996).

17. The preceding part of the conclusions was added by the editor.

Chapter Eight   /   The Greek Religion

1. This introduction was added by the editor.

2. For a brief comparison of Indo-European and Old European burial rites, see Jones-Bley (1990).

3. Greek religion is particularly imbued with influences from the Near East. In fact, several Greek deities and heroic figures seem to be descendants of Near Eastern figures. The Greek hero Herakles, for example, has inherited both the clothing and several labors from the Mesopotamian Gilgamesh, while the Greek goddess Aphrodite is a descendant of the Sumerian-Akkadian Inanna-Ishtar (West Semitic Ashtarte), goddesses of love, war, and several other functions. Although Aphrodite is primarily a love goddess in Greek myth, her warrior function is discernible in her mating with Ares (Homer, *Odyssey,* VIII) and epithets such as the Spartan Aphrodite Areia, "warlike Aphrodite" (Pausanias, *Description of Greece,* III.17:5–6). The *Theogony* of Hesiod, including the "Kingship in Heaven" genealogies, is particularly traceable to the Near East. External origins for other Greek deities are evident as well: Dionysos, according to many scholars, probably originated in Thrace (see Farnell 1896–1909, V:85–86).

4. Hekate was often depicted iconographically in triple aspect, facing in three directions. She was the threefold goddess.

5. Porphyry, *De Antro Nympharum,* 18. Here, Porphyry was speaking of Kore, a maiden aspect of the goddess. As a personification of youth if not virginity, Kore was similar to the virgin Artemis.

6. Pausanias VIII:37.4, on Arcadia.

7. *Homeric Hymn* 28, to Artemis: Ἐλαφηβόλον.

8. Pausanias VII:18, on Achaia.

9. "She [who stands] by the path," "on the wayside." This is similar to Roman *Tri-via,* a common epithet of Hekate, goddess of the crossroads.

10. Porphyry, *de Antrum Nympharum* 18. Here, Porphyry was citing Sophocles, from fragment 795 (Nauck), "the swarm of the dead buzzes and rises up," Βομβεῖ δὲ νεκρῶν σμῆνος ἔρχεταί τ' ἄνω.

11. Ibid.

12. Both the *Oxford Classical Dictionary* and Farnell (1896–1909, II:481) indicate that bees may have been of religious significance in the worship of Artemis at Ephesos. Farnell (591) cites the *Etymologicum Magnum* (1848, 383.30), which gives "The King among the Ephesians" as a definition of "essene," from a metaphor for the king of the bees, who is called an essene (that is, a drone).

13. Homer, *Odyssey,* I:319–20, III:371–72.

14. Homer, *Odyssey,* III:371 et passim. The Greek adjective *glaukōpis* may mean either "bright-eyed" or "owl-faced."

15. According to Sinclair Hood (1971, 112), an inscription whose script runs in a spiral, similar to that on the Phaistos disc, was found on a bronze votive ax excavated from "a sacred cave at Arkalokhori." Hood considers the inscription to be of a religious or magical character.

16. See Della Volpe (in Dexter and Polomé 1997, 103–23) on "The Great Goddess, the Sirens, and Parthenope."

17. Thus, the Sirens were not consistently viewed as negative. Carol P. Christ reminds us that Sirens holding tortoiseshell lyres were also frequently placed as funeral monuments in cemeteries, where their songs comforted the dead; she notes that they are antecedents of the winged, singing harp-bearing angels of Christian iconography (personal communication).

18. Homer, *Iliad,* I:551.

19. *Scholia on Theocritus,* XV:64.

20. Homer, *Iliad,* XIV:345–50. Though the context is war as well as love, there is no doubt that this passage does describe a *hieros gamos* between Hera and Zeus.

21. Plutarch, *Moralia,* XII (943b).

22. On the various possibilities of Indo-European afterworlds, including the gloomy, dark underworld, see Hansen (1987, 8–64).

23. Homer, *Iliad,* XVIII:570.

24. Fragment. Hesiod tells us that Linos is called upon at both the beginnings and endings of feasts and dances.

25. According to Farnell (1896–1909, V:226), there is a fifth century decree that orders the Athenian colonists of Brea to send an annual sacrifice of a phallus to the Dionysia. The ensuing ritual is called the "phallagogia." Farnell (V:225) calls this festival "in some ways the most magnificent of all Attic ceremonies."

26. Farnell translates the name Anthesteria as "the festival that causes things to bloom" (ibid., V:222).

27. In the early ritual, Dionysus was a vegetation (and perhaps fertility) god, but his role as god of wine was a later one. See Farnell (ibid., V:118). On the Orphic Dionysiac rituals, see Nilsson and Rose in Cary et al. (1949, 288–89; 627–28). See also Kerényi (1951, 253–56). Kerényi tells the myth in which Dionysus made the fig-wood phallus, carried in the *liknon,* the winnowing fan (259). See Kern (1922) for texts on Orphic religion and mysteries.

28. See Kerényi (1951, 254–55).

29. If we compare Aphrodite to the Sumerian-Akkadian-Babylonian Inanna-Ishtar, goddess of love, war, and holder of all of the *Mes,* the attributes of civilization, we can understand that Aphrodite has been stripped of much of her pre-Greek power and functionality.

Chapter Nine / The Etruscan Religion

1. Greeks colonized southern Italy and Sicily beginning c. 750 B.C. Earlier evidence of Greek material probably bespeaks sporadic contact rather than colonization. In southern Italy, Rhegium was founded sometime before 720 B.C. The first Greek colony in Sicily, Naxus, was founded c. 734 B.C. Syracuse was colonized c. 733 B.C. See A. J. Graham (1982, III: 91 ff). Greek colonization on the

coasts of France and Spain, by the Greek Phocaeans, probably took place c. 600 B.C. See Graham (139 ff).

2. On Etruscan inscriptions, see Puhvel (1984), Pallottino (1968), and Bonfante (1990, 27–48).

3. Livy, *ab urbe condita libri* (History of Rome), I.xxxiv.9; xxxix.3–4. She was also very wise, as evidenced by her counsel to her son-in-law Servius Tullius (I.xli.3–4) that, since he was unable to function intellectually at the death of her husband, Tarquinius Priscus, and to make himself king, then he should make use of *her* wisdom. And she proceeded to use her intellect to ensure Servius's smooth takeover. In this way, she also functioned as the bestower of sovereignty. See also I.xlvii.6, where she is accused of bestowing the royal power upon both her husband and her son-in-law.

4. This temple actually stood just outside the Etruscan city-state of Veii, in the Portonaccio area. It has been dated to the last quarter of the sixth century B.C. See Bonfante and Bonfante (1985, 32). According to the authors, the temple was dedicated to Minerva (Etruscan Menrva: Latin Minerva). Although it was destroyed in 396 B.C., it continued to be used as an open-air place of worship for at least a century. See Banti (1973, 61).

5. On Etruscan inscriptions, see above.

6. According to Ovid (*Amores,* III:13.35), Halaesus taught the Faliscans the sacred rites of Juno, Iunonia Sacra.

7. Leucothea means, literally, "White Goddess."

8. On Etruscan mirrors—their chemical composition, manufacture, usage, and inscriptions—see de Grummond (1982, 49 ff). Some of the inscriptions are quite charming. For example, on a mirror from Praeneste, a young man and woman are depicted playing a game on a game board. The young woman says, in archaic Latin, *devincam ted,* "I am going to beat you." The young man answers, *opeinod,* "I do believe you are" (75). See also Ernout (1973, 30).

9. Although the Etruscan Turan may have been inherited from Old Europe, Marija Gimbutas was not attempting to connect Aphrodite here with Old European goddesses; she believed that Aphrodite was inherited from the Near East.

10. Compare the Greek (in origin, Thraco-Phrygian) Semele, mother of the vine god Dionysos; she is related linguistically to the Lithuanian Žemyna, the Latvian Zemes Māte, and the Slavic Mat' Syra Zemlya, "mother moist earth." See Dexter (1990, 41–42).

11. For a depiction and discussion of Etruscan tomb paintings, see Moretti (1970); see also Keller (1974, 23–37).

12. From the Etruscans, the Romans borrowed *haruspicy,* and they practiced this form of divination until the end of the fourth century A.D., although in earlier centuries some Romans were skeptical of the practice. See Keller (1974, 398).

13. Pallottino (1968; 1975, 96) cites extant Etruscan literature, in which we may make out votive formulae, liturgical expressions, and prayers. Also see Keller (1974, 397), who cites Lucretius' description of "Tyrrhenian songs" read from right to left. Roman priests adapted Etruscan practices of divination, learning how to divine for themselves; but Romans also turned to Etruscan priests for the interpretation of omens and the foretelling of the future. This practice may have preserved Etruscan ritual formulae.

14. This concluding section was written by the editor.

Chapter Ten / The Basque Religion

1. See Tessier (1917). Among the Basques, the oldest child, male or female, is the heir. A marital relationship between two heirs is an equalitarian one. When a female heir marries a male nonheir, then the female has the greater rights in the marriage. To the situation of Basque female heirs, compare that of the ancient Irish *banchomarbae,* the woman who could inherit; see Dexter (1997a). Further, the high status of the Basque woman is confirmed by Terence Wilbur, author of *Prolegomena to a Grammar of Basque* (1979). Professor Wilbur asserts, "As a matter of fact, *etcheko anderaia* (the 'woman of the house') is the real boss in the Basque Country. She wears the keys to the house" (personal communication, May 1997).

2. This concluding section was written by the editor.

Chapter Eleven / The Celtic Religion

1. Tacitus, *Germania,* 40. For further discussion, see below.

2. The high status and economic viability of Indo-European Celtic women is probably due to their particular influence within the western European matri-patrilineal tribes that assimilated with the Indo-Europeans. See Dexter in Marler, ed. (1997a, 218–36).

3. Bergquist and Taylor (1987) give detailed reasons why the Gundestrup cauldron is thought to belong to the Thracian repoussé sheet-silver-working tradition of southeast Europe. But there is evidence also for a Celtic tradition. See T. G. E. Powell (1958, 154, 167–68). According to Powell, warriors depicted on the cauldron are seen with Celtic warrior equipment; because the stylistic aspects of the animals point to a Middle Danubian origin, Powell believes that the crafters of the cauldron may have been members of a Celtic tribe living in that region, the Scordistae (which Gimbutas called Scordisci). See also Polomé (1989a, 73).

4. Kim McCone has interpreted this plate as depicting a ritual of male initiation. In the lower register, men (probably youths) march to the vessel and are immersed therein. The deity is shown immersing one of the men. (Therefore, this would be not a sacrifice but a ritual immersion leading to "rebirth" into a new class of men.) The upper register shows men mounted on horses, wearing helmets and short tunics, perhaps ready now to be warriors. A wolf faces the uninitiated youths of the lower register. There is much evidence to relate the wolf with Indo-European youths of good birth who are in limbo between childhood and manhood. These youths join a "wolf-band"—a Männerbund—and live together in the woods, as outlaws, before attaining adulthood, with attendant inheritance of property and marriage. The solution to the young Ulster hero Cú Chulainn's unmanageable martial frenzy, that of immersing him into three vats of cold water, serves as a textual parallel to this sort of evidence of a ritual quasi-baptism. See McCone (1986, 16–17).

5. *De Bello Gallico:* a work in seven volumes.

6. According to Celtic folklorist Angelique Gulermovich Epstein (personal communication), *artos* is found in compounds and oblique cases, but not in the nominative case; hence the asterisk.

7. For an interpretation and cognate mythology of Danu, see Dexter (1990a).

8. According to Angelique Gulermovich Epstein (personal communication), her name also appears as uninflected *Anann.*

9. Puhvel (1970) believes that etymologically she is a woman associated with a ritual involving drunkenness due to an intoxicating honey drink.

10. This is now the Hill of Allen.

11. A "woman of the *sidh,* the fairy mound."

12. This concluding section has been added by the editor.

Chapter Twelve / The Germanic Religion

1. On Marija Gimbutas' three-wave migration theory, see introduction. See also Dexter and Jones-Bley, eds. (1997, 195–300).

2. According to the Germanic scholar Professor Edgar C. Polomé (personal communication), the Germanic tribes gelled as a separate ethnic entity around the middle of the first millennium B.C. (Jastorf culture). Further, according to Jürgen Udolph (1994, 935 ff), the Bronze Age Scandinavians may not have been already Germanic; using a mainly hydronymic argument, Udolph hypothesizes that Scandinavia was colonized from the south by Germanic tribes in the first millennium B.C.

3. On runes and magic, see Flowers (1986); on the magical runic term *alu,* "beer," see Polomé (1996).

4. Old Norse Oðin, Old Saxon Wōden, Old High German Wuotan, *from* PIE **u̯āt,* "to be furious."

5. Tacitus, *Germania,* 40. This act of lustration regenerated the vital forces of the goddess. The sacrificed slaves added "fuel" to her own energies and contributed to the fertility of the earth. See Dexter (1990, 99). On the etymology of Nerthus, see Polomé (1987, 460).

6. Many other goddesses also underwent this ritual bathing; for example, the Greek goddess Hera restored her virginity each year by ritually bathing in the river Canathus. See Dexter (1990, 99, 130, 170).

7. *Vǫluspá,* 20.

8. Gullveig (ibid., 21) is the "drunkenness of gold," from Old Norse *gull,* "gold," and *veig,* "intoxicating drink." Like Freyja, Gullveig practices *seiðr,* and Freyja weeps tears of red-gold when her husband goes on long journeys (Snorri Sturluson 1929, 36); Gullveig is probably an epithet for Freyja herself. See Polomé (1989, 60–61).

9. According to Polomé in Eliade, ed. (1987, 438–39), love and sexuality are probably the most important of her functions within the Germanic pantheon. See also Polomé (1989, 61)

10. But we should note that Fulla, in Germanic myth, does not accrue the negativity that surrounds the myth of Pandora. Fulla is not responsible for the woes of humanity.

11. See editor's introduction and chapter 6, above.

Chapter Thirteen / The Baltic Religion

1. Literally a "drive to the east," this phrase indicates the movement of medieval Germans into east-central Europe for the purposes of converting the inhabitants of these countries and conquering them.

2. Thereafter, the Prussian language became extinct. Although Prussia was conquered and converted to Christianity by the thirteenth century, we know that Prussian pagan religious practices continued to be practiced until the language became

extinct in the seventeenth century, since decrees forbidding those practices continued to be issued by the Christian rulers until that time. See Usačiovaitė in Jones-Bley and Huld (1996, 204–17).

3. An excellent selection of Latvian mythological songs is contained in Jonval (1929), in Latvian with French translation. See also Jouet (1989) for translations and discussion of the songs.

4. We may recall that Hera, the Greek goddess of marriage, was also associated with the cuckoo. Before Zeus and Hera were married, Zeus turned himself into a cuckoo and perched at Hera's knee. Seeing it shivering from the cold, Hera put the bird into her blouse. Zeus transformed himself back into his divine shape and attempted to rape Hera. Instead, he married her. The Scholia on Theocritus (XV:64) describes a statue of Hera in her sanctuary at Argos: in one hand she held a scepter topped by a cuckoo.

5. Biezais (1955, 262, No. 29165). Marija Gimbutas translated these and other Latvian folk songs from Biezais' Latvian-German texts.

6. Ibid., 256, No. 32446.

7. Ibid., 327, No. 32447.

8. Ibid., 253, No. 32416, 6.

9. According to Greimas (1979, 35–36) (translated by Irene Luksis Goddard), as late as the beginning of the twentieth century, around (the town of) Švenčionys people used to say that "the bees are weaving honeycombs." This quotation also appears in Dundulienė (1990, 117).

10. The source has not been given.

11. John Malalas wrote about old Lithuanian customs and beliefs in his *Chronicle* (1261). A Bulgarian clergyman, Grigorius, translated Malalas' Greek text, and the translated work found its way to Russia, where it was edited and expanded. In particular, the citations on Lithuanian deities come from the Russian expansion. I am indebted to Irene Luksis Goddard, a member of the Los Angeles, California, Lithuanian community, for information on this early source. For the past several years Ms. Goddard, a former chemist, has been writing about her youth in Lithuania, which was contemporaneous to Marija Gimbutas'.

12. See Pokorny (1959, 13), *aig* (1). I am indebted to Martin Huld for pointing out both the proto-form and the Polish cognate, *jȩzda*, "witch," the meaning of which throws much light on the semantic turn taken by the word.

13. According to Irene Luksis Goddard (personal communication), there was a similar panacea made of whiskey or vodka and a snake. It was called *gyvatinė*, from *gyvate*, "snake." Goddard writes that she remembers seeing bottles with snakes in clear liquid at the outdoor market in her childhood town in Lithuania, and that the belief was that the contents would cure "whatever ails you."

14. For a detailed description of Vily and Rusalki, see Barber in Dexter and Polomé, eds. (1997, 6–47).

15. *Omphalos* is the Greek word for "navel"; the ancient Greeks considered the holy cave at Delphi to be the navel—the center—of the world.

16. This is a Near Eastern phenomenon as well. In ancient Sumer the earth mother goddess was Nin-Hursag, "mountain lady."

17. Marija Gimbutas gives as her source Greimas (1993), but the text does not appear to be contained either in *The Semiotics of Passions* (Minneapolis: University of Minnesota Press, 1993) or in Festschrift, *A. J. Greimas and the Nature of Meaning* (London and Sydney: Croom Helm, 1993). Further, it does not seem to be included

in *Of Gods and Men* (Bloomington: Indiana University Press, 1992) or the earlier Lithuanian version, *Apie dievus ir žmones: Lietuvių mitoligijos studijos* (Chicago: A and M Publications, 1979). Irene Luksis Goddard has found a description of a similar ritual, involving pairs of animals and fowl offered to the god *Žemininkas.* The priest and then the other participants beat the animals with sticks until they were dead (personal communication).

18. Greimas (1979, 35–36).

19. See Greimas (1979, 36). Irene Luksis Goddard believes that *kaukoratis* refers to a "mushroom ring," which she compares to a fairy ring (personal communication).

acropolis   a citadel or fortified site on an elevated location.

askos (plural: *askoi*)   bird-shaped vase.

bucranium   the head and horns of a bull; bull, ox, cow skull rendered in clay or other material.

cairn   a tomb consisting of a group of stones covered by a large mound of dirt, turf, or rocks.

cap stone   the horizontal topmost stone of a dolmen.

court tomb   tomb with semicircular courtyard in front, typical of Ireland and Shetland Islands.

cromlech   a circle of flat stones, usually enclosing a mound.

disarticulation   separation of a body part or body parts at the joints.

dolmen   a prehistoric megalithic monument consisting of two or more large upright stones holding a horizontal stone, the cap stone (q.v.).

enclosure   a fenced-in or walled-in area; prehistoric enclosures include roundels, hedges, square enclosures, and causewayed enclosures, all probably used as places of ritual.

excarnation   the deceased body was exposed outdoors on a platform. There, birds of prey would strip the body of its flesh. The remaining bones would then be buried.

ex voto (or *votive*)   offered or dedicated to a deity in accordance with a prayer or vow.

gallery grave   simple long, rectangular tomb, typical of Brittany.

Indo-European   a family of languages and cultures, including ancient Greek, Latin, Indic, Iranian, Slavic, Baltic, Celtic, Germanic, Albanian, Armenian, Hittite, and Tocharian; the prehistoric parent language and cultural group is called *Proto-Indo-European*. The Proto-Indo-Europeans were seminomadic, patriarchal, patrilineal, and patrilocal. Their religion honored sky deities and warrior deities, and it was male-centered.

The glossary was prepared by the editor.

231

interment	burial.
kerbstones	the stones that form a curb around the outer edge of an earthen mound.
kernos (plural: *kernoi*)	a ring-shaped clay container, usually used for offerings, to which a number of cups or miniature vases have been attached
krater	mixing bowl.
kurgan	a mound, barrow, or tumulus; in Marija Gimbutas' context, this term designates the round barrows of the patriarchal pastoralists of the steppe area of southern Russia, whom she identified with the Proto-Indo-Europeans.
labrys	a Cretan ceremonial symbol that has the appearance of a double ax.
Magdalenian period	the latest Upper Paleolithic period, named for the La Madeleine site in south-western France.
matrilineal	a social structure in which descent and inheritance are traced through the female line.
matrilocal society	a society in which men, upon marriage, go to their wives' family homes; the home territories of a matrilineal kin group.
megalith	a huge stone used in a prehistoric monument.
megalithic monument	large stone monument.
menhir	a large, individual standing stone.
Mesolithic	Middle Stone Age, circa 8300–7000/6000 B.C.; cultures characterized by hunting and gathering.
Neolithic	New Stone Age, circa 7000/6000–circa 3500/3000 B.C.; cultures characterized by crop cultivation and animal domestication. People lived in settlements and used ground-stone tools.
oinocoe, oenocoe	an ancient Greek wine pitcher or jug.
ornithomorphic	bird-shaped.
orthostat	a upright stone, often surrounding a megalithic tomb.
ossuary	a place or container in which bones are buried.
Paleolithic	Old Stone Age; the Upper Paleolithic or later Paleolithic endured from circa 30,000 B.C.–circa 8300 B.C., when the ice sheets receded from northern Europe.

palisade	a fence of stakes, sometimes but not always used for defense. When used in ancient enclosures, palisades probably served to mark ritual areas.
parthenogenesis	birth from a mother with no male participation. In Greek myth, Hera gave birth to Hephaestus without the participation of her husband, Zeus.
passage grave	grave consisting of large upright stones that form a passageway leading to a round or rectangular chamber. These stones are capped with other stones.
phalera	in antiquity, a metal disk worn as a sign of military rank.
pithos	a large ceramic jar.
pre-Indo-European	In archaeological terminology, this refers to indigenous peoples occupying areas to which the Indo-Europeans migrated. In linguistic terminology, this refers to the form of the Indo-European language preceding the proto-phase.
pyxis	an ornate, covered container used in ancient Greece and Rome.
roundel	an ancient circular enclosure that probably marked a ritual area.
sarsen	sandstone boulder; according to Aubrey Burl, a corruption of "saracen"; thus, "heathen stone."
seal	in antiquity, a sign or image often carved into a ring or clay cylinder, whose purpose was to identify a person or group or to represent a mythic subject.
sealing	an impression made by a seal or a small piece of material on which a seal has been imprinted.
steatopygia	a large accumulation of fat on the buttocks; this is often an attribute of ancient female figures.
stela (plural: *stelae*)	an upright stone or slab that has an engraved or sculptured surface.
stereobate	ground floor with round windows.
tholos tomb	circular chamber tomb.
trilithon	an ancient monument consisting of two upright megalithic stones and a third stone placed horizontally over the first two, as a cap stone or lintel.
triple-cella	a space (in this context, in a sanctuary or temple) with three alcoves.
zoomorphic	having the shape of an animal; the use of animal forms in symbolic or mythical representation.

Includes general books, works, articles, catalogs, monographs, and major excavation reports. *Editor's note:* This is a compilation of both Marija Gimbutas's bibliography and my own. All citations to my bibliographic items appear in the notes to the text.

Alexandrescu, P. 1983. "Le Groupe des trésors thraces de nord des Balkans, I." *Dacia* 27.

———. 1984. "Le Groupe des trésors thraces de nord des Balkans, II." *Dacia* 28.

Alexiou, S. 1969. *Minoan Civilization.* Heraklion: Spyros Alexiou.

Ammerman, A. J., and L. L. Cavalli-Sforza. 1984. *The Neolithic Transition and the Genetics of Population in Europe.* Princeton: Princeton University Press.

Andersen, Niels H. 1988. "The Neolithic Causewayed Enclosures at Sarup, on Soth-Wets Funen, Denmark." In *Enclosures and Defences in the Neolithic of Western Europe,* edited by Colin Burgess, Peter Topping, Claude Mordant, and Margaret Maddison. International Series 403. Oxford: British Archaeological Reports.

Anthony, David W. 1986. "The 'Kurgan Culture,' Indo-European Origins, and the Domestication of the Horse: A Reconsideration with CA Comment." *Current Anthropology* 27 (4): 291–313.

———. 1991. "The Archaeology of Indo-European Origins." *Journal of Indo-European Studies* 19 (3–4): 193–223.

Arnal, Jean. 1976. *Les Statues-menhirs, hommes et dieux.* Paris: Éditions des Hesperides.

Atkinson, R. J. C. 1965. "Wayland's Smithy." *Antiquity* 9:126–233.

Atzeni, Enrico. 1981. "Aspetti e sviluppi culturali del neolitico e delle prima eta dei metali in Sardegna." Vols. 27–41 of *Ichnussa: La Sardegna dalle origini all-eta classica.* Milan: Libri Scheiwiller.

Banner, Janos. 1959. "Anthropomorphe Gefässe der Theisskultur von der Siedlung Kökénydomb bei Hódmezövásárehely (Ungarn)." *Germania* 37:14–35.

Banti, Luisa. 1973. *Etruscan Cities and Their Culture.* Translated by Erika Bizzarri. Los Angeles: University of California Press.

Barandiarán, Jose Miguel de. 1960. *Mitologia Vasca I.* Madrid: Editiones Minotauro.

Barber, E. J. W. 1989. "Archaeolinguistics and the Borrowing of Old European Technology." *Journal of Indo-European Studies* 27 (3–4): 239–51.

———. 1991. *Prehistoric Textiles.* Princeton: Princeton University Press.

———. 1994. *Women's Work: The First 20,000 Years; Women, Cloth, and Society in Early Times.* New York: Norton.

———. 1997. "On the Origins of the vily/rusalki." In *Varia on the Indo-European Past: Papers in Memory of Marija Gimbutas,* edited by Miriam Robbins Dexter and Edgar C. Polomé, 6–47. Washington, D.C.: Institute for the Study of Man.

Baring, Anne, and Jules Cashford. 1991. *The Myth of the Goddess: Evolution of an Image.* London: Viking Arkana.

Barker, Graeme. 1985. *Prehistoric Farming in Europe.* Cambridge: Cambridge University Press.

Baroja, Julio Caro. 1975. *The World of the Witches.* Translated from the Spanish by O. N. V. Glendinning. Chicago: University of Chicago Press.

Bar-Yosef, Ofer. 1986. "The Walls of Jericho: An Alternative Interpretation." *Current Anthropology* 27 (2): 157–62.

Batović, Šime. 1966. *Stariji Neolit u Dalmaciji.* Societa Archaeologia Iugoslaviae. Zadar: Museum Archaeologicum.

Battaglia, Frank. 1993. "A Common Background to *Lai de Graelent* and *Noínden Ulad?*" *Emania* 11:41–48.

Becker, H. 1989. "Die Kreisgrabenanlage auf dem Aschelbachäckern bei Meinertal—ein Kalenderbau aus der mittleren Jungsteinzeit?" *Das archäologische Jahr in Bayern 1989:* 27–32.

Behrends, Rolf-Heiner. 1991. "Erdwerke der Jungsteinzeit in Bruchsal." *Neue Forschungen 1983–1991.* Stuttgart: Baden-Württemberg.

Behrens, H. 1973. *Die Jungsteinzeit im Mittelelbe-Saale Gebiet.* Landesmuseum für Vorgeschichte in Halle. Neuöffentlichungen. Berlin: Deutscher Verlag der Wissenschaften.

———. 1981. "The First 'Woodhenge' in Middle Europe." *Antiquity* 55:172–78.

Beier, H. J. 1988. *Die Kugelamphorenkultur im Mittelelbe-Saale Gebiet und in der Altmark.* Berlin: Deutscher Verlag der Wissenschaften.

———. 1991. *Die megalithischen, submegalithischen und pseudomegalithischen Bauten sowie die Menhire zwischen Ostee und Thüringer Wald.* Beiträge zur Ur- und Frühgeschichte Mitteleuropas. Wilkau-Hasslau: Verlag Beier and Beran.

Beltran, Antonio. 1979. *Da cacciatori ad allevatori. L'arte rupestre del Levante Spagnolo.* Milan: Jaca Book.

Benac, Alojz. 1973a. "Obre I. Neolitsko naselje Starčevacko-Impresso i Kakanjski kulture na Raskršču." (Obre I. A Neolithic Settlement of the Starčevo-Impresso and Kakanj Cultures at Raskršce.) *Glasnik Zemaljskog Muzeja* 5 (27/28): 5–171.

———. 1973b. "A Neolithic Settlement of the Butmir Group at Gornje Polje." *Wissenschaftliche Mitteilungen der Bosnisch-Herzegowinischen Landesmuseums* (Sarajevo) Vol. 3A. (Archaeology Series): 1–327.

Benac, Alojz, et al., eds. 1979. *Praistorija jugoslavenskih zemalja.* Vols. 1–4. Sarajevo: Academy of Sciences of Bosnia and Herzegovina.

Berciu, Dumitru. 1966. *Cultura Hamangia: noi contributii.* Bucharest: Editura Academiei Republicii Socialiste Romania.

Berger, Pamela. 1985. *The Goddess Obscured: Transformation of the Grain Protectress from Goddess to Saint.* Boston: Beacon Press.

Bergquist, Anders, and Timothy Taylor. 1987. "The Origin of the Gundestrup Cauldron." *Antiquity* 61 (231): 10–24.

Bernabó Brea, Luigi. 1957. *Sicily before the Greeks.* London: Thames and Hudson.

Best, R. I., and Osborn Bergin, eds. 1954. *The Book of Leinster (LL)* I-II-III. Dublin: Thom and Co.

Bevan, Elinor. 1986. *Representations of Animals in Sanctuaries of Artemis and Other Olympian Deities.* International Series 315. Oxford: British Archaeological Reports.

Biaggi, Cristina. 1994. *Habitations of the Great Goddess.* Manchester, Conn.: Knowledge, Ideas and Trends.

Biaggi, Cristina, Norman Simms, Guy Ventouillac, Robert Liris, and Joseph Grivel. 1994. *Glozel: Les Graveurs du Silence.* Villars, France: Editions BGC Toscane.

Bibikov, S. N. 1953. "Poselenie Luka-Vrublevetskaya." *Materialy: Issledovaniya po Arkheologii SSSR* 38:1–408.

Biezais, Haralds. 1955. *Die Hauptgöttinnen der Alten Letten.* Uppsala: Almquist and Wiksells.

———. 1987. "Baltic Mythology." *The Encyclopedia of Religion,* edited by Mircea Eliade. New York: Macmillan.

Bintliff, John, ed. 1984. *European Social Evolution: Archaeological Perspectives.* Bradford, West Yorkshire, England: University of Bradford.

Blegen, Carl W. 1928. "The Coming of the Greeks II: The Geographical Distribution of Prehistoric Remains in Greece." *American Journal of Archaeology* 32:146–54.

Bloch, Maurice. 1981. "Tombs and States." In *Mortality and Immortality: The Anthropology and Archaeology of Death,* edited by S. C. Humphreys and H. King. London: Academic Press.

———. 1991. *Prey into Hunter: The Politics of Religious Experience.* Cambridge: Cambridge University Press.

Bober, Phyllis Fray. 1951. "Cernunnos: Origin and Transformation of a Celtic Divinity." *American Journal of Archaeology* 55:13–51.

Bogucki, P. 1982. *Early Neolithic Subsistence Production in the Polish Lowlands.* International Series 150. Oxford: British Archaeological Reports.

Bökönyi, Sándor. 1970. "Animal Remains from Lepenski Vir." *Science* 167 (3926): 1702–4.

———. 1974. *History of Domestic Mammals in Central and Eastern Europe.* Budapest: Akadémiai Kiadó.

———. 1976. "The Vertebrate Fauna of Anza." In *Neolithic Macedonia, as Reflected by Excavation at Anza, Southeast Yugoslavia,* edited by Marija Gimbutas, 313–63. Monumenta Archaeologica 1. Los Angeles: University of California, Institute of Archaeology.

———. 1986. "The Faunal Remains of Sitagroi." In *Excavations at Sitagroi: A Prehistoric Village in Northeast Greece,* edited by Colin Renfrew, Marija Gimbutas, and Ernestine S. Elster, 63–133. Monumenta Archaeologica 13, vol. 1. Los Angeles: University of California, Institute of Archaeology.

———. 1987. "Horses and Sheep in East Europe in the Copper and Bronze Ages." In *Proto-Indo-European: The Archaeology of a Linguistic Problem,* edited by S. N. Skomal and E. C. Polomé, 137–44. Studies in Honor of Marija Gimbutas. Washington, D.C.: Institute for the Study of Man.

———. 1989. "Animal Remains." In *Achilleion: A Neolithic Settlement in Thessaly, Greece, 6400–5600 b.c.,* edited by Marija Gimbutas, Shan Winn, and Daniel Shimabuku, 315–32. Monumenta Archaeologica 14. Los Angeles: University of California, Institute of Archaeology.

Bonfante, Giuliano, and Larissa Bonfante. 1985. *Lingua e cultura degli Etruschi.* Rome: Riuniti.

Bonfante [Warren], Larissa. 1973. "The Women of Etruria." *Arethusa* 6 (1): 91–101.

———. 1990. *Etruscan: Reading the Past.* Berkeley and Los Angeles: University of California Press.

Borgeaud, Phillippe. 1988. *The Cult of Pan in Ancient Greece.* Chicago: University of Chicago Press.

Boulotis, Ch. 1981. "Nochmals zum Prozessionsfresko von Knossos." In *Sanctuaries and Cults in the Aegean Bronze Age,* edited by Robin Hägg and Nanno Marinatos. Proceedings of the First International Symposium at the Swedish Institute in Athens, 12–13 May 1980. Stockholm: Svenska Institutet, Athens.

Branigan, K. 1984. "Early Minoan Society: The Evidence of the Mesara Tholoi Reviewed." In *Aux Origines de l'hellenisme: La Crete et la Grece: Hommage Henri van Effenterre,* edited by C. Nicolet, 29–37. Paris: Publications de la Sorbonne.

Branson, Brian. 1964. *Gods of the North.* London: Thames and Hudson.

Bremmer, Jan. 1983. *The Early Greek Concept of the Soul.* Princeton: Princeton University Press.

Brennan, Martin. 1983. *The Stars and the Stones: Ancient Art and Astronomy in Ireland.* London: Thames and Hudson.

Brenneman, Walter L., and Mary G. Brenneman. 1995. *Crossing the Circle at the Holy Wells of Ireland.* Charlottesville: University Press of Virginia.

Brenner, Larsen. 1985. "The Gundestrup Cauldron, Identification of Tool Traces." *Iskos* 5. *Proceedings of the Third Nordic Conference on the Applications of Scientific Methods in Archaeology.* Helsinki.

Brøndsted, Johannes. 1960. *Danmarks oldtid: III, jernalderen.* Copenhagen: Gyldendal.

Brumfield, Allaire Chandor. 1981. *The Attic Festivals of Demeter and Their Relation to the Agricultural Year.* Monographs in Classical Studies. Salem, N.H.: Ayer Co.

Bujna, Josef, and Peter Romsauer. 1986. "Siedlung und Kreisanlage der Lengyel-Kurtur in Bučany." *Internationales Symposium über die Lengyel-Kultur, 1984,* Nitra-Wien: 27–35.

Burgess, Colin, Peter Topping, Claude Mordant, and Margaret Maddison, eds. 1988. *Enclosures and Defences in the Neolithic of Western Europe.* International Series 403. Oxford: British Archaeological Reports.

Burkert, Walter. 1985. *Greek Religion: Archaic and Classical.* Translated by John Raffan. Oxford: Basil Blackwell.

Burl, Aubrey. 1979. *Prehistoric Avebury.* New Haven: Yale University Press.

Cameron, Dorothy O. 1981. *Symbols of Birth and Death in the Neolithic Era.* London: Kenyon Deane.

Cann, J. R., and Colin Renfrew. 1964. "The Characterization of Obsidian and Its Application to the Mediterranean Region." *Proceedings of the Prehistoric Society* 30:111–25.

Cary, M., et al., with the assistance of H. J. Rose, H. P. Harvey, and A. Souter. 1949. *The Oxford Classical Dictionary.* Oxford: Clarendon Press.

Castleden, Rodney. 1990. *The Knossos Labyrinth: A New View of the "Palace of Minos" at Knossos.* London: Routledge.

Chadwick, John. 1976. *The Mycenaean World.* Cambridge: Cambridge University Press.

Chantraine, Pierre. 1966–70. *Dictionnaire étymologique de la langue grecque.* Paris: Klincksieck.

Chapman, John. 1981. *The Vinča Culture of Southeast Europe.* International Series 117. Oxford: British Archaeological Reports.

———. 1987. "The Early Balkan Village." In *Neolithic of Southeastern Europe and Its Eastern Connections,* 33–53. International Conference 1987 Szolnok-Szeged, Varia Archaeologica Hungarica II, Budapest.

Chernykh, E. N. 1980. "Metallurgical Provinces of the 5th–2nd Millennia in Eastern Europe in Relation to the Process of Indo-Europeanization." *Journal of Indo-European Studies* 8 (3–4): 317–36.

Chippindale, Christopher. 1983. *Stonehenge Complete*. Ithaca, N.Y.: Cornell University Press.

Christ, Carol P. 1995. *Odyssey with the Goddess: A Spiritual Quest in Crete*. New York: Continuum.

———. 1997. *Rebirth of the Goddess: Finding Meaning in Feminist Spirituality*. New York: Addison-Wesley.

Cipollini Sampo, Mirella. 1982. *Scavi nel villaggio neolitico di Rendina, 1970–1976*. First published in *Origini* XI (Rome, 1977–1982), 183–354.

Clarke, D. V. 1976. *The Neolithic Village at Skara Brae, Orkney: 1972–73 Excavations*. London: HMSO.

Cowan, Wesley, and Patty Jo Watson, eds. 1992. *The Origins of Agriculture: An International Perspective*. Smithsonian Series in Archaeological Inquiry. Washington, D.C.: Smithsonian Institution Press.

Csálog, József. 1959. "Die anthropomorphen Gefässe und Idolplastiken von Szegvár-Tüzköves." *Acta Archaeologica* (Budapest) 2:7–38.

———. 1972. "Thronende Frauen-Idol von Szegvár-Tüzköves." *Idole. Prähistorische Keramiken aus Ungarn*, 20–24. Vienna: Naturhistorisches Museum.

Cucoş, St. 1973. "Un complex ritual cucutenian descoperit la Ghelaeşti (Jud. Neamt)." *Studi şi Cercetari de Istorie Veche* 24 (2): 207.

Cunliffe, Barry. 1974. *Iron Age Communities in Britain*. London: Routledge and Kegan Paul.

———. 1986. *The Celtic World*. New York: Crown Publishers.

Dames, Michael. 1976. *The Silbury Treasure: The Great Goddess Rediscovered*. London: Thames and Hudson.

———. 1977. *The Avebury Cycle*. London: Thames and Hudson.

———. 1992. *Mythic Ireland*. London: Thames and Hudson.

Danforth, Loring M. 1982. *The Death Rituals of Rural Greece*. Photography by Alexander Tsiaras. Princeton: Princeton University Press.

Daniel, Glyn, and Poul Kjaerum, eds. 1973. *Megalithic Graves and Ritual: Papers Presented at the 3rd Atlantic Colloquium, Moesgard, 1969*. Jutland Archaeological Society Publications, 11. Copenhagen: Gyldendal.

D'Anna, A. 1977. *Les Statues-menhirs et stèles anthropomorphes du midi méditerranéen*. Paris: Editions du Centre National de la Recherche Scientifique.

Dannheimer, H. 1985. *Idole, frühe Götterbilder und Opfergaben*. Ausstellungskataloge der prähistorischen Staatssammlung, Band 12. Mainz am Rhein.

Davidson, Donald. 1979. "The Orcadian Environment and Cairn Location." In *Investigations in Orkney*, edited by Colin Renfrew, 7–20. Society of Antiquaries of London, no. 38. London: Thames and Hudson.

Davidson, Hilda Ellis. 1969. *Scandinavian Mythology*. New York: Hamlyn.

———. 1988. *Myths and Symbols in Pagan Europe: Early Scandinavian and Celtic Religions*. New York: Syracuse University Press.

Davis, E. 1981. "The Knossos Miniature Frescoes." In *Sanctuaries and Cults in the Aegean Bronze Age*, edited by Robin Hägg and Nanno Marinatos. Proceedings of the First International Symposium at the Swedish Institute in Athens, 12–13 May 1980. Stockholm: Svenska Institutet, Athens.

De Grummond, Nancy Thomson. 1982. *A Guide to Etruscan Mirrors*. Tallahassee, Fla.: Archaeological News.

Della Volpe, Angela. 1997. "The Great Goddess, the Sirens, and Parthenope." In *Varia on the Indo-European Past: Papers in Memory of Marija Gimbutas,* edited by Miriam Robbins Dexter and Edgar C. Polomé, 103–23. Washington, D.C.: Institute for the Study of Man.

Demoule, Jean-Paul, and Jean Guilaine. 1986. *Le Néolithique de la France: Hommage à Gerard Bailloud.* Paris: Picard.

Dennell, Robin. 1983. *European Economic Prehistory.* London: Academic Press.

Dergachev, Valentin A. 1986. *Moldaviya i Sosednie teritorii v ëpokhu eneolita.* Kishenev: Shtiintsa.

De Valera, R., and Sean O Nualláin. 1961–82. *Survey of the Megalithic Tombs of Ireland.* Vols. 1–4. Dublin: Stationery Office.

Dexter, Miriam Robbins. 1980. "The Assimilation of Pre-Indo-European Goddesses into Indo-European Society." *Journal of Indo-European Studies* 8 (1–2): 19–29.

———. 1990. *Whence the Goddesses: A Source Book.* New York: Teachers College.

———. 1990a. "Reflections on the Goddess *Donu.*" *Mankind Quarterly* 31 (1–2): 45–58.

———. 1997. "The Frightful Goddess: Birds, Snakes and Witches." In *Varia on the Indo-European Past: Papers in Memory of Marija Gimbutas,* edited by Miriam Robbins Dexter and Edgar C. Polomé, 124–54. Washington, D.C.: Institute for the Study of Man.

———. 1997a. "The Brown Bull of Cooley and Matriliny in Celtic Ireland." In *From the Realm of the Ancestors: Essays in Honor of Marija Gimbutas,* edited by Joan Marler. Manchester, Conn.: Knowledge, Ideas, and Trends.

Dexter, Miriam Robbins, and Karlene Jones-Bley, eds. 1997. *The Kurgan Culture and the Indo-Europeanization of Europe: Selected Articles from 1952–1993,* by Marija Gimbutas. Monograph No. 18. Washington, D.C.: Institute for the Study of Man.

Dexter, Miriam Robbins, and Edgar C. Polomé, eds. 1997. *Varia on the Indo-European Past: Papers in Memory of Marija Gimbutas.* Monograph No. 19. Washington, D.C.: Institute for the Study of Man.

Dillon, Myles. [1954] 1969. *Early Irish Society.* County Cork, Ireland: Mercier Press.

Diodorus Siculus. 1866–68. *Diodori Bibliotheca Historica.* Ex Recensione et cum Annotationibus Ludovici Dindorfii. Leipzig: Teubner.

Dixon, J. E. J. R. Cann, and Colin Renfrew. 1968. "Obsidian and the Origins of Trade." *Scientific American* 218 (3): 38–46.

Dixon, Phillip. 1988. "The Neolithic Settlements on Crickley Hill." In *Enclosures and Defences in the Neolithic of Western Europe,* edited by Colin Burgess, Peter Topping, Claude Mordant, and Margaret Maddison. International Series 403. Oxford: British Archaeological Reports.

Doan, James E. 1987. *Women and Goddesses in Early Celtic History, Myth, and Legend.* Working Papers in Irish Studies, 87–4/5. Boston: Northeastern University, Irish Studies Program.

Dombay, J. 1960. "Die Siedlung und das Gräberfeld in Zengővárkony." *Archaeologia Hungarica* (Budapest): 37.

Dumézil, Georges. 1939. "Mythes et dieux des Germains: Essai d'interprétation comparative." In *Collection mythes et religions,* edited by P.-L. Couchoud. Vol. 1. Paris: Presses Universitaires de France.

———. 1958. *L'Ideologie tripartie des indo-européens.* Vol. 31. Brussels: Collection Latomus.

Dumitrescu, Hortensia. 1961. "The Connections between Cucuteni-Tripolie and Near East Cultures." *Dacia* 5:72–77.

———. 1968. "Un modèle de sanctuaire découvert dans la station énéolithique de Căscioarele." *Dacia* 12:381–94.

Dumitrescu, Vladimir. 1954. *Hăbăşeşti*. Bucharest: Institute of Archaeology.

———. 1965. "Căscioarele: A Late Neolithic Settlement on the Lower Danube." *Archaeology* 18:34–40.

———. 1968. *L'Art néolithique en Roumanie.* Bucharest: Meridiane.

———. 1970. "Édifice destiné au culte découvert dans la couche Boian-Spanţov de la station-tell de Căscioarele." *Dacia* 14:5–24.

———. 1979. *Arta Culturii Cucuteni.* Bucharest: Meridiane.

———. 1980. *The Neolithic Settlement at Rast.* International Series 72. Oxford: British Archaeological Reports.

Dundulienė, Pranė. 1990. *Senovės lietuvių mitologija ir religija.* Vilnius: Mokslas.

Efstratiou, Nikos. 1985. *Agios Petros: A Neolithic Site in the Northern Sporades.* International Series 241. Oxford: British Archaeological Reports.

Eliade, Mircea. [1951] 1991. *The Myth of the Eternal Return: Or, Cosmos and History.* Translated from the French by Willard R. Trask. Bollingen Series 46. Princeton: Princeton University Press.

Ellis, Linda. 1984. *The Cucuteni-Tripolye Culture.* International Series 217. Oxford: British Archaeological Reports.

Eogan, George. 1985. *Knowth and the Passage-Tombs of Ireland.* London: Thames and Hudson.

Ernout, Alfred. 1973. *Recueil de textes latins archaïques.* Paris: Klincksieck.

Evans, Arthur. 1921–36. *The Palace of Minos at Knossos.* 4 vols. London: Macmillan.

Evans, Christopher. 1988a. "Excavations at Haddenham, Cambridgeshire: A 'Planned' Enclosure and Its Regional Affinities." In *Enclosures and Defences in the Neolithic of Western Europe,* edited by Colin Burgess, Peter Topping, Claude Mordant, and Margaret Maddison. International Series 403. Oxford: British Archaeological Reports.

———. 1988b. "Monuments and Analogy: The Interpretation of Causewayed Enclosures." In *Enclosures and Defences in the Neolithic of Western Europe,* edited by Colin Burgess, Peter Topping, Claude Mordant, and Margaret Maddison. International Series 403. Oxford: British Archaeological Reports.

Evans, Estyn. 1966. *Prehistoric and Early Christian Ireland.* New Jersey: Barnes and Noble.

Evans, John Davies. 1959. *Malta.* Ancient Peoples and Places, vol. 11. London: Thames and Hudson.

———. 1971. *The Prehistoric Antiquities of the Maltese Islands: A Survey.* London: Athlone Press.

Everson, Michael. 1989. "Tenacity in Religion, Myth, and Folklore: The Neolithic Goddess of Old Europe Preserved in a Non-Indo-European Setting." *Journal of Indo-European Studies* 27 (3–4): 277–97.

Farnell, Lewis R. 1896–1909. *Cults of the Greek States.* Vols. 1–5. Oxford: Clarendon Press.

Ferguson, C. W., B. Huber, and H. E. Suess. 1966. "Determination of the Age of Swiss Lake Dwellings as an Example of Dendrochronologically Calibrated Radiocarbon Dating." *Zeitschrift für Naturforschung* 21a (7): 1173–77.

Fernandes-Miranda, M. 1983. *Neolitizacion en la peninsula Iberica.* Actes du Col-

loque "Premières communautés paysannes en Mèditerrranée occidentale."
Montpellier.

Fiala, F., and M. Hoernes. 1898. *Die neolithische Station von Butmir.* Part II. Vienna:
Verlag von Adolf Holzhausen.

Filip, Jan. 1962. *Celtic Civilization and Its Heritage.* New Horizons. Prague: Publishing House of the Czechoslovak Academy of Science.

Finlay, Ian. 1973. *Celtic Art: An Introduction.* London: Faber.

Fischer, Ulrich. 1956. *Die Gräber der Steinzeit im Saalegebiet.* Studien über neolithische und frühbronzezeitliche Grab-und Bestattungsformen in Sachsen-Thüringen.
Berlin: W. de Gruyter.

Flowers, Stephen. 1986. *Runes and Magic: Magical Formulaic Elements in the Older
Runic Tradition.* New York: P. Lang.

Fol, Alexander, Ivan Venedikov, Ivan Marazov, and Dimiter Popov. 1976. *Thracian Legends.* Sofia: Sofia Press.

Foster, Mary LeCron, and Lucy Jayne Botscharow, eds. 1990. *The Life of Symbols.*
Boulder, Colo.: Westview Press.

Fox, Robin Lane. 1988. *Pagans and Christians.* San Francisco: Harper and Row.

Frank, Roslyn M., and D. P. Metzger. 1989. *The Mother Goddess in Basque Oral Tradition.* University of Iowa.

Frank, Roslyn, Monique Laxalt, and Nancy Vosburg. 1977. "Inheritance, Marriage,
and Dowry Rights in the Navarrese and French Basque Law Codes." *IV Proceedings of the Western Society of French Historians:* 22–42.

Fraser, David. 1983. *Land and Society in Neolithic Orkney.* British Series 356. Oxford:
British Archaeological Reports.

Gallay, Alain, and Marie-Noelle Lahouze. 1976. "Pour une préhistoire de la met-
allurgie (Europe, Proche-Orient)." *Archives Suisses d'Anthropologie Générale* 40
(2): 137–200.

Gallis, K. J. 1985. "A Late Neolithic Foundation Offering from Thessaly." *Antiquity* 59:20–23.

Georgiev, Georgi I., N. Y. Merpert, R. V. Katinčarov, and D. G. Dimitrov. 1979. *Ezero,
rannobronzovoto selišče.* Sofia: Bulgarian Academy of Sciences.

Georgoulaki, Eleni. 1990. "The Minoan Sanctuary at Koumasa: The Evidence of
the Material." *Aegaeum* 6:5–23.

Giedion, Sigfried. 1962. *The Eternal Present: A Contribution on Constancy and Change.*
Bollingen Series 6, vol. 1, pt. 1. New York: Bollingen Foundation.

Giglioli, G. Q. 1935. *L'Arte Etrusca.* Milan.

Gimbutas, Marija. 1963. *The Balts.* Ancient People and Places, vol. 33. London:
Thames and Hudson.

———. 1974. *The Gods and Goddesses of Old Europe: 7000–3500 B.C.* London:
Thames and Hudson; Berkeley: University of California Press.

———. 1974a. "An Archaeologist's View of PIE* in 1975." *Journal of Indo-European
Studies* 2 (3): 289–307.

———. 1977. "The First Wave of Eurasian Steppe Pastoralists into Copper Age
Europe." *Journal of Indo-European Studies* 5 (4): 277–338.

———. 1980. "The Kurgan Wave # 2 (*c.* 3400–3200 B.C.) into Europe and the
Following Transformation of Culture." *Journal of Indo-European Studies* 8 (3–4):
273–315.

———. 1985. "Primary and Secondary Homeland of the Indo-Europeans: Comments on Gamkrelidze-Ivanov Articles." *Journal of Indo-European Studies* 13 (1–2): 185–202.

———. 1988. "The Pre-Christian Religion of Lithuania." *La Cristianizzazione della Lituania,* 13–25. Vatican: Libreria Editrice Vaticana.

———. 1989. *The Language of the Goddess.* San Francisco: Harper and Row.

———. 1991. *The Civilization of the Goddess: The World of Old Europe.* San Francisco: HarperSanFrancisco.

———. 1997. *The Kurgan Culture and the Indo-Europeanization of Europe.* Edited by Miriam Robbins Dexter and Karlene Jones-Bley. Monograph No. 18. Washington, D.C.: Institute for the Study of Man.

Gimbutas, Marija, ed. 1976. *Neolithic Macedonia (as Reflected by Excavations at Anza, Ovče Polje).* Monumenta Archaeologica 1. Los Angeles: University of California, Institute of Archaeology.

Gimbutas, Marija, Daniel Shimabuku, and Shan Winn et al. 1989. *Achilleion: A Neolithic Settlement in Thessaly, Northern Greece, 6400–5600 B.C.* Monumenta Archaeologica 14. Los Angeles: University of California, Institute of Archaeology.

Ginzburg, Carlo. 1991. *Ecstasies: Deciphering the Witches' Sabbath.* New York: Pantheon.

Giot, Pierre Roland. 1960. *Brittany.* Ancient Peoples and Places, vol. 13. London: Thames and London.

———. 1981. "The Megaliths of France." In *The Megalithic Monuments of Western Europe,* edited by Colin Renfrew, 18–29. London: Thames and Hudson.

Giot, Pierre Roland, Jean L'Helgouach, and Jean-Laurent Monnier. 1979. *Prehistoire de la Bretagne.* Rennes: Ouest-France.

Gitlin-Emmer, Susan. 1993. *Lady of the Northern Light: A Feminist Guide to the Runes.* Freedom, Calif.: Crossing Press.

Gjerstad, Einar. 1973. "Veiovis—a Pre-Indo-European God in Rome?" *Opuscula Romana* 9 (4): 35–42.

Gordon, Cyrus H. 1955. *Ugaritic Manual.* Rome: Pontifical Biblical Institute.

Gorodtsov, V. A. 1907. "Dnevnik arkheol. issledovanii v Bakhmutskom uyezde, Ekaterinoslavskoi gub. 1903 goda." *Trudy XIII Arkheol. Syezda* 1:286–378.

Göttner-Abendroth, Heide. 1983. *Die Göttin und ihr Heros.* Die Matriarchalen Religionen in Mythos, Märchen und Dichtung. 3rd ed. Munich: Frauenoffensive.

Graham, A. J. 1982. "The Colonial Expansion of Greece." In *The Cambridge Ancient History,* 83–162. Vol. 3. 2nd ed. Cambridge: Cambridge University Press.

Graham, J. W. 1987. *The Palaces of Crete.* Princeton: Princeton University Press.

Graves, Robert. 1955. *The Greek Myths.* 2 vols. Baltimore: Penguin Books.

Grbić, Miodrag, et al. 1960. *Porodin. Kasnoneolitsko naselje na Tumbi kod Bitolja.* Bitola: Archaeological Museum.

Green, Miranda. 1989. *Symbol and Image in Celtic Religious Art.* London: Routledge.

Greeves, T. A. P. 1975. "The Use of Copper in the Cucuteni-Tripolye Culture of South-East Europe." *Proceedings of the Prehistoric Society* 41:153–66.

Greimas, Algirdas Julien. 1979. *Apie dievus ir žmones: lietuvių mitoligijos studijos.* Chicago: A and M Publications. (French trans. by Edith Rechner: *Des dieux et des hommes: Études de mythologie lituanienne.* Paris: Presses Universitaires de France, 1985. English trans. by Milda Newman: *Of Gods and Men: Studies in Lithuanian Mythology.* Bloomington: Indiana University Press, 1992.)

Grygiel, R. 1986. "The Household Cluster as a Fundamental Social Unit of the

Brześć Kujawski Group of the Lengyel Culture in the Polish Lowlands." *Prace i Materiały* (Museum of Archaeology and Ethnology, Lódź) 31:43–271.

Guilaine, J., ed. 1976. *La Préhistoire française. 2: Civilisations néolithiques et proto-historiques*. Paris: Centre National Res. Sc.

Guyan, W. 1955a. *Das jungsteinzeitliche Moordorf von Thayngen-Weier*. Monographien zur Ur- und Frügeschichte der Schweiz. Vol. 2. Basel: Birkhäuser Verlag.

Guyan, W., ed. 1955b. *Das Pfahlbauproblem*. Basel: Birkhausen.

Haarmann, Harald. 1990. *Universalgeschichte der Schrift*. Frankfurt–New York: Campus Verlag.

————. 1990a. *Language in Its Cultural Embedding: Explorations in the Relativity of Signs and Sign Systems*. New York: Mouton de Gruyter.

————. 1996. *Early Civilization and Literacy in Europe: An Inquiry into Cultural Continuity in the Mediterranean World*. Berlin: Mouton de Gruyter.

Hägg, Robin, and Nanno Marinatos, eds. 1981. *Sanctuaries and Cults in the Aegean Bronze Age: Proceedings of the First International Symposium at the Swedish Institute in Athens, 12–13 May 1980*. Stockholm: Svenska Institutet, Athens.

————. 1987. *The Function of Minoan Palaces: Proceedings of the Fourth International Symposium at the Swedish Institute in Athens, 10–16 June 1984*. Stockholm: Svenska Institutet, Athens.

Haley, J. B. 1928. "The Coming of the Greeks I. The Geographical Distribution of Pre-Greek Place-Names." *American Journal of Archaeology* 32:141–55.

Hallam, B. R., S. E. Warren, and C. Renfrew. 1976. "Obsidian in the Western Mediterranean: Characterization by Neutron Activation Analysis and Optical Emission Spectroscopy." *Proceedings of the Prehistoric Society* 42:85–110.

Hanfmann, George M. A., and Jane C. Waldbaum. 1969. "Kybele and Artemis: Two Anatolian Goddesses at Sardis." *Archaeology* 22 (4): 264–69.

Hansen, Leigh Jellison. 1987. *Indo-European Views of Death and the Afterlife as Determined from Archeological, Mythological, and Linguistic Sources*. Ph.D. diss., University of California, Los Angeles.

Harrison, Jane Ellen. [1912] 1963. *Themis: A Study of the Social Origins of Greek Religion*. London: Merlin Press.

————. [1922] 1980. *Prolegomena to the Study of Greek Religion*. London: Merlin Press.

Hatt, Jean-Jacques. 1970. *Celts and Gallo-Romans*. Translated by James Hogarth. Archaeologia Mundi. Geneva: Nagel.

Hawkes, Jacquetta. 1969. *Dawn of the Gods: Minoan and Mycenaean Origins of Greece*. New York: Random House.

Hedges, John W. 1983. *Isbister. A Chambered Tomb in Orkney*. British Series 115. Oxford: British Archaeological Reports.

————. 1984. *Tomb of the Eagles*. London: J. Murray.

Hegedüs, Katalin, and J. Makkay. 1987. "Vésztö-Mágor: A Settlement of the Tisza Culture." In *The Late Neolithic of the Tisza Region*, edited by P. Raczky, 82–103. Budapest-S. Szolnok: Kossuth Press.

Hensel, W., and T. Wiślański, eds. 1979. *Prahistoria Ziem Polskich. Neolit*. Wrocław: Ossolineum.

Hensel, Zdzisław. 1991. "Copper Alloys in the Globular Amphorae Culture against a Comparative Background." In *New Tendencies in Studies of Globular Amphorae Culture*, 201–17. Warsaw University: Archaeologia Interregionalis.

Henshall, A. S. 1963. *The Chambered Tombs of Scotland*. Vol. 1. Edinburgh: Edinburgh University Press.

————. 1972. *The Chambered Tombs of Scotland*. Vol. 2. Edinburgh: Edinburgh University Press.

Herberger, Charles F. 1991. "The Labyrinth as an Emblem of the Womb, the Tomb, and Lunisolar Cyclical Time." *Griffith Observer* (March): 2–19.

Herity, Michael, and George Eogan. 1977. *Ireland in Prehistory*. London: Routledge and Kegan Paul.

Herodotus. [1920] 1975. *The History*. Translated by A. D. Godley. London: Heinemann.

Hirvonen, Kaarle. 1968. *Matriarchal Survivals and Certain Trends in Homer's Female Characters*. Annales Academiae Scientiarum Fennicae, Series B. Helsinki: Suomalainen Tiedeakatemia.

Hoddinott, B. 1989. "Thracian Goddesses and Priestesses in the Rogozen Treasure." In *The Rogozen Treasure*. Papers of the Anglo-Bulgarian Conference, 12 March 1987. Edited by B. F. Cook. London: British Museum Publications.

Hodgson, John. 1988. "Neolithic Enclosures in the Isar Valley, Bavaria." In *Enclosures and Defences in the Neolithic of Western Europe*, edited by Colin Burgess, Peter Topping, Claude Mordant, and Margaret Maddison. International Series 403. Oxford: British Archaeological Reports.

Hood, M. S. F. 1968. "The Tartaria Tablets." *Scientific American* (May): 30–37.

Hood, Sinclair. 1971. *The Minoans: Crete in the Bronze Age*. London: Thames and Hudson.

————. 1996. "Thera," in the 1996 *Grolier Multimedia Encyclopedia*.

Horský, Zdenek. 1986. "Vorläufige Untersuchungen über vermutliche astronomische Orientierung der neolithischen Kreisgrabenanlagen." *Internationales Symposium über die Lengyel-Kultur, 1984, Nitra-Wien*: 83–87.

Horváth, Ference. 1987. "A Survey on the Development of Neolithic Settlement Pattern and House Types in the Tisza Region." *Neolithic of Southeastern Europe and Its Eastern Connections*, 85–101. International Conference 1987 Szolnok-Szeged, Varia Archaeologica Hungarica II, Budapest.

Huld, Martin. 1990. "The Linguistic Typology of the Old European Substrate in North Central Europe." *Journal of Indo-European Studies* 18 (3–4): 389–423.

Ivanov, Ivan S. 1978. "Les Fouilles archéologiques de la nécropole chalcolithique à Varna, 1972–1975." *Studia Praehistorica* 1–2:13–27.

Ivinskis, Zenonas. 1986. *Rinktiniai rašai*, II. Rome.

Jacobsen, T. W., ed. 1988–91. *Excavations at Franchthi Cave, Greece*. Fascicles 1–7. Bloomington: Indiana University Press.

Jażdżewski, Konrad. 1981. *Pradzieje Europy środkowej*. Warsaw: Zakład Ossolińskich.

Jones, G. D. B. 1987. *Neolithic Settlement in the Tavoliere*. Vol. 1, *Apulia*. Society of Antiquaries Research Report 44. London: Thames and Hudson.

Jones-Bley, Karlene. 1989. *The Earliest Indo-European Burial Tradition in Neolithic Ireland*. Ph.D. diss., University of Michigan Microfilms Int., Ann Arbor.

————. 1990. "So That Fame Might Live Forever—the Indo-European Burial Tradition." *Journal of Indo-European Studies* 18 (1–2): 215–24.

————. 1997. "Defining Indo-European Burial." In *Varia on the Indo-European Past: Papers in Memory of Marija Gimbutas*, edited by Miriam Robbins Dexter and Edgar C. Polomé, 194–221. Washington, D.C.: Institute for the Study of Man.

Jonval, Michel. 1929. *Latviešu Mītoloģiskās Daiņas*. Paris: Picart.

Jouet, Philippe. 1989. *Religion et mythologie des Baltes: Une tradition indo-européenne*. Paris: Archè.

Joussaume, Roger. 1988. "Analyse Structure de la Triple Enceinte de Fossés Inter-rompus à Champ-durand, Nieul-Sur-L'Autize, Vendée." In *Enclosures and Defences in the Neolithic of Western Europe*, edited by Colin Burgess, Peter Topping, Claude Mordant, and Margaret Maddison. International Series 403. Oxford: British Archaeological Reports.

Jovanović, Borislav. 1969. "Chronological Frames of the Iron Gate Group of the Early Neolithic Period." *Archaeologia Iugoslavica* 10:23–38.

———. 1971. "Elements of the Early Neolithic Architecture in the Iron Gate Gorge and Their Functions." [Journal unknown.]

———. 1975a. "Les tumuli de la culture de steppes et fosses funéraires dans le bassin danubien." *Starinar* 26.

———. 1975b. "The Scordisci and Their Art." *The Celts in Central Europe, Alba Regia XIV*. Székesfehérvár.

———. 1978. "Early Gold and Eneolithic Copper Mining and Metallurgy of the Balkans and Danube Basin." *Studia Praehistorica* (Sofia) 1–2:192–97.

———. 1980. "The Origins of Copper Mining in Europe." *Scientific American* 242 (5): 152–68.

———. 1982. *Rudna Glava: Najstašije rudarstvo kadra na centralnom Balkanu*. Summary in German: Rudna Glava: Die älteste Kupferbau im Zentralbalkan. Belgrade-Bor: Institute of Archaeology Publications 17.

———. 1990. "Archaeometallurgy and Chronology of the Eneolithic Cultures of Central and South Balkans." *Macedoniae Acta Archaeologica* 10 (1985–86): 447–54.

Kaelas, Lili. 1981. "Megaliths of the Funnel Beaker Culture in Germany and Scandinavia." In *The Megalithic Monuments of Western Europe*, 77–91, edited by Colin Renfrew. 2nd ed. London: Thames and Hudson.

Kahil, L. 1979. "La Déesse Artémis: Mythologie et iconographie." In *Greece and Italy in the Classical World: Acta of the XI International Congress of Classical Archaeology, on Behalf of the International Association for Classical Archaeology, London, 3–9 September 1978, under the Sponsorship of the British Academy*, edited by J. N. Coldstream and M. A. R. Colledge, 73–87. London: National Organizing Committee, XI International Congress of Classical Archaeology.

Kalicz, Nándor. 1970. *Dieux d'argile*. Budapest: Corvina.

———. 1985. *Kökorifalu Aszódon*. Summary in German: Neolithisches Dorf in Aszód. Aszód: Petőfi Museum.

Kalicz, Nándor, and János Makkay. 1972. "Gefässe mit Gesichtsdarstellungen der Linienbandkeramik in Ungarn." *Idole, Prähistorische Keramiken aus Ungarn*. (Naturhistorisches Museum, Vienna) 7:9–15.

———. 1977. *Die Linienbandkeramik in der grossen Ungarischen Tiefebene*. Budapest: Akadémiai Kiadó.

Kandyba, O. 1937. *Schipenitz. Kunst und Geräte eines neolitischen Dorfes*. Bücher zur Ur- und Frühgeschichte, 5. Vienna and Leipzig: A. Schroll and Co.

Karmanski, Sergej. 1978. *Katalog antropomorfne idoloplastike i nalazi sa lokaliteta Mostonga I, II*. Odžaci: National University.

Kaul, Flemming, Ivan Marazov, Jan Best, and Nanny de Vries. 1991. *Thracian Tales on the Gundestrup Cauldron.* Publications of the Holland Travelling University, vol. 1. Amsterdam: Najade Press.

Keller, Werner. 1974. *The Etruscans.* Translated by Alexander Henderson and Elizabeth Henderson. New York: Alfred A. Knopf.

Kerényi, Carl. 1951. *The Gods of the Greeks.* Translated by Norman Cameron. New York: Thames and Hudson.

———. 1967. *Eleusis: Archetypal Image of Mother and Daughter.* Bollingen Series 65:4. New York: Pantheon Books.

———. 1976. *Dionysos: Archetypal Image of the Indestructible Life.* Translated by Ralph Mannheim. Bollingen Series 65:2. Princeton: Princeton University Press.

Kern, Otto. 1922. *Orphicorum Fragmenta.* Berlin: Weidmann.

Keuls, Eva C. 1985. *The Reign of the Phallus: Sexual Politics in Ancient Athens.* New York: Harper and Row.

Kośko, Aleksander. 1991. "Globular Amphorae Culture versus Funnel Beaker Culture." In *New Tendencies in Studies of Globular Amphorae Culture,* 87–113. Warsaw University: Archaeologia Interregionalis.

Kruts, V. A., and S. N. Ryzhov. 1983. "Raboty Talvanskogo otryada." *Arkheologicheskie Otkrytiia 1981 goda.*

Krzyszkowska, O., and L. Nixon, eds. 1983. *Minoan Society: Proceedings of the Cambridge Colloquium, 1981.* Bristol: Bristol Classical Press.

Kutzián, Ida Bognár. 1944. *The Körös Culture.* Vol. 1. Budapest: Dissertationes Pannonicae 2.

———. 1947. *The Körös Culture.* Vol. 2. Budapest: Dissertationes Pannonicae 23.

———. 1968. *The Early Copper Age in Hungary.* Budapest: Akadémiai Kiádo.

Lagodovska, O. F., O. G. Shaposhnikova, and M. L. Makarevich. 1962. *Mikhailivsk'e poseleniya.* Kiev: Akadema Nauk Ukrajins'kij SSR.

Larsson, Mats. 1985. *The Early Neolithic Funnel-Beaker Culture in Southwest Scania, Sweden: Social and Economic Change, 3000–2500 b.c.* International Series 264. Oxford: British Archaeological Reports.

Lasicius, Jan. [16th century] 1969. *De diis Samagitarum caeterumque Sarmatarum et falsorum christianorum* (About Samogitian, other Sarmation and false Christian gods). Vilnius.

Lazarovici, Gheorghe. 1979. *Neoliticul Banatului.* Muzeul de Istorie al Transilvaniei. Bibliotheca Musei Napcensis IV. Cluj: Napoca.

———. 1989. "Das neolithische Heiligtum von Parţa." In *Neolithic of Southeastern Europe and Its Eastern Connections,* 149–74. International Conference 1987 Szolnok-Szeged, Varia Archaeologica Hungarica II, Budapest.

———. 1991. "Venus de Zăuan. Despre credinţele şi practicile magico-religioase." *Acta Musei Porolissensis* 14–15:11–36.

Le Bonniec, Henri. 1958. *Le culte de Cérès à Rome, des origines à la fin de la République.* Paris: Klincksieck.

Leick, Gwendolyn. 1994. *Sex and Eroticism in Mesopotamian Literature.* London and New York: Routledge.

Leisner, Georg, and Vera Leisner. 1943. *Die Megalithgräber der Iberischen Halbinsel.* Vol. 1, *Der Süden.* Berlin: Walter de Gruyter.

———. [1956] 1959. *Die Megalithgräber der Iberischen Halbinsel.* Vol. 2, *Der Westen.* Berlin: Walter de Gruyter.

Lerner, Gerda. 1986. *The Creation of Patriarchy.* New York and Oxford: Oxford University Press.

Leroi-Gourhan, André. 1967. *Treasures of Prehistoric Art.* New York: H. N. Abrams.

Le Roux, Charles-Tanguy. 1985. *Gavrinis et les îles du Morbihan: Les mégalithes du golfe.* Guides Archéologiques de la France. Paris: Impr. National.

L'Helgouach, J. 1965. *Les Sépultures mégalithiques en Armorique, dolmens à couloir et allées couvertes.* Rennes: Travaux du Laboratoire d'Anthropologie Préhistorique de la Faculté des Sciences.

Lichardus, Ján, M. Lichardus-Itten, G. Bailloud, and J. Cauvin. 1985. *La Protohistoire de l'Europe: Le Néolithique et le Chalcolithique entre la Méditerranée et la mer Baltique.* Paris: Nouvelle Clio.

Lincoln, Bruce. 1991. *Death, War, and Sacrifice: Studies in Ideology and Practice.* Chicago: University of Chicago Press.

Lottner, C. 1870–72. "The Ancient Irish Goddess of War." *Revue Celtique* 1:32–55.

Lubell, Winifred Milius. 1994. *The Metamorphosis of Baubo.* Nashville: Vanderbilt.

Luca, S. A. 1990. "Festlegungen zur chronologischen und kulturgeschichtlichen Eingliederung der Statuete von Liubcova (Bezirk Caras-Severin)." In *Le Paléolithique et le Néolithique de la Roumanie en contexte européen,* edited by Vasile Chirica and Dan Monah. Iaşi: Institut d'Archéologie.

Lüning, J. 1967. "Die Michelsberger Kultur. Ihre Funde in zeitlicher und räumlicher Gliederung." *Berichte der Römisch-Germanischen Kommission* 48:3 ff, 297 ff.

———. 1982. "Research into the Bandkeramik Settlement of the Aldenhovener Platte in the Rhineland." *Analecta Praehistorica Leidensia* 15:1–29.

MacCana, Proinsias. 1970. *Celtic Mythology.* London: Hamlyn.

MacNamara, Ellen. 1991. *The Etruscans.* Cambridge: Harvard University Press.

MacNeill, M. 1962. *The Festival of Lughnasa.* Oxford: Oxford University Press.

Madsen, Torsten. 1979. "Earthen Long Barrows and Timber Structures: Aspects of the Early Neolithic Mortuary Practice in Denmark." *Proceedings of the Prehistoric Society* 45:301–20.

———. 1988. "Causewayed Enclosures in South Scandinavia." In *Enclosures and Defences in the Neolithic of Western Europe,* edited by Colin Burgess, Peter Topping, Claude Mordant, and Margaret Maddison. International Series 403. Oxford: British Archaeological Reports.

Makkay, J. 1969. "The Late Neolithic Tordos Group Signs." *Alba Regia* (Annales Musei Stephani Regis) 10:9–49.

———. 1976. "Problems Concerning Copper Age Chronology in the Carpathian Basin." *Acta Archaeologica Academiae Scientiarum Hungaricae* 28:251–300.

Malalas, John. 1691. *Joannis Antiocheni, cognomento Malalae, Historia chronica. Bibliothecae Bodleianae nunc primum edita cum interpret. and notis.* Oxford: E Theatro Sheldoniano.

Mallory, J. P. 1989. *In Search of the Indo-Europeans. Language, Archaeology, and Myth.* London: Thames and Hudson.

Malone, Caroline, Anthony Bonanno, Tancred Gouder, Simon Stoddart, and David Trump. 1993. "The Death Cults of Prehistoric Malta." *Scientific American* (December): 76–83

Mannhardt, Wilhelm. 1936. *Letto-Preussische Götterlehre.* Magazin der Lettisch-Literärischen Gesellschaft 21. Riga: Lettisch-Literärische Gesellschaft.

Manning, Stuart. 1989. "A New Age for Minoan Crete." *New Scientist* (Corpus Christi College, Cambridge) 11 February.

Marazov, I. 1979. *The Treasure from Yakimovo.* Sofia: Sofia Press.

———. 1988. "Neue Deutungen thrakischer Denkmäler." In *Der thrakische Silberschatz aus Rogosen, Bulgarien.* Sofia: Sofia Press.

———. 1989. "The Procession of Fantastic Animals." In *The Rogozen Treasure, Papers of the Anglo- Bulgarian Conference, 12 March 1987,* edited by B. F. Cook. London: British Museum Publications.

———. 1989a. *The Rogozen Treasure.* Sofia: Sofia Press.

Marinatos, Nanno. 1984. *Art and Religion in Thera: Reconstructing a Bronze Age Society.* Athens: Mathioulakis.

———. 1987. "Role and Sex Division in Ritual Scenes of Aegean Art." *Journal of Prehistoric Religion* 1:23–34.

———. 1993. *Minoan Religion: Ritual, Image, and Symbol.* Columbia: University of South Carolina Press.

Marinatos, Spiridon. 1972. *Treasures of Thera.* Athens: Commercial Bank of Greece.

Marinescu-Bîlcu, Silvia. 1974. *Cultura Precucuteni pe Teritoriul Romăniei.* Bucharest: Institutul de Arheologie.

Marinescu-Bîlcu, Silvia, and Barbu Ionescu. 1968. *Catalogue sculpturilor eneolitice din Muzeul raional Olteniţa.* Olteniţa.

Markale, Jean. 1979. *La Femme celte. Mythe et sociologie.* Paris: Payot.

Markevich, V. I. 1981. *Pozdne-Tripol'skie plemena Severnoi Moldavii.* Kishinev.

Marler, Joan, ed. 1997. *From the Realm of the Ancestors: Essays in Honor of Marija Gimbutas.* Manchester, Conn.: Knowledge, Ideas, and Trends.

Marshack, Alexander. 1972. *The Roots of Civilization: The Cognitive Beginnings of Man's First Art, Symbol, and Notation.* New York: McGraw-Hill.

———. 1976. "Some Implications of the Paleolithic Symbolic Evidence for the Origin of Language." *Current Anthropology* 17:274–82.

———. 1992. "The Origin of Language: An Anthropological Approach." In *Language Origin: A Multidisciplinary Approach,* edited by J. Wind et al., 421–48. The Netherlands: Kluwer Academic Publishers.

Mataša, C. 1946. *Frumuşica. Village préistorique à céramique peinte dans la Moldavia du Nord.* Bucharest.

———. 1964. "Asezarea eneolitica Cucuteni B de La Tîrgu Ocna-Podei (raionul Tîrgu Ocna, reg. Bacau)." *Arheologia Moldavei* (Bucharest) 2–3:11–66.

Matyushin, G. N. 1982. *Éneolit yuzhnogo Urala.* Moskva: Nauka.

Matz, Friedrich. 1962. *La Crète et la Grèce primitive: Prolégomènes à l'histoire de l'art grec.* Paris: Éditions Albin Michel.

McCone, Kim. 1986. "Werewolves, Cyclopes, *Díberga* and *Fíanna:* Juvenile Delinquency in Early Ireland." *Cambridge Medieval Celtic Studies* 12:1–22.

McPherron, Allan, and D. Srejovic. 1988. *Divostin and the Neolithic of Central Serbia.* Pittsburgh: Dept. of Anthropology, University of Pittsburgh.

Meaden, George Terence. 1991. *The Goddess of the Stones: The Language of the Megaliths.* Foreword by Marija Gimbutas. London: Souvenir Press.

Megaw, R., and V. Megaw. 1989. *Celtic Art.* London: Thames and Hudson.

Meisenheimer, Marita. 1989. *Das Totenritual, geprägt durch Jenseitsvorstellungen und Gesellschaftsrealität. Theorie des Totenrituals eines kupferzeitlichen Friedhofs zu Tiszapolgár-Basatanya (Ungarn).* British Archaeological Reports International Series, no. 475. Oxford: British Archaeological Reports.

Mellaart, James. 1967. *Çatal Hüyük: A Neolithic Town in Anatolia.* New York: McGraw-Hill.

Mellaart, James, Udo Hirsch, and Belkis Balpinar. 1989. *The Goddess from Anatolia*. Vols. 1–4. Milan: Eskenazi.

Menozzi, P., A. Piazza, and Luigi Luca Cavalli-Sforza. 1978. "Synthetic Maps of Human Gene Frequencies in Europeans." *Science* 201:786–92.

Mercer, R. J. 1988. "Hambledon Hill, Dorset, England." In *Enclosures and Defences in the Neolithic of Western Europe,* edited by Colin Burgess, Peter Topping, Claude Mordant, and Margaret Maddison. International Series 403. Oxford: British Archaeological Reports.

Merpert, N. 1991. "Die neolithisch-äneolithischen Denkmäler der pontischkaspischen Steppen und der Formierungsprozess der frühen Grubengrabkultur." In *Die Kupferzeit als historische Epoche,* edited by Jan Lichardus, 35–47. Bonn: R. Habelt.

———. 1992. "The Problem of the Transition between the North Balkan Eneolithic to the Early Bronze Age in the Light of New Exploration of the Upper Thracian Valley." Lecture. Europa Indo-Europea: The VI Conference of Thracology, Palma, Mallorca.

Midgley, M. S. 1985. *The Origin and Function of the Earthen Long Barrows of Northern Europe.* International Series 259. Oxford: British Archaeological Reports.

Milisauskas, Sarunas. 1978. *European Prehistory.* New York: Academic Press.

Milisauskas, Sarunas, and Janusz Kruk. 1991. "Utilization of Cattle for Traction during the Later Neolithic in Southeastern Poland." *Antiquity* 65:562–66.

Modderman, P. J. G. 1970. *Linearbankderamik aus Elsloo und Stein.* The Hague: Staatsuitgeverij.

Monaghan, Patricia. 1994. *O Mother Sun: A New View of the Cosmic Feminine.* Freedom, Calif.: Crossing Press.

Monah, Dan. 1990. "L'Exploitation du sel dans les Carpates Orientales et ses rapports avec la culture Cucuteni-Tripolye." In *Le Paléolithique et le Néolithique de la Roumanie en contexte européen,* edited by Vasile Chirica and Dan Monah. Iaşi: Institut d'Archéologie.

Moretti, Mario. 1970. *New Monuments of Etruscan Tomb Painting.* University Park: Pennsylvania State University Press.

Morgunova, N. L. 1986. "Khozyaistvo naseleniya volgo-uralskoi i samarskoi kul'tur." In *Problemy epokhi neolita stepnoi i lesostepnoi zony Vostochnoi Evropy,* 12–14. Orenburg.

Morris, Sarah P. 1989. "A Tale of Two Cities: The Miniature Frescoes from Thera and the Origins of Greek Poetry." *American Journal of Archaeology* 93 (4): 511–35.

Motz, Lotte. 1984. "The Winter Goddess: Percht, Holda, and Related Figures." *Folklore* 95 (2): 151–56.

Movsha, T. G. 1971. "Sviatilishcha tripol'skoi kul'tury." *Sovetskaya arkheologiia* (1): 201–5.

Movsha, T. G., and G. F. Chebotarenko. 1969. "Ėneoliticheskoe kurgannoe pogrebenie u st. Kainary v Moldavii." *Kratkie Soobshcheniya Instituta Arkheologii* 115:45–49.

Müller-Beck, Hansjürgen. 1961. "Prehistoric Swiss Lake Dwellers." *Scientific American* 205 (6): 138–47.

———. 1965. *Seeberg, Burgäschisee-Süd.* Vol. 5, *Holzgeräte und Holzbearbeitung.* Acta Bernensia II. Bern.

Müller-Karpe, Hermann. 1968. "Jungsteinzeit." *Handbuch der Vorgeschichte.* Vol. 2. Munich: C. H. Beck.

———. 1984. "Kupferzeit." In *Handbuch der Vorgeschichte*. Vol. 3. Munich: C. H. Beck.

Murray, Jacqueline. 1970. *The First European Agriculture*. Edinburgh: Edinburgh University Press.

Nauck, Augustus. 1886. *Porphyrii Philosophi Platonici*. Leipzig: Teubner

———. 1889. *Tragicorum Graecorum Fragmenta*. Leipzig: Teubner.

Necrasov, Olga. 1981. "Les Populations de la period de transition du Néo-Enéolithique à l'Âge du Bronze romaine et leurs particularités anthropologiques." In *Anthropologie et archéologie: Les cas de premiers âges de Metaux*, edited by Roland Menk and Alain Gallay. *Actes du Symposium de Sils-Maria 25–30 septembre 1979*. Geneva.

Němejcová-Pavúková, V. 1986. "Siedlung und Kreisgrabenanlagen der Lengyel Kultur in Svodin (Südslowakei)." *Internationales Symposium über die Lengyel-Kultur, 1984, Nitra-Wien:* 177–83.

———. 1986a. "Vorbericht über die Ergebnisse der systematischen Grabung in Svodin in den Jahren 1971–83." *Slovenska Archeologia* 34:133–73.

Nemeskéri, János. 1978. "Demographic Structure of the Vlasac Epipaleolithic Population." In *Vlasac, Mezolitsko naselje i Džerdapu*, edited by M. Garašanin, 97–133. Belgrade: Srpska Akademija Nauka i Umetnosti.

Neugebauer, J. W. 1983–84. "Befestigungen und Kultanlagen des Mittelneolithikums in Niederösterreich am Beispiel von Falkenstein-Schanzboden und Friebritz." *Mitteilung der österreichischen Arbeitsgemeinschaft für Ur- un Frühgeschichte* 33–34:175–88.

———. 1986. "Erdgrossbauten der älteren Stufe der Lengyel-Kultur." *Internationales Symposium über die Lengyel-Kultur, 1984, Nitra-Wien:* 185–94.

Nielsen, Paul Otton. 1985. "The First Farmers from the Early TRB Culture at Sigerstad." *Tilegnet Carl Johan Becker. Aarbøger for nordisk Oldkyndighed og Historie 1984*. Danish with English summary. Copenhagen.

Niemeier, W.-D. 1986. "Zur Deutung des Thronraumes im Palast von Knossos." *Mitteilungen der deutschen archäologischen Instituts, Athenische Abteilung* 101:63–95.

Nikolov, Bogdan. 1974. *Gradechnitza*. Sofia: Nauka i Iskustvo.

———. 1976. "Mogilni pogrebeniya ot rannobronzovata epokha pri Tarnava i Knezha, Vrachanski okrag." *Arkheologija* (Sofia) 3:38–51.

Nikolov, V. 1987. "Das Flusstal der Struma als Teil der Strasse von Anatolien nach Mitteleuropa." In *Neolithic of Southeastern Europe and Its Eastern Connections:* 191–99. International Conference 1987 Szolnok-Szeged, Varia Archaeologica Hungarica II, Budapest.

———. 1990. "Die neolithische Siedlung Slatina in Sofia (Ausgrabungen im Jahre 1985)." *Studia Praehistorica* 10:77–85.

Nilsson, M. P. [1927] 1950. *The Minoan-Mycenaean Religion and Its Survival in Greek Religion*. Lund: C. W. K. Gleerup.

Nosek, Stefan. 1967. *Kultura amfor kulistych w Polsce*. Wrocław-Warsaw-Kraków: Ossolineum.

O'Kelly, Michael J. 1982. *Newgrange: Archaeology, Art, and Legend*. London: Thames and Hudson.

Olària, Carme. 1988. *Cova Fosca. Un asentamiento meso-neolítico de cazadores y pastores en la serrania del Alto Maestrazgo, Castellon*. Monografies de Prehistoria i Arquelogia Castellonenques 3.

O'Sullivan, Muiris. 1986. "Approaches to Passage Tomb Art." *Journal of the Royal Society of Antiquaries of Ireland* 116:68–83.

Özdoğan, Mehmet. 1987. "Neolithic Cultures of Northwestern Turkey: A General Appraisal of the Evidence and Some Considerations." In *Neolithic of Southeastern Europe and its Eastern Connections,* 201–16. International Conference 1987 Szolnok-Szeged, Varia Archaeologica Hungarica II, Budapest.

Özdoğan, Mehmet, and Nilgün Özbaşaran Dede. 1989. "1989 Yili Toptepe Kurtarma Kazisi." (Excavation at Toptepe in eastern Thrace, 1989.) *Arkeoloji ve sanat* 13 (46–49): 2–24.

Özdoğan, Mehmet, Yutaka Miyake, and Nilgün Özbaşaran Dede. 1991. "An Interim Report on Excavations at Yarimburgas and Toptepe in Eastern Thrace." *Anatolica* 17.

Packard, David W. 1974. *Minoan Linear A.* Berkeley and Los Angeles: University of California Press.

Pallottino, Massimo. [1954] 1968. *Testimonia Linguae Etruscae.* Florence "La Nuova Italia" Editrice.

———. [1955] 1975. *The Etruscans.* Translated by J. Cremona. Bloomington: Indiana University Press.

Panajotov, Ivan. 1989. *Yamnata kultura v bulgarskite zemi.* Razkopki i Prouchivaniya. Sofia: Bulgarian Academy of Sciences.

Panajotov, I., and V. A. Dergačev. 1984. "Die Ockergrabkultur in Bulgarien." *Studia Praehistorica* 7:99–116.

Passek, T. S. 1949. "Periodizatiia tripol'skikh poselenii." *Materialy i issledovaniya po arkheologii SSSR* (Moscow) 10:194–275.

Pavúk, Juraj. 1990. "Siedlung der Lengyel-Kultur mit Palisadenanlagen in Žlkovce, Westslowakei." *Jahresschrift für Mitteldeutschen Vorgeschichte* 73:137–42.

———. 1991. "Lengyel-Culture Fortified Settlements in Slovakia." *Antiquity* 65:348–57.

Peltenburg, E. J. 1988. "A Cypriot Model for Prehistoric Ritual." *Antiquity.*

Peltenburg, Edgar, and Elizabeth Coring. 1991. "Terracotta Figurines and Ritual at Kissonerga-Mosphilia." *Terracottas:* 17–26.

Pestrikova, V. I. 1987. *Khvalynski éneoliticheski mogil'nik kak istorichesky i istochnik.* Aftoreferat Diss. Moscow.

Petrenko, A. G. 1984. *Drevnee in srednevekovoe zhivotnovodstvo srednego Povolzh'ya i Predural'ya.* Moscow: Nauka.

Petrescu-Dîmboviţa, Mircea. 1963. "Die wichtigsten Ergebnisse der archäologischen Ausgrabungen in der neolithischen Siedlung von Truşeşti (Moldau)." *Prähistorische Zeitschrift* (Berlin) 41:172–86.

———. 1966. *Cucuteni. Monumentele Patriei Nostre.* Bucharest: Editúra Republicii Populare Romîne

Phillips, Patricia. 1975. *Early Farmers of West Mediterranean Europe.* London: Hutchinson.

———. 1982. *The Middle Neolithic in Southern France: Chasseen Farming and Culture Process.* International Series 142. Oxford: British Archaeological Reports.

Piazza, A., S. Rendine, P. Menozzi, J. Mountain, and Luigi Luca Cavalli-Sforza. 1992. *Genetics and the Origin of Indo-European Languages.* Stanford: Stanford University Press.

Piggott, Stuart. 1962. *The West Kennet Long Barrow.* London: HMSO.

———. 1965. *Ancient Europe, from the Beginnings of Agriculture to Classical Antiquity: A Survey.* Chicago: Aldine.

———. 1992. *Wagon, Chariot, and Carriage.* London: Thames and Hudson.

Platon, N. 1968. *Crete*. Paris: Nagel.

———. 1971. *Zakros: The Discovery of a Lost Palace of Ancient Crete*. New York: Scribners.

———. 1983. "The Minoan Palaces: Centres of Organization of a Theocratic Social and Political System." In *Minoan Society: Proceedings of the Cambridge Colloquium, 1981*, edited by O. Krzyszkowska and L. Nixon, 273–76. Bristol: Bristol Classical Press.

Pleslová-Štiková, Emilie. 1980. "Square Enclosures of Old Europe, 5th and 4th Millenia B.C." *Journal of Indo-European Studies* 8 (1–2): 61–74.

Pleslová-Štiková, Emilie, František Marek, and Zdenek Horský. 1980. "A Square Enclosure of Funnel Beaker Culture (3500 B.C.) at Makotřasy (Central Bohemia): A Palaeoastronomic Structure." *Archaeologické rozhledy* 32.

Podborský, Vladimir. 1985. *Těšetice-Kyjovice*. Vol. 2. Brno: Masaryk University.

———. 1988. *Těšetice-Kyjovice*. Vol. 4. Brno: Masaryk University.

———. 1989. "Neolithische Kultsitten der Bevölkerung im mährischen Gebiet." In *Religion und Kult*, 175–191. Berlin.

Poetscher, W. 1990. *Aspekte und Probleme der minoischen Religion*. Religionswissenschaftliche Texte und Studien, Band 4. Hildesheim: Georg Olms Verlag.

Pokorny, Julius. 1959. *Indogermanisches Etymologisches Wörterbuch*. Vol. 1. Bern: Francke.

Polomé, Edgar C. 1987. "Freyja." In *The Encyclopedia of Religion,* edited by Mircea Eliade. Vol. 5. New York: Macmillan. "Njǫrðr" in Vol. 10.

———. 1989. "Divine Names in Indo-European." In *Essays on Germanic Religion,* 55–67. Journal of Indo-European Studies Monograph, no. 6. Washington, D.C.: Institute for the Study of Man.

———. 1989a. "Germanic Religion: An Overview." In *Essays on Germanic Religion,* 68–137. Journal of Indo-European Studies Monograph, no. 6. Washington, D.C.: Institute for the Study of Man.

———. 1990. "The Indo-Europeanization of Northern Europe: The Linguistic Evidence." *Journal of Indo-European Studies* 18 (3–4): 331–38.

———. 1996. "Beer, Runes, and Magic." *Journal of Indo-European Studies* 24 (1–2): 99–105.

Popov, D. 1980. "Artemis Brauro (déese thraco-pélasgique)." In *Interaction and Acculturation in the Mediterranean,* edited by Jan G. P. Best and Nanny M. W. de Vries. Proceedings of the Second International Congress of Mediterranean Pre- and Proto-History, Amsterdam, 19–23 Nov. 1980. Amsterdam: B. R. Grüner.

Popov, R. 1916–1918. "Kodža-Dermenskata mogila pri gr. Šumen." *Izvestije na Bulgarskoto Arkheologičesko Družestvo* 6:71–155.

Powell, T. G. E. 1958. *The Celts*. New York: Praeger.

Preuss, Joachim, ed. 1992. *Das Neolithikum in Mitteleuropa*. Berlin: Deutscher Verlag der Wissenschaften.

Puhvel, Jaan. 1970. "Aspects of Equine Functionality." In *Myth and Law among the Indo-Europeans,* edited by Jaan Puhvel, 159–72. Berkeley and Los Angeles: University of California Press.

———. 1984. "Etruscan Inscriptions at the J. Paul Getty Museum." *The J. Paul Getty Museum Journal* 12:163–66.

Quitta, Hans. 1958. "Die Ausgrabungen in der bandkeramischen Siedlung Zwenkau-Harth, Kr. Leipzig." *Neue Ausgrabungen in Deutschland*. Mann and Berlin: Verlag Gebr.

Raczky, Pal, ed. 1987. *The Late Neolithic of the Tisza Region*. Budapest: Kossuth Press.

Radimsky, W., and M. Hoernes. 1895. *Die neolithische Station von Butmir*. Vol. 1. Vienna: Verlag von Adolf Holzhausen.

Ray, B. C. 1987. "Stonehenge: A New Theory." *History of Religions*: 226–78.

Renfrew, Colin. 1972. "The Autonomy of the Southeast European Copper Age." *Proceedings of the Prehistoric Society* 35:12–47.

———. 1972a. *The Emergence of Civilisation: The Cyclades and the Aegean in the Third Millennium B.C.* London: Methuen and Company.

———. 1984. *Approaches to Social Archaeology*. Cambridge: Harvard University Press.

Renfrew, Colin, ed. 1974. *British Prehistory, a New Outline*. London: Duckworth.

———. 1979. *Investigations in Orkney*. Society of Antiquaries of London, no. 38. London: Thames and Hudson.

———. 1983. *The Megalithic Monuments of Western Europe*. London: Thames and Hudson.

Renfrew, Colin, Marija Gimbutas, and Ernestine S. Elster, eds. 1986. *Excavations at Sitagroi: A Prehistoric Village in Northeast Greece*. Vol. 1. Monumenta Archaeologica 13. Los Angeles: University of California, Institute of Archaeology.

Renfrew, Jane M. 1973. *Palaeoethnobotany: The Prehistoric Foodplant of the Near East and Europe*. London: Methuen and Company.

Reusch, Helga. 1961. "Zum Problem des Thronraumes in Knossos." In *Minoica und Homer*, 39 ff. Berlin.

Rezepkin, A. D. 1992. "Paintings from a Tomb of the Majkop Culture." *Journal of Indo-European Studies* 20 (1–2): 59–71.

Rice, Patricia C. 1981. "Prehistoric Venuses: Symbols of Motherhood or Womanhood." *Journal of Anthropological Research* 37 (4): 402–14.

Richardson, Emeline. 1964. *The Etruscans: Their Art and Civilization*. Chicago: University of Chicago Press.

Rimantienė, Rimutė. 1984. *Akmens amžius Lietuvoje*. Vilnius: Mokslas.

Rodden, R. J. 1965. "An Early Neolithic Village in Greece." *Scientific American* 212:82–92.

Roska, Márton. 1941. *Die Sammlung Zsófia von Torma in der numismatisch-archaeologischen Abteilung der Siebenbürgischen National Museum*. Koloszvàr-Cluj.

Ross, Anne. 1967. *Pagan Celtic Britain: Studies in Iconography and Tradition*. London: Routledge and Kegan Paul.

———. 1970. *The Everyday Life of the Pagan Celts*. New York: Putnam.

———. 1986. *The Pagan Celts*. New Jersey: Barnes and Noble.

Ruggles, C. L. N. 1984. *Megalithic Astronomy: A New Archaeological and Statistical Study of 300 Western Scottish Sites*. International Series 123. Oxford: British Archaeological Reports.

Rutkowski, B. 1986. *The Cult Places of the Aegean*. New Haven: Yale University Press.

Säflund, Gösta. 1981. "Cretan and Theran Questions." In *Sanctuaries and Cults in the Aegean Bronze Age,* edited by Robin Hägg and Nanno Marinatos, 189–212. Proceedings of the First International Symposium at the Swedish Institute in Athens, 12–13 May 1980. Stockholm: Svenska Institutet, Athens.

Sakellarakis, Y., and E. Sakellarakis. 1981. "Drama of Death in a Minoan Temple." *National Geographic* 159:205–22.

Scarre, Christopher, ed. 1984. *The Neolithic of France.* Edinburgh: Edinburgh University Press.

Schmandt-Besserat, D. 1979. "An Archaic Recording System in the Uruk-Jemdet Nasr Period." *American Journal of Archaeology* 83:19–48, 375.

Schmidt, H. 1903. "Tordos." *Zeitschrift für Ethnologie* 35:438–69.

———. 1932. *Cucuteni in der oberen Moldau, Rumänien. Die befestigte Siedlung mit bemalter Keramik von der Stein-Kupferzeit bis in die vollentwickelte Bronzezeit.* Berlin: Walter de Gruyter.

Schmidt, R. R. 1945. *Die Burg Vučedol.* Zagreb: Ausgabe des Kroatischen Archäologischen Staatsmuseums.

Shackleton, N., and Colin Renfrew. 1970. "Neolithic Trade Routes Re-aligned by Oxygen Isotope Analysis." *Nature* 228:1062.

———. 1970a. "Neolithic Trade Routes." *Nature* 228:1062–65.

Shapiro, M. 1983. "Baba Jaga: A Search for Mythopoeic Origins and Affinities." *International Journal of Slavic Linguistics and Poetics* 27:109–35.

Shilov, V. P. 1975. "Modeli skotovodcheskikh khozyaystv stepnikh oblastei Evrazii v ėpochu ėneolita i rannego bronzovogo veka." *Sovetskaya Archeologiya* 1:5–16.

Shishkin, K. V. 1973. "Z praktyky Deshyvruvannya aerofotoznimkiv u arkheologichnykh tsilyakh." *Arkheolohiya* (Kiev) 10:32–41.

Shmaghi, Nikolai M. 1986. "O sotsial'no-demograficheskoi rekonstruktsii krupnykh tripol'skikh poselenii." *Internationales Symposium über die Lengyel-Kultur, 1984, Nitra-Wien:* 257 ff.

Shnirelman, Victor A. 1992. "The Emergence of a Food-Producing Economy in the Steppe and Forest-Steppe Zones of Eastern Europe." *Journal of Indo-European Studies* 20 (1–2): 123–45.

Shtiglits, M. S. 1971. "Razvedki tripol'skikh pamyatnikov v rayone Umani." *Arkheologicheskie Otkrytiia.*

Simon, Erika. 1969. *Die Götter der Griecher.* Munich: Hirmer.

Simon, Erika, ed. 1989. *Minoische und griechische Antiken.* Die Sammlung Kiseleff im Martin-von-Wagner-Museum der Universität Würzburg 2. Mainz: Philipp von Zabern.

Simoska, Dragica, and Vojislav Sanev. 1976. *Praistorija vo centralna Pelagonija.* Bitola: Naroden Muzej.

Smith, Isobel F., ed. 1965. *Windmill Hill and Avebury: Excavations by Alexander Keiller, 1925–1939.* Oxford: Oxford University Press.

Sokal, Robert R., Neal Oden, and Barbara Thompson. 1992. "Origins of the Indo-Europeans: Genetic Evidence." *Proc. National Acad. Science [Population Biology]:* 7669–73.

Srejović, Dragoslav. 1969. "The Roots of the Lepenski Vir Culture." *Archaeologia Iugoslavica* 10:13–21.

———. 1972. *Europe's First Monumental Sculpture: New Discoveries at Lepenski Vir.* London: Thames and Hudson.

Srejović, Dragoslav, and L. Babović. 1983. *Umetnost Lepenskog Vira.* Belgrade: Narodni Muzej.

Srejović, Dragoslav, and Zagorka Letica. 1978. *Vlasac: A Mesolithic Settlement in the Iron Gates.* Vlasac: Mezolitsko Naselje u Derdapu, Belgrade: Serbian Academy of Sciences and Arts.

Stanković, Svetozar. 1986. *Žrtvenici i prosopomorfni poklopci iz Vinče.* Archeological Research. Vol. 7. Belgrade: University of Belgrade.

Strabo. 1866–77. *Strabonis Geographica,* edited by Augustus Meineke. Leipsig: Teubner.

Sturluson, Snorri. 1929. *The Prose Edda.* Translated by Arthur Brondeur. New York: American Scandinavian Foundation.

Tanda, Giuseppa. 1984. *Arte e religione della Sardegna preistorica nella necropoli di Sos Furrighesos-Anela (SS).* Vol. 1–2. Sassari: Chiarella.

Tasić, N. 1957. "Praistorisko naselje kod Valača." (Prehistoric settlement at Valač.) In *Glasnik Muzeja Kosova i Metohije,* 4–5. Vol. 1. Priština: Muzej.

———. 1973. *Neolitska plastika.* Belgrade: Gradskij Muzej.

Telegin, Dmitriy Yakolerich. 1973. *Seredn'o-Stogivs'ka kul'tura ĕpokhi midi.* Kiev.

———. 1986. *Dereivka: A Settlement and Cemetery of Copper Age Horse Keepers on the Middle Dnieper.* International Series 287. Oxford: British Archaeological Reports.

Telegin, D. Yakolerich, and I. D. Potekhina. 1987. *Neolithic Cemeteries and Populations in the Dnieper Basin,* edited by J. P. Mallory. Translated from the Russian by V. A. Tikhomirov. Internationals Series 383. Oxford: British Archaeological Reports.

Tessier, Albert. 1917. *De la condition de la femme au pays basque dans l'ancien droit.* La Chapelle-Montligeon (Orne): Montligeon.

Theocharis, D. R. 1973. "The Neolithic Civilization: A Brief Survey." In *Neolithic Greece,* edited by S. Papadopoulos. Athens: National Bank of Athens.

Thimme, Jürgen, ed. 1980. *Kunst und Kultur Sardiniens von Neolithikum bis zum Ende der Nuraghenzeit.* Catalog of the exhibit.

Thom, A., and A. S. Thom. 1978. *Megalithic Remains in Britain and Brittany.* Oxford: Clarendon Press.

Thom, A., A. S. Thom, and A. Burl. 1980. *Megalithic Rings.* International Series 80. Oxford: British Archaeological Reports.

Thomas, C. G. 1973. "Matriarchy in Early Greece: The Bronze and Dark Ages." *Arethusa* 6 (2): 173–95.

Thomas, Julian. 1991. *Rethinking the Neolithic.* Cambridge: Cambridge University Press.

Thorsson, Eldred. 1987. *Runelore.* York Beach: Samuel Wieser.

Tiné, Santo. 1983. *Passo di Corvo e la civiltà neolitica del Tavoliere.* Genoa: Sagep Editrice.

Titov, V. S. 1969. *Neolit Grestsii. Periodizatsiya i khronologiya.* Moscow: Nauka.

Todorova, Henrieta. 1974. "Kultszene und Hausmodell aus Ovčarovo, Bez. Targovište." *Thracia* (Sofia) 3:39–46.

———. 1976. *Ovčarovo. Praistoričeska selištcna mogila.* Sofia: Bulgarian Academy of Sciences.

———. 1978a. "Die Nekropole bei Varna und die sozialäkonomischen Probleme am Ende des Äneolithikums Bulgariens." *Zeitschrift für Archäologie* 12:87–97

———. 1978b. *The Eneolithic Period in Bulgaria in the Fifth Millennium B.C.* Translated by Vessela Zhelyaskova. International Series (Supplementary) 49. Oxford: British Archaeological Reports.

———. 1989a. "Ein Korrelationsversuch zwischen Klimaänderungen und prähistorischen Angaben." *Praehistorica* (Praha) 15:25–28.

———. 1989b. *Tell Karanovo und das Balkan-Neolithikum.* Institut für Klasische Archälogie, Universtät.

Todorova, Henrieta, S. Ivanov, V. Vasilev, H. Hopf, H. Quitta, and G. Kohl. 1975. *Seliščnata Mogila pri Goljamo Delčevo*. Sofia: Bulgarian Academy of Sciences.

Todorovič, Jovan. 1971. "Written Signs in the Neolithic Culture of Southeastern Europe." *Archaeologia Iugoslavica* 10 (1969): 74–84, tables 1–11.

Todorovič, Jovan, and Aleksandrina Cermanovič. 1961. *Banjica, naselje vinčanske kulture*. (Banjica, Siedlung der Vinča-Gruppe). Belgrade: City Museum.

Torma, Zsófia. 1894. *Ethnographische Analogieen: Ein Beitrag zur Gestaltungs- und Entwicklungsgechiete der Religionen*. Jena: H. Costenoble.

Tringham, Ruth, and Dušan Krstić. 1990. *Selevac: A Neolithic Village in Yugoslavia*. Monumenta Archaeologica 15. Los Angeles: University of California, Institute of Archaeology.

Trump, David H. 1972. *Malta: An Archaeological Guide*. London: Faber and Faber.

———. 1983. *La Grotta di Filiestru a Bonu Ighinu, Mara (SS)*. Quaderni della Soprentendenze ai Beni Archeologici per le provincie di Sassari e Nuoro, 13: Dessi, Sassari.

Tsountas, Christos. 1908. *Proistorikae Akropolis Diminiou kai Sesklou*. (The prehistoric Acropolis of Dimini and Sesklo.) Athens: A. D. Sakellariou.

Turville-Petre, E. O. G. 1964. *Myth and Religion of the North*. New York: Holt, Rinehart, Winston.

Twohig, Elizabeth Shee. 1981. *The Megalithic Art of Western Europe*. Oxford: Clarendon Press.

Udolph, Jürgen. 1994. *Namenkundliche Studien zum Germanenproblem*. Berlin and New York: Walter de Gruyter.

Ursachi, V. 1990. "Le Dépot d'objects de parure énéolithique de Brad, com. Negri, dép. de Bacău." In *Le Paléolithique et le Néolithique de la Roumanie en contexte européen*, edited by Vasile Chirica and Dan Monah. Iași: Institut d'Archéologie.

Usačiovaitė, Elvyra. 1996. "Customs of the Old Prussians." In *The Indo-Europeanization of Northern Europe*, edited by Karlene Jones-Bley and Martin E. Huld, 204–17. Washington, D.C.: Institute for the Study of Man.

Van Berg, P. L. 1990. "Aspects de la recherche sur le Néolithique de la Roumanie en contexte européen." In *Le Paléolithique et le Néolithique de la Roumanie en contexte européen*, edited by Vasile Chirica and Dan Monah. Iași: Institut d'Archéologie.

Van de Velde, Pieter. 1979. *On Bandkeramik Social Structure: Analysis of Pot Decoration and Hut Distributions from the Central European Neolithic Communities of Elsloo and Hienheim*. Analecta Praehistorica Leidensia, 12. Leiden: Leiden University Press.

Vankina, L. V. 1970. *Torfyanikovaya stoyanka Sarnate*. Riga: Zinatne.

Vasić, Miloje M. 1932–36. *Preistoriska Vinča*. 4 vols. Belgrade: Izdanje Drzavne Stamparije.

Vasil'ev, I. B. 1981. *Eneolit Povolzh'ya: step' i lesotep'*. Kuibyshev: Kuibyshevskii Gosudarstvennyi Pedagogic'eskij Institut.

Vasil'ev, I. B., and A. A. Bybornov. 1986. "Nizhnee Povolzh'e v epokhu kamnya i bronzy." *Drevnyaya i Srednevekovaya Istoriya Nizhnego Povolzh'ya* (Saratov University): 3–20.

Vasil'ev, I. B., and G. Mat'eeva. 1976. "Poselenie i mogil'nik u sela S'ezzhee." In *Ocherki istorii i kul'tury Povolzh'ya*. Kuibyshev: Kuibyshevskii Gosudarstvennyi Pedagogic'eskij Institut.

Vėlius, Norbertus. 1983. *Senovės baltupasaulēžiūra.* (The world outlook of the ancient Balts.) Vilnius: Mintis.

Vogt, E. 1951. "Das steinzeitliche Uferdorf Egolzwill 3 (Kt. Luzern)." *Der Zeitschrift für schweizerische Archäologie und Kunstgeschichte* 12 (4): 193–215.

———. 1954. "Pfahlbaustudien." In *Das Pfahlbauproblem,* edited by W. V. Guyan, 199–212. Basel: Birkhausen.

Vosniak, Z. 1975. "Die Kelten und die Latènekultur auf den Thrakischen Gebieten." In *The Celts in Central Europe, Alba Regia XIV.* Székesfehérvár.

Vries, Nanny M. W. de 1984. "Die Stellung der Frau in der thrakischen Gesellschaft." In *Dritter Internationaler Thrakologischer Kongress zu Ehren W. Tomascheks, 2–6 Juni 1980, Wien.* Vol. 2. Sofia: Swjat.

———. 1991. See Kaul, Flemming, et al.

Vulpe, R. 1957. *Izvoare: Sapaturile din 1936–1948.* (Summaries in Russian and French: Izvoare: Les Fouilles de 1936–1948.) Bucharest: Biblioteca de Arheologie.

Wace, A. J. B., and M. S. Thompson. 1912. *Prehistoric Thessaly.* London: Cambridge University Press.

Wainwright, G. J. 1968. "Durrington Walls: A Ceremonial Enclosure of the 2nd Millennium B.C." *Antiquity* 42:20–26.

———. 1969. "A Review of Henge Monuments in the Light of Recent Research." *Proceedings of the Prehistoric Society* 35:112–33.

———. 1970. "Woodhenge." *Scientific American* 223:30–38.

———. 1971. "The Excavation of a Later Neolithic Enclosure at Marden, Wiltshire." *Antiquaries Journal* 51:177–239.

———. 1979. *Mount Pleasant, Dorset: Excavations 1970–71.* Reports of the Research Committee of the Society of Antiquaries of London, no 37. London: Society of Antiquaries.

———. 1989. *The Henge Monuments: Ceremony and Society in Prehistoric Britain.* London: Thames and Hudson.

Wainwright, G. J., and L. H. Longworth. 1971. *Durrington Walls: Excavations 1966–68.* Reports of the Research Committee of the Society of Antiquaries of London, no 29. London: Society of Antiquaries.

Walberg, Gisela. 1986. *Tradition and Innovation: Essays in Minoan Art.* Mainz: Verlag Philipp von Zabern.

Warren, Peter. 1981. "Minoan Crete and Ecstatic Religion." In *Sanctuaries and Cults in the Aegean Bronze Age,* edited by Robin Hägg and Nanno Marinatos. Proceedings of the First International Symposium at the Swedish Institute in Athens, 12–13 May 1980. Stockholm: Svenska Institutet, Athens.

———. 1988. *Minoan Religion as Ritual Action.* Studies in Mediterranean Archaeology and Literature, pocket-book 72. Göteborg: Paul Åströms förlag.

Weinberg, Saul S. 1962. "Excavations at Prehistoric Elateia, 1959." *Hesperia* 31:158–209.

Whittle, Alasdair. 1977. "Earlier Neolithic Enclosures in North-West Europe." *Proceedings of the Prehistoric Society* 43:329–48.

———. 1985. *Neolithic Europe: A Survey.* Cambridge: Cambridge University Press.

———. 1988. "Contexts, Activities, Events—Aspects of Neolithic and Copper Age Enclosures in Central and Western Europe." In *Enclosures and Defences in the Neolithic of Western Europe,* edited by Colin Burgess, Peter Topping, Claude

Mordant, and Margaret Maddison. International Series 403. Oxford: British Archaeological Reports.

Wijnen, Marie-Helene Josephine Marcell Nicole. 1982. *The Early Neolithic I Settlement at Sesklo: An Early Farming Community in Thessaly, Greece.* Analecta Praehistorica Leidensia, no 14. Leiden: University Press.

Willetts, R. F. 1965. *Ancient Crete: A Social History.* London: Routledge.

Willms, C. 1983. "Obsidian im Neolithikum Europas." *Germania* 61:327–51.

———. 1985. "Neolithischer Spondylusschmuck. Hundert Jahre Forschung." *Germania* 63:331–43.

Winn, Shan Milton McChesney. 1973. *The Signs of the Vinča Culture: An Internal Analysis; Their Role, Chronology, and Independence from Mesopotamia.* Ph.D. diss., University of California at Los Angeles. Ann Arbor: University Microfilms.

———. 1981. *Pre-Writing in Southeast Europe: The Sign System of the Vinča Culture, ca. 4000 B.C.* Calgary: Western Publishers.

———. 1990. "A Neolithic Sign System in Southeastern Europe." In *The Life of Symbols,* edited by Mary Le Cron Foster and L. J. Botscharow, 263–85. Boulder: Westview Press.

Wiślański, T., ed. 1970. *The Neolithic in Poland.* Wrocław-Warsaw-Kraków: Inst. Hist. Kultury Mat. Polsk. Akad. Nauk.

Wyss, René, and Jakob Bill. 1978. "An Ancient Lakeshore Settlement at Egolzwil Helps Clarify Europe's Neolithic Past." *Archaeology* 31:24–32.

Yarovoy, E. V. 1990. *Kurgany ėneolita ėpokhi bronzy nizh'nevo Podnestrov'ya.* Kishenev.

Zălai-Gaál, István. 1986. "Mórágy-Tüzködomb: Entwurf Sozialarchäologischer Forschungen." *Internationales Symposium über die Lengyel-Kultur, 1984, Nitra-Wien:* 333–38.

———. 1988a. *Soziarchäologische Untersuchungen des mitteleuropäischen Neolithikum aufgrund der Gräberanalyse.* Béri Balogh Ádám Múzeum Évkönyvebol XIV. Szekszárd.

———. 1988b. "Közép-europai neolitikus temetök sociál-archaeologiai elemzése." *Bi Balogh Ádam Múzeum Évkönyve* 14:5–178.

Zápotocká, M. 1983. "Circular Ditches of the Stroked-Pottery Culture at the Site of Bylany, Distr. of Kutná Hora." *Archaeol. Rozsledy* 35:475–85.

Zürn, Hartwig. 1965. *Das jungsteinzeitliche Dorf Ehrenstein (Kreis Ulm). Ausgrabung 1960. Die Baugeschichte.* Stuttgart: Staatliches Amt für Denkmalpflege.

Note: Page references in italics indicate figures.

Bergquist, Anders, 226n3

Best, Jan, 182

bezdukai. See Kaukai (Baltic manikins)

Biaggi, Cristina, 116, 218n25

Bibikov, S. N., 16

bi-lines (symbol), 75

bird goddess: in Baltic culture, 203; figurines of, 14; hairstyles on, 91; in Mycenaean culture, 152; rituals dedicated to, 66, 86; signs associated with, 14, 45; Sirens and Harpies associated with, 158–59; temples dedicated to, 77–79, 87–88

birds: Athena associated with, 158; as death images, 19–21, 24, 42, 58–59, 66, 71, 186, 193; diversity and richness of, 41–42; fairies associated with, 207–8; goddesses as, 201, 205, 206–7; in grave goods, 176–78; as life-sustaining symbol, 14; in peak sanctuaries, 140; as regenerative images, 40, *41*, 42, 66, 142; on sarcophagi, 147; signs associated with, 54, 75; Sirens and Harpies associated with, 158–59; symbolism of, 194; temple models shaped like, 81, 83, 87–88; on vessels, 14, 69. *See also* bird goddess; *specific birds*

birth: of animals, 202–3; cave sanctuaries associated with, 139; creativity in, 201; festivals for, 156, 200; god associated with, 195–96; models of, 140; rituals of, 12, 87, 200; sacredness of, 11–14, 87, 135, 200; stool for, 220n7; symbols of, 11, 87, 96–97; temple dedicated to, 135, 136–38. *See also* birth canal; birth-giving goddess; womb

birth canal: cave as, 60; passageway of tomb as, 66, 68, 70; represented in shrine structure, 58

birth-giving goddess: animals associated with, 12–14, 144; Artemis as, 12, 139, 151, 155–57, 193; cave sanctuaries associated with, 139; deer associated with, 13–14; Freyja as, 193; in Ireland, 184–85; Laima as, 200; as life-giving image, 11–12, 143; offerings to, 200; temples dedicated to, 96–97. *See also* birth; regenerative goddess; womb

bison, 44

Bjerggård enclosure (Denmark), dog skulls at, 108

black (color), 202, 208

Blegen, Carl W., 222n2

blood types, for establishing kinship, 116

blouse, on costumed figurines, 89, *91*

boars, 193, 195, 212

boats, 147. *See also* ship

Boeotia (Greece), vases from, 31, 156–57

Boginki (Polish fairies), 208

Boian culture, 47

bones: disarticulated in burials, 59; in enclosures, 109; entombment of, 64, 66, 109; equalitarian treatment of, 61, 63, 71; for establishing blood group, 116; in grave goods, 178; images and signs on, 20, 30, 43; missing in burials, 66, 222n12; in roundels, 103, 107. *See also* burial practices; skulls

Bonfante, Giuliano, 225n4

Bonfante, Larissa, 225n4

Bonu Ighinu culture: death goddess from, *22*; rock-cut tombs of, 62–64, 71

Book of Leinster, battle in, 186

Borsod (Hungary), symbolic signs from, *48*

Boudicca (Celtic queen), 123–24

Boyne River Valley (Ireland), 67–68. *See also* Newgrange (Ireland)

Branigan, Keith, 115

Brauronian Artemis, festival of, 156, 217n5

Brautsteine (bride stones), 209

bread, offerings of, 76, 203, 208–9

bread baking: by Basque goddess, 173; consecration of, 79; location of, 16, 79; models of, 84–86; as sacred, 16, 73, 74, 75

breasts: absence of, 95, *96*; on clay drums, 109; death imagery and, 26; as regenerative image, 6–7, 63, 185; on ritual equipment, 81, *82, 83*; on sarcophagi, 147; on seals, 142–43; on temple walls, 136–37; of vulture goddess, 144

Brigid/Brighid/Bride (Irish/Scottish goddess), 184–85, 187

Brimos-Dionysus (divine child), 161

Britain: earth mother worshiped in, 209; matrilineal customs in, 122–24; migrations to, xvi; Old European deities in, 183–86; roundels in, xviii, 100, 103–5, 220n4 (chap. 5); walls

caves: as sanctuaries, 138–39, 149–50; as tombs, 60–70

Cel (mother goddess), 169

Celsclan (son of Cel), 169

Celtic culture: description of, 178–86; formation of, 179; goddesses and gods in, xix, 179–86; great-goddess in, 182–83; Gundestrup cauldron from, 180–81, 186; Old European cultural persistence in, 130, 179, 186–87; sacred marriage rite in, 118; social structure in, 123–24, 129; spread of, 170, 178–79, 189; women's status in, 179, 226n2; writing in, 184

cemeteries: dog images from, 32–33; emergence of use of, 113; grave goods from, 114–15; kinship evidence from, 115–17; masks from, 9; vases from, 177. *See also* burial practices

ceramics. *See* figurines; pottery

ceremonial centers: British, 99–100, 103–7; causewayed enclosures as, 107–10; central European, 101–3; ritual evidence from, 99–100, 111; square enclosures as, 110; towns as, 110. *See also* roundels

Cernavoda (Romania), vegetation goddess/god from, 17–18

Cernunnos (stag god, Celtic), 180–82

Chadwick, John, 133

chairs, 79, 220n7

Champ-Durand enclosure, burials in, 108

Champollion, Jean-François, 51

Charlemagne (Frankish emperor), 189–90

Charon (ferryman of dead), 169

Charun (Etruscan demon), 169

checkerboard (symbol): on pottery, 81; on skirts, 89, *92*; on temple model, 83, *84*, 87

chevrons (symbol): on figurines, 6, *13*, 14, *37*, 45, 81, 86, 119–20; on pottery, 39, *40*, 45, *48*, *78*, 79; on sculptures, *31*; in temples, 75, 78

chickens. *See* hens

childbearing: skirts associated with, 220n8. *See also* birth

children: burials of, 103, 106, 108; care for, 98; figurines of, 12–13, *49*; protection for, 193; ritual role of, 60; snakes and, 204

Christ, Carol P., 218n21, 219n3, 220n2 (chap. 4), 224n17

Christianity: in Baltic culture, 197, 198; in Basque culture, 173; conversion to, 173, 189–90, 197, 198; individualism in, 55; offerings in, 50; triangular images in, 38; writing development and, 184

Cimbri tribe, 180

circles (symbol): associated with animals, 43, 46; on figurines, 8; on grave goods, 177; on Hera's dress, 159; on pottery, 26, 77; as regenerative symbol, 26; on sarcophagi, 147; on temple models, 83, *84*; in temples, 77; on tomb walls, 68. *See also* eggs; roundels

"civilization," definition of, 132

Civilization of the Goddess, The (Gimbutas), xv, xvi

clans, burials as reflection of, 146

clothing. *See* adornment; costume

coil (symbol): on figurines, 15, 120; on pottery, 177; on sarcophagi, 147; in temples, 75, 77; on tomb walls, 68–69

colors: black, 202; purple, 61; red, 11, 57–58, 61, 66, 70, 221n12; white, 222n5; yellow, 61

community: ceremonial centers for, 99–100, 111. *See also* settlements

Corded Ware culture, 188–89, 197

costume: blouse, 89, *91*; on Celtic cauldron, 181; on ceremonial figurines, 88–93; as gender identifier, 222n5; hairstyles, 89, 91, 93; on *phalera,* 180; Roman, influenced by Etruria, 171; skirts, 89, *90–92*, *96*, 177; of Vǫlva (magician-priestess), 194. *See also* adornment

court tombs, 64, *65*

Cow Laima (goddess), 202–3

cows: goddesses associated with, 159, 202–3; as regenerative images, 218n21; snake as protector of, 203–4. *See also* bulls

crafts: Athena associated with, 158. *See also* metallurgy; pottery; spinning; tools; weaving

cremation, 66, 106, 177–78

crescents (symbol), 68

Crete: agricultural communities on, 132; burials on, 144, 146–48, 177; cave sanctuaries on, 138–39, 149–50; circular tombs on, 115; decline of, 133; hedgehog goddess from, *32*;

Diodorus, 28

Diodorus Siculus, 123

Dionysian festivals, 37, 162

Dionysus (Greek god), 145, 151, 161–62, 168, 210

ditches: around enclosures, 107–8; around roundels, 99, 101–2, 106

divination, in Etruscan culture, 168–69, 171

Dnieper culture, 197

dog: goddess as, 206; Hekate associated with, 110, 155, 206; as regenerative symbol, 32–33; on Rogozen jug, 181; sacrificial, 32–33, 108, 110, 155; Uni associated with, 168

Dölauer Heide enclosure, 109

dolmens, 20, 64–65, 174

dolphins, 136–37, 170

Donja Branjevina (former Yugoslavia), artifacts from, 7, 82

Dorian tribes, 153

dots (symbol), 43, 89, 92, 120

double axes: as butterfly-shaped, 157; in Minoan culture, 135–36, 139–40, 142–44, 147–48, 149–50; in Mycenaean culture, 152; symbolism of, 135–36, 139–40, 142–43

double eggs, symbolism of, 7

double triangles. See hourglass shapes; triangles

Drang nach Osten, 198, 227n1 (chap. 13)

drums, in temple models, 88

ducks, 170, 176–78

Dumézil, Georges, xvi, 121, 196

Dumitrescu, Vladimir, 77

Dumuzi (Mesopotamian god), 196, 211

Dupljaja (former Yugoslavia), grave goods from, 177–78

Durrington Walls (Britain), 100, 105–6

Early Bronze Age, 146–47

Early Iron Age, 176, 189

earth: deities associated with power of, 145–46, 161, 196, 208–13; as justice, 209; Kaukai as manifestations of, 211–13. See also agriculture; fertility; nature

earth fertility goddess: approach to, 5, 217n1; in Baltic culture, 118, 198, 199, 208–13, 225n10; in Germanic religion, 191, 192; male partner of,

118; Nerthus as, 145–46, 178, 191, 192; objects associated with, 142; offerings to, 146; ritual dedicated to, 120; stones representing, 209. See also pregnant vegetation goddess; specific names

ecology, influences on, 215

Edda (poetry and prose vols.), 190, 191

eggs: double image of, 7; legs shaped as, 94; painted red, in temples, 77; signs associated with, 46; symbolism of, 14, 58; on temple models, 84, 85; temples shaped as, 95; tombs shaped as, 60–61, 70–71. See also circles

Egypt: deities in, 28, 196, 223n14; languages in, 50, 51

Eileithyia cave (Crete), 138–39

Eileithyia (goddess), 139, 143, 168, 184, 193

Elbe River, vegetation festival along, 192

Elder Futhark (Runic writing), 190

elephants, 181

Eleusis, Mysteries of (Greece), 136, 153, 161

Eliade, Mircea, 217n12

elk. See deer

enclosures: British, 107–8; causewayed, as ceremonial centers, 107–10; dating of, 221n1; shape of, 107–8, 110; tombs related to, 115–16

Endröd-Szujóskereszt (Hungary), goddess from, 37

England: ceremonial centers in, 99; Christianization of, 189; enclosures in, 107–8; frog goddess in, 30; graves in, 65; Sanctuary in, 104–5. See also Stonehenge; Woodhenge

Enodia (Thessalian goddess), 156

Ensisheim (Upper Rhein), owl goddess from, 20

Ephesus, 155, 157

Epona (Gaulish-Celtic goddess), 183, 187

Epstein, Angelique Gulermovich, 226n6, 226n8

Ereshkigal (Sumerian goddess), 42, 219n2

Estonia. See Baltic culture

Esus (god), 181

Eteocypriot language, 53

Ethelred, 221–22n13

Etruscan culture: decline of, 170–71, 179; divination in, 168–69, 171;

food: vegetation goddess associated with, 15–16. *See also* bread; feasts and festivals; honey

forests: goddess of, 209–10; Kaukai in, 211–12; Pan associated with, 163. *See also* trees

Forst Wötz (Germany), graves from, *65*

fortified settlement: use of term, 101. *See also* settlements

France: figurines from, 8; goddesses in, 30, 183; matrifocal customs in, 122–23; owl goddess from, 35–36; toads in, 29. *See also* Brittany; Burgundy; Gaul

frescoes: on Crete, 137–38, 141–42; Minoan goddess in, 142; Mycenaen, 158; on Thera, 118–19, 221n5

Freyja (Germanic goddess), 118; death and regeneration associated with, 120, 191, 193–96

Freyr (Germanic god), 118, 195–96

Friebritz (Austria), roundel at, 102

Frigg (Swedish goddess), 194

frogs/frog goddess: Artemis as, 156; as regenerative symbol, 27–30; signs associated with, 27, *28*, 46, 54; temple dedicated to, 84, *85*

Fufluns (Etruscan god), 168, 169

Fulla (Frigg's handmaiden), 194, 227n10

Funnel-necked Beaker culture. *See* TBK culture (Trichterbecherkultur)

G̈abija (Baltic goddess), 203

Gaia-Demeter (Greek goddess), 208

Galatians, origin of, 179

gallery graves, 64, *65*

games: represented in Etruscan tombs, 170; represented on mirrors, 225n8. *See also* sport

Gaul: deities of, 182; Germanic tribes in, 189; matrilocal customs in, 123–24; ram-headed serpent from, 182

Gavrinis passage grave (Brittany), 69–70

Gefion (Danish goddess), 193

gender: agricultural labor division by, 98; white as symbol of, 222n5. *See also* men; sexuality; women

Gepidae (tribe), 189

Germanic culture: Christianity and, 189–90, 198; deities in, xix, 130, 146, 191–96, 209; graves from, *65*; migrations and, xvi; Old European cultural per-

sistence in, 130, 191; origin of, 188–89; social structure in, 124, 129; spread of, 189, 227n2

Ġgantija temples (Malta): materials for, 93–94; structure of, 95, 96

Ghajn Abul cave (Gozo Island), 60

Ghar Dalam cave (Malta), 60, 71

Ghelaești-Nedeia (Moldavia), temple model from, 79–80

Giedion, Sigfried, 8

Giedraitis, Bishop Merkelis, 198

Giltinė (Baltic goddess), 204–5, 213

Gitlin-Emmer, Susan, 190

Gladnice (Kosovo-Metohije), masks from, *10*

Globular Amphora culture, 188

Glozel (France), possible script controversy and, 218n25

goats: birth of, 200; as death images, 193; in peak sanctuaries, 139–40; as regenerative symbol, 33, *34,* 147

goblins, in Basque culture, 174

Goddard, Irene Luksis, 228n11, 228n13, 228–29n17, 229n19

goddesses: diverse shapes of, xviii, 37; double, 73, 76–77, 95, *96,* 161; embodied in temple models, 83–84; healing and, 62, 182–83; as mistress of beasts, 31, 156, 181; meanings/roles of, 5–10; militarization of, 154, 158, 168, 186; parthenogenetic, 112–13; rapes of, 160–61, 164; ritual bathing of, 192, 227n6; on sarcophagi, 147–48; subordination of, 153–55, 164; triple, 11, 37–41, 192–93, 199, 200, 205, 223n4; water symbols on, 12. *See also* great-goddess; *specific cultures and goddesses*

gods: associated with death, 195–96, 207, 210–11; as master of beasts, 182; roles of, 117–19; warrior type, 152. *See also specific cultures and gods*

Gods and Goddesses of Old Europe (Gimbutas), xvi

Goljamata Mogila (Bulgaria), dog images from, *33*

Gorgon, as death goddess, 24–26, 42. *See also* Medusa

Goths (tribe), 189, 197

Gozo Island: caves on, 60, 95, *96*; temples on, xviii, *93*

Gradešnica (Bulgaria), sacred script from, *48,* 51

Hercules (Roman hero; equivalent to Greek Herakles), 180

Hermes (Greek god), 37, 162–63, 168, 195

Hermigisil (king of Saxon Varini), 221–22n13

Herodotus, 28, 165

Herpály (Hungary), temple at, 74, 75

Hesiod, 154, 161, 223n3

hierarchical social structure, spread of, xvi, 121, 124, 129, 176

hieroglyphs. See symbols

hieros gamos. See marriage, sacred

Hill of Allen (Ireland), 227n10 (chap. 11)

hip belts, 89, 90

History of Denmark (Saxo Grammaticus), 190

History of the Bishops of Hamburg (Adam of Bremen), 190

Holla (Germanic goddess), 120, 173, 195

Homer, 154; on Artemis, 156; on Athena, 158; on birth-giving goddess, 143; on Demeter, 145, 160; on Hera, 159, 160; on Hermes, 163; on Linos, 161; on Mycenaean culture, 151, 153–54; on Persephone, 160; on Sirens, 158–59

honey, as offering, 139, 143

Hood, M. S. F., 51

Hood, Sinclair, 137, 223n16, 224n15

hooks (symbol), 26, 36, 177

horned god, symbolism of, 182

horns (symbol): Hera associated with, 159; in Minoan culture, 139–41, 149–50; in Mycenaean culture, 152; on pottery, 177; on sarcophagi, 147. See also bucranium (bull head and horns); sheep

horse(s): goddess as, 183, 187; in Indo-European culture, 176; in migration, 131; Poseidon associated with, 145; representation of pregnant, 44

hourglass shape(s) (double triangles): dancing women depicted in, 63–64; goddess as, 37, 39–40; on pottery, 63–64, 109; as regenerative images, 37, 38–41

houselike temples (southeast Europe): for bird or snake goddess, 77–79; clay models of, 73–74, 78, 79–80, 83–88,

119; daily activities at, 73–74; functions of, 75–83; miniatures of, 88; overview of, 72–73; for pregnant vegetation goddess, 79–80; for regenerative goddess, 75–77

houses: goddess as protector of, 203; Kaukai in, 211; size differences in, 116–17; snakes in, 203–4; temples in, xviii; women buried under, 113–14. See also houselike temples (southeast Europe); settlements

Huld, Martin, 219n5 (chap. 2), 228n12

humans: animals fused with, 11; exaggerated body parts of, 6–8; figurines of, 84–86; sacrifice of, 140, 181; schematic forms of, 5–6; symbolic significance of, 5. See also bones; female body; male body; skulls

Hungary: burials in, 115; goddesses in, 17, 18, 28, 37; symbolic signs from, 47, 48; temples in, 74, 75, 80–81. See also Kökénydomb

Hyakinthos (pre-Greek god), 131, 145

Hypatius, 210

Hypogeum tomb (Malta), figurines from, 31

Iasion (god), 145

Iberian culture: matrifocal customs in, 122–23; Old European cultural persistence in, 172

Iceland, Edda compiled in, 190

Idean cave (Crete), 139

Ile Longu (Brittany), engravings from, 69

Ilgės (festival), 210

Imbolc, Brigid's feast, 185

Inanna-Ishtar (Sumerian-Akkadian goddess), 223n3, 224n29

India: migrations to, xvi; phallic images in, 38; sacred marriage in, 118

Indo-European culture: bull images in, 35; burial practices in, 176, 221n3; deities of, 16, 121, 183, 199; hierarchy of, xvi, 121, 124, 129, 176; individualism in, 55; Old European culture disrupted by, 52–54, 121, 129–30, 149; religion of, 124; sacred marriage in, 118–19. See also Indo-European languages; warfare

Indo-European languages: families of, 189; formation of, 188–89; Old Euro-

furnishings of, xviii, 79, 81, 88, 97, 220n7; location of, xviii, 117; miniatures of, 4, 88, 120; models of, 73–74, 78, 79–81, 83–88, 119; for pregnant vegetation goddess, 79–80; for regenerative goddess, 75–77, 95–96, 135–38; structure of, 134, 136–37; tripartite, 140, 167; women buried under, 113–14. *See also* megalithic temples; ritual equipment

La Tène culture, burials from, 124

Těšetice-Kyjovice (Moravia), roundel at, 102

Teutonic culture, 123, 198

Themis (Greek), 209

Theopompus, 122

Thera: in Aegean cultural group, 131, 133; frescoes on, 118–19, 221n5; goddess from, 142, 157, 168; jewelry from, 157; natural disaster on, 148–49; temple on, 142

Theseus (god), 169

Thesmophoria, ritual of, 120

Thessaly: goddess in, 156; temple model from, 85–87, 119. *See also* Dimini culture; Sesklo culture

thinking, abstract and symbolic, 54

tholoi (circular tombs), 115

Thor (Germanic god), 191

Thrace: Celtic cauldron influenced by, 180; vessel-shaped deity from, 78, 79

three (number): sacredness of, 167. *See also* Norns (Triple Fates); Moirai; Parcae

thrones: for figurines, 110, 120; room for, 137–38; shape of, 137; succession to, 124, 221–22n13

Thuringian culture, 124

time, symbols associated with, 68

Tin/Tinia (Etruscan goddess), 167, 169, 171

Tîrgu Ocna-Podei (Moldavia), symbolic script from, 47

Tisza culture: altar from, 38; frog symbols from, 27, 28; houses from, 117; pottery from, 77; script from, 47, 51; sculpture from, 76; temples from, 75, 80–81; vegetation goddess/god from, 17, 18

Tivr (Etruscan moon), 169. *See also* moon

toads: drink with, 207; goddesses as, 206, 207, 213; as regenerative and death image, 156, 207. *See also* frogs

Todorović, Jovan, 50

tomb goddess. *See* death goddess

Tomb of the Double Axe (Crete), 144

"Tomb of the Eagles," 66–67

Tomb of the Lionesses (Etruscan), 170

tombs: astronomical alignments of, 67–68, 71; bucrania on, 36–37, 63; in caves and rock-cut spaces, 60–70, 138, 146–48; circular-chamber *tholos,* 146–47; in Etruscan culture, 169–70, 171; importance of, 55–56; moon symbols on, 63; new life from, xvii; structure of, 55–56; uterine and egg-shaped, 60–71; for wealthy, 166; as womb, 60–61, 66, 68. *See also* burial practices; megalithic tombs

tools: loom weights, 50, 73, 156; manufacturing of, 80; in men's burials, 114. *See also* spindle whorls

Toptepe tell (Thrace), vessel-shaped deity from, 78, 79

Torma, Zsófia, 50

torques, Celtic, 180–82

towns. *See* settlements

Traian-Dealul Viei (Romania), symbolic signs from, 48

Transylvania, signs and script from, 45, 50

Traostalos peak sanctuary (Crete), 139

TRB culture. *See* TBK culture (Trichterbecherkultur)

trees: of life, 33, 37, 139, 147, 150; sacred, 190, 192, 200–201, 210

triangles (symbol): on figurines, 13, 120; as goddess' body, 66; on grave goods, 24, 177; on pottery, 48, 63, 77, 79, 109; pubic, 37, 38–41, 57, 144; as regenerative symbol, 26, 38–41; on sculpture, 76; on temple models, 84. *See also* double axes; hourglass shapes (double triangles); triangular shrines

triangular shrines: altars in, 57–59; figurines from, 31; floor plans of, 57; structure of, 55–56; symbolism of, 55, 57–59, 70

Triballoi tribe, 180

Trichterbecherkultur. *See* TBK culture (Trichterbecherkultur)

tri-lines (symbol): on figurines, 13, 14, 81, 86, 119; on pottery, 48, 177; in temples, 75

Tripartite theory, xvi, 196

Les Trois Frères cave (France), death images in, 19

Troy, abstract signs from, 45

Indexer:	Margie Towery
Designer:	Kathleen Szawiola
Compositor:	Integrated Composition Systems
Printer/Binder:	Malloy Lithographing
Text:	10/14 ITC Berkeley Oldstyle Book
Display:	ITC Berkeley Oldstyle Book Italic